Slavery Unseen

A book in the series   LATIN AMERICA OTHERWISE

Languages, Empires, Nations

Series editors   Walter D. Mignolo, Duke University
Irene Silverblatt, Duke University
Sonia Saldívar-Hull, University of Texas, San Antonio

Slavery Unseen

Sex, Power, and Violence in Brazilian History

LAMONTE AIDOO

Duke University Press : Durham and London : 2018

Printed in the United States of America on acid-free paper ∞
Interior designed by Courtney Leigh Baker; cover designed by Heather Hensley
Typeset in Garamond Premier Pro by Copperline Book Services

Library of Congress Cataloging-in-Publication Data
Names: Aidoo, Lamonte, [date] author.
Title: Slavery unseen : sex, power, and violence in Brazilian history / Lamonte Aidoo.
Description: Durham : Duke University Press, 2018. | Series: Latin America otherwise |
Includes bibliographical references and index. | Description based on print version
record and CIP data provided by publisher; resource not viewed.
Identifiers: LCCN 2017043431 (print) | LCCN 2017046595 (ebook) |
ISBN 9780822371168 (hardcover : alk. paper)
ISBN 9780822371298 (pbk. : alk. paper)
ISBN 9780822371687 (ebook)
Subjects: LCSH: Slavery—Brazil—History. | Brazil—Race relations—History. | Slaves—
Abuse of—Brazil. | Slaveholders—Sexual behavior—Brazil.
Classification: LCC HT1126 (ebook) | LCC HT1126 .A728 2018 (print) | DDC
306.3/620981—dc23
LC record available at https://lccn.loc.gov/2017043431

Isabel Löfgren & Patricia Gouvêa, *Ways of Seeing*, 2016. Interference on print
by J. M. Rugendas. Source image: "Negras do Rio de Janeiro," lithograph
first published in *Voyage Pittoresque dans le Brésil*, by J. M. Rugendas (1802–1858),
Paris, 1835. Part of the project Mãe Preta | Black Mother (www.maepreta.net).

Whatever is unnamed, undepicted in images, whatever is omitted from biography, censored in collections of letters, whatever is misnamed as something else, made difficult-to-come-by, whatever is buried in the memory by the collapse of meaning under an inadequate or lying language—this will become, not merely unspoken, but unspeakable.

—ADRIENNE RICH, *On Lies, Secrets, and Silence: Selected Prose, 1966–1978*

Contents

Acknowledgments : ix

INTRODUCTION. Secrets, Silences, and
Sexual Erasures in Brazilian Slavery and History : 1

ONE. The Racial and Sexual Paradoxes of
Brazilian Slavery and National Identity : 11

TWO. Illegible Violence: *The Rape
and Sexual Abuse of Male Slaves* : 29

THREE. The White Mistress and the Slave Woman:
Seduction, Violence, and Exploitation : 67

FOUR. Social Whiteness: *Black Intraracial Violence
and the Boundaries of Black Freedom* : 111

FIVE. *O Diabo Preto* (The Negro Devil): *The Myth of
the Black Homosexual Predator in the Age of Social Hygiene* : 149

AFTERWORD. Seeing the Unseen:
The Life and Afterlives of Ch/Xica da Silva : 187

Notes : 197   Bibliography : 227   Index : 249

Acknowledgments

Writing *Slavery Unseen* has been a journey, and I consider myself truly grateful to have had several people who have helped, encouraged, and supported me along the way.

I would like to thank my editor at Duke University Press, Gisela Fosado. Gisela is a brilliant and compassionate editor who supported, encouraged, and stood by me to see this book come to fruition, and to her I am most grateful. I would also like to thank the staff at Duke University Press, especially Sara Leone, my production editor, for the care, enthusiasm, and work that she has put into my book.

While researching and writing *Slavery Unseen*, I was greatly assisted by the staff at the Arquivo Nacional, Torre do Tombo in Lisbon, Portugal; Museu do Crime in São Paulo, Brazil; Museu Paulista; Fundação Rui Barbosa; Duke University Library; Associação Dos Investigadores de Polícia do Estado de São Paulo; Arquivo Histórico Municipal de Salvador; the New York Public Library; and the Schomburg Center for Research in Black Culture.

I am also grateful to Walter D. Mignolo, Irene Silverblatt, and Sonia Saldívar-Hull, editors of the Latin America Otherwise Series, for including *Slavery Unseen* in the company of so many important and distinguished works in Latin American studies. I would also like to thank three anonymous Duke reviewers for their time, feedback, and support of my work.

Daniel F. Silva has been a true friend, collaborator, and colleague from our days as graduate students at Brown and has been a constant source of support. GerShun Avilez has been a fun, supportive friend and colleague, and I am grateful to have met him. Danielle Carmon has been a friend, motivator, supporter, and constant source of laughter. I am glad to have her as a friend.

Among my colleagues in the Department of Romance Studies at Duke, I would like to thank Esther L. Gabara, Roberto Dainotto, Richard Rosa, Claudia Milian, Helen Solterer, David Bell, Michèle Longino, Valeria Finucci, Stephanie Sieburth, Deborah Jenson, and Laurent Dubois, Elvira Vilches, Luciana Fellin, and N. Gregson Davis. I am also thankful to the staff in Romance Studies.

I would also like to thank the Franklin Humanities Institute for awarding me the Junior Faculty Book Manuscript Workshop Fellowship. The fellowship allowed me to convene some of the most brilliant minds in several different fields to engage my work. I would especially like to thank Sander L. Gilman and Farah Jasmine Griffin for attending the workshop and their enthusiasm, support of the manuscript, and invaluable feedback. I would also like to thank Karla F. C. Holloway, Esther Gabara, David Bell, Richard Rosa, and John D. French for attending the book workshop, and for their time and valuable suggestions.

I would like to thank former director Ian Baucom and Christina Chia. And a very special thank you to Beth Monique Perry for her help and support, and for organizing a wonderful workshop. I am grateful to count her as a friend.

I would also like to thank Richard Powell, Kevin W. Moore, and Valerie Ashby, the late Srinivas Aravamudan, and Laura Eastwood for their administrative support.

I would like to give a special thank you to Valerie Petit-Wilson, who served as the associate dean of the Graduate School at Brown while I was a graduate student. Valerie was a tireless supporter and champion and I am most grateful to her. Margaret Copeley has also been a friend and an unwavering source of support from the very beginning of my academic journey.

During my time at Duke, I have been fortunate to have had many wonderful and inspiring students. A very special thank you to Giulia Ricco, Anna Tybinko, Chelsea Grain, Janani Arangan, Alison Dos Santos, and James Sanderson.

My professors and advisors at Brown University, Nelson H. Vieira, Luiz Valente, Anani Dzidzienyo, and Keisha-Khan Y. Perry, encouraged me as a graduate student and provided me with the historical, literary, and theoretical tools to take on a project of this nature. They were and are inspiring professors, advisors, mentors, and friends.

I would like to especially thank my family for their love and support and a very special thank you to my dear mother, Peggy Thomas, for her love, patience, and prayers.

INTRODUCTION.

Secrets, Silences, and Sexual Erasures
in Brazilian Slavery and History

Perhaps the pioneers in the slave's cause will be as much surprised as any to find that with all *their* looking, there remained so much unseen.—SOJOURNER TRUTH, *Narrative of Sojourner Truth*, 1850

[The slave] Luke was appointed to wait upon his bed-ridden master, whose despotic habits were greatly increased by exasperation at his own helplessness. He kept a cowhide beside him, and, for the most trivial occurrence, he would order his attendant to bare his back, and kneel beside the couch, while he whipped him till his strength was exhausted. Some days he was not allowed to wear anything but his shirt, in order to be in readiness to be flogged. . . . As he lay there on his bed, a mere degraded wreck of manhood, he took into his head the strangest freaks of despotism; and if Luke hesitated to submit to his orders, the constable was immediately sent for. Some of these freaks were of a nature too filthy to be repeated. When I fled from the house of bondage, I left poor Luke still chained to the bedside of this cruel and disgusting wretch.—HARRIET A. JACOBS, *Incidents in the Life of a Slave Girl, Written by Herself*, 1861

Slavery is not a single, uniform institution. There is not one slavery, but there are many slaveries. Each period and incident of slavery is shaped by its cultural, geographical, and social contexts, which determine the specific conditions to which slaves are subjected and the particular character of relations between master and slave. *Slavery Unseen* brings to the surface stories, testimonies, and violations that were often endured in silence and behind closed doors, abuses of power that "remained unseen." In many instances these events were too vile, too unbelievable, "too filthy to be recorded," named, or included in official historical accounts. This book examines aspects of Brazilian slavery that ranged from the barbaric to the ludicrous: the rape of male slaves by their white male masters; white mistresses who exploited their slave women for sex and forced them into prostitution to support the household; formerly enslaved blacks who became slaveholders, tortured slaves, and campaigned against abolition; social whitening (a system of designating certain blacks as white, thereby controlling which blacks could participate in white society while restricting their marriage and sexual access to white women). By the late nineteenth century Brazilian whites would also resort to pseudoscientific theories to prove blacks' racial inferiority and would use medical studies to cast black men as homosexuals who preyed on white men.

Slavery as an institution was defined on the surface by differences that created a stark power differential: between free and enslaved, black and white, men and women, wealthy and impoverished, elite and marginalized. Yet slavery also depended on relationships of sameness that are less obvious in our traditional understanding, that is, relationships between men, between women, and between blacks. Those relationships served to sustain difference and inequality, as in the rape of male slaves by their masters, the sexual exploitation of female slaves by white mistresses, and black ownership of slaves. All of these relationships derived from and bolstered the overarching structures of white male supremacy.

The habitual focus on difference and heteronormative reproductive sex can cause us to overlook forms of sex and racial violence that do not fit neatly into these models. Each chapter in this book examines one of these less conspicuous relationships of sameness. Sex, violence, and exploitation that occurred in the context of sameness, though less widely known, had a profound impact on the lives of slaves and on how race and sexuality would come to be articulated in the aftermath of slavery. These same-sex relationships deviated from heteronormative reproductive sexuality, and yet they worked in tandem with those socially and religiously sanctioned forms of sex. Paradoxically, the master's right to rape a male slave derived from his white male heterosexual privilege over *all* bodies, while the white mistress's sexual exploitation of her female slaves was enabled by her relationship to that same privilege through her husband and father. By the same token, free blacks drew their privilege of owning slaves from the white master's power to free them and the white elite's authority to grant them official whiteness—which never included unfettered sexual access to white women, demonstrating that the white male social hierarchy prevailed even when it was invisible.

Thus by considering relations of sameness within an institution invested in maintaining racial difference, we can observe how two men, two women, or two blacks sought to actively wield power over one another and reproduce inequality through physical violence, discrimination, exploitation, and sex with the ultimate goal of sustaining the social order even as they appeared to veer so flagrantly away from it.

The idea of widespread interracial sex was central to the construction of Brazilian racial exceptionalism and the myth of racial democracy. Sex and its traditional connection to intimacy and interracial reproduction were used to create a racially complex society and as an effective weapon of subjugation for the enslaved. Sex was attributed a transcendental meaning by many of the nation's white elite and racial theorists; that is, sex and reproduction had the capacity to erase barriers and served as proof that race could be and had been transcended. This conceptualization of sex and its connection to race was central to Portuguese colonialism and became the very basis of Brazilian racial exceptionalism and the myth of racial democracy.[1] The silencing and sanitization of the nation's history of rape, sexual violence, and abuse during slavery and its aftermath laid the foundation for an enduring legacy of erasure that then created the illusion of equality and racial progressivism, while in reality, solidifying an antiblack, racist system that preserved white male supremacy in Brazil's past and present.

The themes that form the heart of this book all revolve around power and control: the determination of the white elite, and even free blacks and mulattos, to maintain their base of power and wealth and unfettered domination over the black body—entrenched since the beginning of Brazilian slavery in the sixteenth century—as radical political, economic, and social changes mitigating against slavery swept across Europe and the Americas in the nineteenth century.

These mechanisms of white supremacy and the stories of the lives of Brazilian slaves presented here challenge our commonplace assumptions about what slavery was and how it worked. They reveal the many contradictions between the image of harmonious race relations that Brazil presented to the world during slavery and the unseen and oftentimes horrific sexual abuse and exploitation of slave men, women, and children. At the end of the nineteenth century these structures of white supremacy were surreptitiously folded into the Brazilian national identity under the guise of an exceptional national identity that cast Brazilian slavery as less malevolent, almost beneficent compared to other countries. These enduring structures and myths are part of what has made modern Brazil.

This book sheds new light on unfamiliar and obscured aspects of Brazil's sexual and racial histories from the beginning of slavery in the 1500s through the early twentieth century. Throughout this book we will explore the myriad contradictions and anxieties that emerged during this time around race and sexuality. Elite white Brazilians were unprepared for massive social change after 350 years of reaping the benefits of slavery. They had established a racial, social, and economic order that depended entirely on the ownership and domination of slaves. One of the primary mechanisms of control employed by many slaveholders across the Americas was the sexual exploitation of enslaved women, men, and children, which will be explored at length in this book.

This conflation of sex and intimacy at the center of Brazilian racial exceptionalism suggested the consent of blacks to what was often in reality sexual exploitation and abuse. This book will explore the many meanings and strategic uses of interracial sex by white Brazilian slaveholders, politicians, writers, and scientists, revealing sex to be an apparatus that controlled many different aspects of Brazilian society, politics, and the economy.

Slave owners needed to retain control over women and reproduction in order to ensure constant replenishment of their slave supply. During slavery throughout the Americas, the status of the mother, whether free or enslaved, determined the status of the child. All children of slave women were born into inherited servitude. Thus sex was central to the perpetuation of slavery, and race, enslavement, and freedom were reproduced through women. Beyond reproduction, however, sex during slavery was a violent mechanism of power and control used to degrade, torture, and kill slave men, women, and children and to solidify white male supremacy.

In order to justify the longevity of Brazilian slavery and divert attention away from Brazil's position as the last slaveholding nation in the Western Hemisphere, members of Brazil's dominant class, including plantation owners, politicians, and intellectual leaders, needed to somehow rewrite the country's history of slavery, in particular the sexual abuse of slaves. The above quotes from Sojourner Truth and Harriet Jacobs about the "unseen" and "filthy" parts of slavery convey that some aspects of slavery and certain forms of violence were purposely concealed by both masters and slaves, as they were too unspeakable to put into words or commit to paper.

White elites were especially interested in camouflaging sexual violence of a taboo nature that fell outside the heteronormative. The trial records of the Portuguese Inquisition in Brazil reveal numerous instances of same-sex sexual violence against slaves, cloaked beneath language that denies the real nature of these events. Moreover, certain forms of sexual exploitation and violence went undetected because they were not recognized, legible forms of sexual violence, such as the rape of male slaves by the master or sex between slave mistresses and their female slaves.

The title of this book, *Slavery Unseen*, refers to the difficulty of detecting and understanding the real conditions under which Brazilian slaves lived due to willful concealment by whites, lack of a vocabulary to describe what took place, and blaming slaves for their own victimization. In order for historical events to be better understood, people and their experiences must be seen, must be made visible. The language of victims is very different from the language of perpetrators, allowing, for example, for rape to be cast as consensual sex by the rapist. A language is needed that renders the experiences of slaves visible so that they may be understood and victims may be clearly distinguished from perpetrators. My goal in this book is to make violence against Brazilian slaves legible by renaming it, removing the exculpatory terms used by the Portuguese Inquisition, slaveholders, and the Brazilian government.

These acts of racially motivated sexual violence were committed with a cognizance that they fell outside the paradigm of commonplace forms of slave bodily exploitation and that by their very nature they would be undetectable. A master or mistress could confidently say to a slave about these deeds, "Who would believe you?" The unbelievability or unspeakability of certain forms of violence inflict shame and degradation on the victim while providing protection, invisibility, and omnipotence to the perpetrator, leaving these stories in the dark recesses of the historical archive.

The approach of this book is interdisciplinary in an effort to more fully examine the complexities of Brazilian slavery, race relations, interracial sexual violence, and the racialized and pathological constructions of male homosexuality in the late nineteenth century. The book draws on many original sources from the sixteenth through the early twentieth centuries, specifically from the regions of Bahia, Pernambuco, Pará, Rio de Janeiro, São Paulo, and Minas Gerais, to reconstruct a detailed picture of racial relations in Brazil during and after slavery. Among the most important of these sources are confessions and denunciations from the Portuguese Inquisition from the sixteenth through the early nineteenth centuries. Narratives of sexual violence are culled from the very explicit, verbatim Inquisition transcripts of the trials of slaves who were accused of committing sexual sins. These cases clearly reveal that the accused were victims of cruel sexual violence committed by their white masters.

The stories of slave women and men found in the archives of the Portuguese Inquisition render a striking portrait of the obscured and unseen history of Brazilian slavery. These documents are invaluable, as after the Inquisition there was no further official recording of sexual crimes against slaves. These records help us to piece together a history of sexual violence committed against slaves that extended well beyond the domain of the heteronormative. The cases presented in chapters 2 and 3 in many instances relate not only the story of a single victim or confessant, but also reports of other victims that point to the pervasiveness of same-sex sexual violence in the everyday lives of slaves. Yet, while these documents record stories of abuse, violation, and degradation, many of these testimonies equally show enslaved men's and women's resistance to slavery and sexual abuse as they risked their lives to tell their stories.

In Inquisition records the sexual violation of slaves was concealed by recording the occurrences in a vocabulary that made slaves culpable for their oppression and by portraying rape either as a sin committed by slaves or as consensual sex. These records would set precedents for how the rape of slaves would later be encoded in Brazilian law and for the pathologization of the sexuality of black men and women in Brazilian medical studies.

Though *Slavery Unseen* is not the first book to study same-sex relationships in Brazil, it departs from other studies in that it examines the role of nongenerative sex in shaping the history of slavery in Brazil, the construction of race relations, and the subsequent racialized pathological constructions of homosexuality that would emerge two centuries after the close of the Inquisition. I do not use cases of same-sex relations to examine sexual orientation or to document a genealogy of male and female homosexuality, but to understand same-sex sexual relations and violence committed by masters against slaves as a mechanism of reproducing gender, racial, and sexual inequality. In fact what appears on the surface as homosexual exploitation of slaves by their masters will be revealed, paradoxically, to be expressions of heterosexual norms that played a fundamental role in reinforcing white racial and sexual supremacy.

This book uses a narrative rather than statistical approach. It is virtually impossible to quantify how frequently enslaved men were raped and sexually abused, or how often slave mistresses engaged in sexual acts with slave women. During the Inquisition, as we will see in the first two chapters, both black and white Brazilians were skilled at keeping secrets, as they had strong reasons to do so. But at the same time, this was an era when important events such as the Inquisition trials were dutifully recorded and archived. The Inquisition depended on people watching others and reporting real, suspected, or imagined incidents of heresy, and then much pressure was put on the accused to confess their sins. The testimony of denouncers and witnesses, the confessions of the accused, and the sentences were all recorded by court scribes with an astonishing degree of voyeuristic detail in cases of sexual sins.

In recent years, a number of very important studies have used inquisitional documents to examine the history of colonial Brazil and slavery.[2] These scholars have all argued for the importance of these documents in exploring the private lives of men and women in colonial society. Yet the use of Inquisition records and their validity as historical evidence have also been the source of much debate in the academic community, and I approach their use cautiously. While numerous historians, anthropologists, and cultural studies scholars have used and heralded Inquisition records as important historical documentation of early modern Catholic societies across the world, other scholars, such as historian Edward Muir and anthropologist Renato Rosaldo, have argued against their validity and use as historical evidence in cultural history and anthropology.[3] Though these scholars do not write directly about the reliability of inquisitional records as they pertain to the testimony of slaves, and though work questioning their validity in relation to the topic of same-sex sexual violence is sparse, the issues that they raise can also be validly examined in a context such as the present study.[4]

While Inquisition documents have been an invaluable source for historians and cultural studies scholars, discerning the voices and stories of enslaved men and women in these records is challenging. We must contend with their inherent silences and erasures, and acknowledge, as does historian Antoinette Burton, that "*all* archives are provisional, interested, and calcified in both deliberate and unintentional ways; that *all* archives are, in the end, fundamentally unreliable."[5]

While it is irrefutable that the records of the Portuguese Inquisition contain testimony by and about slaves, they are not direct first-person accounts but reports authored by the inquisitional court. The format of the proceedings was rigid and formulaic. The accused in most cases were not allowed to speak directly to the court. Their testimonies were dictated and recorded by a scribe in the third person as "he said," "she replied," or "he confessed." The accused were instructed to deliver a "whole," "truthful," and "full" confession and were threatened with punishment by the court and by God if they did not. The transcripts reveal that the inquisitors had prejudices and a priori assumptions about confessants, especially slaves, and often constructed their questions according to these presumptions. They often practiced what we would call today "leading the witness," posing questions to educe particular responses. The scribe may have recorded only what he deemed relevant to the case, distorting or discarding other information.

Thus, in the Inquisition documents we have multiple contending voices and discourses of the slave, master, court, and scribe. Historian John Arnold argues that Inquisition documents should be read within a heteroglossic framework, recognizing that it is impossible to entirely disentangle these myriad and competing voices.[6] That slaves had little control over what was recorded in the trial transcripts points to a weakening of their voice in favor of the slave master and the court itself. And yet these transcripts paint a vivid picture of extreme violence against slaves. We can validly wonder what more was left out.

These testimonies were given in a climate of fear and intimidation. Slaves, particularly male rape victims and women who engaged in same-sex sexual activity, were wholly cognizant that they were exposing a crime or sin for which they could be severely punished, and that slaves had been murdered by their masters for exposing them. These fears may have conditioned the slaves' testimony.

I am not suggesting that all white masters and mistresses coerced their male and female slaves into nonconsensual sex. But while the surviving inquisitional archives cannot prove the exact extent of sexual violence against slaves, they unequivocally prove that it occurred and that it was often of a gruesome and taboo nature. The fact that sources are in some ways flawed does not diminish the importance of what they do reveal. Among the numerous competing voices, entrenched in discourses of criminality and sin, the stories and voices of slaves are present and can be heard if we are willing to listen.

Throughout the nineteenth century, many Europeans traveled to Brazil, establishing businesses and schools and living there for short or long periods of time. Some of these travelers were gifted writers and recorded their observations of the country and its people, including relations between slaves and slave owners, in published journals. The writings of travelers such as Charles Expilly, Adèle Toussaint-Samson, Maria Dundas Graham, Reverend Robert Walsh, and Henry Koster are quoted throughout this book not to validate their social and political opinions about Brazil as white Europeans—indeed some of their remarks are decidedly racist—but because they are a rich source of information regarding the history of slavery. The writings of Expilly and Toussaint-Samson are particularly revealing of the intersections of race, gender, and sexuality. They depict the daily lives of slaves in great detail, giving readers a complex and often disturbing picture of relations between the races and the suffering of slaves. They expose exactly the type of information that the Brazilian government sought to conceal from the eyes of the world. They provide a counternarrative, showing us the difference between, on the one hand, what Brazil wanted to believe about itself and how it projected itself internationally, and on the other hand, what outside observers actually witnessed. These European writers felt no particular affiliation with white Brazilians and therefore had no motive for disguising what they saw and experienced in Brazil. I also use period newspapers, medical literature (which addressed race and sexuality extensively), the law, art, letters, memoirs, literature, and Senate and parliamentary debates, as well as writings in psychology, sociology, and anthropology, to piece together and interpret the history.

Many previous studies on race have examined Brazil's so-called racial democracy as a myth about harmonious racial relations, but most studies have not examined nongenerative forms of sex and sexual violence as fundamental yet concealed components of the myths of Brazil's exceptional slavery and racial democracy.[7] Here I move the focus specifically to the major role of nongenerative sex in shaping slavery, inter- and intraracial and intragender inequality, and the emergence of pathological and racialized studies of homosexuality. Interracial sex throughout Brazilian history will be exposed as a place of crime, violation, nation making, and myth. I have chosen to investigate "interracial sex" rather than "miscegenation" (*miscigenação* or *mestizaje*) in the interest of specificity and historical recovery. The term *miscegenation*, meaning racial mixing, has taken on innumerable meanings that work on ambiguous and conflicting assumptions. When we commonly talk about it in relation to Brazilian history, miscegenation works almost exclusively within a heteronormative framework—we think of it mainly as sex between black or indigenous women and white men. Miscegenation as it relates to Brazil's so-called racial democracy is also attached to interracial reproduction, which was claimed to prove racial harmony. The relatively benign term *miscegenation* has often served in Brazilian history to mask the true aims of racial mixing, which was engineered by whites to fulfill their purposes for power, control, pleasure, economic gain, reproduction, humiliation, and annihilation. This term has kept us from discerning the often-violent mechanisms that structured racial mixing and how sex between the races served as a catalyst for other forms of racial violence. The heteronormative workings of miscegenation and its connection to reproduction have also concealed forms of sex and sexual violence during slavery that had nothing to do with reproduction.

For some readers, some of the content of this book may be disturbing. I do not include the facts and stories of sexual violence here for their sensational value, but rather to unearth the lived experiences of Brazilian slaves and to show, in human terms, how the ever-present reality of sexual and racial violence and exploitation by the white elite broke enslaved people. Their stories and pain are brought to light throughout the pages of this book because they deserve to be told and warrant our attention. Sex in the universe of slavery was a weapon, a mechanism of torture, a calculated means of reproducing slaves and slavery, and the consummate form of annihilation. None of us today will ever be able to truly understand the extent of the atrocities, the day-to-day erasure of humanity endured by enslaved men, women, and children. The discomfort that many feel when approaching questions of race and sex is a testament to their continuing significance today.

Though similarities and differences between slavery in Brazil and the United States are examined here, this is not a comparative study. Brazilian officials continually drew comparisons between Brazil and the United States during slavery and well into the twentieth century. The contentious racial history of the United States provided an important counterpoint for Brazil to construct its racial exceptionalism. However, contrary to nineteenth- and twentieth-century claims of racial democracy and exceptionalism, Brazilian slavery was no less brutal than in any other country.

The goal of this book is to read the story of Brazilian slavery against the silence, contradictions, shame, and concealment surrounding the black body. As Michel-Rolph Trouillot makes us aware, "The ultimate mark of power may be its invisibility; the ultimate challenge, the exposition of its roots."[8] Institutions change, but slavery has exercised an unrelenting hold on all Brazilians that has endured beyond the formal abolition of slavery. This book is an attempt to look back in order to move forward. It is my hope that these pages will unsettle but press toward greater understanding.

ONE

The Racial and Sexual Paradoxes of
Brazilian Slavery and National Identity

"If I had been Minister [when abolition was passed], I would have ordered, as part of the Law, the burning of all slave registration books so that no one would know who was a slave in Brazil," declared Bahian senator José Antônio Saraiva in July of 1888, just months after the abolition of slavery. Saraiva's wish was realized two years later on December 14, 1890, when finance minister Rui Barbosa, citing the "stain" of slavery on Brazil's past, issued a proclamation ordering the immediate destruction of all of the government records related to slavery, including the slave registers. Barbosa's decree read:

> Given that the Brazilian nation, in the greatest step toward its historical evolution, has abolished from its homeland the most fatal institution of slavery that for so many years paralyzed the development of society, and perverted the social atmosphere; . . . the Republic is thereby obligated to destroy [the] vestiges [of slavery] in the name of national honor, and in honor of our duties of brotherhood and solidarity with the great mass of citizens who through the abolition of slavery became members of the Brazilian family.
>
> It is decided that:
>
> 1 All existing papers, books, and documents pertaining to slaves, the registration of slaves, slave children freed under the Law of the Free

Womb, free children born to slave women, and slaves freed under the Sexagenarian Law will be requisitioned from all plantation treasuries and should be immediately remitted to the capital and collected and stored in the appropriate place in the depository.

2 A commission composed of Senhores João Fernandes Clapp, President of the Abolitionist Confederation, and the Director of the Capital Depository will oversee the collection of the aforementioned books and papers and will proceed to immediately burn and destroy them, in the municipal warehouse of the capital city, in whatever way is deemed most convenient to the commission.[1]

The records were so extensive that it took several years to destroy them. The burning of the slave records was supposedly done in the name of redemption and progress, but it can only be understood as an attempt to obliterate the former enslaved by removing all trace of their existence and their oppression from the official history of Brazil and to promote Brazil as "exceptional" among former slaveholding nations for its more benign form of slavery.

Following its independence from Portugal in 1823, Brazil needed to define itself as a nation both internally and in the image that it presented to the world. The destruction of the slave records allowed Brazil to declare itself finally purged of its history of slavery. But the mere burning of the nation's archives was not enough to erase four hundred years of slavery and its complex outcomes throughout Brazilian society.

Interracial sex was integral to slavery as a means of reproducing slaves and maintaining white dominance. The propagation of the notion of Brazil's exceptional slavery gave rise to complex connections among interracial sex, racial formation, and citizenship. In this view of democratic Brazilian race relations, interracial sex and reproduction dissolved racial barriers and produced a system of equality that offered a more promising future for Afro-Brazilians than blacks had in the United States. This chapter will provide a brief overview of the history of slavery in Brazil and summarize the events that led up to the abolition of slavery and the formation and propagation of Brazil's myth of racial and sexual exceptionalism.

History of Brazilian Slavery and Abolition

Slavery and its bitter realities served as the cornerstone of nation building throughout the Americas. At the beginning of Brazil's colonization by the Portuguese in the sixteenth century, indigenous people were used as slaves for farming. A substantial number of the early slave population died due to severe working conditions and diseases contracted from the Portuguese. The enslavement of indigenous people was strongly opposed by the Jesuit priests in Brazil, who had initially come to convert them to Catholicism. In large part due to their efforts, indigenous slavery was officially abolished in 1757.

By the beginning of the nineteenth century slavery had been firmly established throughout the Americas for more than four centuries in the former and present Portuguese, British, French, Spanish, and Dutch colonies. The exact number of slaves who were forcibly brought to Brazil is unknown, but it is estimated that from the beginning of the slave trade to the abolition of slavery in 1888 Brazil imported close to four million slaves—the largest number of any country in the Americas. The total number of slaves brought to British North America between 1701 and 1860 has been estimated at five hundred thousand. In other words, Brazil imported perhaps ten times more slaves than the United States, over a much longer period of time.

Brazil received its first known shipment of African slaves in 1538. From 1570 onward it carried out the mass importation of African slaves to support the country's vast agricultural market. They came primarily from West Africa (Ghana, Nigeria, Benin, and Togo) and the former Portuguese colonies of Angola and Mozambique. The black population during Brazilian slavery was very diverse. Until massive immigration of white Europeans in the late nineteenth century, Brazil was a mix of newly imported African slaves, *crioulos* (native-born Afro-Brazilians), mulattos (those of mixed black and white ancestry), and *cafusos* (mixed African and indigenous people). These differences would become important, and whites would amply exploit the divisions and conflicts among blacks to prevent them from uniting.

From 1600 to 1650 sugar was the primary export of the Brazilian colony, and from the mid-sixteenth century and throughout the seventeenth century enslaved Africans worked primarily on sugar plantations in the northeastern region of Brazil in the states of Bahia and Pernambuco. Toward the end of the 1600s gold and diamond deposits were discovered in the southeastern state of Minas Gerais and slaves were imported to work in the mines. The mining industry began to decline substantially in the second half of the eighteenth century. Cattle ranching and foodstuff production proliferated after the population of Brazil began to increase, and both relied heavily on slave labor. At the beginning of the nineteenth century the rise of coffee and tobacco production in the southern states of São Paulo and Rio de Janeiro also led to an increase in the importation of slaves.

Underscoring the importance of slaves in Brazilian society, Félix Peixoto de Brito, president of the state of Alagoas, wrote in 1870, "The slave occupies a very important place in all the conditions of the existence of the country; the slave represents labor, the source of wealth; he represents capital through his value and through his production; he represents small industry, because, aside from agricultural and domestic labor, he is employed in all crafts. Ultimately, the slave is an integral part of Brazilian society, which has thus been organized over the long span of three centuries."[2] But slavery in Brazil was not merely about economic profit. Slaves were above all property that elevated the social standing of their owners. Luiz Peixoto de Lacerda Werneck, a wealthy slaveholder and politician of Rio de Janeiro, wrote in 1855 that the slave was more than "an agent of labor and production," but also "an object of luxury, a means of satisfying certain vanities and certain vices of the nature of man. Just as owning land has certain attractions, so does the slave offer to the master a certain pleasure of command and authority that exists in the human heart, of which we know not whether for good or for evil."[3] Werneck's words are striking for their unexamined assumption that slaves were to be used however the master saw fit, whether for work or for pleasure. His ambiguous yet ominous references to undefined "vanities and vices" and "pleasure of command and authority" are at the heart of this book. In these phrases we seize the unquestioned free agency of the slave master and the complete lack of agency of the slave.

By 1819 the population of Brazil had reached 3.6 million, one-third of which was made up of slaves. With the continuation of the slave trade, the population of slaves and free blacks and mulattos reached almost 56 percent in 1860.[4] It is doubtful that white Brazilians ever imagined that as a result of their sustained efforts to create wealth through slave labor, blacks would one day outnumber whites and Brazil would be thrown into social disarray as it tried to come to terms with an unintended racial mixture and the permanent legacy of slavery that the country still struggles with today.

Slavery and World Opinion

As a newly independent country Brazil was especially concerned about its international reputation among nonslave nations. "How can Brazil, isolated and the only of its kind on the globe, resist the pressure of the entire world?" asked Bahian politician José Tomáz Nabuco.[5] Writer and politician José de Alencar, a member of Parliament and minister of justice during the time of the abolitionist debates, remarked, "The cause of emancipation in our country gained force due to this panic. Many spirits were gravely frightened by the idea that

Brazil was in this moment the last country where slavery existed. . . . No noble country would allow itself to be last in the line of civilized nations, to be almost mistaken with semibarbaric states of the Orient and the object of aversion to all mankind."[6] Brazilians began to feel fearful as the social landscape of the Americas was changing before their eyes. Many knew that the days of slavery were numbered, but the thought of losing the power, labor, and financial benefits of slavery was intolerable. It took pressure from the French Emancipation Committee to induce the Brazilian government to make its first formal statement on slave emancipation in 1866. The government assured the French that emancipation was merely "a question of form and opportunity"[7] and that at the culmination of the Paraguayan War (1864–70) emperor Dom Pedro II would devote significant effort to abolishing slavery. During that war many masters sent their slaves to fight with the promise of manumission, meaning that slaves were expected to risk their lives, above and beyond their servitude, in order to become full citizens.

Under the watchful eyes of Europe and ever concerned with their public image, Brazilians made deliberate attempts to hide the evils of slavery from European visitors. In 1869 Parliament passed a law prohibiting the sale of slaves in public and the separation of husbands and wives and parents and children under the age of fifteen. Additionally, many masters were cautious not to punish their slaves in the presence of visiting foreigners, who would write accounts, like those excerpted in this book, about these occurrences and publish them abroad. Adèle Toussaint-Samson, a French woman traveling through Brazil in the 1830s, remarked, "Everything is done mysteriously in these impenetrable abodes, where the lash has made the slaves as silent as the tomb."[8] Though Brazil attempted to cover up the realities of slavery, many visitors from Europe quite readily discerned that there was a stark disconnect between the consciously confected portrait that Brazil sold to foreigners and the insidious reality of masked violence. Many Europeans were shocked by what they saw. Shortly after arriving in Rio, Toussaint-Samson relates her horror upon encountering a slave auction while walking the streets:

> At every instant my heart revolted or bled when I passed before one of those [places], where the poor negroes, standing upon a table, were put up at auction, and examined by their teeth and their legs, like horses or mules; when I saw the auction over, and that a young negress was being handed over to the [plantation owner], who would reserve her for his "intimate" service, while her little child was sometimes sold to another master. Before all of these scenes of barbarism my heart would rise up and

generous anger would boil in me, and I was obliged to do me violence in not screaming to all these men who were making a traffic in human flesh.[9]

Such European criticism was one of the driving forces among the elite that led to the curious and complicated Brazilian abolitionist movement. Abolitionist clubs and organizations began to emerge in several cities throughout Brazil and gained momentum through the end of the nineteenth century. After independence in 1822, many Brazilian citizens felt ashamed to be the object of European scrutiny. Many did not believe that slavery was fundamentally wrong, but they were concerned about the country's precarious reputation out of bourgeoning nationalist sentiment. Those against slavery believed that the institution of slavery and slaves themselves were an impediment to Brazil's modernization. The desire for acceptance by Europe and for modernity were important motives of Brazilian abolitionism. Abolition was turned into an issue of national honor, and as famous abolitionist Joaquim Nabuco made clear, "Abolitionist propaganda . . . was not directed toward the slaves . . . but against an institution." Thus, the emancipation movement was not about freeing slaves but about freeing the nation from slavery and slaves.[10]

The interference of Great Britain and France in the affairs of the new nation incited a good deal of hostility. Among proslavery supporters and writers who expressed opposition to abolition and the end of the slave trade was highly influential writer and politician, José de Alencar. Alencar saw European intervention as hypocritical and disingenuous, given the Europeans' own history of slavery. "I do not fear that our country will be dishonored for maintaining slavery for some time yet, after it has generally been abolished," Alencar wrote in an 1865 letter. "We will be the last to emancipate ourselves from this necessity; but is there any one among us who can cast a stone at us for this crime of civilization? If such a people exists, of clean consciousness, let them stand up."[11]

Brazilian slaveholders were especially incensed by the fact that some European nationals residing in Brazil owned slaves. Alencar criticized the former slaveholding Europeans for now forcing the Brazilians to abolish slavery. He describes sardonically the hypocritical position of the European philanthropist toward the last two slaveholding nations in the Americas: "The European philanthropist, between the smoke of the fine tobacco of Havana and a fine cup of Brazilian coffee, gets caught up in his humanitarian utopia and hurls at these countries a great many insults for maintaining slave labor. But why don't these moralists reject with disgust the fruit of African labor?"[12] Alencar and many proslavery supporters saw the Brazilian abolitionist movement as fundamentally fueled by foreign pressure. Manoel Vitorino, who would later become governor of Bahia and vice president of the republic, confirmed their belief as he recalled, "My trip to Europe showed me just how much [European philanthropists] were slandering us and how our reputation bedeviled us, for the fact that we were a country that still had slaves. After returning home my abolitionist feelings became insistent and uncompromising, and on this issue I never again conceded."[13]

Supporters of slavery saw abolitionism as an antinationalist movement that threatened to jeopardize the future of the new nation and the security of slaveholders, who saw their slaves as legitimate property. Attributing the greater part of Brazil's economic growth and stability to slave labor, they maintained that it would be to Brazil's detriment to emancipate slaves. They further criticized Brazilian abolitionists for cowering to European pressure and regarded them as traitors to the nation. Slavery, they maintained, was a necessary evil, essential to Brazil's growth as a nation.

Brazilian slaveholders and planters were determined not to be overly idealistic like the United States, whose drastic approach to abolition ended in the virtual demise of plantation owners. The history of abolition throughout the Americas had proven to the Brazilians that all immediate, unconditional emancipation was followed by economic disaster: a decline in production, loss of land values, and the weakening of agricultural industries. In their view, abolition in the United States brought chaos, panic, vagabondage, and increased racial hostility to the Southern states, all of which Brazil wanted to avoid.

Brazil's "Exceptional" Slavery

Though many among Brazil's elite had a consistent preoccupation with keeping up appearances for the Europeans, slave emancipation was a tough sell because the majority of Brazilian citizens did not believe that slavery was wrong. Humanitarian pleas that spoke of slavery's cruelty and injustice fell on deaf ears, as many staunchly held the belief that Brazilian slavery was more genteel, more humane, than in other parts of the Americas, and that slavery was mutually beneficial for slave owners and slaves.

Paternalism pervaded proslavery arguments. Slaveholders saw themselves as both fathers and property owners who retained the legitimate right to protect their interests and decide whether their slaves were fit to possess freedom. They believed themselves to be benevolent masters. They insisted that Brazilian slavery was a far cry from the cruel form of slavery practiced in the United States and that domestic relations on the plantations were peaceful. They maintained that their slaves were treated well, fed, and clothed, and that by "innate feeling and custom"[14] masters were more like fathers to their slaves, so that to some degree the slaves were already free.

Alencar, in an 1869 letter in support of slavery, illustrates the belief in the benefits of slavery for all concerned and even propounds the notion that slavery will free Africa: "Even though the slave came through the brutal means of the slave trade, to compensate, he brought the energy to fight great Mother Nature. . . . Here is a benevolent result of the slave trade. . . . The white race, despite reducing the African to a commodity, ennobled him not only through contact, but also through the transfusion of the civilized man. The future civilization of Africa is right here, in this embryonic fact. If someday, as expected, civilization bursts through the African continent, penetrating the peoples of the black race, . . . [it] will be thanks to slavery. It was slavery that prepared the precursors of African freedom."[15] But before the enslaved were emancipated, Alencar argued passionately before the Senate, it was first necessary "to clear their blunted intelligence, elevate their humiliated consciousness, so that one day, when they are granted their freedom, we can say: you are men, you are citizens. We have redeemed you as much from slavery as from ignorance, from vice and misery, and the animalism in which you wallow."[16]

National claims of the genteel and exceptional nature of Brazilian slavery and the quasi-paternal relations between master and slave were undermined by the reality of slave mortality. First of all, as many as two million slaves, or *peças* [pieces], as they were called by slavocrats, are believed to have died during or as a result of the Middle Passage due to malnourishment, abuse, and infections.[17] Many died within days or weeks of arriving on Brazilian shores. Slaves who died before or soon after arriving in the port city of Rio were buried in the Cemetério dos Negros Novos (New Negro Cemetery) near the Valôngo Street slave market. So many slaves were buried in the cemetery that in 1811 police chief Paulo Fernandes Vianna reported that he had received numerous complaints that the corpses were so "poorly buried, that in all of the neighborhood one perceived a foul smell."[18]

Under plantation conditions, 75 percent of slaves died within the first three years of their servitude, before they were habituated to the rigors of the climate and the work. An editor of the English-language newspaper *Rio News*, published in Rio de Janeiro, stated, "Those who say that slavery is milder and more humane in this country than formerly in the United States are either grossly ignorant, or else they are guilty of deliberate falsehood—and the evidence is in favor of the latter supposition."[19] The mortality rate of slaves in Brazil was one of the highest in the Americas. Malnutrition, severe physical punishment, unsanitary food and living conditions, and poor or nonexistent medical care all contributed to their high death rate. As early as the sixteenth century there were numerous reports of slaves dying from starvation. Italian Jesuit Jorge Benci confirmed this in 1700, remarking that masters would make "use of the miserable slaves during the entire week without giving them anything for their sustenance or anything to cover themselves."[20] Benci noted that on some plantations, after working the entire week, slaves were allowed to grow their own food on Sundays and holy days "so that at that time they may obtain their required food and clothing."[21] As historian James Sweet has shown, in times of drought, slaves were often not able to grow enough food to survive, and when plantation owners encountered economic hardship or wanted to cut costs, they eliminated slave rations.[22]

Historian Robert Conrad estimates that in 1798 the slave population was about 1,582,000 and that between 1800 and 1850 1,600,000 new slaves were imported. He argues that if the slave population had been sustained through natural reproduction, it should have reached somewhere near three million by 1871, the year in which the Law of the Free Womb was passed, but in fact only 1,540,829 slaves were registered under the provisions of the law, indicating a very high mortality rate among slaves.[23]

Many Brazilian slaveholders neglected their slaves in the extreme, especially at the height of the slave trade. With the constant influx of new slaves at cheap prices, slave owners would simply work their slaves to death and replace them. Brazilian senator Cristiano Otoni told the chamber of the legislature in 1883 that slave owners were "careless as to the duration of the life of their slaves." The masters perceived that the "proceeds of the first year's labor of a slave were at least enough to cover his cost; that the second and following years were clear profit. Why then, said they, should we bother ourselves about them, when we can so easily get fresh ones at such a low price?"[24] Thomas Nelson, a British physician living in Rio de Janeiro in the 1840s, reported that the slave population was "found to dwindle away, and would shrink into insignificance, except for the shoals of doomed Africans who are annually drawn from the opposite shore" to replace those who had died.[25]

Mahommah Gardo Baquaqua (1824?–1857?), a slave born in Benin, lived in Pernambuco in the early nineteenth century. In 1854 he published the only known biography by a former slave from Brazil. His biography is significant given the paucity of Brazilian slave narratives. Baquaqua recounts his desperation at the extent of his master's brutality, which drove him to attempt escape and suicide and to contemplate killing his master, for "I would rather die than live to be a slave." He continues, "After this sad attempt upon my life, I was taken to my master's house, who tied my hands behind me, and placed my feet together and whipped me most unmercifully, and beat me about the head and face with a heavy stick, then shook me by the neck, and struck my head against the door posts, which cut and bruised me about the temples, the scars from which savage treatment are visible at this time, and will remain so as long as I live."[26]

Despite the harsh realities of Brazilian slavery, slaveholders were outraged by reports indicting them of cruelty. Accounts of the high death rate of Brazilian slaves from malnutrition, whipping, and other acts of violence were nothing but "exaggerations and lies," declared Senator Antônio Coelho Rodrigues.[27] Brazilian slaveholders and proponents of slavery claimed that the masters were generous and compassionate, and that emancipation was not needed as many masters often took the initiative to liberate their slaves of their own accord. "Slaves are treated better in Brazil than in any other country in the world," said Senator Martinho Campos.[28] He argued that the slaves were treated as human beings and retained their dignity. For this reason, Campos exclaimed before the Senate, "slavery ought to continue out of the love of the slaves [for their masters]!"[29]

In the late nineteenth century several laws were passed that gave the impression that the country was moving toward protecting slaves, but these laws were for the most part cosmetic, as noted by Herbert H. Smith, a European traveler well acquainted with Brazil:

> Practically they are almost useless, because they are not enforced. Everybody knows that there are cases of cruelty to slaves, maltreatment even to death, which are visited only by a light punishment, or with none. But no one knows, few even imagine, the vast number of *hidden* crimes which are yearly perpetrated under the slave system, and which never see the light of a court of justice. A slave may be maimed or killed on an island plantation, and no outsider will know of it; the master and the overseer, interested persons, will not proclaim their own crime, and the other slaves dare not give information, or have no one near to appeal to, or being brutalized by the hardships of their life, they do not care.[30]

Two laws that led up to the abolition of slavery yielded paradoxical results. In 1871 the Lei do Ventre Livre (Law of the Free Womb), first proposed by viscount Rio Branco, stipulated that children would remain under the authority of the master and their mother, and that the master had the legal obligation to care for them until the age of eight. At that point the master had the option of either receiving an indemnity payment from the government or continuing to use the child as a slave until the age of twenty-one. Of course, these young children could not care for themselves, and therefore they remained on the plantation. The master did not have to accept the payment from the government, and in most cases it was more beneficial to enslave the child until the age of twenty-one than to accept the money. Additionally, many plantation owners, in league with parish priests, continued to register black infants with an earlier date of birth to prevent them from being freed. In 1885 the Sexagenarian Law unconditionally freed slaves over the age of sixty, but only a small portion of elderly slaves were registered as such and actually freed.[31] Elderly slaves who were freed were abandoned and in many cases left destitute and homeless, without food or any means of supporting themselves.[32]

Gilberto Freyre and the "Myth of Racial Democracy"

The origin of what most know today as Brazil's infamous "myth of racial democracy" has been the source of much speculation. The myth of racial democracy is commonly attributed to Brazilian sociologist Gilberto Freyre in his influential 1933 work *Casa-Grande e Senzala* (The Masters and the Slaves). But Freyre did not invent this myth, nor did he invent the term or use it in *The Masters and the Slaves*. Recently a number of Brazilianist scholars have sought to set the record straight regarding the conflation of the man and the myth.[33] Idelber Avelar has shown that the first time the term *racial democracy* was employed was by Arthur Ramos in 1943, ten years after the publication of *The Masters and the Slaves*. Brazilian sociologist Antônio Sérgio Guimarães asserts that it appeared in Roger Bastide's account of his travels in northeastern Brazil in 1944 in which Bastide wrote about his observations of race relations and Brazilian culture, with references to Freyre's work.[34] Historian Jerry Dávila and Guimarães have argued that Freyre started using the term only in the early 1960s, when he began working with the Portuguese government and endorsed Lusotropicalism (the ideology that the Portuguese were superior colonists due to their climate and history).[35]

Gilberto de Mello Freyre was born in 1900 in the northeastern city of Recife to an old and wealthy family descended from the first colonizers of Brazil. He studied extensively in the United States and received an undergraduate degree from Baylor University and a master's degree in sociology from Columbia University. At Columbia, Freyre studied under the tutelage of Franz Boas, who is often referred to as "the father of American anthropology." Boas was one of the most prominent opponents of the then-popular ideology of scientific racism, which asserted that race was a biological concept and that human behavior was best understood through biological characteristics. Boas influenced Freyre's thinking about the connection between race and culture, and genetics and environment. Freyre's interdisciplinary work in sociology, history, and anthropology provides a historical account of Brazilian slavery and shows how that history was reinterpreted and repurposed by the Brazilian elite in postabolition Brazil. His best-known work is *The Masters and the Slaves*, followed by two sequels, *The Mansions and the Shanties: The Making of Modern Brazil* (1938) and *Order and Progress: Brazil from Monarchy to Republic* (1957). In the 1920s Freyre traveled extensively throughout the American South. Upon returning to Brazil, Freyre drew on his experiences with the contentious nature of US race relations in writing *The Masters and the Slaves*.

Only fifty-five years after the abolition of Brazilian slavery, Freyre was among a number of early twentieth-century scholars, theorists, and scientists who were seeking to understand the nation's past, particularly Portuguese colonialism and slavery and their implications for the present. Freyre was especially interested in demonstrating what he saw as Brazil's uniqueness—what distinguished Brazil from the rest of the world and made it exceptional. His investment in depicting Brazil's exceptionalism greatly influenced his interpretation of the nation's past. This led him to romanticize certain aspects of Brazilian slavery and Portuguese colonialism, which, upon the publication of the book, ultimately garnered him an onslaught of criticism that continues today.

Freyre emerged at a critical moment when racial pathology and hetero- and homosexuality were being studied with intense interest, and doctors and scientists were attempting to diagnose, cure, and criminalize those who did not fit into the nation's future. The importance of Freyre's work for the history of Brazilian race relations and this book is his attempt to analyze how Brazil's unique brand of race relations evolved through contact between the three races (white, black, and indigenous).

Freyre also grew up and came of age in a time in which the Brazilian elite and the government lamented the country's history of slavery and actively sought to erase and destroy it, as we saw with the burning of the slave registers. But at the same time many elite white Brazilians also greatly resented the nation's history of miscegenation and the predominantly black population, which they sought to rectify through the mass importation of European immigrants to whiten the country over time.

When Freyre was eleven years old, physician and president of the National Academy of Medicine João Batista de Lacerda reported, "The importation, on a vast scale, of the black race to Brazil has exercised a harmful influence on this country's progress. For a long while it has been a brake on its material development and has made it difficult to exploit its immense natural wealth. The character of the population has suffered from the failings and vices of this imported, inferior race."[36] For this, many of Brazil's politicians, writers, and intellectuals blamed the Portuguese colonizers. Elite whites were infuriated at Portugal for the mass importation of Africans over centuries that now left them surrounded by an overwhelming black population—a "black stain" that they needed to somehow wipe out. Joaquim Nabuco also remarked in 1881,

> According to one of the most eminent spirits of Portugal [Oliveira Martins], "The enslavement of blacks was the painful cost of colonization in America, because without it, Brazil would not have become what we see today." . . . But who paid this price, and continues to pay, was not Portugal, it was us; and this price in all regards is too hard, and too expensive for the [limited] development that we had. The africanization of Brazil through slavery is a stain that our homeland has engraved on her face and on her tongue, and it is the only truly and long-lasting national project that she was able to found.[37]

In *The Masters and the Slaves*, Freyre broke with the late nineteenth- and early twentieth-century cynicism that the black presence and miscegenation had done irreparable damage to the nation. He celebrated Brazil's racial history and argued that what made Brazilian society so exceptional was precisely its miscegenation. He claimed that the absence of racism in Brazil was due to the nation's history of peaceful miscegenation between European, indigenous, and African peoples, which he held to be one of the country's defining characteristics, especially in contrast to the segregationist system that existed in the United States. Freyre, like many of his predecessors, ascribed to the long-standing belief that Brazilian slavery was more benign and humane as a result of these intimate relations among the races. He describes this process in the preface to *The Master and the Slaves*, asserting that "miscegenation and the interpenetration of cultures—chiefly European, Amerindian, and African culture—together with the possibilities and opportunities for rising in the social scale that in the past have been open to slaves, and individuals of colored races, . . . the possibility and the opportunity of becoming free men and, in the official sense, whites and Christians . . . all these things, from an early period, have tended to mollify the interclass and interracial antagonisms."[38] Brazilian historian Ronaldo Vainfas shows that Freyre portrays sex as an "instrument of power" but at the same time a "terrain of negotiation and a way of cushioning the contradictions at the heart of slavery and the colonial hierarchies."[39] Miscegenation, in Freyre's view, was inherited from the Portuguese colonizers and had created a society that was both racially and sexually fluid. Sexual contact between the races had created a distinct sense of intimacy among all of the nation's people.

The fundaments of what we know as the myth of racial democracy or Brazilian racial and sexual exceptionalism evolved with the Brazilian nation itself. The need to depict Brazil as exceptional is rooted in the nation's independence and its history of slavery. With Brazil's official independence in 1822 and the foreign pressure to abolish slavery in the second half of the nineteenth century, many of the Brazilian elite began to reflect on what distinguished Brazilian slavery and race relations from those of Europe and the United States in light of widespread emancipation throughout the Americas. What appeared initially as a defensive tactic to resist abolishing slavery turned into a critical part of defining national identity. The overt segregationist structure of the United States and its well-known racial antagonism provided an important counterpoint to construct the exceptional nature of Brazilian race relations.

It is important to acknowledge that the belief in Brazil's exceptional slavery and race relations, as well as the transcendental power of miscegenation, was espoused not only by the white elite but also by many free blacks, who were both for and against slavery. José do Patrocínio, a mulatto born as the illegitimate child of a manumitted slave woman and a white priest, was one of the most prominent voices in the abolitionist movement. Because of his race and illegitimate birth he suffered a great deal of discrimination over the course of his life. In 1887, a year before abolition, he curiously remarked in an editorial in his newspaper *Gazeta da Tarde*, a paper devoted to the abolitionist movement, "We [Brazilians] have been able to fuse all races into a single native population because Portuguese colonization assimilated the savage races instead of trying to destroy them, thus preparing us to resist the devastating invasion of race prejudice."[40]

In 1879 Joaquim Nabuco entered the Brazilian parliament and became the leader of the bourgeoning abolitionist movement. In his classic work *O abolicionismo* (Abolitionism), published in 1883, five years prior to abolition, Nabuco detailed several of what would become the key concepts of Brazilian racial exceptionalism, which Freyre would also expound upon in his work. He observed that Brazilian slavery was inherently different from the slavery practiced in the United States, where blacks were separated from whites and barred from being active participants in society:

> In Brazil the exact opposite happened: slavery, although founded on differences between the two races, never made race a barrier, and in this sense, Brazilian slavery was infinitely more skilled. The contact between the two races from colonization to today produced a mixed-race population, as we have seen, and the slave upon receiving his freedom receives the title of citizen. Slavery in our country remained open and extended

her privileges to all indiscriminately: white or black, *ingênuos* [freeborn children born after the Law of the Free Womb], slaves, foreigners, or national citizens, rich or poor, in this way it acquired at the same time an incomparably flexible amalgamation and elasticity much greater than what would have happened had there been a racial monopoly, as in the southern states of the United States. This system of absolute equality certainly opened up a better future for the black race in Brazil than in North America.[41]

It is notable that Nabuco believes that although Brazilian slavery was founded on "differences," which he purposefully avoids naming, these differences were automatically overcome through interracial sex, which was harmonious and consensual, unlike in the United States, creating a mostly mixed-race population. According to Nabuco, slavery in Brazil, although based on whites owning blacks, was nondiscriminatory, somehow affording black Brazilians a wealth of opportunities that were denied to blacks in the United States. For many abolitionists like Nabuco, and even supporters of slavery, Brazilian slavery was curiously not seen as a racist or discriminatory institution; it was somehow conceived to exist without race or racism. Under Brazilian law, blacks could and did own slaves. This complicated the racial dynamics of slavery. Though black slaveholders were not in the majority and all slaves in Brazil were black, the possibility for blacks to own slaves contributed to the deracialization of Brazilian slavery and racial relations by the white elite, making slave ownership a question of property rather than a matter of race or racism. The view of racism as a product of North American society and of Brazil as a racially exceptional country obscured the extreme oppression suffered by the black masses.

Slavery, Interracial Sex, and the Brazilian National Narrative

Sex was necessarily central to both the institution of slavery and to the construction of the myth of racial democracy. Interracial sex came to serve as proof of racial harmony. Historian Gerald Bender has shown that the Portuguese colonizer did not use "the [same] exploitive motivations of his counterparts from the more industrialized countries in Europe"; instead he "entered into 'cordial relations' with non-European populations he met in the tropics." Bender concludes that "the ultimate proof of the absence of racism among the Portuguese" is found in Brazil, "whose large and socially prominent *mestiço* [mixed race] population is living testimony to the freedom of social and sexual intercourse between Portuguese and non-Europeans."[42] Bender's use of the term *cordial relations* is a reference to Sérgio Buarque de Holanda's theory of the Cordial Man, who asserts his dominance under the guise of intimacy (in this case sex), making it possible for violence to coexist with intimacy. Sex became the Portuguese weapon of colonization and vehicle of exploitation. Holanda has argued that throughout Brazilian history there has been a confusion of the private and the political, so that "private desires continue to dominate within an environment of closed circles that are impermeable to impersonal order."[43] Brazilian slavery as an institution was intimately connected to individual white male supremacist desire. This confusion between the private desires of white men and the political during slavery created what anthropologist Erica Lorraine Williams refers to as "ambiguous entanglements" in which power, exploitation, and violence are both concealed and enacted through intimacy.[44]

Ronaldo Vainfas has shown that the Catholic Church had strict rules governing sexual conduct for both men and women in colonial society. Fornication, promiscuity, and all sexual activity outside of marriage were prohibited by the church. Vainfas writes that many openly disobeyed and subverted these laws, proclaiming their "right to pleasure" and their "male privileges" over vulnerable women and slaves.[45] Sexual desires, as Ann Laura Stoler writes, "were never about sex alone. . . . Sexual desire in colonial and postcolonial contexts has been a crucial transfer point of power, tangled with racial exclusions in complicated ways."[46] By reshaping the rules around sex to fit their own needs and desires, white men were also shaping the historical archives of slavery and colonialism and how sex would be recorded in the archives. This is key to understanding that interracial sex under slavery as it would later become narrated as part of the nation's history of race and miscegenation was entangled with white male desire and identity.

Sex under colonialism and slavery was only one mechanism of control and domination. Sex had a very important role in concretizing and physicalizing white male gender, racial, and sexual supremacy both in the home and in society. Portuguese colonizers assimilated blacks by "colonizing them in bed," writes Albert Gomes.[47] The Portuguese, according to anthropologist Vale de Almeida, were seen as "half-breeds who generate yet more half-breeds, and proximity leads to both contact, and conflict and cruelty."[48] What is important is the conception of the act of sex. In the context of slavery and colonialism, sex took on deeply personal and political meanings for colonizers and later slave masters.

For the theorists of Brazilian racial exceptionalism, interracial sex came to symbolize intimacy and equality. The mulatto, whom Portuguese sociologist Boaventura de Sousa Santos derisively referred to as the fruit of a "harmonious reciprocal elision" between blacks and whites, came to serve as proof of the absence of racism and of Brazilian racial exceptionalism. Mulattos, Sousa Santos contends, "contributed against their will and own interests to legitimize racial and social inequality. Deracializing social relations permitted colonialism and Brazilian politics to displace blame and to effectively produce social inequality."[49] Santos calls attention not only to the significance of the mixed-raced body but also, more importantly, to how essential interracial sex is to defining the Brazilian difference and sustaining uniquely Brazilian forms of inequality. Political and national mythology constructed on or through the body is indeed the most enduring, because with procreation comes the reproduction of the body's meaning and visibility in relation to national myth.

The myth of racial democracy, which anthropologist Angela Gilliam has acerbically termed the "Great Sperm Theory of National Formation,"[50] was a conscious rescripting of the historical sexual exploitation, rape, and humiliation suffered by slave women at the hands of white men. Sex with white men became the means of inclusion of blacks in the nation. In this sense, to borrow historian Paulina Alberto's term, white men historically defined the "terms of inclusion"[51] and created a hegemonic discourse around how all bodies—those of black women, black men, and white women—were included in the nation's historical narrative. If the nation's story is defined only in relation to white male supremacist desire, what stories and experiences have been discarded or left out?

In a society in which black men and all women, whether black or white, were the legal property of white men, sex was construed only in terms of white male desire both socially and legally. During Brazilian slavery, the term *rape* was applied only in certain contexts with certain bodies. A white woman, only of a particular class, could be legally raped, although not by her husband, because she was owned by him. Slaves could not be raped for the same reason. Thus there was no social or legal prohibition against the rape of slaves, and certainly there was no understanding of the possibility of same-sex rape. This meant that in most cases sexual relations between white men and slaves were claimed to be consensual even when they involved coercion and violence. This presumed consent of slaves became the sexual basis of the harmonious myth of Brazilian slavery, racial exceptionalism, and the myth of racial democracy, which denied the rape of black women and men and other forms of racial violence. Thus rape and racial violence go hand in hand.

In examining relationships between poor black women from a Rio favela and wealthy white men, Donna Goldstein has shown how the conflation of interracial sex and antiracism still persists today and obscures forms of exploitation and violence.[52] Thus even today what is more powerful and dangerous than the sexual act itself is the narrative that is created about it, who controls it, and what it continues to conceal.

We cannot understand the history of Brazil's complex racial relations without looking at its complex sexual history. Race was made through sex—the act itself, the personal and political meanings ascribed to it, and its use as a mechanism of power and white supremacy. Sex, like the nation, becomes the discourse that we create about it.

Brazil's untenable contradiction was that rape and racial violence could never be reconciled with racial harmony and consensual miscegenation. For Brazilian racial exceptionalism to be sustained, violence against slaves in all forms had to be silenced. This was not difficult to achieve: slaves did not own their bodies; they did not control the narrative made about their bodies; and the law provided them with very little recourse for naming what was done to them.

As Frantz Fanon has demonstrated in the context of colonialism and enslavement, the white man projects "his own desires onto the Negro" and behaves "as if the Negro really had them."[53] The projection of white male desire (sexual, racial, political), its fusion with the black body, and the blurring of lines between the two are critical to silencing racial, sexual, and gender violence throughout Brazil's history of slavery. The power of sexual and racial violence lies not only in the physical overpowering, humiliation, or defilement of the victim, but also in controlling the victim's individual story. Proponents of Brazilian racial exceptionalism correctly attributed meaning to sex between the races—though not, of course, its true meaning—and throughout Brazilian history interracial sex took on forms that were both personal and political in meaning.

TWO

Illegible Violence:
The Rape and Sexual Abuse of Male Slaves

[Francisco] repeated some ten times the Holy Name of Jesus, saying that he was not a woman to satisfy his master's sexual whims. —FRANCISCO, Mozambican slave of Jacinto Ferreira dos Campos, Vila Rica, Brazil. From the Torre do Tombo National Archive of the Portuguese Inquisition, Lisbon, 1758

On June 10, 1767, a twenty-year-old unmarried Angolan slave named Joaquim Antonio went into the city of Belém, in the northeastern state of Pará, Brazil, with a group of slaves to sell firewood. Taking advantage of this time away from the plantation, Joaquim went to the Collegio de Santo Alexandre, where the trials of the Portuguese Inquisition were being held, with the intention of telling his story to the inquisitors. Upon being sworn in, he confessed that he had been violently raped by his master, Francisco Serrão de Castro. Joaquim Antonio's case is very significant because it reveals the painful details of his own rape and the fact that Francisco Serrão de Castro routinely and sadistically raped more than twenty of his male slaves. His victims ranged from small boys and adolescents to married men. Due to his master's brutality, Joaquim Antonio testified, several men contracted infections and suffered severe bleeding, leading to the deaths of five slaves.[1] Transcripts from trials of the Portuguese Inquisition show that this case was not unusual and that the sexual violation of male slaves by their masters was employed as a tool of domination in Brazil.

The Portuguese Inquisition and Sexual Violence

The Portuguese Inquisition was formally established in Portugal in 1536 at the request of King João III and lasted until 1821. It later expanded to the Portuguese colonies of Brazil, Cape Verde, and Goa, where the inquisitors investigated reputed offenses against Roman Catholicism. The main targets of the Inquisition were New Christians—Iberian Muslims as well as Jews and their descendants who had converted to Catholicism and were suspected of clandestinely practicing Judaism. Although initially the Inquisition's main focus was religious matters, its reach eventually extended to every aspect of society, such as book censorship, witchcraft, bigamy, and sexual crimes.

Unlike the Spanish Inquisition, which established courts throughout Spanish America, the Portuguese Inquisition never established a tribunal in Brazil.[2] Trials were presided over by bishops in Brazil or, in more severe cases, adjudicated by the inquisitional court in Lisbon, which held jurisdiction over Brazil, the Atlantic Islands, Africa, and Asia.[3] Many of the early cases from the Portuguese Inquisition in Brazil from as early as the fourteenth century, when Portugal was still under Spanish rule, were presided over by representatives sent from Portugal.[4] The first visitation of inquisitorial officials to Brazil occurred in Salvador de Bahia, the capital of the Brazilian empire from 1591, then in Pernambuco in 1595, followed by Rio de Janeiro in 1605, again in Salvador from 1618 to 1620, and the southern regions in 1627. The inquisitors also visited the states of Pará, Maranhão, Paraíba, and Minas Gerais between 1763 and 1769.[5] As the eighteenth century progressed and the Inquisition drew to a close many cases were adjudicated by local officials in Brazil.

The written proceedings of the Portuguese Inquisition in Brazil preserved in the Torre do Tombo National Archive in Lisbon provide some of the earliest and most extensive documentation of same-sex sexual violence during Brazilian slavery and throughout the colonial period. The Inquisition cases of sexual violence committed by white male masters to be examined in this chapter show that the rape and sexual abuse of enslaved men and boys was a reality of Brazilian slavery. We will never know for certain how often these acts occurred or how many enslaved men and boys were subjected to rape and sexual abuse at the hands of their white masters. But the recorded cases do unequivocally provide us with a glimpse into the experiences of some male rape victims and suggest that there may have been more incidents that were not reported, or perhaps were reported but not documented. Given the range of sodomy cases found in the record, each case must be examined in its specific context—freedom or enslavement, class position, consent or coercion—to completely understand the overt and concealed complexities of each case.

Sodomy in the early modern period was, as Foucault puts it, an "utterly confused category."[6] Sodomy referred to highly sinful and heretical acts, offenses that encapsulated a host of nonprocreative sexual practices condemned by the Catholic Church.[7] The category of "sodomy" included anal and oral sex between a man and a woman or between two men, masturbation, the penetration or stimulation of a woman with the hands by either gender, sex between women, and sex or sexual stimulation using objects. Any form of sex in which conception was not possible was deemed sinful and heretical in the eyes of God by the Catholic Church.

The sodomy cases brought before the Portuguese Inquisition in Brazil are striking for their diversity. These cases include the rape of male slaves by white masters, sex between clergymen and young boys, and numerous instances of incest (brothers engaging in consensual anal sex, mutual masturbation, and oral sex with each other). The diversity of these cases evinces the pervasiveness of anal sex and shows that sodomy did not follow an exclusive pattern of offenders and their motivations. Men who engaged in or fell victim to the "nefarious sin" of sodomy, as it was called, belonged to a number of different races, classes, and social stations.

For the most part, the Inquisition prosecuted and punished most severely the male who was penetrated, whether voluntarily or involuntarily. Inquisitors took into account a number of factors in their evaluation of sodomy cases.[8] They considered whether the sodomy was consensual or forced, the age of the accused, and the specific circumstances under which the act occurred. Though each sodomy case was recorded in great detail, judging from the results of most cases, the church appeared primarily concerned with the act as a sin and gave very little importance to the violent and coercive conditions under which these offenses occurred. This was especially true for cases involving enslaved men and the poor.

Those found guilty of heresy, including sexual sins, were sentenced at an auto-da-fé. Clergymen would preside over the proceedings and deliver punishments. The auto-da-fé served as a grandiose public display of the power of the Inquisition in which the accused were punished and reconciled with the church. Punishments included confinement in dungeons, torture, abuse, and, in the most severe cases, being burned alive at the stake. Historian Luiz Mott reports that after New Christians, sodomites were the social group most persecuted by the Portuguese Inquisition.[9] The most vigorous prosecutions against sodomites occurred in the seventeenth century, and the last prisons for sodomites were built in 1711 in Coimbra, Portugal.[10]

Article 13 of the 1603 Filipine Code of Portuguese criminal law, titled "Of Those Who Commit the Sin of Sodomy and with Animals," stated, "Anyone, regardless of their rank, who in any way commits the sin of sodomy, will be burned until they have turned to ashes so that there will never be any memory of their body or grave, and all of their property will be confiscated by the Crown of the Kingdom if they have descendants, and in the same way their children and grandchildren will lose their rights and become as infamous as those who commit the crime of treason."[11] In Portugal five thousand cases of sodomy or sexual acts between men were confessed or denounced.[12] Of this total, more than thirty accused were burned at the stake. The largest number of cases of sodomy in the Brazilian colony was found among the most vulnerable of the society: slaves, dependent workers, and servants made up 43 percent of documented cases.[13]

In Brazil, despite the severe punishment stipulated in the Filipine Code, no one was burned at the stake. For those convicted of sodomy, punishments varied greatly, most commonly including public defamation, whippings, fines, confiscation of assets, public prayer and fasting, deportation to other regions of Brazil or Angola, and imprisonment.

Sinners were encouraged by the Catholic Church to confess their sins. Many avoided punishment by openly confessing their sins during what was called the Tempo da Graça (Grace Period), a period of a few weeks in which people could confess their sins in exchange for clemency or lighter punishments. There are indications in the trial transcripts that a number of people, including white masters who had sexually abused their male slaves, may have brought their cases before the inquisitors proactively as a means of self-protection before a denunciation could be brought against them.

The church proclaimed that every Catholic had a duty to denounce all crimes and heretical acts against the church. The edict assigned this duty to "any person, man or woman, clergy or religious person, of whatever state, condition, dignity, or class."[14] This clause gave slaves both the freedom and the moral duty to make confessions or denunciations against their masters. But this did not mean that all testimonies were valued equally or that the inquisitors were not prejudiced by a person's race, gender, or social standing.

The inquisitorial edict on denunciations incited an atmosphere of extreme distrust and espionage. Neighbors, relatives, friends, wives, husbands, siblings, and slaves all spied on each other and would not hesitate to inform the church of any perceived wrongdoing by others, no matter how insignificant. Confessions and denunciations ran the gamut from clandestinely practicing Judaism to eating meat on a Friday, blasphemy, bestiality, and female sodomy.

Though according to Catholic doctrine sodomy was considered one of the gravest sins, as historian Ronaldo Vainfas has argued,[15] the Inquisition's stance on sodomy confessions and denunciations made by free and enslaved blacks was characterized by indifference toward the suffering of the victim on the part of most inquisitors. Their voyeuristic penchant for sexual detail is obvious and they were satisfied if the slave provided a detailed confession, seeing no need to mete out strict punishments. In some instances, a guilty party's assets were seized, and in the most severe cases, punishment for sodomy convictions consisted of deportation and confinement in the galleys, but those cases were the exception. As Vainfas argues, even though the inquisitors found sodomy to be extremely sinful, they were wholly aware that it was virtually impossible to "separate the institution of slavery from sexual abuse."[16] As a result, since the sixteenth century the inquisitors had decided not to punish masters or slaves accused of sodomy, save for a few masters who were formally charged. In Minas Gerais, for example, one hundred individuals were accused and only four were prosecuted during the entire Inquisition.[17]

Confessions by slaves, such as those to be examined in this chapter, were viewed with even more indifference. As slaves were legal property and masters had the right to use them in any way they wanted, it was virtually impossible for the church to hold masters accountable for the sexual abuse of their male and female slaves.[18] This confirms the involvement of the Catholic Church in slavery and places the church at the center of legitimating—or at the very least turning a blind eye to—sexual abuse inflicted on enslaved men and women. Sex was considered the duty of slaves or justifiable use by the master of property, and thus the church chose not to intervene when it became aware of the sexual violation of slaves. In this sense, confessions made by male rape victims were little more than a pornographic display in which the slave related his violation and humiliation, only to realize that there would be no real punishment of the perpetrator. There is an obvious contradiction between church law, which prescribed severe punishment for sexual sins, even burning at the stake, and the indifference of the inquisitors toward male slaves who were raped by their masters. Examining the victims' confessions and denunciations, one gets the sense that many slaves were aware of the severity of the sin and thought that their confession might provide some sort of protection for themselves or punishment of their masters, but most were mistaken.

The Inquisition prosecuted cases of *sodomia perfeita* (ejaculation inside the anus) and *sodomia imperfeita* (sodomy without ejaculation), with the former being the most egregious. It condemned but did not prosecute instances of *molície* ("softness," meaning feminine qualities), which referred to consensual or forced sexual acts between men and between women such as oral sex and masturbation. Given that homosexuality did not exist as a sexual category during this period, the inquisitors were solely interested in consummated anal sex, or sodomia perfeita, and not any form of romantic or intimate relationship between men. A number of elite and even common white men, believing themselves to be powerful and unpunishable, lured young enslaved and free black men and boys by offering them food, alcohol, lodging, and even opium in exchange for anal intercourse, masturbation, or oral sex.[19]

Male Rape Cases from the Inquisition Records

LUIZ DA COSTA

On the morning of July 30, 1743, a twenty-year-old unmarried slave named Luiz da Costa, born in Costa da Mina, present-day Ghana, was taken from a prison cell, where he had been held for eight days, and was tried by the Holy Office of the Portuguese Inquisition in Lisbon for his own rape. Upon being sworn in by inquisitor Manoel Varejão Távora, Luiz was admonished to "confess his misdeeds," for only telling the truth would "clear his conscience, save his soul, and satisfactorily resolv[e] his case." He testified to the inquisitors that he had accompanied his master, Manoel Alves Cabral, and parish priest Manoel de Lima on a hunting trip to a remote area in Pernambuco. Luiz told the inquisitors that when they found themselves alone his master raped him at gunpoint, "threatening and intimidating him with the shotgun" and "saying that he would kill him if he did not consent to what he wanted." Luiz added that despite the "repugnance that he felt, out of fear he consented." He described the act as "penetration and ejaculation in his anus, with Luiz performing the passive role and his master the active."

Luiz worked as a domestic slave in the town of Vila da Boa Vista in the northeastern state of Pernambuco, Brazil. Luiz fled and told the priest what had transpired, perhaps thinking that Lima would help him. Though Lima had not witnessed the act, he brought Luiz da Costa rather than his master to the attention of the inquisitors. One year after the event, Luiz was transported to Lisbon to stand trial for his own rape.

According to Luiz's testimony, prior to the day in question, Alves Cabral had attempted to rape him many times. To avoid this, Luiz was forced to agree to perform other nonpenetrative sexual acts which could have included oral sex and masturbation, which the transcriber renders as *molície*, on numerous occasions. He does not state exactly what kinds of sexual acts he engaged in. Luiz's story also reveals that sexual violence included various forms of abuse as the term *molície* referred to all forms of nonpenetrative sex that caused ejaculation outside of the anus.

Luiz's case is important, as he reveals not only his own story, but also that of José, another victim of rape and sexual abuse. Luiz recalls that Alves Cabral would come repeatedly to be with them at night, getting into the bed between them. Luiz states that on many occasions he witnessed firsthand Alves Cabral "realizing acts of consummated sodomy with José, which José later intimated to him that it was exactly in fact what he had perceived." This case shows again that male rape was not an isolated incident during Brazilian slavery. All slaves, male and female, were vulnerable to sexual assault.

The inquisitors heard Luiz's confession and did not punish him, but cynically "strongly recommended that he dissociate himself entirely and flee the company of anyone who might pervert him and induce him in any way . . . to commit again similar crimes, because should he not emend his ways he [would] be punished with the full force of the law."[20]

JOAQUIM ANTONIO

The trial transcript of the slave Joaquim Antonio, who "confessed" to his own rape, illustrates the inquisitors' habit of recording the rape of slaves in great detail. The inquisitors instructed Joaquim that he must fully "confess his transgressions" so that "his soul might be saved." Joaquim related that six years earlier, in June 1761, his master, Francisco Serrão de Castro, summoned him to his room and ordered him to sit on the bed. Suspicious of his intentions, Joaquim hesitated, which caused Serrão de Castro to forcefully grab him and pin him facedown on the bed. Serrão de Castro began to remove his pants. Joaquim told the inquisitors that he "instantly understood the evil aim that Serrão de Castro had in these actions, because at that time several male slaves on the plantation had complained that he had sodomized them," the trial transcript reads. Joaquim felt forced to submit to his master: "Seeing that the door was closed and there was nowhere for him to escape, fearful of some severe punishment, Joaquim agreed to what he wanted," upon which Serrão de Castro "forcefully thrust his penis into Joaquim's anus." Joaquim related that he was "unable to tolerate the pain," yet Serrão proceeded to "penetrate him as much as he could," intending to ejaculate inside him, but "was only able to do so on the outside, covering Joaquim's legs with semen." He then dismissed Joaquim, giving him four coins with the promise of more if he did not tell anyone of the incident. Joaquim told the inquisitors that Serrão de Castro remained angry with him for the imperfect ejaculation and "would regularly send him to be severely whipped under other pretexts." Joaquim reported that he was only one of numerous rape victims and that Serrão de Castro had "sodomized almost all, or the majority of, the male slaves on the plantation."

Serrão de Castro's enduring anger over this incident of sodomia imperfeita is laden with meaning. Sodomia perfeita was considered more sinful, but in the case of the rape of a male slave by his master, the sin accrued to the victim rather than the perpetrator. Thus ejaculation was the greater form of degradation and forced a higher degree of culpability on the slave. As with rape in the modern age, the rape of male slaves was not solely or perhaps even primarily about the rapist's gratification, but also about the conscious use of sodomy as a form of degradation, terror, and defilement that left the slave culpable and sinful in the eyes of the church.

In his confession Joaquim names more than fifteen other male slaves, including "two young slave boys," who were sexually brutalized by the master, and he describes their injuries in graphic detail. He states that prior to their deaths, slave men Manoel Fagundo and Pedro showed him their wounded rear-ends, which he describes as "swollen" and "pouring with blood." Five men died as a result of infections. He adds that "those who remain alive live in fear that they will also die in the same manner" and thus they "flee from Serrão de Castro whenever possible."

Joaquim further attempts to provide evidence of Francisco Serrão's nefarious character by divulging to the inquisitors that while Serrão presented himself publicly as a devout Christian by attending church, he "did not allow the slaves to pray or direct them spiritually in any way" and "in his everyday life he regularly fornicates with all of the slaves on the plantation in the way that [Joaquim] just described." It is curious that the inquisitors did not take more interest in Serrão de Castro's prohibition against prayer. A number of slave confessions that I have come across show that slaveholders refused to allow their slaves to be baptized or to practice Catholicism. Unbaptized slaves had less visibility in the eyes of the Catholic Church, and the church was less inclined to protect them. White masters may have intentionally denied their slaves baptism and prayer in order to render them less moral, less deserving of the church's protection, and therefore more sexually available to the master.

The fact that Joaquim Antonio came forth to confess of his own volition meant that he was able, despite his lot as a slave, to juxtapose himself as morally good, in contrast to his heretical master, who was a sinner and tried to deceive the church. Among the most important and striking aspects of the inquisitorial testimonies of slaves against white masters is the slaves' cognizance of their vulnerability as well as of the limits of their believability and capacity for morality in the eyes of the Catholic Church. Using faith and their knowledge of church doctrine and what constituted sin in stating their claims against their masters proved to be a powerful form of resistance against shame and abjection. This testimony demonstrated to the inquisitors—who concerned themselves primarily with the fact that the sin had occurred rather than that it had caused injury and humiliation—that the slaves knew what sin was, were forced to engage in it against their will, and were now using the church to hold their masters accountable for their actions.

While on the one hand we should read Joaquim's story as a heart-wrenching confession of an enslaved man who was violently raped, and who also bravely exposed the murders of his fellow slaves who were literally raped to death, his confession and a number of other confessions in this chapter, regardless of their outcome, show unmistakable resistance. In these inquisitional confessions and denunciations, male slave rape victims are daring to use the precepts of the religion used to justify their enslavement to expose and record for posterity the abuses of white slaveholders and the institution of slavery.

Joaquim's statement that his master attempted to buy his silence with four coins points to the purposely deceptive behavior of the slaveholder, who was very protective of his public image yet savagely raped male slaves in private and then sought to conceal his actions.[21] The rape of slaves almost always occurred in private. This fact holds significant implications for the history of same-sex rape under slavery as the master's shame and active attempts at erasure contradict the so-called unrapability of slave men—the claim that they could not be raped because they were both men and property frames the same-sex archive of slavery. Masters were anxious not about being viewed as homosexual—since homosexuality was not yet an identified sexual category—but as errant Catholics, which was the primary concern of the Inquisition. Thus a slave could claim some measure of agency by attempting to prove that a master was a heretic, a conscious sinner.

Joaquim ended his confession by intimating to the inquisitors that because of all he had suffered, he could not "help but feel hatred and ill will, as he certainly does not want to belong to Francisco Serrão because of the sins and harm that he causes in order to satisfy his appetite."[22] After hearing Joaquim's story, the inquisitors deliberated and based their judgment on the fact that he did not entirely consent to the act and that his master was unable to commit perfect sodomy. They released Joaquim back to his master's custody, telling him that it was good that he had come before them to take accountability for the crimes that *he* had committed. They reprimanded him, admonishing him to "never again commit such an abominable, dirty, ugly, and vile crime that is sodomy and in which he performed the passive role that greatly offends the Divine Majesty," intimating that Serrão de Castro was less guilty because he had played the active role.

Joaquim Antonio's denunciation was not the first brought against Serrão de Castro. Nine years earlier, in 1759, João Marimba, a recently arrived Angolan slave, was also raped by Serrão de Castro and brought his case before the Inquisition. Serrão de Castro ordered João Marimba to accompany him deep into the woods where no one could see them. There Serrão de Castro exposed himself and ordered João to touch his penis. João complied out of fear. Serrão de Castro then ordered João to lie facedown on the ground and proceeded to rape him. A year later Serrão de Castro offered João a glass of liquor and tobacco and then ordered him to "give him his ass," the transcript reads. João replied that he was not a "slave woman for him to fornicate with, but that he was still a man even though he was slave, and that the first time had caused him a great deal of pain, and he did not want to suffer any more." Serrão de Castro tried to grab him and rape him, but João managed to escape.[23] After his confession was heard, João was released. Serrão de Castro went unpunished and continued to sexually abuse his male slaves, as the first case illustrates.

CORROBORATING CASES IN THE INQUISITIONAL RECORD

The archives of the inquisitional proceedings provide additional evidence of enslaved men who were raped by their masters in several states throughout Brazil. In all of these cases the connection between ownership, domination, and forced sex is apparent. Gaspar Rodrigues, a plantation owner in the northeastern state of Bahia, was accused of raping twenty-five-year-old Matias, born in Guinea. According to Matias, Rodrigues forcefully raped him on several occasions, holding him down and choking him to prevent him from calling for help.[24] Also in Bahia, Felipe Thomaz de Miranda, another wealthy plantation owner, became infamous for raping his male slaves. Years earlier, Miranda had fled Pernambuco, where he had murdered one of the victims whom he had regularly raped for fear that the slave would denounce him to the Inquisition. In Bahia, he continued his malevolent behavior and was later denounced by a mulatto slave named Francisco, whom he had also raped.[25]

Pero Garcia, a plantation owner in Bahia, confessed in 1618 that he had raped three of his male slaves "innumerous times," including two mulatto house slaves named Joseph and Bento, ages fourteen and fifteen, and Jacinto, who was six or seven at the time of the confession.[26] Joseph confessed to the inquisitors that "they committed the abominable sin [sodomy] together in the master's bed once or twice at night, after the evening meal, and the other times were in the morning and in the afternoon after lunch."[27] The documents also state that Garcia raped Joseph so frequently that the boy was referred to by the slave women as "master's little girl."[28] Garcia also admitted to having raped a freed slave on several occasions.

Miner Manuel Álvares Cabral confessed in 1739 (some twenty years after the fact) in Mariana, Minas Gerais, that he had sodomized six slave boys between the ages of four and eight over a period of eight years. They were José Coura, João Gago, João Ladano, Luiz Mina, Antonio Jorge Ladano, and Francisco Angola. After Cabral's confession, five of the slaves came forth to testify about these acts. José Coura, who was twenty-eight years old at the time, confessed that he had "served as the passive recipient during anal sex with his master, forced by the fear of being a slave and respect for his master, who virtually ordered him to do it." Antonio Jorge similarly stated that he had acquiesced to being raped for "fear of punishment and out of respect for his master." João Gago stated that he also had complied out of "fear of punishment."[29]

Luiz Delgado, a Portuguese guitarist and tobacco merchant, was infamous for engaging in sexual activity with men, for which he was deported from Portugal to Brazil by the Inquisition. Though married, Delgado openly carried on sexual exploits with several men in Salvador. He raped a recently arrived slave from Angola in 1674 whom he found fleeing from his master. The slave did not speak Portuguese and told his story to a translator, saying, "This is a bad white man, because on that night he had wanted to make me a woman, fighting with me and promising that he would let me go and would give me money if I agreed to play the part of a woman." Delgado "committed imperfect sodomy with the black slave as the passive one."[30]

Several cases expose the fact that white slave owners purchased male slaves, as was the case with enslaved women, based on physical attributes for the sole purpose of sexually exploiting them. In 1742 João da Silva, twenty-one years old and a slave of Manuel Alves Carvalho, declared before the Inquisition that on the very night that Carvalho purchased him he "ordered him to come to bed with him." João said that he was fully aware that Carvalho planned to rape him, which Carvalho confirmed by stating that "he bought him for this purpose [sex], and that if he did not comply he would sell him."[31] In 1762 a creole slave by the name of Anselmo from the city of Taubaté in São Paulo, who worked in the diamond mine in Arraial do Tijuco, accused his master, Inácio Geraldes, of raping him for several years. According to Anselmo, immediately after buying him Geraldes began to treat him like a "son" and at night would bring him to sleep in bed with him, whereupon he would "grope his private parts and penetrated him from behind."[32] Geraldes was also very violent and possessive and held Anselmo virtually as a sex slave. According to Anselmo, on one occasion when Geraldes observed him conversing with a solider, he became enraged and "tied him up with chains" and "ordered him to suck his penis, which he did many times and also served as an instrument with his hands until he ejaculated."[33]

In 1743 Filipe Santiago, a mulatto slave, accused his master, José Ribeiro Dias of Minas do Paracatu, a wealthy priest who owned twenty-seven slaves, of rape and several other sexual acts, such as oral sex and masturbation, performed against his will. Father Dias was also reputed to have engaged in anal sex on numerous occasions with young men and children, many of them his own slaves. In his denunciation Filipe reveals a clear understanding of his vulnerability as an enslaved man when he discloses that he was raped by the priest "with the power and respect of a master" and that he "fearfully acquiesced to his master's will because of his slave condition."[34] Father Dias was one of the few slaveholders who was punished. He was sentenced to imprisonment in the galleys for ten years.[35] Filipe's testimony directly condemns Dias's hypocrisy and abuse of power as a Catholic priest who, rather than upholding the doctrine of the church, instead used his positions as priest and slaveholder to rape his male slaves.

The proceedings of the Portuguese Inquisition in Brazil are replete with instances of priests coercing slave men and women and young white boys to engage in anal sex. The case of Filipe Santiago shows the complicated relationship between the Catholic Church and the institution of slavery in Brazil as well as the inherent contradictions between the church's dogma and its practices. Though slaves may have been portrayed as inherently sinful and morally depraved, Filipe, like many of the enslaved men and women in this book, dared to tell his story, revealing that he knew what sin was and that he was unwilling to accept his degradation in silence.

Also in Bahia in the second half of the eighteenth century, slaveholder Garcia Dávila Perreira Aragão, one of the wealthiest and most illustrious men in the state, was denounced for his extreme cruelty toward his slaves. His denunciation lists countless victims, ranging from small children to elderly men and women who suffered a range of cruel punishments, including whippings, mutilations, burnings, and lynchings. One victim was a young slave boy by the name of Manoel. The denunciation states that Aragão made Manoel "lie down with his head to the floor and arse in the air, drawing back both of his buttocks with his hands, while Garcia Dávila Perreira Aragão held a lit candle, and when a good amount of melted wax was gathered he poured it into the boy's anal cavity, who with a scream from the pain of the fire, jumped off the floor, combined with a scream from the pain suffered. With this, Aragão laughed with pleasure."[36]

In 1792 a miner, Manuel Pereira Guimarães of Congonhas, Minas Gerais, confessed before the inquisitors to engaging in a host of obscene sexual acts and to forcing his slaves to participate in orgies. This case shows that slaves were in an extreme sense what Saidiya Hartman calls "vehicles of white enjoyment, in all its sundry and unspeakable expressions,"[37] existing for the pleasure and sexual gratification of the master, as forms of human pornography. Manuel tells the inquisitors that to "arouse his flesh"[38] he ordered his black slave, Ventura, to "fondle his private parts" while he did the same with several different slave women. He also admits to engaging in sexual acts with other men whom he either summoned or paid. Manuel Pereira was a consummate voyeur who also admitted that he ordered his slave men to have sex with slave women while he watched and masturbated. He stated, "While in bed with one woman, that he had vaginal and anal sex with, and other times placed his penis in the mouth of some men and women, but never ejaculated in their mouth, and sometimes masturbating myself. [He stated,] I ordered my male slave to masturbate men with their hands and I did it to him, and I ordered many *crioulos* [a native-born black Brazilian] and *cabras* [a child of a mulatto and a black woman] to also do the same." Despite these confessions, Manuel Pereira was not charged with any offense. He asked for forgiveness and promised to never do it again.[39]

Slavery and the Catholic Church

The Old Testament firmly establishes the right to own slaves. Leviticus 25:44–46 reads, "Your male and female slaves are to come from the nations around you; from them you may buy slaves. You may also buy some of the temporary residents living among you and members of their clans born in your country, and they will become your property. You can bequeath them to your children as inherited property and can make them slaves for life, but you must not rule over your fellow Israelites ruthlessly." The prescription that "fellow Israelites" should not be treated ruthlessly implies that slaves from other nations could be treated ruthlessly.

There were voices opposing slavery. Saint Augustine challenges slavery in *City of God*, written in the fifth century. He begins by pointing out that in Genesis God gave humans dominion over animals but not over other humans, and thus he concludes that "the condition of slavery is the result of sin," meaning the sin of the slaveholder. This apparent condemnation of slavery is muddled by his later advice to slaves: "And therefore the apostle admonishes slaves to be subject to their masters, and to serve them heartily and with good-will, so that, if they cannot be freed by their masters, they may themselves make their slavery in some sort free, by serving not in crafty fear, but in faithful love, until all unrighteousness pass away."

The position of church officials in Rome swung dramatically back and forth between condemning and sanctioning slavery. Several papal bulls were issued prohibiting the enslavement of natives in the Canary Islands in the early fifteenth century, but in the middle of the century the church reversed its course. Two papal bulls illustrate the authority that the Catholic Church gave to itself to dole out global slavery rights. The *Dum Diversas*, issued by Pope Nicholas V in 1452, gave King Alfonso V of Portugal "full and free power . . . to invade, conquer, fight, [and] subjugate the Saracens and pagans, and other infidels and other enemies of Christ . . . and to lead their persons [into] perpetual servitude." The reason given for this permission was to encourage the spread of Christianity. The intent was to give Portugal favored status in seizing these lands. The 1454 *Romanus Pontifex* gave Alfonso V the right to control and enslave all lands south of Cape Bojador in Morocco—virtually the whole of Africa. These bulls imply that the Catholic Church had some type of authority over these areas, that they were there for the taking.

In 1686 the Holy Office of the Inquisition denounced slavery in its *Response of the Congregation of the Holy Office*. Pope Gregory XVI condemned slavery in his *In supremo apostolatus* in 1839. Yet in the United States, the Jesuits, a Roman Catholic order of priests and brothers, enslaved blacks for 160 years, beginning around 1700. In 1838 they sold 272 slaves from their plantations in Maryland to bolster the faltering finances of Georgetown University and shipped them to a plantation in Louisiana.

In May 1888, eight days before slavery was abolished in Brazil, Pope Leo XIII issued *In Plurimis*, a seven-thousand-word encyclical addressed to the bishops of Brazil enjoining them to help ensure that the freeing of the slaves would take place peacefully. This document exposes much of the church's denial of its role in slavery over the preceding five centuries, couched in language that can only be described as self-congratulatory for the church's role in the humane treatment of slaves and their manumission. Pope Leo intended this encyclical as a strong condemnation of slavery, writing, "In the presence of so much suffering, the condition of slavery, in which a considerable part of the great human family has been sunk in squalor and affliction now for many centuries, is deeply to be deplored; for the system is one which is wholly opposed to that which was originally ordained by God and by nature." Most importantly for this chapter, noting that slavery had flourished "even among the most civilized peoples," including the Greeks and Romans, Leo acknowledges the sexual abuse of slaves: "Owing to this state of moral confusion it became lawful for men to sell their slaves, to give them in exchange, to dispose of them by will, to beat them, to kill them, to abuse them by forcing them to serve for the gratification of evil passions and cruel superstitions; these things could be done, legally, with impunity, and in the light of heaven." But Leo never acknowledges the church's role in sustaining slavery or its failure to condemn the sexual abuse of slaves during the Inquisition, when the Catholic Church doggedly hunted for sinners and brought them to trial but attributed sexual sins to slaves who were violated rather than to slave masters who violated them. Leo makes many claims about the positive role of the church in protecting and aiding slaves, such as, "The care of the Church extended to the protection of slaves, and without interruption tended carefully to one object, that they should finally be restored to freedom, which would greatly conduce to their eternal welfare. . . . There are also many other good deeds of the Church in the same behalf. For she, indeed, was accustomed by severe penalties to defend slaves from the savage anger and cruel injuries of their masters." Leo recounts a long history of the church's positive efforts against slavery going back to the fifteenth century but does not mention the church's direct involvement in slavery via papal orders sanctioning the slave trade. Leo exhorts the Brazilian slaves about to be freed to be grateful for their freedom, to not resent the wealthy, and to act lawfully, avoiding rebellion. He makes no mention of the slaveholders, failing to hold them accountable for their cruelty toward their slaves.

The Dilemma of the Catholic Church and Brazilian Slaves

Were slaves human? If so, what was the nature of their humanity and what were their rights compared to other human beings? What was their standing in the Catholic Church compared to their owners? These questions were of utmost importance to the church's response to reports it received of the rape and sexual abuse of male slaves during the Inquisition. The question of slave humanity and personhood in Catholic doctrine and practice is complex and illustrates a fundamental disconnect between religious dogma and the reality of slavery.

The religious and legal recognition of the slave as a moral human being has been traditionally considered a distinctive quality of Latin American slavery compared to other areas of the world where slavery was practiced.[40] The Catholic Church recognized slaves as human beings with souls, possessing the capacity to distinguish right from wrong and therefore to sin. Thus, they could be held accountable for sins committed against Catholic doctrine. Yet the church also recognized and respected the legal property rights of slaveholders. The dilemma for the church was to somehow reconcile those two deeply conflicting notions of the slave's status as both human and legal property.

Slaves in Brazil and throughout Latin America had the right to be baptized and were strongly encouraged to convert to Christianity. Baptism was the slave's entrance into the Christian community and formal recognition by the Catholic Church. However, until slaves received sufficient instruction in the Catholic faith to be baptized, they were not considered part of the Christian or even human community.[41] Thus, without conversion to the Catholic faith and baptism, the slave was to some degree devoid of humanity and remained unseen by the church and bereft of its protection. By referring to the slave's soul in the inquisitional documents and beseeching slaves to confess their sins so that their souls might be saved, the church was acknowledging their humanity and that they were members of the Christian faith. Once they were baptized, the church claimed that slaves and masters were equal in the sight of God, which was greatly contradicted by the reality of slavery. Also, as historian James Sweet points out, "Operating side by side by these doctrines of equality were deeply held assumptions that Africans were incapable of completely grasping the Church tenets."[42] The slaves' status as legal property informed their humanity and personhood and how those were lived on a quotidian basis.

The relationship between master and slave constructed by the Catholic Church was fundamentally paternalistic. It was the master's responsibility to protect the spiritual integrity of slaves, instruct them in Christianity, and help them avoid sin.[43] Italian Jesuit priest Jorge Benci, who first arrived in Brazil in 1683 and spent a significant amount of time in northeastern Brazil during the time of the Inquisition, maintained that under slavery the master and slave had mutual obligations to one another in the eyes of God. In 1705 he published a collection of sermons in Europe, which he delivered during his stay in Bahia, titled *Economia cristã dos senhores no governo dos escravos* (Christian Economy of Masters in the Governing of Slaves). In these sermons Benci condemns the abuses of slave owners to some degree while biblically justifying slavery. He lays out the responsibility of the master to the slave in these words: "As slaves are rational creatures, that consist of a body and soul, the master should not only give them sustenance to nourish their bodies so that they do not perish, but also spiritual sustenance so that their souls do not die."[44]

Thus master and slave were not on equal footing, as the master was construed as morally superior to the slave. Some male rape victims point out in their testimony to the Inquisition that by forcing them to engage in the sin of sodomy, their masters were deliberately imperiling the victims' spiritual integrity. The church's narrative of the master-slave relationship would be fundamental to the romanticization of the master-slave relationship in the myth of Brazil's genteel slavery—a myth that would be proliferated during the late nineteenth century as a means of denying the need for slave emancipation while concealing violence perpetrated against slaves.

In a number of cases in the Inquisition records, slaves openly denounced their masters for preventing them from being baptized, attending church, or marrying. The benefit of not baptizing slaves was that it left them with no visibility in the Catholic Church and therefore no protection. In several instances, white men or masters who raped or sexually abused slave men showed a particular preference for the recently arrived slave men from Africa known as the *boçal*.[45] Most of these slaves did not speak Portuguese and could not defend themselves or tell anyone about what was done to them; they were unaware of Brazilian customs; and they were likely unbaptized, which would make them not yet part of the Catholic community. But this was not the case for the male rape victims described above. Many had been established in Brazil, spoke Portuguese, and had an understanding of church doctrine and the nature of sin. Thus even as they "confessed" their sins, they were able to expose their masters.

The Catholic Church was a cornerstone of the institution of slavery throughout Latin America for centuries. The church may have attributed humanity to slaves in its dogma, but it also unwaveringly supported an institution that denied the humanity of slaves through their ownership and exploitation. The humanity ascribed to enslaved women and men was not that of whites but a strategic racialized humanity, which gave way to a racial construction of humanity in church and civil law. The Inquisition cases make it evident that the recognition of slaves' humanity neither constituted equality nor provided them with any sort of protection or justice but was instead used to legitimate an institution rooted in violence and exploitation.

The sermons of Jesuit priest António Vieira (1608–1697), a notable theologian, philosopher, and orator, illustrate the irresolvable conflict in the church's relationship to slavery. Vieira was raised in the east central state of Bahia and was officially ordained in 1635. He consecrated his life to the conversion of Amerindians and Africans in Brazil to Christianity until his death in 1697. Vieira was active during the Portuguese Inquisition.[46] As a witness to the suffering and exploitation of the enslaved population, he felt compelled to speak out against slavery. He was known for his fiery sermons denouncing the abuses of slave masters, particularly against the Amerindian population.

Vieira's sermons show him torn between his realization that slavery was wrong and his duty to uphold the teachings of the Catholic Church. In fact a number of his sermons justify slavery.[47] A sermon addressed to the slaves of Bahia in 1633 encapsulated the church's stance regarding the abuse that slaves suffered at the hands of their masters. He admonished them, "Slaves, you are subjects and obedient in everything to your master, not only the good and modest one, but also the bad and unjust."[48] In another sermon to slaves he offered up words of consolation by telling them that their lives as slaves were "imitations of the passion of Christ," meaning that their pain and humiliation were noble reflections of Christ's crucifixion. Thus while white masters were inherently morally superior, the enslaved were Christlike because of the abuse they suffered. Vieira tells the slaves, "There is no work, or way of life in the world more similar to the cross and passion of Christ, than yours on these plantations. . . . On a plantation you are the imitators of the crucifixion of Christ." He elaborates, "During the passion of Christ part of the night he went without sleep, part of the day without rest; such are your nights and days. Christ naked, you naked: Christ subjected to every abuse, you, also subjected to every form of abuse. The chains, the prisons, the whippings, the wounds, the offensive names, all of this part of your imitation, that if accompanied by patience, you will also be deserving of martyrdom."[49] Vieira's message to the slaves is that they should accept their suffering as Jesus accepted his crucifixion, because it is what God has ordained for them. Resistance to their suffering is depicted as disobedience to God. Thus slaves become spiritual martyrs as the price to be paid for their eternal salvation. The explanation for their abuse is shifted from slaveholders to God's will, leaving slaveholders blameless. Vieira's sermon does not give slaves a way out of their physical and spiritual dilemma: how can they simultaneously avoid sin and be subjects and obedient to their master, who forces them to commit sin by raping and sexually abusing them? How can they gain eternal salvation by obeying the Bible and the church while obeying this command to accept the sins forced on them by their masters?

In another sermon delivered to slaves in Bahia, Father Vieira goes so far as to refer to slavery as a "great miracle" because it exposed the slaves to Christianity and saved them from eternal damnation:

O! black people torn from the jungles of your native Ethiopia,[50] and transported to Brazil, if you only knew how much you owe God and his most Holy Mother for this condition that may seem like exile, bondage, and disgrace, but is really nothing more than a miracle, a great miracle! . . . Your parents, that were born in the darkness of paganism, and in it they live and die without the light of faith, and without the knowledge of

God, where shall they go after they die? . . . They are going to hell and there they are burning and will burn for all of eternity."

Vieira tells the slaves that those who have been baptized and professed the Christian faith "have saved your selves because you recognized, honored, and obeyed God: and this is the greatest joy of this truly miraculous condition in which you live."[51]

Curiously, Vieira's inclination to see the "bright" side of slavery is strikingly similar to the position taken by proslavery supporters two centuries later. Renowned author José de Alencar wrote in an 1869 letter defending slavery at the height of the abolitionist movement, "The white race, despite reducing the African to a commodity, ennobled him not only through contact, but also through the transfusion of the civilized man. The future civilization of Africa is right here, in this embryonic fact."[52] Here we can see how Catholic and proslavery thought intersect. Vieira and Alencar both contend that even though slaves suffered abuse, torture, and even death, slavery had in fact been beneficial for African people. While Vieira believed that the slaves received Christian salvation, many supporters of slavery such as Alencar maintained that the Africans had received civilization via contact with the white race through slavery, and through this contact had learned how to govern themselves. Civilization and salvation go hand in hand. For the Catholic Church and supporters of slavery, slavery had prepared the slaves for a better future.

In a sermon delivered in 1653, however, Vieira shows that he has grown weary of witnessing the abuses of the Portuguese colonists against the enslaved. He harshly rebukes them: "All of you are in mortal sin; all of you live in a state of condemnation [for living off the blood of enslaved Indians] and all of you are going directly to Hell. Indeed, many are there now and you will soon join them if you do not change your life."[53]

It appears that religious critics such as Fathers Vieira and Benci found in the Bible a way of double speaking, both condemning slavery and justifying its existence while rationalizing the abuses of white slave masters. This may have been a mechanism by which they absolved themselves of the personal and moral guilt they felt without completely disavowing slavery. Their views show the relative indifference with which both inquisitors and members of the clergy viewed slave reports of abuse and sexual violence.

The trial transcripts make it clear that the enslaved men in the above cases understood their powerlessness and vulnerability as human property. Some naively believed that the public revelation of their masters' conduct would protect them and other slaves from future sexual abuse. The mere fact that these men would risk imprisonment, punishment, or even death to tell their stories illustrates the complete misery and helplessness in which they lived.

Slavery was an institution constructed around white male desire, and white male desire and rights were protected under the law. The Inquisition in Brazil was primarily concerned with regulating white morality, not protecting slaves from the moral offenses of white slaveholders. A master could compromise slaves' souls by forcing them to engage in sinful acts such as sodomy, but these acts were also deemed a legitimate use of the master's legal property, and therefore the church rarely prosecuted masters for sodomy. The slave's position as property effaced the vulnerability under which the sin was committed, but never the sin itself, which was ascribed to the slave.

Since the Middle Ages blacks had been associated with evil, the devil, and crime and, as Frantz Fanon has asserted, "whether one is thinking of physical dirtiness or moral dirtiness . . . the Black man is the equivalent of sin. . . . Whether concretely or symbolically, the Black man stands for the bad side of the character."[54] Whites, in contrast were associated with virtue, purity, holiness, and beauty. These conflations would endure beyond the institution of slavery in Brazil.[55] Moreover, as Sander Gilman argues, the religious conflation of blacks and sexual depravity, especially as it pertains to same-sex acts, was rooted in the biblical confrontation of Ham with his father's nakedness: "For blacks, the sons of Ham, all sexual license is permitted because their nature was revealed (or formed) in the most heinous of all sexual acts, the same-sex gaze."[56] If sodomy was part of the construction of blackness, formed through the same-sex gaze and inherited by the descendants of Ham, then the rape of male slaves merely reaffirmed their innate moral depravity.

The recognition of slaves' humanity by the Catholic Church was deformed by this historical association between the black race and depravity, sin, and crime such that when they were victimized by sin and crime, the church's response was tempered by this narrative of blacks as inherently prone to sin even when they were baptized into the Catholic faith. A crucial part of slave resistance in the inquisitional archive is the extent to which they were aware of the narrative of sin already attached to them and attempted to prove that they were good Christians despite being forced to consent to sinful acts against their will, risking punishment to confess that they had been subjected to these acts involuntarily.

To fully imbue slaves with humanity and personhood meant allowing them to be violatable and vulnerable in religious and civil law and in society. White men—both slaveholders and church officials—benefited from the conflation of sin, sex, and race, as they controlled who could be vulnerable and violated and under what terms.

If slaves were endowed with humanity, they had the capacity to commit sin, and if they were already inherently sinful according to the biblical narrative, the sinful deeds committed against them by white slaveholders—who were both racially and morally superior in the eyes of the church—had to be deemed less severe. This convoluted logic of religious and civil law, rooted in the disparate power relations of slavery, gave rise to a notion of culpability that constructed slaves as embodying the crimes and sins of their masters. Through slavery's criminalization of captivity, slaves paradoxically become both the victims and the agents of their own violation and enter into the historical archive as criminals and sinners rather than victims of rape.

In both the United States and Brazil the slave's humanity and will were admitted only in these negative contexts of sin and crime and served only to protect the slave master from prosecution, as Saidiya Hartman writes: "The slave was recognized as a reasoning subject who possessed intent and rationality solely in the context of criminal liability; ironically, the slave's will was acknowledged only as it was prohibited or punished. It was generally the slaves' crimes that were on trial, not white offense and violation, which were enshrined as legitimate and thereby licensed, or, obviously, the violence of the law, which in the effort to shift the locus of culpability is conceptualized here in terms of the crimes of the state."[57]

It is important to contextualize the word *consent* in the inquisitional proceedings, as many of the slaves in the above cases claimed to have consented to rape out of fear. The use of the verb *consentir*—to give permission, permit, tolerate, or admit—in the inquisitional documents connects male rape to desire, the willingness to commit sin and to be violated. The humanity given to the slave allows for the assumption of agency, confirmed by the inquisitors' admonishment that the slaves should never allow someone to pervert them in such a way again. In the view of the Inquisition judges, the fact that these acts occurred meant that the slaves had consented to rape. But in modern terms, in order for consent to exist one must first be acknowledged as a violatable body, the possibility of violation must be recognized under the law, and refusal must be an option. None of these prerequisites for consent existed for slaves. Whether the slaves enjoyed these acts or allowed themselves to be subjected to them repeatedly is irrelevant, for they had no legal or practical possibility of refusing them.

Few masters were prosecuted or held accountable for their crimes by the Portuguese Inquisition in Brazil. The slave—the victim—was made to confess to participating in the violation of his body so that the judges might mete out an appropriate punishment and forgive his transgressions and his soul might be saved. Victimhood did not factor significantly into the equation. This reality holds significant implications for the historical record. The myth of slave bodily agency, consent, and desire for their own violation led to the systematic erasure from and sanitization of sexual violence in Brazil's history of slavery, becoming fundamental to the construction of the narrative of harmonious sex between the races in the myth of racial democracy.

Legal, Religious, and Social Constructions of Rape

Today, with the push toward greater gender equality, the law in many countries, including Brazil, recognizes that rape can be committed by both men and women against any other person, of either gender. In premodern Europe and Brazil and throughout the Americas, the understanding and legal codification of rape were much more restricted. By modern standards, the law favored perpetrators and punished victims according to gender, race, and socioeconomic status in support of existing power relations. To understand how the violent rape of male slaves was tolerated by the Catholic Church and the law and went unrecognized historically, we need to examine how rape laws evolved from the constitution of gender roles and notions of humans as property.

The legal understanding of male rape has its roots in rape law as it relates to women. From the time of the Inquisition until the early nineteenth century, Brazilian law was based on the Filipine Code, promulgated between 1580 and 1640 during the reign of King Philip I of Portugal. Under the Filipine Code rapists were put to death, and in theory—but most certainly not in practice—the code regarded all women as potential victims of rape and all men as possible offenders. Title XVIII of the Filipine Code defines a rapist as "one who sleeps with any woman against her will, constrains, or takes her against her will" and further states, "Any man, regardless of his state or condition, that forcefully sleeps with any woman even if she earns money with her body, or if she is a slave, the perpetrator shall die."[58]

With the declaration of Brazilian independence, officials undertook a radical revision of the law that they maintained would be "founded on the basis of justice and equality."[59] Until 1940, Brazilian law explicitly defined rape as a crime that could be committed only by a man against a woman—not just any woman, but a *mulher honesta*, an honest women. Article 222 of the 1830 Brazilian Imperial Criminal Code defined rape as "carnal copulation by means of violence or threat with an honest woman."[60] Two years after the abolition of slavery, the criminal code was modified slightly, and article 268 defined rape as "the act by which a man violently abuses a woman, virgin or not, but *honest*."[61] It was only in 1940 that the term *honest* that dictated a woman's legitimacy as a plausible victim of rape was removed. Article 213 of the 1940 penal code states that rape is "to force a woman into having sexual intercourse, through violence or serious threat."[62]

The vulnerability of slave women to legalized rape turned around this word *honest*. The longevity of the term *honest woman* in Brazilian rape law shows that the legal system had a strong investment in its meaning from the very beginning of Brazil as a nation, throughout slavery, and well into the twentieth century.[63] A dishonest and impure woman was not protected. There was no understanding that a dishonest and impure woman—much less a man—could be violated.

Honesty under the law had a direct correlation to biblical sin. Brazilian law never explicitly defined what constituted female honesty. Until the late twentieth century *honest* was understood to mean chaste, modest, and virtuous—words that were applied almost exclusively to white middle- and upper-class married women. Black sexuality was constructed as impure, salacious, and abnormal, and therefore not honest. This limited definition of *honest women* excluded the possibility for sexual violence to be committed against black bodies, which inherently fell outside the realm of honesty warranting protection. The construction of honesty held direct racial and class implications, and its ambiguity allowed elite white men, from colonial times and for centuries after, to designate which bodies were legally violatable and which were not in ways that exclusively benefited themselves.

In nineteenth-century US law, rape was defined as the "forcible carnal knowledge of a female against her will and without her consent."[64] This definition of rape, as in Brazil, had virtually no application to enslaved women, who were seen by society and the law as property and thus not legitimately violatable. Sociologists Lorenne Clarke and Debra Lewis trace the beginning of rape law to the view of women as private property belonging to men. A woman's honesty in the eyes of the law derived from the socioeconomic status of her father and her husband. It was the husband or father, not the woman, who was wronged by rape, and therefore any recompense stemming from the rape was paid to him. Clarke and Lewis explain that the "legal system confirmed, supported and perpetuated unequal relationships between individual men, and between sexes. Women simply were not considered to be 'persons' under the law. They could not own property; . . . and within marriage, they and their children were the property of their husbands. Their economic status was determined by that of their father or husband, and their unique status as women within this system was determined by their sexual and reproductive capacities."[65] During slavery and well into the twentieth century, rape legislation focused exclusively on heterosexual intercourse in order to protect male property and to guarantee that any children from the marriage were of the husband so as to secure legitimate heirs.

Race, gender, and white male supremacy over the course of history have systematically shaped legal visibility, that is, who is seen or invisible in the law and under what terms. Slavery allowed oppressors to retain the exclusive right to define victimhood, giving way to the creation of the myth of black hypersexuality and hyperavailability as a strategic means of effacing rape and sexual violence against black men and women. As the enslaved in Brazil transitioned to freedom, their race and poverty would come to delineate them as not meeting the definition of legally honest or rapable under the law; therefore they would have no more protection against sexual violence than they had as slaves.

Though rape law was modified over time, it could not erase the sociohistorical, gendered classifications of rapability. It was not until five centuries after the Filipine Code, in 2009, that the Brazilian government attempted to make rape law gender neutral, to apply to both men and women as possible rapists and victims. The revision of the 1940 law defining rape as "to force a woman into having sexual intercourse, through violence or serious threat" was revised to read, "to force *someone* into having sexual intercourse, through violence or serious threat," although it does not explicitly recognize men as possible victims of rape.

This change in modern consciousness has significant implications for how we understand sexual violence during and after slavery. It makes possible and real what was once held to be impossible and nonexistent and points to voids in what we know about the everyday experience of slaves. It urges us to uncover stories of male rape concealed in the historical archive and to give new interpretations to terms such as *sodomy* that hid the true nature of these acts as crimes of rape and sexual abuse, erasing sexual violence even as it was being described by its victims.[66]

The history of rape law, with its deep roots in Roman Catholicism and the 1603 Filipine Code, shows us how the law sustains race, class, and gender with respect to bodily vulnerability. The implications for the Brazilian historical record and national identity if enslaved rape victims could not legally be raped are profound. Legal visibility is inherently linked to historical visibility. The harmonious myth constructed around interracial sex in Brazilian history is dependent on the legal impossibility for sexual violence to occur to black men and women or for white men to be rapists of black men and women. The mere idea that a male slave and rape victim would be admonished to not "put himself in such a position again" illustrates the disavowal of slave violability and the construction of an unsustainable myth of consent, desire, and agency.

The shortsighted cultural and religious narratives around sex as exclusively an act of intimacy, denying its frequent use for violent domination and degradation, framed sex between master and slave and in turn framed narratives around race. Because of the limited definition of what constituted rape or sexual violation, forced sodomy was not considered a form of violence against men, even though the above cases illustrate the extreme violence of these incidents.

The fact that rape throughout the early modern world, but particularly in the context of Brazilian slavery, was treated legally as a question of abuse of *male* property meant that women of any race and enslaved men had limited control over what was done to their bodies, and their bodies held legal meaning and value only in relation to white men, not in and of themselves. This shows that sex during this era was not merely about pleasure but also had personal, political, and legal meaning for white men as property owners.

Perhaps the most prominent Roman Catholic theologian of the early modern era, Saint Thomas Aquinas (1225–1274) described sodomy in his highly influential *Summa Theologica* as a form of *luxuria* or lust and deemed it the second most egregious sin, after bestiality. Sodomy was categorized as an "unnatural vice" for its impossibility of procreation. As Aquinas explains, with sodomy "man transgresses that which has been determined by nature with regard to the use of venereal actions; it follows that in this matter this sin is gravest of all."[67] Sodomy, therefore, is a conscious act of sin and gender transgression, an expression of desire or will. Sodomy was a sin for two reasons: it transgressed or perverted gender—arguably one of the most important identities in the early modern world as prescribed by the Bible—and it did not lead to procreation. These two reasons framed the limited conception of sodomy, excluding an understanding of its use for power and control over men. The conflation of sodomy between men and conscious transgression against nature (gender), the church, and God would lead to the notion of sodomy or homosexuality as a predatory perversion during the rise of medical science in the nineteenth century.

During the Portuguese Inquisition in Brazil it was virtually impossible for people to conceive of sodomy as a form of nonconsensual sex or rape. In cultural and religious logic, sodomy was considered consensual, as it was conflated with sin, and sin as a manifestation of lust or desire was a matter of conscious choice. The rape of a woman was viewed as the theft of male property (her virtue), but with men, there was no virtue to be stolen. Even today, as many studies of prison rape have shown, many continue to doubt the possibility of male rape, considering it a manifestation of latent homosexuality on the part of the victim and the assailant.

Rape laws were based on the assumed vulnerability of women and the invulnerability of men. Moreover, sex was associated with procreation. These two views together, grounded in restricted gender constructions, made it impossible to conceive of the rape of male slaves by their masters. While same-sex sexual relations were not unknown, there was no framework for understanding them as nonconsensual rape.

Sexual coercion was framed within a classed heteronormativity rooted in narratives of gender power that gave men power over defenseless women as the weaker sex. In this framing men could not be viewed as predators of other men because of the myth of male invulnerability. Moreover, at Inquisition trials rape was always recounted as a confession of sin, whether by the victims or the perpetrators, indicating that the confessor was aware of the sinful nature of the act and, in the minds of the Inquisition judges, had consciously chosen it. The judges ascribed degrees of culpability, but male slaves who were victims of rape remained guilty of the sin of sodomy.

The evidence of male rape found in the Inquisition trial transcripts allows us to see that the rape of black men and women served distinct purposes in relation to the slave economy and white-master identity. As historian Winthrop Jordan points out, "Sexually, as well as in every other way, Negroes were utterly subordinated. White men extended their dominance over their Negroes to the bed, where the sex act itself served as a ritualistic enactment of the daily pattern of social dominance."[68] Through the practice of male rape, black men and their sexuality entered into the Brazilian national narrative in sexual submission to white men.

Male Rape and the Sexual Initiation of the White Master

According to some observers, male rape became a part of the sexual initiation of young white masters. Gilberto Freyre documents in *The Masters and the Slaves* how acts of sexual violence against young slave boys became part of this process of coming-of-age in what he describes as the sexual initiation of the slave master's son, in which the young white master gained sexual experience by raping a slave boy:

> Through the submission of the black boy in the games that they played together, and especially the one known as *leva-pancadas* [taking a drub-

bing], the white lad was often initiated into the mysteries of physical love. As for the lad who took the drubbing, it may be said of him that, among the great slave-holding families of Brazil, he fulfilled the same passive functions toward his young master as did the adolescent slave under the Roman Empire who had been chosen to be the companion of a youthful aristocrat: he was a species of victim, as well as a comrade in those games in which the "premiers élans génesiques" [first sexual impulses] of the son of the family found an outlet.[69]

Englishman Henry Koster, traveling through Pernambuco in the early nineteenth century, observed, "As soon as a child begins to crawl, a slave of about his own age, and of the same sex, is given to it as a playfellow, or rather as a plaything. They grow up together, and the slave is made the stock upon which the young owner gives vent to passion."[70] Journalist José Veríssimo wrote, "There was not a house where there was not one or more *moleques* [slave boys], one or more *curumins* [indigenous slave boys], who were the victims specially devoted to the young master's whims."[71] An inquisitional trial transcript reveals that Estevão Velho Barreto, from Pernambuco, the son of a wealthy plantation owner, admitted that at the age of thirteen he regularly raped two young slave boys.[72]

In accounts by Freyre, Koster, and Veríssimo of the young master's initiation into the "mysteries of physical love," male rape becomes concealed in a pretext of familial intimacy, and the roles of the participants are inculcated in the master's son and the slave boy beginning in childhood. Through this seemingly incestuous process the slave boy is made to submit, is rendered passive, serving as both the friend and sexual victim of the slave master's son.

This sexual initiation occurred in a formative stage for both the young master and the slave child and was central to the construction of the sexual and racial identities of both boys. The master and slave boy assumed their places in the hierarchy of slavery through rape. Under slavery, white male supremacy was dependent on the existence of a male sexual and racial inferior, and male rape served as a way of manifesting that supremacy physically beginning in childhood. Historian Richard Trexler has argued that in colonial Latin America masculinity was perceived as the assertion of control and superiority over others and was maintained through domination over men, women, and boys. Power, as Trexler has shown, was evinced by dominance as the ultimate proof of one's masculinity.[73]

The sexual initiation of the slave boy was above all an instance of intimate violence. Although it was couched in terms of intimacy, that intimacy served as the vehicle to inflict abuse, rendering the slave boy both a "species of victim" and a "comrade." Freyre justifies this practice or attempts to sanitize it by comparing it to sodomy in the Roman Empire. This historical rationale, coupled with an emphasis on intimacy or friendship between the slave boy and young white master—which also included an element of force, since the slave boy was chosen for the master's son as a playmate—functioned to euphemistically insinuate that sexual abuse was taking place. The rape of the slave boy is seemingly romanticized in Freyre's writing, as his concern is only for the young master's experience of sexual pleasure, distorting the reality of the rape of the slave. Freyre's description appears as a sort of rape fantasy in which the master's narrative shrouds the violence of the act and the master's pleasure is narrated as that of the slave.[74] The slave boy's role was to provide the young slave master with practice in penetration—ostensibly for future heterosexual sex, although the above Inquisition cases make it clear that this same-sex abuse that began in childhood continued into adulthood in a number of instances. Freyre makes sure to inform his readers that the slave boy was sexually passive to the young master. Thus racial and sexual supremacy were being made manifest through sex beginning in childhood. As in the inquisitional cases, Freyre's account makes it appear as if the slave boy consented by failing to note any resistance on his part, but as with their fathers, resistance to white domination was not an option for the slave boy. The slave boy's experience of rape is not Freyre's concern.

As historian Jeffrey Needell has shown, "sadism, sexuality, and racial domination" are tied together both "implicitly and explicitly" in Freyre's works on slavery to render a "gendered account in which the Brazilian white male creates Brazil through a dominating sexual intercourse." Needell further adds that the while male child from an early age "learns to look for sensual gratification and sadistic pleasure," and that in Brazilian slave society as Freyre describes it, "power, penetration, and punishment were naturally arranged from the top down."[75]

Slavery and white male supremacy were made and sustained through the sexual exploitation of black men and women of all races. The sexual initiation of the master's son reveals how important the sexual domination of not only women's bodies but of all bodies was to the solidification of white mastery and white master identity.

The Penetrability of the Slave Body

Powerlessness and penetrability were deeply intertwined in the institution of slavery. In a society that was fundamentally rooted in white male racial and sexual supremacy, both gender and race were constructed in the active/passive, penetrator/penetrated binaries. In seventeenth-century Portugal it was common to hear the saying, "There is no chicken that does not lay eggs, nor servant who does not commit sodomy."[76] The meaning of this saying is multifarious in that it establishes that sodomy with one's owner or employer was very common and even an expected obligation of slaves and servants. The adage places blame on the servant, as it is he who commits sodomy. In this adage we see the conflation of labor, forced penetration, and captivity. The power dynamic between owner and servant frames the terms of culpability and also the sexual positions of both the slave (the penetrated) and the master (the penetrator). The adage purposely points to the initiative of the servant and not the employer, and this coerced act between superior and inferior becomes even a desired and habitual act on the part of the slave, as the stigma and criminalization of the act befall the body of the slave while absolving the master.

As narratives around race and white supremacy in relation to blackness were being developed as part of slavery as an institution, rape had a crucial role in physicalizing racialized gender subordination for enslaved men and women. By using the enslaved to engage in sinful forms of sex and making that part of their job or duty as slaves as well as part of their identity, white masters were also giving physical form to the abject, sinful stereotypes associated with black sexuality. In the vast majority of the forced sodomy cases involving enslaved men and white men reported to the Inquisition in Brazil, it is the white master or white man who forcibly rapes the male slave. Inquisitors made a clear distinction between the "active" and "passive" positions in same-sex acts. They demanded to know who performed which role in order to determine the degree of culpability for each participant. Being penetrated was more egregious in the eyes of the Catholic Church than actively penetrating because it deviated from the natural role of males as sexually dominant prescribed by the Bible.

In the Inquisition transcripts male rape victims who are penetrated are referred to as "passive" or "performing the female duty," embodying the sin and stigma of sodomy and a crime against nature. Meanwhile the perpetrator, although equally engaging in a highly sinful act, maintained his gender integrity and masculinity in the eyes of society and the church. As we have seen, the presumption of consent to be penetrated by another male, even in the face of obvious violence, is recorded as willful, as is the cognizance on the part of the penetrated male slave that he is undermining his natural gender role, thus rendering him more deserving of blame and punishment.

The rape cases presented in this chapter provide important revelations about sexuality and Brazilian definitions of homosexuality that would appear centuries later. When theories of homosexuality began to be developed in the late nineteenth century, this history of apparent black male passivity or penetrability during slavery would provide a fertile terrain for the development of pathological and racialized theories of homosexuality and the supposed predisposition of men of color to homosexuality. But sodomy between men during the time of the Inquisition had no correlation with what we know today as homosexuality or any alternative form of sexual identity. The concept of sexual identity—that is, the hetero/homosexual binary—would emerge only in the late nineteenth century. In this sense, during the early modern period it can be said that for practicing Catholics who adhered to biblical mandates, there was what could be called a "presumptive heterosexuality" based on an understanding that sex should occur only between a man and woman rather than being based on physical or sexual desire for the opposite sex. The only concepts of sex that existed during the time of the Inquisition were sanctioned sex between a man and a woman within the confines of marriage for the sole purpose of procreation, and its opposite: all forms of sinful, heretical sex that served any other purpose. This presumptive heterosexuality is more rooted in social constructions of gender than in desire. Brazilians' understanding of sex would later be transformed with the rise of pseudoscientific studies of human sexuality.

Historian Pete Sigal, in his volume dedicated to same-sex sexual relations in colonial Latin America, has shown that a number of men engaged in sex with both men and women, and even though some evinced a strong preference for men, there is no evidence to suggest that these individuals espoused a sexual identity that was "ingrained in the individual psyche."[77] Colonial and early modern Latin American historians Richard Trexler and Serge Gruzinski argue similarly that while sodomy between men was quite common, its meaning did not carry the same implications that it would today. Both scholars maintain that homosexuality as we understand it today is a modern construction of sex and sexual desire that could not have existed in the early modern world.[78] Others, such as noted Brazilian historians Luiz Mott, João Silvério Trevisan, and Amílcar Torrão Filho, go against the grain to argue that homosexuality as a defined sexual identity did exist during the colonial period and that a number of men formed communities around their sexual desire for men. Though these authors do acknowledge the existence of violence in some instances of sodomy, they contend that Inquisition cases can be read as early instantiations of male homosexuality or as part of a queer or gay genealogy.[79] Male rape activist and survivor Michael Scarce, however, cautions us against using early premodern archives of same-sex sexual relations and relating them to modern-day LGBT culture. He asserts, "Historians must begin to ask themselves if same-sex rape should be considered homosexual behavior. If so, what are the modern-day implications of using a past of sexual violence to inform and strengthen today's gay male culture and community?"[80]

Given the time period and cultural perceptions of intragender sex as a highly sinful act, it is important to underscore that neither the master nor the slave would have viewed the act as what we would know to be homosexual today. Both were aware, however, that sodomy was a grave sin, as the record indicates, which is why most slaveholders sought to conceal their engagement in these acts. Their fear was of being outed not as a homosexual but as a sinner in a world in which the Catholic Church reigned supreme and in theory punished heretics. As the Inquisition's primary grievance per the Bible was that sodomy between men was a grave sin because it undermined gender roles and the essential procreative purpose of sex, we can deduce that there was an awareness on the part of both the slave and the master of the gravity of the sin, and a cognizance on the part of the master that he was defiling the male slave by undermining his gender integrity through sinful sex. What is evident, however, is that through being penetrated, the male slave, in his own eyes and in the eyes of the Inquisition, had been feminized by sodomy, as the slave Jacinto Ferreira dos Campos protested in the opening epigraph of this chapter, proclaiming that "he was not a woman to satisfy his master's sexual whims."

A possible interpretation of the acts of sodomy recounted in the Inquisition trial transcripts is that slave masters were aware of the stigmatization and greater sinfulness of playing the passive role in same-sex relations, and therefore they chose the role of penetrator. I did not find any cases in which a male slave was forced to penetrate his master. Both same-sex and heterosexual sodomy were taboo, illicit forms of sex that may have heightened the desire of some entitled white masters to engage in it with male and female slaves and even with their wives against their will.

A number of recent works by social scientists working in Brazil and the United States have sought to understand in present-day sexual culture how same-sex relations can function for some men as an expression of heterosexuality and demonstration of masculinity. Taking historical differences into account, these studies can help elucidate the uses of sodomy and male rape under slavery, prior to the existence of homosexuality as a sexual category, as a mechanism for physicalizing and reinforcing white male gender, sexual, and racial supremacy. These studies show that what is important is not only the nature of the incidents of male same-sex relations reported to the Inquisition, but also the narrative that was created around them, which paradoxically construed as heterosexual and hypermasculine, without transgressing into homosexuality, acts that would be defined as homosexual today.

Sociologist Jane Ward, in her provocative study *Not Gay: Sex between Straight White Men*, writes that straight white men reinforce their heterosexuality, masculinity, and race by engaging in homosexual sex while simultaneously appearing to both control and reject it. In fact she claims that homosexuality is often an important element of heterosexual masculinity. This "male sexual fluidity"—as evinced in the male rape cases presented in this chapter and Freyre's description of the sexual initiation of the master's son—is closely connected to whiteness, functioning as a source of power that enables white men to engage in racially privileged forms of nonheteronormative sex that are denied to men of color.[81]

In his study of contemporary sexual culture in Brazil anthropologist Richard G. Parker has similarly shown how the gendered views of penetrability and passivity or the penetrator/penetrated dyad that existed during the Portuguese Inquisition remain in force today and have come to shape Brazilian constructions of masculinity and homosexuality. Sex between men can function as an expression of male heterosexual supremacy and domination even today, when homosexuality is a recognized sexual identity, as long as a man performs the active role during sex and maintains his expected male role socially. The sexually penetrated male, on the other hand, abandons his masculine role and becomes a "symbolic female."[82]

One of Parker's research informants, a twenty-eight-year-old man living in Rio de Janeiro, said candidly, "What really matters is what you do in bed, whether you like being *ativo* [active] or *passivo*. An *homem* [man] fucking another *homem* isn't really that much different than if he was screwing a *mulher* [woman]. . . . As long as he's the one who is doing the fucking, who is penetrating the other guy, it doesn't really matter. He's still an *homem*—even a '*machão*' [a real macho man]."[83] Don Kulick's groundbreaking study *Travesti: Sex, Gender, and Culture among Brazilian Transgendered Prostitutes* argues similarly, "The bed is the arena where some males make themselves into 'men,' by penetrating their partner, and other males make themselves into 'women,' by allowing themselves to be penetrated by those men. It is thus in bed where gender is truly established. But it is also in bed that the risk for gender slippage is most acute."[84]

The white master who sodomized his male slaves not only did not compromise his masculinity or heterosexuality but also elevated his masculine gender status in the ultimate performance of masculine power and domination while emasculating his slave victims. He escaped stigmatization because the sexual role he performed with another man conformed to and enhanced his socially constituted gender role while repudiating and usurping the masculinity of the male slave.

Social worker and feminist theorist Florence Rush has argued, "Men rape other men because they feminize their victims within heterosexual patterns of dominance and subordination."[85] Still today we do not have a language to speak of male sexual domination or rape—that is, the forced penetration of a male by another male—that does not conflate with the feminine or the female body.[86] Maleness and femaleness are mutually constituted by notions of penetrability: the hyperpenetrability and vulnerability of the female body and the impenetrability and invulnerability of maleness. This absence of language to refer to the rape of a male by another male that does not conform to this structure has served historically and legally to conceal same-sex violence in the archive of slavery.[87] As in other slave societies, the rape of male and female slaves in Brazil served to preserve white male power and privilege.

The Psychology of Male Rape

Male rape is not an expression of homosexuality, just as the rape of a woman by a man is not an expression of heterosexuality. Rape and sexual violence are not about sex, sexuality, or repressed sexual desire, but about power. Several studies on male rape have called attention to the abiding myth that the perpetrators of male rape are always homosexual men.[88] This myth confuses the forced sexual act between two men with sexual orientation (male homosexuality) and has come to exculpate socially dominant heterosexual males, allowing society to overlook the problem of male rape.[89] This view continues to place emphasis on sex between men, rather than the extreme violence under which these acts occur, contributing to silencing of the history of the rape of male slaves.

To insert these cases of male slave rape into a genealogy of homosexuality is also to suggest that male homosexuality bears a connection to rape and is rooted in pathology. This view of male homosexuals as violent and pathological would be fully developed in Europe and Brazil and throughout the Americas in the late nineteenth century and throughout the twentieth century. Here the importance of naming sexual violence between persons of the same gender becomes crucial, as the historical ambiguity surrounding sodomy did not register the reality or context in which the act occurred.

Slaves not only had no control over what was done to their bodies but also were not allowed to name the violence perpetrated against them. The law presupposed that they must suffer in different (lesser) ways than whites and did not acknowledge the violence committed against them. When rape, violence, and humiliation cannot legally be called exactly what they are, they may be registered as something else, allowing perpetrators to define these acts of violence and their victims in ways and in language that serve themselves.

Power, domination, and violence have no allegiance to heteronormativity but violate fluidly across racial, gender, and sexual boundaries. A number of studies by psychiatrists documenting cases of sexual violence between men provide critical insight into the underlying psychic and cultural structures that legitimated male rape during Brazilian slavery. Psychologists A. Nicholas Groth and Ann Burgess have identified several motivational components that call attention to the centrality of masculinity in male rape cases. A number of the male rape cases presented in this chapter bear characteristics of what psychologists have defined as "power rape." According to Groth, for the power rapist, sex is a means of expressing mastery, strength, control, authority, identity, and capability.[90] Rape is purposely used as a means to degrade and emasculate the male victim and affirm the masculinity of the rapist. Here, rape is used to prove to the victim first, that the rapist is not a homosexual, as the rapist assumes the dominant role, and second, that the victim, through his subjugation, *is* a homosexual.[91] In the context of the Inquisition, by penetrating the male slave, the master could have been proving to the victim that the slave was the sodomite and the sinner, and not the master himself.

In a study of twenty-two cases of male rape, Groth and Burgess found that for the offenders, rape is an "expression of power and an assertion of their strength and manhood," and that the victim comes to symbolize "what they want to control, punish and/or destroy, something they want to conquer and defeat."[92] Like the slave-master rapist, power rapists select their victims based on their accessibility and vulnerability, often experiencing a feeling of omnipotence through their assaults. To achieve a sense of conquest, the rapist resorts to any means necessary to overcome his victim's resistance and render him helpless. One rapist described his motivation in simple terms: "I wasn't really interested in sex. I felt powerful, and hurting him really excited me."[93]

In a lecture titled "Sex among Male Prisoners and Its Implications for Concepts of Sexual Orientation: A Million Jockers, Punks and Queens," male rape victim advocate Stephen Donaldson argues that male rape in prison is deemed primarily a "male activity" and is used to emasculate the victim while enhancing the masculinity of the penetrator. More importantly, Donaldson states that male rape is "psychologically heterosexual to [the perpetrator] (as well as to most of their partners, willing or not)."[94] In prisons male rape is "wielded as a tool for aggression, domination, and literal enslavement of others,"[95] writes Michael Scarce. These modern conceptions of rape, power, and masculinity shine a bright light on the motivations of the slave-master rapist in actual slave societies.

Slavery, Reproduction, and the Visibility of Sexual Violence

The cases presented in this chapter show that enslaved men were no less vulnerable to sexual violence than enslaved women, and that rape was not an exclusively female domain but a reality of enslavement for both genders. Historical resistance to documenting and prosecuting the rape of male slaves, and to calling it by its rightful name, has been shaped by what sociologists Denise Donnelly and Stacy Kenyon have termed the "myth of male invulnerability."[96] Our understanding of sexual violence during slavery throughout the Americas has been largely conditioned by the notion that men are innately less vulnerable to sexual violation than women both physically and psychologically, such that they cannot actually be victims of rape and sexual violence. This distortion has dictated what forms of violence were documented and entered into the archive, and ultimately it has sustained the erasure of male slave rape. If male slaves were not vulnerable to rape, then the logical conclusion was that they desired and were willing participants in these violent acts. The Inquisition trial transcripts clearly show that this was not the case, yet the inquisitors' reprimands emphasized that the slaves "allowed" themselves to be raped.[97] There was no acknowledgement at the time that sex could be used as a weapon against male slaves.

An additional belief at the time was that rape and sexual violence occurred only in the context of generative sexuality, specifically between white men and black women. Sexual violence under slavery has been exclusively bound to generative sex and its potential to leave proof of its occurrence through reproduction, that is, the pregnancy of a female rape victim. Reproductive sex was the only kind of sex that society and the law acknowledged for centuries. Sex was understood to be about desire and reproduction. There was no social framework or language for understanding a form of sex that was about violence and degradation rather than desire, that did not end in reproduction, and that left no evidence behind.[98] There was no social or legal language to account for sodomy as a mechanism to inflict violence against men. The term *sodomy* alone does not imply coercion, as was the case also for sex or miscegenation between white masters and Brazilian women of color. The very fact that we must use the term *male rape* signifies how deeply gendered the crime of rape was and still is.

The heteronormative myth of sexual violence also undergirds the fact that rape was viewed as a sexual crime rather than a violent crime about power: reducing the act to sexual gratification meant that it must be sexual in nature. Therefore the Catholic Church and the law dealt with sodomy exclusively as a form of sin and an unnatural act, not as sexual violence.

Scholars have long argued that slavery feminized enslaved men. They were emasculated by their inability to assume traditional gender roles as husbands and fathers, and by the fact that they were unable to protect their mothers, sisters, wives, and daughters from being raped. But the evidence of the rape of male slaves points to a more complex sexual trauma embedded in the history of black men's emasculation under slavery. Scholars of American slavery and literature throughout the Americas have analyzed at length the deeper sexual and sadistic meanings of lynchings, castrations, beatings, and whippings that, as Frantz Fanon argues, served as forms of "sexual revenge."[99] These physical and symbolic performances were documented and survived because this violence could be fitted within a white supremacist heteronormative framework of racial oppression that was made to be culturally legible and comprehensible.

Torturing enslaved men did not always have to do with sex, but when it did, it was made culturally legible through white male supremacist anxieties surrounding black men's purported lust for white women. The American myths of black male hypersexuality and the predatory black male rapist, along with the spectacular public torture that was designed to punish the slave, could have functioned strategically to camouflage and deflect attention away from the rape of male slaves and the white masters who raped them in private.

Male Rape, Trauma, and Black Masculinity

The existence of male slave rape adds new dimensions to our understanding of pre- and postabolition black masculinities, as well as of the impact of this concealed history of sexual violence on the sexualities and identities of black men today. The explicit painful details recounted to the Inquisition judges allow us to clearly imagine the trauma of the rape victims. Psychiatrists Groth and Burgess, as well as Gillian Mezey and Michael B. King, have shown the devastating effects that rape can have on victims' perceptions of their masculinity and sexuality. They have found that victims of male rape often doubt their masculinity, believing that they are not real men because they were unable to defend themselves against rape.[100] P. L. Huckle reports that many male rape victims experience feelings of shock, humiliation, embarrassment, behavioral changes, and phobias, in addition to anger, confused sexual orientation, and loss of self-respect.[101]

The trauma of slavery constituted for the enslaved and for the nation a history that Shoshana Felman and Dori Laub describe as essentially "not over," a history "whose repercussions are not simply omnipresent (whether consciously or not) . . . but whose traumatic consequences are actively evolving."[102] The national fashioning of black men as sexual and gender others displaced them and their sexuality from the national miscegenation narrative while solidifying white male racial and sexual supremacy at its center.[103] Though Brazil wanted to conceive of itself as a land of racial equality that stood apart from the horrors of slavery in the United States, the rape of male slaves firmly establishes a different national story.

THREE

The White Mistress and the Slave Woman:
Seduction, Violence, and Exploitation

The popular Brazilian colonial adage "branca para casar, mulata para fornicar, negra para trabalhar" (white women for marriage, mulatto women for fornication, and black women for work) describes a hierarchy of women's bodies and how they were designated to be used by white men during the colonial period and throughout the history of slavery in Brazil. In short, white women were essential to white men for reproducing purely white offspring and legitimate heirs so that the wealth of the white elite could be passed from generation to generation. Slave women worked on the plantations to create that wealth, but they also reproduced the slave workforce that perpetuated it because the law in Brazil and other slave societies such as the United States stipulated that children inherited the legal status of their mother rather than their father. Thus all children born to slave mothers were slaves. In this sense, slave women reproduced slavery itself and passed it on to their children. Thus both black and white women's bodies under slavery were framed in an economy of use. White men dominated women of both races, but the mechanics of white male power also overshadowed the relationship between black and white women. To conceal the role of white men in this hierarchy of power, race, and sex, narratives were created around the purity of white women and the depravity of slave women, ascribing culpability to black women for the deviant sexual behaviors and violence of the white master and mistress.

White mistresses and their female slaves shared a closely entwined existence that was a convoluted fusion of intimacy, sex, exploitation, and violence embedded in the white patriarchal structures of slavery and coloniality. Slave women were their white mistresses' laborers, rivals (real and imagined), wet nurses, sexual partners, and prostitutes[1]—and their brutalized victims. Significant attention has been given to the cruelty of the slave master toward his slaves, but the work of a number of historians and recent archival findings have brought to light the fact that white mistresses participated with astonishing ferocity in these acts.[2] The violence perpetrated by white women and mistresses was a critical part of the life of slavery and also simultaneously affected the construction and meaning of notions of black and white womanhood that would endure long after slavery's official abolition in 1888.

Ironically, although under the domination of their husbands and families and having limited freedom, a number of white women nonetheless found ways to avail themselves of the same mechanisms of power, control, and gratification used by their husbands, fathers, and brothers, played out in their relationships with other women. Perhaps most surprising to the modern reader are the sexual encounters and relationships between white women and between white mistresses and their female slaves. The cases of the Portuguese Inquisition in Brazil provide clear documentation of these same-sex relationships, as people were pressured by the Catholic Church to confess them, and some women appear to have been all too eager to denounce those who engaged in them. Within these relationships, white women transgressed the patriarchally defined limitations of their gender and threatened to displace white men in the latters' role as the sole sexual gratifiers of women.

Framing Sex between Women and the Female Body

There is extensive documentation in the Inquisition case records in Brazil going back as far as the 1500s of numerous instances of white women engaging in sex with other white and slave women. In order to interpret these records, we need to understand how sex between women was conceptualized at the time and the language that was constructed to describe it. These relationships were termed *amizade deshonesta* (dishonest friendship), *amizade nefanda* (nefarious friendship), *amizade tola* (foolish friendship), or *amizade de pouco saber* (friendship of little knowledge). This terminology employed by the Inquisition was used to designate the transgression of the platonic homosocial bond or intimacy between women, becoming sexual in nature and therefore sinful, "dishonest," or "nefarious" in the eyes of God, the church, and society. Sexual contact perverted the purity of "friendship," ostensibly the only kind of relations women should have with other women.

As historian Sueann Caulfield shows, in the late nineteenth century "honor was associated with sexual virtue and loyalty to husbands, not individual autonomy and public authority."[3] There was a significant difference in the conceptualizations of male and female honor, which was synonymous with honesty. Both words carried a strong religious connotation of obedience to God. Female honesty had an almost exclusively sexual basis (sexual virtue) that was not applied to men. It did not recognize women as autonomous beings or bestow on them any public or political power, while it mandated absolute obeisance to their husbands.[4] The term *honest*, as we saw in our review of Brazilian rape law in the previous chapter, referred to a woman's virtue in the eyes of the law. *Dishonest* described acts that threatened a woman's virtue. The terms used to refer to sex or sodomy between men do not carry a connotation of platonic intimacy or friendship, perhaps revealing that the church considered that only nonphysical interactions could exist between women.

The Catholic Church and Brazilian society were perplexed as to how to define sex between women, and during the Inquisition there was no concrete language to describe these acts. Sex between women in Europe and throughout the Americas was viewed by many as virtually impossible. In a court case from Scotland in 1811 alleging oral sex between two women, it was determined by the court that "the crime here alleged has no existence."[5] In the United States, in the Plymouth Colony in 1649, Sara Norman and Mary Hammon were convicted of unspecified "lewd behavior each with [the] other upon a bed," and Norman was required by officials to make public acknowledgement of her "unchaste behavior."[6] In the Massachusetts Bay Colony in 1642, Elizabeth Johnson, a female servant, was sentenced to pay a fine and to be severely whipped for "unseemly practices betwixt her and another maid."[7] Like the word *dishonest*, the terms *lewd*, *unchaste*, and *unseemly* used in the trial transcripts of the Portuguese Inquisition are very vague, and none of the alleged acts are clearly described. But clearly these words are ridden with contempt, and the behaviors associated with them offended moral, religious, and gender protocols. This lack of precise language to describe sex between women and concealing it beneath vague terms associated with shame extended well into the nineteenth century and would become characteristic of male attitudes toward female homosexuality.

In the Inquisition transcripts, sex between women is consistently expressed in heteronormative language. In all cases, the confessors and denouncers describe the two women as pleasuring themselves "like a man would with a woman." As with the male cases described in the previous chapter, there was no language to describe same-sex relations outside the male/female, active/passive dyad. The language used is rather vague and may camouflage what actually occurred, or may conceal a wider variety of unspecified practices.

As was the case with the rape of enslaved men, sex between women during the Portuguese Inquisition was collapsed into the category of sodomy. Because sodomy involved penetration, the biggest question that loomed in the minds of the inquisitors was whether in fact a woman was capable of penetrating another woman. A number of inquisitors weighed in on the issue and attempted to provide some insight into how women could effectively commit sodomy like their male counterparts. Inquisitor Álvaro Soares de Castro and Deputy Sebastião de Fonseca maintained that sodomy could occur only if there was both penetration and ejaculation in the vagina or the anus, and they believed that women could penetrate other women only through the use of an instrument, but even with an instrument, ejaculation would be impossible. With this, they concluded that women could commit only *molície* (nonpenetrative sexual acts), and that real sodomy could be committed only between men. Inquisitor Manoel de Magalhães and deputies Manoel do Valle and João Estaço believed that female sodomy could be committed only through the use of instruments that were capable of "injecting semen outside or inside of the anus."[8] Inquisitor Mateus Homem Leitão advised that when the hands or mouth were used "as a vessel," or if a man or woman were to use a finger "in place of the male penis in the other's anus," these would all be, in his view, molícia."[9]

Female sodomy entered into ecclesiastical legislation in Brazil in 1707 in the First Constitutions of the Archbishop of Bahia, which detailed all of the potential punishments for sodomy. The First Constitutions made a distinction between sodomy committed by women and men. All sexual acts between women fell into the domain of *molície* or *sodomia impópria*, which was also deemed a "very severe sin" but not as serious as *sodomia própria* committed by men.[10] However, title XVIII, paragraph 964, stipulated that female sodomy, or molície, was an act "against the order of nature as grave as sodomy and bestiality" and "upon being proven and given the quality of proof and circumstances the most severe punishment would be deportation for a maximum of three years."[11]

Several period priests and theologians speculated that a woman could in fact penetrate another woman with her clitoris as, they argued, it was very similar to the male penis. Italian Franciscan priest Ludovico Maria Sinistrari (1622–1701) wrote an extensive treatise on the clitoris and female sodomy,[12] stating that African women's clitorises are abnormally large from birth and then grow to the size of a penis. He claimed that in Ethiopia and Egypt genital mutilation was used "so that [the clitoris] does not start to approximate a male penis."[13] Though

Sinistrari's treatise was written a century after the start of the Portuguese Inquisition and was not used by the Inquisition in the prosecution of same-sex crimes against women, it provides an important documentation of the pathological racist fictions of the period created around black women's bodies and women's bodies more generally. Sinistrari believed that women who engaged in female sodomy were just as culpable as men and should be "punished by death and burned."[14]

Historian Bernadette J. Brooten in her study *Love between Women: Early Christian Response to Female Homoeroticism* argues that sex between women presented a conundrum for period Christian authors because if they tried to fit women within the framework of penetrator and penetrated, they would inevitably run into the problem that women do not have penises, which would undermine the active/passive dyad. As Brooten shows, period theologians' response to this quandary was to "depict one of the two women as having become like a man, that is, as having a physical organ wherewith to penetrate her female partner (an enlarged clitoris, a dildo, or some unnamed phallus-like appendage)."[15] Sinistrari confirms this perspective in his statement that the clitoris "is made up of the same elements as the male penis" and that it "takes the shape of a penis when it is swollen."[16]

Tibérius Décianus, an Italian lawyer cited in Sinistrari's studies, also claimed that a woman could not be seduced by another woman unless she had "inside the vulva a large 'nymphium' [clitoris]: that is to say a slight fleshy excrescence/ outgrowth, that can become erect like a penis and through which women become aroused during sex like men."[17]

These pathological views of women of African descent supported the idea that black women were more capable of penetrating other women and must have some predisposition to engage in female sodomy.[18] As Sander Gilman states, if black sexual parts could be shown to be inherently different, "this would be a sufficient sign that blacks were a separate (and, needless to say, lower) race, as different from the European as the proverbial orangutan."[19]

Sex between Women in the Inquisitional Records

Before delving into individual cases of sex between women in the inquisitional records, we need to consider one important shortcoming of these documents: the majority of the confessions and denunciations were brought by white women or men, and thus we only have their side of the story. The voices of black, mixed-race, and indigenous women are virtually absent, in contrast to cases involving enslaved men presented in the previous chapter. We do not have the words of slave women to counter or corroborate how and under what conditions the sexual acts occurred, or whether the slave women may have been coerced by white women or the sex occurred consensually.

Identifying overt instances of sexual abuse by white women of enslaved women in this archive proves even more difficult because of the nature of the Inquisition trials and the understanding of what constituted sex and sodomy. Legally and culturally, just as it was believed that men could not be raped, it was considered impossible for a woman to rape or sexually abuse another woman, due in large part to prescribed gender narratives and male assumptions about the limitations of the female sex. Same-sex sexual relations were treated by the inquisitors as sinful acts on the part of both participants, even in contexts of violence and coercion. It was believed that the fact that the act occurred was evidence of consent even when the victim said otherwise.

Historian Nell Irvin Painter has argued that famous nineteenth-century slave woman Sojourner Truth alludes several times, albeit in deeply veiled language, in her 1828 slave narrative to sexual abuse that she suffered at the hands of two of her white mistresses, Sally Dumont and Ann Folger.[20] When left alone with Truth, Folger would get into her bed and kiss and fondle her.[21] Truth's writing about her sexual abuse by Dumont is shrouded in shame and ambiguity. She writes, "It would seem to others, especially the uninitiated, so unaccountable, so unreasonable, and what is usually called so unnatural, . . . they would not easily believe it. 'Why, no!' she says, 'they'd call me a liar! they would, indeed! and I do not wish to say anything to destroy my own character for veracity, though what I say is strictly true.'"[22] The language she uses to refer to the abuse she suffered—"so unnatural," "unreasonable," "unaccountable"—is almost identical to the language employed by the Inquisition to refer to acts of female sodomy and in the few early US colonial cases to describe sexual acts between women. Painter also points out that the exposure of sexual abuse by white masters was fairly common in slave narratives—seen most notably in *Incidents in the Life of Slave Girl*,[23] written by Harriet Jacobs under the pseudonym Linda Brent—and audiences were aware of this reality. Painter argues that if Truth had been abused by her master, she would have said so, as audiences would have expected it, but they would not have accepted the idea of an enslaved woman being raped or sexually abused by a white mistress. In the context of US slavery, most people were not able or willing to conceive of the sexual abuse of a slave woman by a white mistress. Truth states that "especially the uninitiated" would not believe her story, implying that what she suffered was indeed known to "the initiated"—to other slave women. Reading Truth's narrative alongside the cases found in the Portuguese Inquisition records in Brazil reveals striking parallels.

Acts that fell outside the rigid religious, heteronormative, and classed definition of rape were consensual in the minds of the inquisitors, the church, and society. But the absence of overt force in the trial transcripts should not lead us to assume that force was uncommon. If sex between women did occur under coercive conditions, most women would likely not have willingly confessed to it—in one of the cases presented below a white woman pleaded with her denouncers to not expose her sexual affairs with two slave women.

A number of factors prevent us from knowing exactly what happened in these cases regardless of what is written in the record. First, confessions were given in a climate of intense fear under threat of punishment for failing to confess to heresies, for the gravity of one's sins, or for failing to denounce others who committed sins. Punishments varied from public shaming to excommunication, seizure of property, banishment, imprisonment, lashing, torture, and burning at the stake. Beyond the punishment meted out by the inquisitors, women who were denounced for same-sex relationships may also have feared their husbands' and families' reactions to the exposure of their sexual heresies and damage to their social standing, which depended on their roles as wives and mothers.

Thus people had strong motivations to avoid confessing or may have "minimized the acts, only telling inquisitors what they wanted to hear," as Ronaldo Vainfas points out.[24] Women who were accused of or confessed to repeated "dishonest indiscretions" were at heightened risk of being punished. Under pressure from their denouncers, they may have confessed to only one or two same-sex sexual experiences out of many, or perhaps they confessed only to the times when they were caught. We have no way of telling empirically how frequently sexual acts took place between women. We must read each of these cases with a degree of scrutiny, including attention to what is not being said. Given the time period, we can imagine that it must have been very intimidating and humiliating for these women to divulge their sexual encounters with other women before male inquisitors.

A salient difference between male and female "sodomy" cases, as they were called, especially those between white women, is the degree of affection involved in the female cases, including kissing, hugging, and caresses, in contrast to the overt violence that we see in cases between men. In cases involving white women there is often an element of courting or seduction. In some instances, especially those involving two white women, there was an extended period of exchange of letters and gifts before engaging in sex. Affection and courting are less common in the few available sodomy cases between white mistresses and enslaved women, which in most cases were denunciations made by outside observers rather than confessions.

Women who engaged in "dishonest friendship" were required to divulge all of the details to the inquisitors, who judged female cases within the same heteronormative active/passive dyad applied to men. In the cases that we have available to us the most documented forms of sexual contact between women were tribbing, kissing, and touching. The women were forced to describe their sexual positions so the inquisitors could determine the specific role of each partner. The woman who was on top was referred to as the *íncuba* (incubator), meaning the aggressor or active partner, who performed as the man in the eyes of the inquisitors. The woman who was on the bottom was known as the *paciente* (the passive woman). In most cases the woman who assumed the passive role during sex was less culpable because she did not breach her assigned gender role.[25] This is the opposite of cases involving men, where the passive penetrated male was more culpable and sinful than the active partner.

Women were also pressured to divulge whether pleasure was received from the act. Most importantly, maintaining the ejaculatory model applied to men, the inquisitors wanted to know whether either party reached orgasm. Many women openly confessed that they did, while others claimed they could not recall. Pleasure and orgasms between women are described exclusively in heterosexual terms in the Inquisition documents, "as a woman tends to orgasm with a man." Sex between women was viewed as only a simulation of heterosexual sex, and it was believed that only men could give this sort of pleasure to women, even though the women in these cases were clearly stating that another woman did so.

There is also mention in the Inquisition cases of women's anatomy, but only as it relates to the sexual act. The vagina is referred to as the *vaso natural* (natural vessel) and *natura*, and vaginal sex is often described as *por diante* (from the front). Curiously there are virtually no references to other parts of the female body, such as breasts, buttocks, or even the clitoris.

Regardless of any linguistic obfuscation, the Inquisition record clearly shows white women consciously transgressing gender conventions. In some instances, women were known to use phallic-shaped instruments or dildos made out of different materials, such as velvet, wood, glass, or leather. Those who used such instruments were judged more severely, because these instruments that attempted to simulate a penis were considered more unnatural.

The inquisitors' obsession with instruments, pleasure, and orgasms reveals that they were primarily concerned with the sexual acts themselves and whether gender conventions—what it meant to be a woman in the cultural and religious senses—were being transgressed rather than what these acts meant personally to the women or their motivations. Their questions also point to anxiety around replacing men, which would later appear in the literature on female homosexuality in the late nineteenth century.

Though same-sex desire within the white supremacist ideology of slavery became attributed to black women who corrupted white women, of the cases we have available to us, white women predominate in the confessions and denunciations and are mostly depicted as the initiators.

FIVE DISHONEST WOMEN IN THE PORTUGUESE INQUISITION

The following cases give a sense of the types of confessions and denunciations received by the Inquisition and how they were narrated and recorded.

In Bahia, Guiomar Pisçarra, a thirty-eight-year-old white mistress, confessed to the Inquisition during the grace period in 1592 that at the age of twelve or thirteen she engaged in sexual activity on at least two or three different occasions with Mécia, an eighteen-year-old Guinean slave.[26] Recalling their first encounter, Guiomar relates that they "stood before one another with their skirts raised, embracing each other, joining and rubbing their bodies and vaginas against each other, and in this way they pleasured themselves like man and woman."[27] Guiomar reported that she "can neither confirm nor remember if she orgasmed, on any of the occasions, as a woman tends to orgasm with a man, nor if Mécia orgasmed." Isabel Marques, a mixed-race woman, also confessed that at the age of ten she performed similar acts with Catarina Baroa, who was fourteen or fifteen at the time. Catarina Quaresma, nineteen, daughter of a wealthy Bahian planter and married to a rich plantation owner, confessed that before her marriage she regularly had sexual relations with girls under the age of ten.[28]

Maria Roiz was denounced in Pernambuco in 1593 by neighbor, Manoel Fernandes. Fernandes reported to the inquisitors that from his house he had observed Maria Roiz, a married white woman, and an eleven-year-old black girl named Ana at the latter's house. The documents do not indicate whether Ana was free or enslaved. Fernandes, who was a bit of a Peeping Tom, went to "spy on them through a hole in the door and saw Maria Roiz lying on a mat on her back and Ana lying facedown on top of her, with their undergarments rolled up, doing to one another as if they were man and woman." After watching them for a while, he told the inquisitors, he burst open the door and Ana hastily stood up while Maria Roiz remained on the floor. He reported that they exclaimed, "Oh, our shameful behavior!" He did not witness them using any "penetrating instruments."[29]

Maria Rangel confessed that at the age of seven or eight she was molested by Felipa Dias, who was fifteen or sixteen at the time. According to her testimony, one day when she arrived at Felipa's home, Felipa "took her by force, and closing the door, both of them were alone, she threw her back-down on the bed, and got on top of her straddling her waist, joining her vagina with her own, without the use of any penetrating instrument, she remained there with her being pleasured a bit, but she was so young and this was the first time that this happened to her, she did not understand what was happening."[30]

Madalena Pimentel, a forty-six-year-old white woman from Pernambuco, confessed that between the ages of nine and eleven, she engaged in "foolish friendship of little knowledge with a number of different girls of different races including a white girl named Micia de Lemos, a black girl named Iria Barbosa, and a sixteen-year-old white girl named Ana Fernandes." Madalena reported that "without the use of any penetrating instrument other than their bodies" and "without anyone seeing them" they had "carnal congress, joining their vaginas alternately with one on top and the other on the bottom." Madalena claimed that she had sex with each girl "multiple times on different occasions, but [did] not remember the exact number of times."[31]

MARIA DE LUCENA

This case is of particular importance as it is the only known denunciation of a mistress for female sodomy by a slave woman who was also an eyewitness. In November of 1593, Maria de Lucena, a *mamaluca* (a mixture of white and indigenous) upper-class woman around forty-five years old, was denounced twice to the Inquisition in Pernambuco for her "dishonest" behavior while staying in the home of her relative, Clara Fernandes, and her husband, Cristovão Queixada. Maria was caught on more than one occasion having sex with two slave women named Margayda and Vitória, who belonged to her cousin. The two denunciations were made by a thirty-five-year-old slave woman named Mônica and a white woman by the name of Maria de Hesedo, who was married to Clara de Fernandes's nephew. For unspecified reasons the denunciations occurred ten and fifteen years after the acts. Her denouncers reported that at that time she was a "single woman who already had children."

Mônica told the inquisitors that shortly after Maria de Lucena moved into Clara Fernandes's house it became known throughout the plantation that she was "sleeping carnally with the black female house slaves." She told the inquisitors that one night while everyone was asleep she heard "Maria de Lucena ascend from her hammock and go upstairs to the room where a black slave woman, Margayda, was." Mônica followed her and said she saw them both "on the floor on top of each other making movements and bodily gestures as if they were man and woman." Mônica, "having witnessed for herself both of them having carnal congress" and "unwilling to suffer such depravity," entered the room and "spit on both of them, telling them that what they were doing was not for lack of men." The following morning Maria de Lucena came to Mônica and pleaded with her to not tell anyone.[32]

Throughout her denunciation, Mônica, like Maria de Hesedo, actively incriminates Maria de Lucena, pointing out to the inquisitors that at the time she was "already a mature woman" and had "already given birth." This along with her exclamation that "what she was doing was not for lack of men" suggested to the inquisitors that Maria was wholly aware of what she was doing and that it was sinful, and yet she consciously chose to have sex with another woman. Some other women stated that they were unaware of what they were doing or didn't know that sexual activity with another woman was a sin. In Maria de Lucena's case, the sin was even graver because it was conscious: she deliberately chose physical pleasure over obedience to the Catholic Church.

If the denunciations of Maria de Lucena's multiple transgressions are true, this would mean that she, like white slave masters, saw slave women—even those who didn't belong to her—as sexually available to her. This example also shows how some slave mistresses sexually abused the enslaved as their husbands did, yet reconciled their actions with their marriages. Maria de Lucena's sexual trysts with slave women did not conflict with her being married or having children. As we do not have access to the testimonies of Maria de Lucena or the other slave women, we do not know the full details of how these sexual encounters started or Maria de Lucena's reasons for engaging in them. Though Mônica's denunciation clearly indicts Maria de Lucena as the provocateur, the slave Margayda is not spared, as Mônica denounced her as well. In the context of same-sex relations between women, Mônica's denunciation can be read as a form of slave resistance in which she openly exposes the abuses of a white mistress.

Mônica's denunciation is greatly concerned with her own self-representation and image, presented to the inquisitors through her eloquent command of the Portuguese language and devotion to the Catholic faith. As historian Nicole von Germeten has shown, African-descended women who came before the Inquisition to put forth a confession or denunciation had to confront the prejudice of inquisitors who inherently presumed that they "lacked honor due to their origins in Africa, connections to slavery (even if freed) or manual labor, and [their] doubtful Christianity."[33] Mônica goes to great lengths to establish her credibility, or what Sojourner Truth refers to in her slave narrative as her "character for veracity," as well her position as an upstanding woman of religious faith. She showcases her moral authority, mentioning her baptism, that she was born and reared in the home of Clara Fernandes, and that she is the "aunt of the Governor of Pernambuco." With this information, Mônica also attempts to establish her credibility and social position as a well-established member of Pernambuco society through her mistress. Mônica adds that she "truly isn't a slave but manumitted and free, as was her mother manumitted and free." She depicts herself as different from other slaves, establishing her self-image as a pious, free, and devoted slave woman who works for her mistress by her own free will.

Mônica's self-presentation before the inquisitors is a device found in many slave testimonials throughout the Americas. Her motivation for bringing forth this particular denunciation so many years after the fact is not clear. In narrating their own experiences and denouncing the abuses of white masters to white audiences, slaves such as Mônica, Sojourner Truth, Linda Brent, and the enslaved male rape victims presented in the previous chapter, sought to demonstrate to the inquisitors that they were good Christians and that they had a clear understanding of what constituted sin. Despite their condition as slaves and being perceived as immoral and inherently depraved, they sought to show their innocence and moral integrity in contrast to the aberrant abuses of the white masters they denounced. Slave men and women were aware of how they were perceived by whites and sought even through the rigid confines of the inquisitorial denunciations to refashion themselves through language, religiosity, and autobiography. This was especially the case when a slave accused a mistress of such a serious offense as female sodomy. Establishing a character for veracity was important for enslaved men and women throughout the diaspora, so that their stories and what they witnessed would be believed. Thus many, like Truth, were forced to discard the "unmentionable, unaccountable" aspects of their stories, such as sexual abuse at the hands of their mistresses, so that their entire narrative would not be undermined.

A second denunciation of Maria de Lucena was made by Maria de Hesedo, granddaughter of Clara Fernandes and wife of Matheus de Freitas de Azevedo, the governor of Pernambuco. Maria recounted that while staying in Clara's home while she was away, upon entering the house she saw to her surprise "a black slave woman named Vitória on the floor behind the door laid on her back . . . and on top of her with her undergarments off was Maria de Lucena." Maria stated further that Maria Lucena "was misusing herself straddling Vitoria doing as if she were a man with a woman engaging in the sin of sodomy." After Maria watched them for a while they noticed her standing in the doorway, and the two hastily got up and implored her not to tell anyone.[34] In both cases Maria de Lucena was reported to be the aggressor. Maria de Hesedo recalled that Maria de Lucena was expelled from the house as a result of these acts, and the two slave women were given to Maria Hesedo, possibly to avoid a scandal.

Other such cases of white women having sex with black women were reported to the Inquisition. Guiomar Pinheira, a mixed-race woman and daughter of a Portuguese man and a slave woman, confessed in 1592 that when she was eighteen, Quitéria Seca, a married white slave mistress and wife of Pero Madeira, the mayor of the city of Ilhéus, came to her home with a message from her aunt. According to Guiomar, Quitéria had the express intent of forcing her to engage in dishonest friendship. Guiomar relates that Quitéria "took her in her arms and took off her shirt, and rolled up their skirts." Quitéria then proceeded to "jump on top of her, straddling her, joining her vagina with her own, doing this to her as if she were a man with a woman, and in this way they pleasured themselves for an extended period of time." According to her confession, they had sex at least two more times, with Quitéria always being the "initiator and always on top without the use of any instrument other than their vaginas."[35]

FELIPA DE SOUZA

In addition to inquisitional cases involving slave mistresses and enslaved women, there are instances of married white women who acted out sexual relations with other married women. This was the case with Felipa de Souza, who was twice married and bragged of seducing scores of other married women and of having several girlfriends throughout the northeastern city of Salvador. Felipa is depicted in the inquisitional documents as an aggressive woman who actively pursued her same-sex desires despite her marriage and social and religious repression. She openly declared during her trial that she pursued women who awakened in her "great love and carnal affection."[36] Felipa is described almost like an addict, with the terms *useira* and *costumeira* suggesting that this was her habit or custom—an understanding of same-sex attraction that would later find its way, upon the creation of homosexuality as a medical category, into the medical description of lesbians as deranged sex addicts. Felipa was especially disconcerting to the inquisitors because with her ability to seduce innocent married women who claimed they had not previously engaged in same-sex activity, she embodied what doctors and sexologists three centuries later would see as the corruptive and predatory nature of homosexuality.

Though allegedly Felipa's partners were many and diverse, the cases brought before the Inquisitions in Bahia seem to suggest that she had a penchant for married white women, two of them being in their forties. Felipa made a practice of befriending other married women, gaining their confidence, and later revealing her real intentions. On a few occasions she had even flirted with women during Mass.

In 1591 Paula de Siqueira, a forty-year-old white woman who was twice married, made a confession during the grace period accusing Felipa de Souza of seducing her. Paula paints herself as the victim and prey of a brazen, dishonest woman. According to Paula, Felipa started "writing her many love letters" and making "lascivious gestures and gazes." Felipa's initial advances were not innocent but done "in such a way that she understood that Felipa de Souza had naughty intentions." Paula claims that Felipa pursued her in this way for two years, all the while giving her "some hugs and kisses, without her clearly discerning her objective." Despite Felipa's overtures, Paula claims not to have known exactly what Felipa wanted from her until one Sunday morning when Felipa stopped by her home for a visit and "she suspected and understood without a doubt that Felipa's intention was to have carnal congress with her." She states that Felipa took her to one of the rooms in her home, where she closed the door and "told her in clear words what she intended to do to her." Paula states that they had "carnal congress with one another from the front, joining their vaginas to each other, pleasuring themselves until both of them orgasmed." Then they stopped for a small meal and afterward "returned to engage in so many other times that same vile congress . . . with Felipa using her in the same way as if she were a man, placing her on top." Paula claims that at the time she committed these "vile sins," she was unaware that it was "such a serious sin and against nature." Before heading home, Felipa "drank a lot of wine" and bragged about her many female conquests, including Paula Antunes and Maria de Peralta of Pernambuco, along with "many other girls of both high and low social stations," some of these incidents even occurring in a monastery.

Paula's motives for confessing and denouncing Felipa are not clear. She may have confessed out of guilt, although she claimed to have enjoyed her trysts with Felipa "many other times." She paints Felipa as the aggressor and other accounts corroborate this claim. She offers many incriminating details about Felipa that have nothing to do with her case, such as the names of other women Felipa had sex with. Perhaps she wanted to minimize her culpability by showing that Felipa preyed on many other women. Paula equivocates throughout her confession, initially claiming that she was unaware of Felipa's "naughty intentions" even after her many advances but then saying that she was wholly cognizant that Felipa wanted to have "carnal congress" with her. Was Paula ashamed and repentant for engaging in dishonest friendship? Or was she jealous that she was only one of out many of Felipa's "dishonest pursuits" and vindictive? We cannot be sure of her motives, but we do know that there were similar confessions from several other women, which led to Felipa's banishment from Salvador and public flogging in the street.

Paula ends her confession with some gossip she heard around the city regarding Felipa's relations with another married woman named Paula Antunes. She relates that she heard that Felipa "seduced women and had girlfriends and that she ardently pursued a young girl married to a hunchback." When the husband discovered this he "went to get Felipa de Souza to take her to his home to spank her,"[37] after which Felipa ceased courting his wife and turned to other "dishonest" pursuits.

Eight days later, Maria Lourenço, also a forty-year-old white woman and married to a local artisan, came forward with a confession and denunciation against Felipa detailing for the inquisitors what occurred when Felipa visited her at her home one day while her husband was away. According to Maria, after they had breakfast Felipa suggested that they go to another room in the house, where she locked the two of them inside and began to "speak with seductive and amorous and lascivious words, better than any pimp to his whore." Felipa then proceeded to give Maria "many hugs and kisses and, ultimately threw her face down on the bed, and Felipa de Souza lay face down on top of her with their underwear undone, as such, with their vaginas joined together, they pleasured themselves until Felipa de Souza, who was on top, orgasmed, and they did with one another as if it were a man with a woman, without the use of any penetrating instrument between them, only their vaginas."[38]

Maria also states that on the following night, Felipa was so anxious to have sex with her again that she feigned to be suffering from menstrual cramps in the middle of the night as a ploy to get Maria to come to her house. Felipa woke up her husband and demanded that he go get Maria to come and "lie in bed with her to cure her." Maria, well aware of Felipa's intentions, refused. Five or six days later, however, Felipa came to Maria's house during breakfast and again locked the two of them in the bedroom, where Felipa again proceeded to "speak words of love, caressing her, hugging her, and kissing her." This time however, Maria "threw Felipa down on her bed and climbed on top of her, undoing their undergarments and with their vaginas joined together, they pleasured themselves as if they were man and woman, until Felipa de Souza orgasmed." Maria also states that Felipa told her that she had seduced several other women in Salvador, including Paula de Siqueira, Paula Antunes, and Maria Pinheira, and engaged in the same "dishonest acts" with them.[39] For her dishonest conduct and the numerous accusations brought against her, Felipa was one of the most severely punished of the women who engaged in same-sex sexual activity. She was imprisoned, publicly flogged, and ultimately banished from Bahia.[40]

One of the most striking interracial female sodomy cases brought before the Inquisition in 1592 involved a free black woman named Francisca Luiz and a white woman by the name of Isabel Antônia. Francisca had been abandoned by her husband. She later met Isabel and the two quickly became friends and lovers and remained together until Isabel's death. Their relationship proved scandalous.

Isabel was known throughout the city of Salvador as "a do veludo," the Velvet One. She garnered this curious nickname due to her use of a velvet-covered phallic-shaped instrument during her sexual relations with women. Francisca was denounced by a woman who stated to the inquisitors that it was "public knowledge that Francisca Luiz sleeps carnally with the single woman named the Velvet One and that they engage in nefarious sex with an instrument covered in velvet."[41]

The Velvet One had been previously prosecuted for engaging in female sodomy in Porto, Portugal, and as a result was deported around 1579 to Brazil, where she continued to engage in sex with women. In fact Portugal sent a number of its convicted sexual deviants, both male and female, to Brazil as punishment during the Inquisition.

One afternoon, the relationship between Isabel and Francisca soured when the Velvet One returned from a date with a man. Francisca, furious, cornered Isabel as she was leaving the house where they lived together, and in front of a crowd of onlookers screamed at her, "You tramp! . . . How many kisses and hugs have you given to this lame man, and you don't give me any?! . . . Don't you know that I love one vagina more than all the penises around here?!" Their fight turned physical, and Francisca grabbed the Velvet One by her hair, hitting her and dragging her inside as the neighbors watched in shock.[42]

In 1592, when the Inquisition investigated their affair, Isabel had passed away. Francisca Luiz was called in to make a deposition by the inquisitors. She confirmed that the accusations were true and that the two women had been previously tried around 1580 and sentenced to leave the city but were ultimately allowed to stay. The inquisitors closed the case but punished Francisca, ordering her to pay the fees of the proceedings and imposing the obligatory penances and prayer.

The relationship between the Velvet One and Francisca Luiz is one of the most unique cases in the Inquisition record. It documents a consensual interracial same-sex relationship between two previously married women. Based on the denunciations brought against them, it appears that the Velvet One assumed the active role, penetrating Francisca. It is also possible that they exchanged the active and passive roles, as other cases indicate. Although Isabel was in a relationship with Francisca, it appears it was not entirely to the exclusion of interactions with men. The motive behind the Velvet One's date with a male suitor that caused a public fight leading to a denunciation against them is unclear. It is possible that she could have also engaged in sex with men, or the date could have been an attempt to make Francisca jealous. Francisca's public exclamation that she "loves one vagina more than all the penises around here" is radical and indeed subversive. All of this must have been particularly disconcerting to those who denounced her and to the inquisitors, as it portrayed women as owning their sexuality and displacing men—white men in particular. This anxiety over controlling both black and white women's sexualities, as well as those of black men, would color the emergence of Brazilian studies on homosexuality in the nineteenth century.

The above cases point to a sexual fluidity among women during childhood and adolescence and as mature married women that was not entirely different from the conduct of a number of white men during the period, a fluidity that undermined the heteronormative, generative narrative of nation.

Transgression of the Female Gender Role via Same-Sex Desire

We saw previously that power was a primary motivation behind the rape of slave men in Inquisition cases, functioning within a logic of heteronormativity that served to enhance the masculinity and domination of the white-master rapist. Here we will examine the motivations of white women to engage in sex with other women and how it impacted notions of womanhood and manhood.

My interest here is not to attempt to decipher whether these women were what we could consider lesbians or bisexual, or were merely experimenting sexually, but to examine what these instances of sexual fluidity or transgression may have meant in relation to their position as women and wives in Brazilian slave society. With some exceptions noted above, the documents of the Inquisition do not directly reveal what provoked white women to engage in sex with other women. Although the Catholic Church was aware of their conduct, it did not concern itself with the sinner's personal motivations or the meaning the sinner gave to such acts, but only with the sin itself. For the inquisitors, these relationships did not suggest any deeper correlation to a woman's personality or sexual preference. Interest in those aspects of sexual conduct would only emerge in the late nineteenth century with studies on male and female homosexuality.

The absence of homosexuality as a sexual category in the eyes of society during the time of the Inquisition allowed both men and women to bend the boundaries of heterosexuality without undermining it. Even though engaging in sinful acts such as dishonest friendship or male sodomy was deemed sinful, it is possible that because sex between persons of the same gender was not correlated with a specific sexual category, it was able to occur with more fluidity and the motives and desires to engage in same-sex sexual relations held more fluid meanings, all while not entirely disavowing the participants' presumptive heterosexuality. Dishonest women transgressed their role as women but not necessarily their sexual identity. As scholars such as historian Ligia Bellini have shown, none of the women charged with female sodomy in the archives of the Portuguese Inquisition confessed to or assumed what we would consider today to be a gay or lesbian identity. They did not see themselves as part of a collective of women who shared same-sex desire.[43] We know that they had strong reasons for not publicly assuming what would have been considered a subversive identity.

The closest to admissions of same-sex desire came from Felipa de Souza, who admitted to pursuing women who awakened in her "great love and carnal affection," and from Francisca Luiz, who exclaimed to her lover the Velvet One that she loved her vagina more than all the penises in Salvador. But all of the women who either confessed to or were denounced for engaging in dishonest friendship were or had been previously married or in a relationship with a man. It would have been virtually impossible to avoid relationships with men given societal scrutiny and control of women. From the limited information available to us, we cannot draw any direct conclusions about how these women saw their own sexuality or sexual identities. Their sexual practices, much like those of many of the white masters analyzed in the previous chapter, embodied a fluidity that was part and parcel of the institution of slavery and libidinous life in the colony.

In the female sodomy cases reported to the Inquisition in Brazil there was deep concern with gender—womanhood, the feminine—on the part of both inquisitors and confessants rather than with sexual or romantic desire for women. Same-sex sexual acts were considered above all crimes against nature, meaning against gender prescriptions defined by the church. Marital sex for white women within the confines of a rigidly patriarchal society was not about pleasure, but expressly about reproducing legitimate white heirs, which in some instances was characterized by control, domination, and violence, just as for women of color.

Ever the romantic, Father António Vieira cautioned that love or passion was not supposed to exist in a marriage, and those who thought so would surely be condemned to hell. In 1651 he professed in a sermon, "I declare ... that this thing in the world that people call love is a something that isn't real and doesn't even exist. It's a fairytale, a lie, a deception, a sickness of the imagination, and for this reason it is only a form of torment ... It is a death for which one will go to hell."[44]

Arranged marriages at the age of eleven or even younger were also common-place. The church and period theologians had strict rules governing the sexual conduct of married couples, which was critical for the perpetuation of gender hierarchies. It was the duty of married women to have sex with their husbands and to produce progeny. Because husbands were the legal owners of their wives, women were required to obey their husbands in all matters. As historian Eman-uel Araújo has shown, "Moderation, and the control of the senses and the flesh, was what was expected of both [husband and wife]. . . . Not that [sex] should be avoided. On the contrary, husbands and wives should actively insist on the payment of the 'matrimonial debit.'"[45] Women were not supposed to outwardly express sexual desire; rather, desire should always "be intimated" and it was the husband's duty to "be aware of the oblique, modest, and shameful signs of his wife."[46] Women were made to feel ashamed of their sexual desire and bodies.

The church, like medical doctors and sexologists of the late nineteenth century, extended its reach into couples' bedrooms, concretizing the societal gender hierarchy of man over woman by condemning a host of sexual posi-tions. Couples were not to engage in intercourse while standing or seated, and a woman was not to be on top of her husband during sex, as in such positions sperm could be wasted and not reach its destination.[47] Lust, or sex simply for physical pleasure, was considered dangerous and morally reprehensible. Thus gender was made through sex, and the church found in sex a way of cementing male supremacy by defining women as penetrable property, as was the case with male and female slaves. Women were literally beneath men at all times. Sueann Caulfield points out that these norms were camouflaged as "sexual honor" when in fact their purpose was to reinforce the supremacy of the white male elite.[48]

Though white women during the colonial period were "enclosed, devalued, watched, beaten," as Ronaldo Vainfas demonstrates, they did not merely "resign themselves to suffering, cornered by the growing misogyny of the customs and laws," but "always reacted to male pressures, challenging men, breaking away from intolerable relationships and taking various initiatives in the field of love and sex."[49] The fact that some women repeatedly engaged in sexual acts with other women even though they knew those acts were considered unnatural and sinful suggests that these relations may have had personal meanings and moti-vations rooted in their experiences as women that are not clearly represented in the documents. The women confess to having derived physical pleasure from sexual acts with other women, a type of gender subversion as they shifted away from sex for procreation to sex for pleasure—a privilege reserved exclusively for white men. The women in the inquisitional cases alternate fluidly between sexual positions of dominance and passivity, from aggressors to initiators, transgressing their rigidly prescribed gender roles. White women who engaged in sex with other women did so because they wanted to.

Reproductive sex defined the male-female relationship and cemented gender hierarchies. If the purpose of sex for white women was transformed from the reproduction of whiteness and white male supremacy to pleasure, men could be displaced. Thus dishonest friendship also becomes a contravention against men and male domination over women.

Anxieties over gender are present in the language and the framing of sexual relations between women as a crime against gender and nature. In case after case women are said to be acting "like a man with a woman," revealing anxiety around the simulation of heteronormativity between two women, maintenance of gender roles through sex, and the displacement of men. Other than the inquisitors' own voyeuristic impulses, this is perhaps another reason why they evinced so much concern over orgasms, the use of phallic-shaped instruments, and the potential for women's clitorises to grow to penis size.

People of the time were unwilling to see white female sexuality as anything other than passive. Given the period restrictions, sex with other women may have been a way for white women to explore dominance or to have sex solely for the purposes of pleasure. These acts may have been a means of transcending the fiction of white female passivity and openly defying the white male patriarchy. Moreover, they undermine the myths that white women were victims and prey to black women's bestial sexuality, myths that would be propagated throughout the nineteenth century and the history of slavery and that were central to the nation's antislavery movement. White women were not mere victims, and their transgression of female passivity in some cases took the form of physical violence and sexual exploitation of enslaved black women.

Perhaps this gender subversion, the opportunity for white women to explore dominance, could only have occurred between women. I want to make clear that this pleasure seeking by white women could have included violence and coercion of enslaved women that may not be accounted for in the archive. If they could not exert power in relation to white men, white women could feel powerful with their equals or subalterns. In a number of documented instances, this power subversion would also result in physical violence against black women, who often bore the brunt of white women's anger toward their husband's philandering. With other women, they could be violent, sexually deviant, aggressive, or passive on their own terms, expanding the definition and terrain of white womanhood.

Bahian poet Gregório de Matos, popularly known as the Boca do Inferno (Hell's Mouth) (1636–1696), penned one of the first works of Brazilian literature to address the sexual desire of a woman for another woman. The poem, like most of Matos's work, was considered scandalous, which caused him to be deported to Angola. It was titled "A huma dama que macheavea outras mulheres" (To a Woman Who Copulates with Other Women). There is no direct English translation for the verb *machear*; it refers to sex specifically between animals. Matos's poem was addressed to a white female love interest called Nise. The poem's primary concern, consistent with the church's concern, is the displacement and rejection of white men (himself) for women, and more explicitly sex with other women and the subversion of gender norms. Matos exclaims, "I fell in love without knowing of this vice that you engage in, that to no man will you give yourself and you take all of the women!" He asks himself throughout the poem how he could possibly win over this woman if "she is a woman not for men, and is a man for women."

Matos depicts female same-sex desire within the active/passive dyad, masculinizing her for her desire for women. With the verb *machear* he refers to sex between women as sex between animals, an act that he sees as vulgar and unnatural. This poem reveals early white male fears regarding female same-sex desire. Given Matos's reputation for scandal and slander and his penchant for retaliation, we must also consider that he could have been falsely accusing Nise of being a dishonest woman for rejecting him. This poem underlines the place of white women in the colonial adage as being "for marriage." The white woman who rejects white men ruins the white family and becomes a direct threat to white male racial and sexual supremacy.

Slave Women and White Victimhood
in the Nineteenth Century

In the late nineteenth century, when Brazil was forced to confront the reality of the coming abolition of slavery, same-sex desire became increasingly classed and racialized. Homosexuality (both male and female) in many cases was depicted as foreign to white elite Brazilians, and the language used to talk about it changed. Female sodomy and same-sex desire moved from vice to contaminative perversion. Homosexuality as a category emerged during the time when sexually transmitted diseases were being studied, and homosexuality, among other perversions, came to be viewed as a black perversion that could contaminate whites. Black sexuality was inherent to black people, but white sexuality could become blackened through contact with the perversions embodied in black people. At the same time, slave women came to represent everything that was wrong with the nation and that needed to be eradicated.

Despite—or perhaps because of—the pervasive sexual contact between the races that occurred in Brazil, it was important for whites to portray blacks, whites, and their sexuality as fundamentally different and to deflect attention away from their own interracial sexual activity. Sander Gilman has shown that in order to achieve this goal, in the nineteenth century white sexuality became configured as in constant peril of being "contaminated through an external source, rather than by virtue of any inherent failure of the individual."[50] Slave women emerged in nineteenth-century literature, political discourse, and popular culture as a grave moral and physical threat to whites, to the white family, and to the nation. They were framed as inherently degenerate and bent on corrupting white women and families. White women, on the other hand, were depicted as innocent, vulnerable, and defenseless against the destructive influence of slave women.

Ironically, even abolitionists viewed blacks as inherently degenerate. A number of them argued that slavery should be abolished not out of respect for the humanity and rights of slaves but to protect white families from them. On November 11, 1823, during the abolitionist debates, statesman José Bonifácio de Andrada e Silva of São Paulo in a speech to the Brazilian parliament asked bluntly, "What kind of morality can families expect to have, employing these miserable, dishonorable beings without religion? From slave women who prostitute themselves to the first man who seeks them out?" Bonifácio followed his question with a serious warning: "Everything in this life, however, is compensated; we have tyrannized the slaves, and reduced them to brute animals, and in return they inoculate us with all of their immorality and every one of their vices."[51]

Impressionable young white girls were thought to be especially vulnerable to the corrupting influence of slave women. Slavery "influences, from near or far, the life of the young white mistress, disturbing and poisoning the education of these poor victims. The slave woman who walks around unnoticed, poorly judged, and not feared, shocks, causes panic, terrorizes, when her reflection manifests and renders its dark and fatal influence," wrote medical doctor and writer Joaquim Manuel de Macedo in 1869.[52]

Nowhere was white morality thought to be more threatened by slaves than in the bedroom. White girls and women were left for long hours in the constant company of their friends and slave women who bathed, clothed, and groomed them, leading to fears and unsettling suspicions that there might be more than dressing and praying going on in the boudoirs of the wives and daughters of white men.

All of the rampant prejudices, anxieties, and contradictions inherent in Brazilian antislavery literature were united in Joaquim Manuel de Macedo's 1869 collection of stories, *As vítimas algozes: Quadros da escravidão* (Victim Executioners: Portraits of Slavery).[53] It is reputed that the emperor commissioned Macedo to write this work to help prepare the public for the Law of the Free Womb.[54] Macedo tells his readers that although the slaves are certainly to blame for their perverse habits and for the intentional harm that they inflict upon whites, as long as whites own slaves, they too are to blame—not because of the cruelty and violence to which they subject their slaves, but because they have brought these slaves into their homes: "The blame of this great evil is more ours than the slaves' because we all recognize that slavery produces debasement, shame, turpitude, the corruption of men turned into slaves; and in the countries that maintain slavery, parents put depravation, debasement, turpitude, corruption right next to their daughters."[55] In the nineteenth and early twentieth centuries, the nation depended on the family, and the integrity of the family depended on sexual honor. Thus women's sexual honesty was essential to prevent social collapse.[56]

Macedo confirms the intent of slave women to destroy what they could not possess and the grave danger that they posed to young white girls:

> The slave woman left to the contempt of slavery, growing up where some of the most scandalous and repugnant vices are practiced, from childhood, from infancy, witnessing shameful acts of lust, and hearing the most vulgar and nasty speech, becomes perverted long before having consciousness of her perversion, and she cannot live outside of that atmosphere without violently imposing and plaguing others with similar customs and her lustful ideas; thus the slave woman, placed at the feet of the innocent, inexperienced, curious little girl takes her, drags her down as much as possible.... She envies the purity of the young mistress and seeks to destroy it so that she does not have that angelic halo that she never felt in herself.[57]

Antislavery proponents pleaded that what was at stake was the innocence and virtue of all white women. Black women and their sexuality became in the mid-nineteenth century and throughout the abolitionist debates a "phobogenic object, a stimulus to anxiety,"[58] as Frantz Fanon terms it. Slave women were "corrupters of the feminine and masculine offspring," wrote Francisco Pacifico de Amaral, secretary of the Provincial Assembly of Pernambuco, in

1884.[59] They sought to ruin white women by stealing their men and by subjecting them to perversions ranging from extramarital sex to homosexuality. Slave women, warned Joaquim Manuel de Macedo, "infected" white women's hearts; "inspired by their brutal sensualism, sordid greed, their demoralization, their perversion, and even for revenge they go to the extreme of dragging [the white mistress] into dishonor, facilitating the blemish that will forever stain her life."[60]

A common belief was that slave women strategically made themselves sexually available through the seduction of white masters or prostitution with well-to-do white men with the hope of obtaining their freedom. Jesuit priest André João Antonil remarked that the money that slave women used to purchase their freedom "rarely comes out of any other mines than their bodies, with repeated sins; and after they are freed, they continue to be the ruination of many."[61] Though we have no way of knowing the degree to which this pattern occurred, there are several documented cases of illicit relationships, concubinage, and marriages between former slave women and white masters that suggest that there may have been some truth to this (admittedly racist) claim.

Dishonest Friendship in the Mistress's Boudoir

During the Inquisition women who were denounced or who confessed of their own free will told their own stories of same-sex experiences to the inquisitors, although we cannot know whether the (male) scribes recorded them accurately. In the nineteenth century female same-sex desire became narrated exclusively by white men, and the white male narrative in literature, cultural production, and politics was fraught with anxieties about women's sexual activities. Because slave women purportedly seduced white men with their uninhibited sexuality, it was feared that perhaps curious young girls and abandoned wives would become prey to the perversions of slave women as well. One noticeable shift from the time of the Inquisition is that in the wake of the abolition of slavery and bourgeoning studies of homosexuality, white male fictions were created in literature, in political and scientific narratives, and in the general social discourse to explain the motives behind white women's engagement in same-sex sexual activity. The emphasis in many respects remains the same, as the preservation of white female purity and heterosexuality had a direct connection to white male supremacy. Given their own copious sexual relations with their slave women, some white masters were troubled by speculations about what their wives, sisters, and daughters were doing alone with the slave women in their absence.

Gilberto Freyre observes that in some cases it was through her "favorite *negra* or mulatta that the young mistress was initiated in the mysteries of physical love,"[62] employing the same term—"the mysteries of physical love"—that he uses to describe the rape of the young slave boy by the master's son. In the following passage from *As vítimas algozes*, Joaquim Manuel de Macedo describes anxieties surrounding the extensive physical contact between the young mistress and the slave woman and the slave's unfettered access to the white mistress's body:

> In many houses the slave maid sleeps close to the bed of the young mistress, or at the door to her room. In some families this extremely imprudent practice has been done away with; but in any case the slave maid is in charge of dressing the young mistress; she helps her to undress and to dress . . . ; [the slave woman] is a confidant who has privileged access to the secret imperfections of [the young mistress's] body that she disguises and to all of the beautiful forms of her body that stand out. . . . The doctor even in the most severe cases of illness does not get to see the imperfections of her sick body; the slave woman knows her soul as well as the priest, and her body much more than any doctor.[63]

This closeness between the slave woman and the white mistress becomes laden with sexual meaning. Black women were privileged to intimate, almost sexual knowledge of white women's bodies—more privileged, perhaps, than their own husbands. The concerns about this "imprudent practice" suggest a more deep-seated anxiety around the difficulty of policing and containing white female sexual desire. Macedo alludes not so discreetly to potential homoerotic interactions between the slave woman and the naïve young mistress. He does not fully describe the "imprudent practice," perhaps to avoid shocking his public but also because there was little language to describe sex, especially sexual desire between women.

Many white men wanted to believe that white women had no sexual desire at all, or if they did it was a result of contact with black women—a specter that incited fears that if white men could not regulate white and black women's sexualities, the women would be out of their control altogether, anxieties not so different from those mirrored in the Inquisition trials centuries earlier. Anxiety abounded in the idea that black women could potentially encourage white women to access their own sexual nature through lesbian activity, without their husbands.

Slave women's desire for white women in the minds of white men was emulous. Macedo in his short story "Lucinda the Slave Maid" describes the envy of the black woman for her mistress: "The young mistress was not paying attention to her body, and let the collar of her night gown open indiscreetly due to her slanted position in bed, and one of her breasts, white as snow, proudly stuck out, left exposed to the envious eyes of the slave woman."[64] That is, the black woman, in the minds of white male antislavery thinkers, came to desire what she could never embody, and because she could not be it, she desired to enslave it and destroy it with her sexuality.

Specific erotic practices that took place between enslaved women and their white mistresses—at times documented in language bordering on fantasia—intensified these anxieties. Period travel journals from European observers such as Frenchman Charles Expilly and Englishman Thomas Lindley, traveling through Brazil in the early nineteenth century, chronicle in great detail several of these erotic acts. One of these practices was known as *cafuné*, which means "caress" in modern Portuguese. Said to have its origins in southern Africa, cafuné was a practice of gently massaging the head and removing lice. Judging from the effect that it had on the white mistress, Expilly and Lindley thought cafuné to be more erotic than hygienic. For French sociologist Roger Bastide, cafuné was a "substitute for lesbian amusements."[65] Lindley in 1805 referred to cafuné as a "shocking custom" practiced particularly by "females who fill up their vacant hours with this elegant amusement." Witnessing the cafuné ritual proved so disconcerting for Lindley that he prefaced his description of it to his readers by stating, "I am ashamed of recording an instance of the filth and indelicacy of the wretches around us."[66] According to Expilly, it was practiced "hidden away, far from any watchful eyes" and was both "a distraction and pleasure" for Brazilian mistresses. Expilly writes:

> In the heat of the day . . . the *senhoras* retire to the interior of the house and lie down in the lap of their favorite *mucama* [slave maid], presenting their head to her. The *mucama* repeatedly runs her supple, indolent fingers through the thick hair that unrolls in front of her. The *mucama* explores that luxuriant tangle of hair and slowly tosses it in all directions. She delicately caresses the root of each hair, skillfully pinching the scalp and sounding, from time to time, a subtle click between the nails of the pointer and middle fingers. This sensation becomes a source of pleasure for the slave woman's sensual nature. A voluptuous shiver runs through the mistress's body at the touch of the caressing fingers. Invaded, disabled, conquered by the fluid that spreads through her entire body, some succumb to the delicious sensation and swoon with pleasure on the *mucama*'s knees.[67]

Expilly's language describing the cafuné ritual unmistakably simulates sex and orgasm. Lindley's observations mirror Expilly's, as he too observed cafuné to

FIGURE 3.1 Woodcut by Livio Abramo showing a slave woman performing *cafuné* on her white mistress, 1948.

produce a "sort of enjoyment" in the slave mistress.[68] For Expilly, the Brazilian mistress is clearly expressing same-sex desire, to which the slave woman acquiesces, as Expilly also states that some white mistresses had "stronger reasons to so faithfully practice cafuné than simply the desire for a sweet arousal of the senses, followed by a state of pleasurable languishing that reaches ecstasy."[69]

What Expilly describes is a staged scene of seduction in which the erotic desire of the *senhora* and *mucama* are interconnected, with the ritual becoming pleasurable for both. Here the mucama seduces, but the mistress also desires to be seduced. For Expilly, there is a certain subversion of power and physical domination by the slave woman that occurs here, as her touch leaves the mistress in a state of vulnerability, "invaded, disabled, conquered."

Gilberto Freyre also describes the erotic quality of the bathing of the mistress by the slave woman, which "may have provided senhoras constrained by male despotism the opportunity to practice acts that approximated or simulated lesbian acts" in lieu of heterosexual acts "that were sometimes difficult."[70] Thus Freyre regards bathing and other expressions of eroticism between white mistresses and enslaved women as a response to sexual repression and as compensatory for heterosexual acts that were more difficult to engage in due to the separation of the sexes and the constant surveillance of white female sexuality. This separation, according to Bastide, resulted in "the great temptation for same-sex erotic activity, and evidently lesbian love."[71] He continues, "For it was only natural that the senhoras' repressed libido find an outlet, even more so given the lustful environment created by the polygamous affairs of her husband and his slaves. . . . She could only explore her sexuality under such conditions with the women who were around her and dressed her, and who served as confidants and were her company throughout the day, her mucamas."[72]

This archive of interracial same-sex sexual relations between women complicates how we understand the power relations and erotic ties between enslaved women and white mistresses and the interconnectedness of black and white female sexualities under slavery. These accounts, along with the inquisitional cases, provide important information about these relations, but more than anything they describe how white men framed them. White mistresses lived under the watchful eyes of their husbands and families, and the expression of their sexual desire was certainly constrained. But the view of same-sex erotic activity between black and white women as compensatory acts, as Freyre and Bastide have suggested, that protected the white mistress from being dishonored by illicit heterosexual sex seemingly denies some white women's same-sex desire and the fact that white women within the confines of a deeply patriarchal society also partook in slavery's sexual economy. Moreover, in some cases these women did have men available to them.

As Freyre makes us aware, enslaved black women and girls bore the brunt of the slaveholder's sexual domination via rape, in a sense sparing white women from the same fate: "It was the bodies of black women—at times, tiny ten-year-old bodies—that, in the moral architecture of Brazilian patriarchalism, constituted a formidable block of defense against bold attacks by Don Juans on the virtue of the white senhoras."[73] The notion of black women as safeguards of white female morality and an outlet for white women's repressed libidos suggests black female complicity and obscures the reality that white mistresses, like their husbands and fathers, in some cases could have sexually exploited black women.

In all of these accounts the emphasis is on white female sexual desire and pleasure, and it is all but impossible to discern enslaved women's desire or reactions to engaging in these activities. In the descriptions of these erotic practices the authors and analysts do not merely suggest black women's complicity but propagate the idea of slave agency and the notion that slave women got pleasure from pleasing white men and women.

Enslaved women's desire and pleasure became conflated with the desire and pleasure of their oppressors. Reflecting on her experience with her mistress, slave woman Harriet Jacobs wrote in her 1861 narrative, "That which commands admiration in the white woman only hastens the degradation of the female slave."[74] As Jacobs shows, the relationship between the two women was mutually constitutive and fundamental to perpetuating the economy of slavery. Therefore, in order for white women to be pious and virtuous, black women had to be their polar opposites, both physically through sexual exploitation and in writing. For, as Jacobs writes, "She is not allowed to have any pride of character. It was deemed a crime in her wish to be virtuous."[75]

Slavery was an institution of desire that fomented white pleasure through black injury. Enslaved black women and men served as sexual experience and moral safeguards, and through the erasure of their personhood, their pleasure became the pleasure of the black woman. Though as we progress into the nineteenth century, lesbianism within the white supremacist ideology of slavery becomes attributed to black and poor women who seduce white women, the Inquisition cases provide us with another account. I do not mean to suggest that black women did not have same-sex sexual desires and did not willingly engage in same-sex erotic acts, as there are also many instances, as we have seen, of what would appear to be consensual sex between black and white women. However, contrary to the white supremacist view of homosexuality as an exclusively black perversion, none of the reported cases reveal white women engaging in same-sex sexual activity as a result of the coercion of black women.

This exclusive focus on the desire and pleasure of the master and mistress and the idea that slave women enjoyed pleasuring them obscures the slave woman's captivity: she had no choice but to comply with her owners' desires under conditions of coercion and violence. For the captive slave there could be no true consent or agency. The mistress's pleasure—the notion of sex as an act of intimacy—conceals the power dynamic at work. White pleasure obscures black captivity and injury and becomes a false equalizer. The portrayal of sexual acts between enslaved women and white mistresses, as with white men, as an act between equal consenting partners then becomes the basis of the sexual narrative undergirding the myth of racial democracy.

As we saw in our examination of rape law in the Brazilian colony and the independent nation, being deemed an "honest" woman was a primary determinant of rapability or violatability, as a dishonest woman could not be violated. The adage that designates white women for marriage shows how much of white women's worth to white men was embedded in their honesty and virtue. These qualities were often the only sources of power and worth that white women had in relation to white men. We can imagine how the potential loss of virtue or honesty in the eyes of their husbands, families, and society must have informed how white women told their stories or the indiscretions that they may have intentionally secreted.

There is much that we will never know or that remained unseen about the relationship between white mistresses and enslaved women precisely because the narratives created by white men about them—that is, the constructed passivity and piousness (asexuality) of white women and the depravity of black women—often took precedence and overshadowed the reality of their lives and interactions. The narrative of white women's virtue was both a prison and a veil, but also a source of power as it relates to black women, enabling extreme and unchecked forms of cruelty that were not much different from those committed by their husbands, sons, and brothers. If white mistresses did abuse slave women, their mythical virtue would have protected them, just as being white and male protected slave-master rapists. The likelihood of a slave's story of sexual abuse being believed was very low. Admitting sexual abuse would cast shame on both the mistress and the slave woman. The element of disbelief veiled many crimes of white women against black women. Society did not want to accept that a white woman had the capacity to be sexual, promiscuous, dominant, or aggressive. Racialized fictions around gender were as much about suppressing white and black women as solidifying white male supremacy over them. Within the context and logic of slavery it was far easier to blame white women's transgression and deviant behavior on their contact with licentious slave women than to come to terms with the reality that white women had these deviant desires of their own. To accept an expanded notion of white womanhood would be to displace them from their exclusive role of reproducing white legitimacy. The area of sex was where white men controlled both black and white women and concomitantly reproduced slavery and freedom. Blurring the lines between white women for marriage and white legitimacy, and the mulatta or black woman for fornicating and the reproduction of slavery, would undermine their position in white men's (sexual and political) lives and also the very logic and existence of slavery.

The Creation of Lesbianism in the White Male Imagination

At the close of the Inquisition, sex between women ceased to be documented as thoroughly, making only oblique appearances via allusions in novels and short stories. As pseudoscientific studies of sexuality began to proliferate in the late nineteenth and early twentieth centuries and "female homosexuality" became a sexual category, health professionals sought to pinpoint and meticulously document the causes of these women's "unnatural desires." Women who engaged in sex with other women were referred to in the literature as *lesbianistas*, *sáficas*, *viragos*, *fanchonas*, and *tríbades*. Drawing on the late nineteenth-century conflation of race, class, and sexual deviance, José Pires de Almeida stated that *clitorismo*, or *roçadinho*, was most commonly practiced "among poor women and girls,"[76] which becomes depicted in the literature of the period. For some women, perhaps the more experienced lesbians, whom Pires de Almeida refers to as *mundanas* (worldly or carnal women), roçadinho or clitorismo was "not enough to satisfy them as they had already enjoyed it too much." They instead preferred to engage in "oral coitus or vulgarly called *chupadinho* (licking or sucking)."[77]

According to Pires de Almeida, clitorismo was practiced by young women at the age of marriage and by spinsters who did it surreptitiously. Though it was done in private, he argued, as he would of male homosexuals, that these women's secret could be easily found out by a number of physical symptoms, including "soft breasts," "strong and sometimes sour breath," "discolored lips and gums," "eyes without that sweet humidity," a pale complexion, freckles or pimples on the face, or flabbiness. He warned that clitorismo could be fatal and would also lead to loss of memory and reason.[78]

In *Atentados ao pudor: Estudos sobre as aberrações do instinto sexual* (Assaults on Modesty: Studies on Sexual Aberrations) doctor Francisco José Viveiros de Castro, who was also a professor of criminal law and a judge on the High Court of Appeals in Rio de Janeiro, offered a number of potential causes of homosexuality, including "erotic madness." According to Viveiros de Castro, lesbians were mentally ill sex addicts. He argued that their illness and addiction derived from several sources, including a disdain for the "natural" sexual perversions that a man required of his woman partner. He also claimed that modernization, education, and modern literature "brought women out of the silent half-light of the fireplace into the tumultuous upheavals of the world, opening up unknown horizons, initiating them into the secrets of vice and awakening indiscreet curiosity."[79] More importantly, Viveiros de Castro cautioned, "When the addiction is of long duration, its cure is almost impossible, because the nerves in the genital parts have become hyperestheticized (overly sensitive) and the pleasure experienced far exceeds that granted by the embraces of natural love,"[80] an obvious reference to sex with men.

Depending on the severity of a given case, Pires de Almeida recommended a variety of approaches that could be used to cure lesbians. He first suggested speaking to them about it "gently and convincingly." However, if they weren't receptive, he recommended reprimanding them using "hard and severe language," and for a rebellious woman he encouraged haranguing her with the disgust and disdain "that only monsters deserve." Coupled with these forceful vocal methods he also recommended thirty to one hundred sessions of hypnosis in order "to instill in the sick woman repulsion, disgust, and horror of her abnormality." Finally, upon completion of the sessions he prescribed physically directing her "to the caresses of the other sex."[81]

In Aluísio Azevedo's novel *O cortiço* (The Slum, 1890), the first novel in Brazilian literature to openly depict lesbian sex, lesbianism ruins the life of an innocent girl. *The Slum* makes explicit the connection between poverty and homosexuality via two poor white characters: Léonie, a middle-aged French prostitute forces herself on her goddaughter, Pombinha, a virginal adolescent engaged to be married to a respectable man. Homosexuality, regarded as a "perversion," became a locus or catchall for a host of perversions (incest, rape, premarital sex, and prostitution). All of these coalesce in this one same-sex interaction between the two female characters. The rhetoric of the nineteenth century with respect to sexual deviance differed little from the inquisitional view that sin breeds sin and that contact with sinners can cause one to become a sinner, as here perversion breeds perversion. Contact with wayward homosexual women can also cause an innocent virginal girl to fall into the same condition.[82]

In this work we can see how the language and descriptions draw extensively not just from the medical literature but also from the cases reported to the Inquisition. Azevedo reproduces the active/passive or predator/prey dyad through the characters' names: Léonie, meaning "lioness," and Pombinha, "little dove." Azevedo shows how gender can create a false sense of intimacy and can obscure violence between two people of the same sex. On a warm day in the slum Léonie lures the virginal young Pombinha into her bedroom after a luncheon at her home, where she forces her into sex and takes her virginity:

> Léonie pretended to listen, stroking the girl's waist, thighs, and bosom. Then, as though without realizing what she was doing, she began unbuttoning the top of Pombinha's dress.
>
> "Stop!" Why are you doing that? I don't want to get undressed!"
>
> The girl, feeling embarrassed, crossed her arms over her chest and blushed in shame.
>
> "Don't fight me!" Léonie whispered, her eyes half shut.
>
> And despite Pombinha's protests, pleas, and even tears, Léonie pulled her clothes off and pressed against her, kissing her all over and licking her nipples to excite her.
>
> "No! No!" The victim stammered, pushing her away.
>
> "Yes! Yes!" Léonie insisted, clasping her tightly between her arms and pressing her whole naked body against the girl's.

She thrust her stiff tongue into Pombinha's mouth and ears, pressed her wet kisses upon her eyes, bit her shoulder and clutched her hair as though trying to uproot it . . . till finally, with a violent start, she devoured the girl. . . .

Pombinha returned to her senses and rolled over with her back to her adversary, clutching the pillow and smothering her sobs, ashamed and bewildered.[83]

This scene, as per warnings in the medical literature, would have a devastating outcome: Pombinha rejects men and becomes a lesbian and prostitute, like her assailant.

The Prostitution of Enslaved Women by White Mistresses

In several cities throughout Brazil, but most prominently in the major port cities of Rio de Janeiro and Salvador, mistresses would purchase slave women not only for labor in their homes but also for the express purpose of prostituting them. In the second half of the nineteenth century Rio de Janeiro was among the cities that received a substantial number of male travelers and European immigrants, especially from France, Portugal, Spain, Italy, and Eastern Europe. Some of these men arrived seeking sexual favors, which some white mistresses saw as an opportunity for extra profit.[84] Travel journals, police records, and medical literature of the period all provide evidence that some white mistresses supported themselves with the prostitution of slave women. Historian Charles R. Boxer has argued that "the prostitution of slave-girls by their owners, whether male or female, was more common in Portuguese than in Spanish America."[85]

The mistress functioned as a pimp who would force her slave women to prostitute themselves into the late hours of the night, imposing upon them a daily quota of money that they were to bring in, all of which the mistress took for herself. Prostitution took place in the street, in brothels, and in some cases inside the home of the mistress to prevent the slaves from escaping. Documents from the mid- to late nineteenth century report that several mistresses would dress their slave women up and place them in a window in their home, half-naked, to solicit men who passed by.

The prostitution of slave women by white mistresses was observed most perceptively by Expilly at the beginning of the 1860s. In major cities, particularly in Rio de Janeiro, in an effort to prevent illicit activity such as prostitution, the government imposed a curfew requiring all slaves to be in their master's home by seven o'clock in the evening or risk being arrested and taken to prison.[86] Only slaves who had written permission from their masters that they could produce when stopped by police would be allowed to be out in the streets after hours. However, as Expilly wrote, the law proved "useless given the abject greed of the masters." He continues, "Some masters sell the right to walk the streets at night and to be away from home until the next morning to attractive slave women who belong to them. . . . There are some small households that possess only two or three slave women as their entire fortune and yet they live in relatively great comfort. They derive their income from the fruits of these poor creatures' prostitution."[87] Mistresses would circumvent the law by writing fake permission letters indicating that the slave was charged with running an errand to allow them to roam the street in search of clients throughout the night. During his stay in Brazil, Expilly encountered what he ironically called a "pious" old white mistress who "used to be rich but is now ruined, absolutely ruined, because she was only able to keep two girls after selling her numerous slaves."[88] These two slave girls served as both domestic workers and prostitutes, providing the mistress's sole source of income.

Public attitudes regarding the prostitution of enslaved women by their mistresses varied. The practice was apparently pervasive enough to have been mentioned in the Confederate Abolitionist Manifesto of Rio de Janeiro, which stated, "The business of prostituting slave women has been exploited in the largest scale, as can be demonstrated by the police records of the Court."[89] Some were appalled that white women were capable of committing such atrocities toward other women, while others—such as Dr. Herculano Augusto Lassance, who wrote a thesis on prostitution in Rio de Janeiro in 1845—though recognizing that enslaved women were in many cases forced into prostitution, nevertheless blamed them for perverting and infecting white men with sexually transmitted diseases and destroying white families. In 1845 Lassance termed their activities the ultimate affront to national and public morality and decency: "The slave women who prostitute themselves in the street at a cheap price help to feed our moral cancer, running to the first man who calls them, performing the most irreverent and scandalous scenes of debauchery that men who are not black desirously solicit in sordid taverns and whorehouses etc. of the capital city in the eyes of neighboring families, or in front of those who happen to be passing by."[90]

Another Rio de Janeiro doctor, João Álvares de Macedo Junior, in September 1868 reported the case of one his patients, a seventeen- or eighteen-year-old slave girl by the name of Júlia. Júlia was admitted to the Women's Hospital of Santa Casa da Misericórdia by her master because she suffered from attacks of hysteria. Shortly after she was discharged in her "modest-colored cotton dress to her master's house," Macedo Junior was passing through one of the city plazas with a colleague and saw their "modest patient from fifteen days ago sitting on the balcony of a townhouse, wearing a stunning silk dress with her hair powdered and covered with flowers." They inquired about how she had been so radically transformed, and "she told us that her master had gotten rid of her because of her illness and that a mistress who lived in the area bought her and dressed her like this, and ha[d] forced her into prostitution. But the most repugnant of all is that the mistress to whom poor Júlia was sold, fearful of losing her capital, prostituted her from inside her house."[91]

Equally concerned with the affronts to public morality and decency, the police chief of the imperial court,[92] Francisco de Faria Lemos, expressed in 1871 his dismay about the growing number of prostituted slave women in the streets of the nation's capital: "The public outcry has risen in this city against the immoral scandal of the prostitution of slave women, at the behest or consent of their masters, from which they derive exorbitant wealth, forcing these poor slave women to satisfy their destructive greed through acts that are highly offensive to public morality, exposing themselves half naked in the windows, enticing passersby with gestures, words, and almost by force to engage in perverse deeds."[93] Municipal judge Miguel José Tavares interrogated several enslaved women who were taken into custody for questioning because of prostitution in 1871. In his response to chief Francisco de Faria Lemos, Tavares writes of the stories that were told to him by slave women about the cruelty of white mistresses who would beat, threaten, and humiliate them to make them prostitute themselves. Several of these slave women contracted sexually transmitted diseases, yet their mistresses would continue to prostitute them to satisfy their greed. Tavares wrote:

> The slave woman placed in the window is not a woman, but a machine that moves at the command of her mistress, who forces her to smile for the passersby through intimidation and threats of tears of pain caused by the whip, because she is required to bring in a daily earnings at the end of the day of nothing less than ten thousand réis. Ridden with syphilis, she has no right to abstain from perversions, as she has to receive any man that comes along, even if she doesn't want to. Forcing them to get drunk to lower their inhibitions, these slave mistresses are real pimps, selling [sex] in exchange for a thousand réis and the venom of syphilis and the health of the slave woman, who for as strong as she may be cannot resist such excesses. . . . What I have just described is but a pale version of what is told during the interrogations of these poor women. Not only their

bodies are abused, but their souls, because they prostitute their hearts and the most intimate, pure, prudent feeling that every woman has a right to even if she is a slave."[94]

In Rio de Janeiro a sustained effort was mounted by the police chief of the court in conjunction with the second-rank municipal judge to combat what they termed "the immoral scandal of the prostitution of enslaved women." Close to two hundred cases were brought against both masters and slave mistresses based on depositions made by enslaved women. The aim of this effort was to manumit slave women forced into prostitution by their mistresses and masters. As historian Sidney Chaloub has shown, slave mistresses deeply resented police officials meddling in their private affairs and potentially compromising their income by freeing their female slaves. Some, aware that public officials would catch up with them sooner or later, attempted to circumvent their efforts by registering the manumission of their slave women with a stipulation of further indentured servitude for a specific amount of time. This technically freed the slaves on paper but forced them to continue working for the master or mistress as they had always done for the specified time period. This ruse allowed mistresses to evade public officials and secure the labor of their slave-prostitutes for a longer period.[95]

In 1879 in Rio de Janeiro the police received reports that Amélia Francelina Cabral de Azevedo, a white slave mistress, was prostituting her underage seventeen-year-old slave, Catarina Parda. Deputy João Nunes da Costa took a statement from Catarina that reads,

> She said that about a month ago she had arrived from Rio Grande do Norte in the custody of João Fonseca, who sold her to Amélia Cabral. It had been three weeks since she had continuously been at the window receiving clients, and she was deflowered by an individual at the order of her mistress, who received money for it. Her mistress forces her to stand in the window until one o'clock in the morning and she is made to give all of the money that she makes from her visits to her mistress, who threatens her with punishments and with sending her to the house of corrections when she doesn't receive enough paying clients. She said that her mistress punished her by slapping and punching her for not wanting to be a prostitute.[96]

After her deposition Catarina Parda was released back to the custody of her mistress, Amélia Cabral. Because of laws protecting the property rights of masters, Cabral did not receive any form of blame or punishment for prostituting

Catarina. As politician and abolitionist Joaquim Nabuco wrote in 1883, "Masters may force their slave women into prostitution, receiving all of the profits from this business without losing the property rights that they have over them, just as a father can be the master of his own son."[97] Other than provoking the sympathy of a few officials, due to the pitfalls of the Brazilian legal system these depositions did virtually nothing for slave women who had been forced into prostitution, but they do provide us with invaluable information about this unseen practice. As was the case with male rape victims, the property rights of slave owners inevitably took precedence over the rights of slave women who were victimized and exploited by white mistresses.

White women, like their fathers, husbands, and sons, shaped black womanhood through violence, torture, humiliation, and exploitation. By prostituting enslaved women, these white mistresses added a new dimension to the colonial adage that black women were for fornication and labor, showing that they too were complicit in shaping this identity for black women. The hyperviolatability of white women framed the unrapability of black women. Black women did not simply "become" prostitutes; they were made such through quotidian practices of sexual exploitation by white masters and mistresses and the men to whom they were prostituted. The sexual exploitation of enslaved women against their will during Brazilian slavery is referred to constantly and disturbingly in newspapers, literature, and historiography of the period and well into the twentieth century, including in the work of Freyre, as "prostitution," never as "rape." Suffering rape and sexual violence became part of the job of slavery and was perversely scripted as a willful exchange with a client, in which black women were painted as agents and never as victims. White women were invested in protecting white womanhood, but also in shaping black women's experiences as distinct from their own. The unequal economic, political, and social positions that black and white women inhabited in the social construction of slavery were all barriers to any sentiment of solidarity or empathy between white mistresses and enslaved women.[98] While prostituting, sexually exploiting, and beating slave women, white women were at the same time defining themselves as their polar opposites.

White women, who otherwise had little agency or freedom beyond their role as slave mistresses and were completely dependent on their husbands and families, found in prostitution a way of taking control and profiting economically from slavery just as the slave master profited from slave labor. Here again, race, sex, and economic profit were intertwined, just as they were in the plantation fields.

The Invisible Violence of the White Mistress
toward the Slave Woman

White slaveholding women throughout the Americas were cognizant not only of their limited place and function in the male hierarchy, but also of the power they held in relation to slave women. As Harriet Jacobs wrote in 1861, "I knew that the young wives of slaveholders often thought their authority and importance would be best established and maintained by cruelty."[99] Many did not hesitate to avail themselves of that power in the form of violence and sexual exploitation.[100] According to the mostly male scholars of the nineteenth century, white women's violence toward enslaved women in Brazil derived from their lack of education and their forced connection to the domestic sphere. Gilberto Freyre writes that Brazilian mistresses lived in almost "Arabic isolation."[101] While this was true in some cases, it was certainly not the case for all white mistresses, especially those in larger cities. Freyre notes, "Without contacts with the world that would modify in them, as in boys, the perverted sense of human relationships; with no other perspective than that of the slave hut as seen from the veranda of the Big House, these ladies still preserve, often, the same evil dominion over their house maids as they had exercised over the little Negro girls who had been their playmates as children."[102] English traveler Henry Koster confirms this view of the Brazilian mistress as even more violent than her husband toward her slaves and also attributes it to her lack of education and social isolation.[103] But the longevity of Brazilian slavery and the innumerous accounts of violence committed by white masters against slaves point to the failure of education and social integration to mollify the behaviors of slaveholding men. We must seek explanations for white women's violence toward their female slaves elsewhere.

As the title of this book indicates, the perpetuation of white dominance depended greatly on concealing its existence and how it operated. This was achieved by constructing a myth of Brazil's more benign slavery and the gentleness of the master and mistress while devaluing slaves and shifting blame for white violence to them. White mistresses' violence was often unacknowledged because it clashed with the period construction of white womanhood as kind, pious, and defenseless. White women could only be victims, never plausibly victimizers, which opened spaces for them to exert control over black women and men and for their violence to go unchecked and unpunished in many cases.

From nineteenth-century records and reports we know that common forms of violence against enslaved women by white mistresses throughout the Americas included verbal abuse, beatings, burning, genital mutilation, forced prostitution, sexual abuse, and murder.[104] Several regional newspapers, particularly in the second half of the nineteenth century, reported cases of white mistresses physically abusing and even murdering slave women. *O Popular*, an abolitionist newspaper in Recife, published an exposé on April 19, 1883, titled "The Despotism of Slavery" reporting the recent beating of a slave woman by her mistress, Souza Pimentel: "Our informant witnessed the miserable state in which a poor slave woman by the name of Delfina was found on the property of José Machado de Souza Pimentel. . . . Drowned in blood and covered with wounds to the face, the sight of the wretched slave was horrifying and painful. It's shocking, perhaps criminal that a senhora, a mother, cultivates such perversion that she is capable of abusing another woman, all for not having prepared her some potatoes!" On April 7, 1857, the *Correio de Vitória* reported the murder of a slave woman called Cristina in Itabapoana, in the state of Rio de Janeiro. Cristina was murdered by two white sisters at their mother's home. The paper reported that the two sisters whipped Cristina repeatedly and then burned her to death.

In the United States, Frederick Douglass, while living in Baltimore, witnessed the case of a fourteen-year-old slave girl named Mary and her older sister Henrietta, who suffered the abuses of their white mistress: Mary's "head, neck, and shoulders . . . were literally cut to pieces. I have frequently felt her head, and found it nearly covered with festering sores, caused by the lash of her cruel mistress."[105] Douglass also writes of his wife's cousin, who had accidentally fallen asleep while caring for a white baby and was barbarically murdered by her mistress as punishment. The child's mother, Douglass recalls, "jumped from her bed, seized an oak stick of wood by the fireplace, and with it broke the girl's nose and breastbone, and thus ended her life."[106]

The writings of European travelers in nineteenth-century Brazil also provide documentation of the violence suffered by enslaved women at the hands of their mistresses. While living in Rio de Janeiro, Charles Expilly was invited by the widow Dona Francisca to attend the whipping of a slave woman called Luizia several days after Luizia had committed an offense. She was chained naked to the porch and whipped coldly by Dona Francisca. The mistress explained that she did not whip the slave at the time of the offense so as to avoid killing her in a moment of rage: "When several days have gone by, then your hand is firm, your head is cool. The slave who is punished isn't exposed to any harm that diminishes his value. Justice is done without any loss to the slave owner." Expilly concurs ironically that since "a black is a piece of property, exactly like a sack of wheat, like a pair of boots or a ball of wool," it made sense to not maim a slave, just as "you spare your dog and your mule" so they don't lose value.[107]

German traveler Joseph F. Friedrich von Weech writes of a friend who observed his neighbor beat her slaves relentlessly in a spectacle that typically lasted for three hours. When von Weech visited his friend, he personally witnessed her give one slave woman almost fifty blows with the *palmatória*, an instrument of torture used in Brazil and the Portuguese colonies, and whip a girl of fifteen, who already had swollen hands from previous beatings, because she had pleaded not to be beaten.[108] Adèle Toussaint-Samson writes of being awoken late at night by the shrieking cries of young slave girls coming from her neighbor's home: "Every day the most terrible scenes took place over our head. For the least omission, for the least fault of either of [the slave girls], the señora would beat them . . . and we would hear the poor negresses throw themselves on their knees, crying, 'Mercy! Señora!' But the pitiless mistress would never be touched, and gave mercilessly the number of blows she would consider necessary to be given."[109] When Toussaint-Samson called the mistress an executioner, she subsequently gagged the girls to muffle their screams.[110]

These anecdotal accounts by period observers, if true, reveal that Brazilian slaveholding women's treatment of female slaves was no different from men's. To the slave mistress, the slave woman was a piece of property on par with a ball of wool.

Physical violence against female slaves by white mistresses appears in Machado de Assis's 1899 short story "O caso da vara" (The Case of the Whip).[111] Throughout the entire story a white mistress, Sinhá Rita, threatens to whip her eleven-year-old slave girl, Lucrécia, who is described as having a "scar on her forehead and a burn on her right hand" from previous punishments by the mistress. At the end of the story she is whipped yet again. Such fictionalized scenes are tragically similar to actual events witnessed and recorded by observers.

Many of the analyses examining violence inflicted on slave women by their mistresses in Brazil have identified the constant infidelity of white men as a primary cause.[112] In 1845 medical doctor Herculano Lassance wrote, "No one can ignore the domestic turmoil that a slave woman evokes. There are so many men out there who leave their marital bed to go defile themselves in the filthy slave houses where the slave woman sleeps, who is preferred over a tender and loving wife."[113] Expilly wrote similarly, "The master who boasts of not having any black blood coursing through his veins pays his debt to society by marrying a white woman; but just as soon as she gives him an heir, he abandons the woman of his own race for a girl of color."[114] Toussaint-Samson, while staying on a plantation outside Rio de Janeiro, encountered a slave mistress who spoke of her resentment toward the mulatta slave women of the plantation: "My husband forces me to receive these creatures in my own bed; and it is there, right in front of me, that he gives them his caresses."[115]

At the heart of this supposed rivalry between white and enslaved women is the interracial sexual economy that defined the institution of slavery. White and black women sustained slavery in distinct and conflicting ways. Slavery, as Nell Irvin Painter writes, "often made women of different races and classes into co-mothers and co-wives as well as owners and suppliers of labor."[116] White women were essential for the reproduction of legitimate heirs but were constructed as pure and desexualized, while black women reproduced the workforce and had to be sexually available to both the master and the mistress.

This portrayal of black women as hypersexual and sexually deviant greatly conditioned the relationship between the white mistress and the slave woman. The mistress was impotent to prevent her husband's flagrant sexual relations with female slaves, and so in several documented cases she directed her wrath against the slave woman. As Expilly wrote, "How many proud and tender *senhoras* are at first indifferent to the attention that their husbands pay to the slave women, and then after their pride and love are wounded by the constancy of the preference, try to attract him to her. Flirtatious gestures, tears, explosions of anger, all of these means have been employed in vain." The revenge of the white mistress was exacted most violently. Expilly witnessed firsthand one "hated rival" who was "whipped, dragged through the mud, and mutilated." He recalled a mulatta slave woman whose mistress cut off two of her fingers, and added that some of the women had even been poisoned.[117] One mistress had the eyes of an attractive slave woman gouged out and served to her husband for dessert. According to Freyre, white mistresses also kicked out slave women's teeth, burned their faces and genitals, and had their breasts amputated.[118] In São Luís, in the northeastern state of Maranhão, a white mistress stabbed a slave woman to death because she suspected that the slave's newborn son was her husband's offspring.[119]

This view of slave women as the sexual rivals of white women plays to the negation of black victimhood and the impossibility for slave women to be legitimate victims of sexual violence. But a slave who is owned by the master as property cannot legitimately resist the will of the master, and therefore is not a willful rival to the master's wife.

The narrative of white victimhood that permeated Brazilian slavery was a primary cause of the violence inflicted upon enslaved women by white mistresses as punishment for their hypersexuality. Though white mistresses were well aware that slave women were raped by the mistresses' husbands, sons, and brothers, many were unwilling to see slave women as legitimate victims of rape. Turning a blind eye to the victimization of slave women by white men allowed the mistress to justify her own violence toward them. If black women were given sexual agency, they could not plausibly be victims of rape. This violence needed to be sanitized, renamed, and erased to benefit white women and men by reversing and concealing the roles of perpetrator and victim.

The slave woman was not the only victim of the white mistress. Several slave mistresses, as documented in travel journals, newspapers, and police reports during the nineteenth century, murdered the children of slave women who were fathered by the master. In São Paulo, Austrian traveler Johann Baptist Emanuel Pohl wrote of a mistress who savagely murdered the son of one of her female slaves for this reason. The mistress burned the child to death in a fire pit and presented him to her husband.[120]

Depictions of slave mistresses' violence against slave women, despite its relative frequency, appear very little in the literature of the period. Aluísio Azevedo's 1881 novel *O mulato* (The Mulatto) is the only novel to treat the topic directly and realistically. The novel's main character, Raimundo, is the son of Portuguese slaveholder, José, and a slave woman named Domingas. José is married to Dona Quitéria, a rich white Brazilian widow. Shortly after Raimundo's birth she confronts her husband about the child: "'You nigger lover!' she shouted at her husband, contorted with rage. 'If you think I'd permit you to bring up in my home those children begot from the Negresses! That's the last straw! And don't try to get rid of me! I'm the one who'll do the getting rid of—that black boy!—and it will be over there, at the side of the chapel!'"[121] Quitéria is implying that she will kill the black child in the shadows of the church. Shortly afterward she follows through on her threats and whips the slave woman and savagely burns her genitals, enacting her revenge with a hot iron while forcing her son to watch:

> Stretched out on the ground with her feet in the stocks, head shaved and hands behind her, lay Domingas, completely naked and with her genital parts burned by a hot iron. Off to one side her little three-year-old son screamed like one possessed, as he attempted to embrace her. Each time he approached his mother, two slaves, on Quitéria's orders, would flick the whip away from Domingas's back and direct it against the child. The shrew, hideous and drunk with rage, stood there laughing, hurling obscenities and howling with spasms of rage. Domingas, half dead, lay groaning and writhing in pain on the ground. The incoherence in her speech and her uncoordinated gestures already denoted symptoms of insanity.[122]

Conclusion

The role of women in colonial and nineteenth-century Brazil was conditioned by many complex intersecting factors overlying the central constant of white male supremacy. During the Inquisition the long arm of the Catholic Church stretched across the Atlantic Ocean from Lisbon to the Brazilian colony as the inquisitors pried into women's bedrooms and left us with an astonishing written record of same-sex relations heavily laden with labyrinthine meanings about love, desire, and control. That record is narrated in imprecise language and colored by limited knowledge and biases about women's bodies and their sexuality—biases that would only become more bizarre with new medical studies in the nineteenth century.

White slave mistresses were consigned to a restricted role in comparison to men. Slavery was the one venue where they could exert domination over those who were relegated to the bottom of Brazilian society, and in their boudoirs they assumed the sexual agency that was otherwise denied them. Given the deliberately constructed outward image of white women's purity, we are shocked today at their brutality toward their female slaves and by period accounts of their same-sex dalliances. Both can be understood in part as responses to their oppression. Ultimately the violence and exploitation that marked the relationship between the white mistress and the slave woman mimicked or exceeded the master's devices of domination, while blame for Brazil's sexual depravity was thrust upon the slave woman and a heavy cloak of silence was drawn over the white mistress's savagery.

FOUR

Social Whiteness: *Black Intraracial Violence and the Boundaries of Black Freedom*

The preceding chapters have examined the unseen sexual violence and exploitation of blacks by whites that occurred during Brazilian slavery. In this chapter we shift our focus to relations between slaves and free people of African descent to observe how complex white supremacist mechanisms became a catalyst for violence, domination, and self-interest among blacks themselves, rendering some blacks champions of slavery, agents of torture, and slaves turned slaveholders.

By the end of the nineteenth century, three hundred years of importing African slaves, along with unstoppable miscegenation, had had a massive, unplanned impact on Brazil's racial makeup, such that whites found themselves in the minority. Despite growing internal and international pressure to end the slave trade, there still remained a demand for slave labor, and Africans continued to be illegally smuggled into Brazil well into the late nineteenth century, so that the black population was still growing. The anxieties of the white elite about the changing demographics were intensified by the increase in the number of free blacks. In 1798 data suggests that whites numbered 1,000,000, slaves 1,500,000, free blacks 225,000, and Native Americans 250,000 out of a total population of three million.[1] In the late eighteenth century the number of free blacks continued to grow at a substantial rate due to manumissions and slaves purchasing their freedom. Free blacks became a substantial part of the overall population in every region.[2] Historians Francisco Vidal Luna and Herbert S. Klein suggest that free blacks a half-century prior to the formal abolition of slavery "were an important, competitive, and integrated element within imperial society."[3] In regions such as Pernambuco, Bahia, and Minas Gerais, mulattos outnumbered whites, and Rio de Janeiro had a large number of free blacks. By the nineteenth century free blacks outnumbered slaves and Brazil had the largest number of free blacks in the Americas.[4]

In 1872 Brazil's first national census counted 4.2 million free blacks. The national census data, though significant, should be read with caution. While the data does give us a general idea of this large and important sector of Brazil's population, we have no way of determining how accurate these numbers are. Brazil had ample reasons to falsify census data. First, the largest slaveholding empires—England, France, and the United States—had abolished slavery, yet Brazil resisted following suit. It is not difficult to imagine that the government could change the census figures to convey an illusion that the majority of slaves had already been freed and that the nation thus did not need to abolish slavery.

The free black population was diverse in its racial makeup, including mulattos, *pretos* (blacks of pure African descent), and *pardos* (people descended from both pretos and *brancos* [whites]),[5] and mixtures of these. It also included *forros* (people of color who were born free) and *livres* (former slaves who had purchased their freedom or had been manumitted).[6] Mulattos and pardos outnumbered pretos. Often the children of enslaved women and white men, mulattos were more frequently manumitted and received greater privileges, such as learning to read and write and even receiving inheritances, affording them more opportunities for advancement than the rest of the black population.[7]

Like slaves, the nation's free black population could be found throughout the country, with large numbers in Minas Gerais and São Paulo.[8] Though the free black population continued to increase, the economic need for slaves continued, and the censuses of 1872 and 1874 counted over 1.5 million Brazilians of African descent who remained enslaved.[9] The need for labor to maintain Brazil's vast coffee, rice, and sugar industries would continue well beyond the abolition of slavery in 1888.

The 1890 census indicates that just over half (56 percent) of the country's approximately fourteen million inhabitants were of African descent, both mulattos and blacks. By the end of the century Brazil had the largest black population in the Western Hemisphere. Meanwhile, the Haitian Revolution (1791–1804) and a series of violent slave revolts throughout the country, most notably in Bahia, in the first part of the nineteenth century were not forgotten, inciting white fears of further black rebellions.

With emancipation on the horizon, the nation wrestled with the meaning of black freedom and its implications for a multiracial society in which whites were now a minority and the status of blacks was changing in perplexing ways. As historians Luna and Klein point out, though free blacks were integrated in many sectors of Brazilian society, especially in terms of economic mobility, Brazil was still like all other American slave regimes and was "by its very nature racist, and the white elite discriminated in various ways against free persons of color, even as it permitted a very active level of manumission."[10]

Over the course of Brazilian history blacks had become intimately and paradoxically tied to every area of Brazilian society. In the nineteenth century a number of free mulattos and blacks had risen to become prominent lawyers, doctors, government officials, artisans, and writers—but some of these free blacks also became slaveholders, slave torturers, and slave catchers. As Brazil's free black population steadily increased, the idea of including all blacks as full citizens in the newly established nation proved to be a source of extreme contradiction, disquiet, and violence. For white slaveholders the question was, how could they hold onto their privileged status and retain control over the black masses given the inevitability of abolition? What would it mean if blacks could act freely upon their desires and whites could no longer define and control the terms of miscegenation, as had been the case for over three hundred years of slavery?

Blacks faced more complex questions about racial identity and affiliation as they attempted to negotiate the transition between slavery and freedom. Free blacks and mixed-race Brazilians saw an opportunity to take part in whiteness, but for this they needed the consent of whites. Blacks, whites, and mulattos participated together in devising new social rules around race that were unique to Brazil, at times incongruous—permitting the illusory transformation of blacks into whites—and never very far from their origins in slavery and white supremacy.

Black Freedom and the Politics of Passing: Brazil and the United States

Racial passing refers to persons of black ancestry with visibly white features who could assimilate or pass as white, often to escape racial prejudice and to gain access to opportunities otherwise closed to blacks. It is often associated with US society and seldom considered in relation to preabolition Brazil because of Brazil's vision of itself as multiracial and its rejection of nonlinear racial categorization. Passing provides an important racial, social, and theoretical framework for understanding the position in society of free blacks and mulattos throughout the course of Brazilian slavery.[11] How would this practice of passing function in a country where the lines between black and white were often obfuscated, and what would be hailed in the twentieth century as a true example of racial democracy?

In *Neither Black nor White: Slavery and Race Relations in Brazil and the United States*,[12] Carl Degler argues that one of the primary distinctions between Brazilian and US racial histories is that in Brazil there existed an intermediate racial category between black and white that he famously termed the "mulatto escape hatch." He argues that this escape hatch, dating back to the colonial period, was an informal, not institutional, social mechanism by which select mixed-raced men and women (of known black ancestry), by virtue of their education, wealth, culture, or talent, could become socially mobile and gain entry into the ranks of the Brazilian white elite. The mulatto escape hatch, which other scholars have referred to as "social whitening," became an overt form of racial passing. Degler's escape hatch can be extended to include free blacks. Theoretically, this informal social mechanism provided a means of transcending one's black ancestry, allowing millions of free black and mulatto men and women to be designated as white in terms of their social possibilities compared to those who remained in slavery—that is, black in color yet ostensibly white in social privilege.

The privilege and social capital of free blacks and mulattos did not erase the knowledge or physical markings of their black ancestry, but it did allow them to disassociate themselves from blacks by assuming a white public identity. As German painter Johann Moritz Rugendas, who traveled and worked extensively throughout Brazil in the 1820s, observed, "It is true that the law does not confer upon Blacks the right to vote or hold office; but the more or less dark-skinned officials make no difficulty about recognizing as whites all those who wish to so style themselves, and provide them with the necessary documentation to establish the purity of their origins."[13]

The degrees of privilege, opportunity, and whiteness afforded through the "mulatto escape hatch" were by no means uniform, and varied significantly depending on region. Free mulattos and blacks benefited more from this structure in the states of Rio de Janeiro, Bahia, and Pernambuco than in states in the south such as São Paulo.[14] In the state of Bahia—where the African-descended had always been a majority, constituting over 60 percent of the population in the late nineteenth century—even fifty years after the abolition of slavery, the notions of whiteness were significantly more malleable than in states such as São Paulo and other states in the south that contained a sizeable European immigrant population in the late nineteenth and early twentieth centuries. Bahia's black majority, coupled with this singular form of racial designation, gave way to uniquely racial terms such as *branco da Bahia* (Bahian white), persons who looked phenotypically black, but were legally classified as white.[15] In São Paulo and the southern states, because of the larger number of European descendants, definitions of whiteness and the privileges of the mulatto escape hatch were not as pronounced. In 1797 whites made up 56 percent of the population, rising to 63 percent in 1890 due to the influx of European immigrants. Though São Paulo boasted a significant free black population and lighter-skinned blacks or pardos, they did not necessarily receive greater privileges from whites than darker-skinned blacks, and racial relations functioned with a black/white binary similar to the United States.[16]

Such a system of social whitening did not exist in the United States, where racial categories were rooted in skin color (phenotypically) and racial ancestry. One's status as free or enslaved did not alter one's race. Free or enslaved, rich or poor, the US "one-drop rule" dictated that all people with one drop of black blood were legally categorized as black. Color distinctions—such as mulatto, quadroon (one-quarter black), and octoroon (one-eighth black)—existed for individuals of mixed-race heritage, but those intermediate categories were cosmetic, afforded no real social or legal benefits, and did not allow these individuals to avoid being identified as black legally or socially. The legacy of the one-drop rule has continued to the present day in the United States: a person's black ancestry cannot be altered or transcended based on social status. In Brazil color and racial ancestry were never erased, but racial categorization, while initially defined in the traditional phenotypical and ancestral sense, could change fluidly in the social sense according to status (free or enslaved), wealth, and social prestige. There existed a racial meritocracy whereby one's blackness could be in some ways transcended through great effort and one could become socially— and in some cases legally—categorized as white.

Passing in Brazil was part of an overt racial and social system, whereas in the United States it was a clandestine practice. Yet passing in both contexts required public denial of one's black heritage and the assuming of a white social identity. As historian Emília Viotti da Costa points out, although in Brazil passing created opportunities and social mobility for individual blacks and mulattos, the benefits of this system were both "limited and contradictory."[17] Anthropologists João Costa Vargas and Jaime Ampara Alves write, "Docility, thankfulness, and silence around racial matters are expected from the blacks who are the objects of such inclusion."[18] Ultimately, these "special" blacks, or "blacks of white soul," as they were frequently referred to by the white Brazilian elite, were forced to assume white attitudes and perceptions of race and of themselves, as Viotti da Costa points out.[19]

Some of these complexities encountered by free black and mulatto men who passed for white are illustrated in the life of famous nineteenth-century writer Machado de Assis. Shortly after Machado's death, journalist José Veríssimo wrote an article about Machado in which he referred to him as a "mulatto." Machado's close friend, abolitionist and politician Joaquim Nabuco penned a note to Veríssimo in an attempt to prevent the use of that highly offensive word to describe the illustrious author:

> Your article is very beautiful but there is one sentence that gave me chills: "A Mulatto, he was indeed a Greek of the best epoch." I would have never called Machado mulatto and I think that nothing would have hurt him more than your having concluded this. I implore you to omit this remark when you convert your article into permanent form: The word is not literary, it is pejorative. To me Machado was white and I believe he considered himself to be as well: whatever foreign blood he may have had in no way affected his perfect Caucasoid makeup. I, at least, saw only the Greek in him.[20]

Though everyone was well aware that Machado de Assis was a mulatto, to publicly refer to this celebrated Brazilian author as such would be an egregious social blunder. Nabuco in his praise of Machado shows that any mention of his race would diminish his social and literary prominence and his contributions to Brazilian culture. In Nabuco's eyes, Machado's fame and talent could not coexist with his black ancestry. Though many claim Machado as a black or Afro-Brazilian author, the concept of a black or mulatto author did not exist in preemancipation Brazil; it would only emerge in the twentieth century. The profession of writer was conceived as one of elite white men, and writers whom we would today consider black would in many cases not have identified as such during their lifetimes. A mulatto's or black's success as a writer could be enough to allow him to pass and socially identify as white, regardless of his race. Nabuco's letter also makes plain the seemingly illusory nature of social whitening. Despite Nabuco's effort to retain the whiteness of his dear friend, Machado's fame and prominence did not blind people to his race. As Viotti da Costa explains, throughout Machado's life he was constantly haunted by his race, his modest origins, and his epilepsy. Machado was not born white, either phenotypically or socially. He was born into relative poverty and had worked desperately to climb the social ladder and earn and sustain his whiteness. Upon becoming famous, Machado, like many Brazilian passers, severed ties with black

Brazilian friends, family, and neighbors so as to avoid calling attention to his black ancestry. Machado only visited his family at times when he would not be seen, married a white woman, and like many Brazilian passers held a discreet and reserved stance toward abolition.[21]

Machado was well aware of the precariousness of passing and social whiteness in Brazil.[22] Perhaps his own experience of passing could explain why many of the characters in his novels, though predominantly white, are haunted by a secret and are forced into a game of maintaining appearances. Nabuco's letter demonstrates that much like African Americans who attempted passing, in Brazil blackness and whiteness could not be reconciled in their social persona by blacks who had attained a measure of social status—"famous writer" and "black" simply could not coexist.

The foregoing helps us to understand some of the hidden barriers surrounding mixed-race identity in nineteenth-century Brazil, and arguably beyond. As Vargas has noted, the common Brazilian saying, "Passou de branco preto é" (If you're beyond white—meaning, can't pass as white—then you're black) "reveals that underlying the color spectrum is a clear understanding of a white/nonwhite binary system that determines social privileges based on race."[23] The mention of one's black ancestry or maintaining any ties to black identity would undo a painfully constructed social image. Passing in Brazil was what sociologist G. Reginald Daniel calls "inegalitarian integration," which "assigns value to one tradition and one people and seeks the elimination of all others through assimilation.[24] Passing in both Brazil and the United States was a process of silencing that was not merely a question of skin color but was also a form of integration through erasure.

The protocols of social whitening required a complete disassociation from one's black heritage in order to be accepted by whites; there was no in-between space. The actual practice of mixed-race identity or multiracial identity politics, though heralded as part of the Brazilian story, became increasingly problematic throughout the nineteenth century and in the wake of abolition. If free blacks and mulattos were able to embrace both sides of their heritage publicly this would significantly undermine social definitions of race—that is, black as completely distinct from white—and therefore complicate the racial account on which slavery was built. Even though blacks gained freedom or had white blood, the meanings imbued in race that served as the basis of slavery had to remain intact in order to maintain white supremacy.

Complicity between Whites and Free Blacks
in Social Whiteness

What did Brazilian whites gain from blacks and mulattos passing as white? Inherent to Brazilian passing or social whitening is a complicity between blacks and whites, akin to a real-life game of make-believe. This complicity is constructed on an agreement that whites would knowingly allow certain free blacks and mulattos to assimilate into white society. Though this agreement is mutually constitutive, whites retained control over who could pass as white and who could not, to what extent they would be allowed to pass, and under what terms.

At the heart of white complicity in black passing is whites' need for what Homi Bhabha refers to as mimicry of the colonizer by the colonized. Through mimicry of the racist ideals of the colonizer, colonial subjects attempt to emulate the culture and discourse of the colonizer. Mimicry, says Bhabha, is "one of the most elusive and effective strategies of colonial power and knowledge."[25] He shows that while the colonizer requires that the other assimilate the culture and norms associated with whiteness, he must also constantly evoke and maintain the difference between himself, as a white man, and the other to justify and sustain his power. Ultimately, the mimic man, like black Brazilians who passed, becomes "almost the same but not white."[26] Mimicry of whiteness in the end can never really be whiteness. Thus, whites collaborated with black passing because with the inevitable coming of abolition, passing created intraracial division and conflict and therefore functioned as a mechanism of containment, both securing the loyalty of black passers and upholding their preexisting racially based power and privilege. For whites, supporting black passing was preferable to granting blacks full legal and social equality.

This mutual complicity is a lifelong process in which socially white blacks must perform their conferred racial membership, or consciously partake in what Sharon Patricia Holland calls a "project of belonging."[27] Both the rigidity and instability of this agreement lie in the fact that blacks and mulattos are only white as long as whites are in agreement with their whiteness. At no point do they become completely white. Even after his death Machado de Assis depends on Nabuco to aver his whiteness. In essence, Brazilian passing is not a practice of blacks duping whites into thinking they are white, but rather a system of mutual complicity between blacks and whites to maintain an illusion. But at any given moment this complicity, with one wrong step, as Daniel notes, could become a "trap door."[28]

Brazilian passing is both social and biological, and a phenotypically black person's ability to move across racial lines confirms that race is indeed a social construction. While black men and women both benefited from passing, it is important to mention the gendered dimensions of the racial complicity, as the terms of entry differed greatly for each. In many instances, black and mulatto women who were manumitted became socially mobile via illicit consensual sexual relationships as the mistresses of white men or through marriage.

On a collective level this complicity between free blacks and mulattos and whites served as a mechanism of social containment in preabolition Brazil and beyond. Free blacks and mulattos were accorded a status that exceeded that of slaves, yet they were denied the full privileges of whiteness. This mechanism of control by whites won the loyalty of free blacks and mulattos while discouraging them from seeking affiliations with slaves, lest they lose their modicum of privileges, thus preventing them from mounting any opposition to white supremacy.[29]

The passing models of Brazil and the United States mirrored the racial structures of each nation. In both contexts, passing was a form of being included in the dominant culture, although in the United States this inclusion was illicit due to segregation laws. Due to the absence of complicity between blacks and whites in the United States, passing there became a conscious act of transgressing racial boundaries in both the social and legal constructions of race, whereas in the Brazilian context, passing as a function of white consent served as a way of concretizing racial boundaries and racial meaning. Passing in Brazil, unlike in the United States, worked in line with the social order, not against it. Whites controlled the terms of the agreement in passers' simulation of whiteness, but by assuming a socially white identity passers became complicit in reproducing and solidifying white domination.

The system of Brazilian passing and social whitening pandered to blacks' desire to belong, and, more importantly, appeared to make the dream of acceptance and first-class citizenship a possibility. These mulattos and blacks who benefited from the escape hatch stood as testaments to the possibility of white acceptance and to the exceptional nature of Brazilian slavery, while also repudiating the existence of racism and racist practices on a collective level. These few blacks and mulattos, along with whites, become fundamental to the emergence of the narrative of Brazilian exceptional racial relations.

While these exceptional blacks and mulattos represented the possibility of acceptance, they also became the direct target of resentment. As a mechanism of social containment, this system engendered intraracial conflict among people of African descent—blacks, mulattos, Africans, and the socially white—with a rupture between socially white free blacks and mulattos on the one hand, and the larger enslaved black population on the other. In preemancipation Brazil, legal status as free or enslaved was more important than race in determining interactions among people.[30]

White Fears of Black Insurrection

This blurring of lines greatly complicated the racial narrative of slavery and abolition, and on a systemic level functioned as an effective divide-and-conquer strategy. Given the large number of free blacks in nineteenth-century Brazil, Brazilian whites and foreign visitors were incessantly worried about the possibility of black insurrection. British reverend Robert Walsh, who lived in Brazil from 1828 to 1829, remarked that the black population in Brazil was "beyond all ordinary calculation," so much so that his "eye was so familiarized to black visages, that the occurrence of a white face in the streets of some parts of the town, struck me as a novelty."[31] English woman Maria Dundas Graham was "struck by the great preponderance of the black population,"[32] adding that Brazilian whites had "become aware of the prodigious inconvenience, if not evil, they have brought on themselves by the importation of Africans, and now no doubt, look forward with dread to the event of a revolution, which will free their slaves from their authority, and, by declaring them all men alike, will authorise them to resent the injuries they have so long and patiently borne."[33] Given that slaves, free blacks, and mulattos constituted the majority of the population in several regions, many Europeans traveling in Brazil in the nineteenth century observed that it was only a matter of time before Brazil would experience an uprising greater than the Haitian revolution. Adèle Toussaint-Samson echoes these sentiments: "Only the large number of free negroes is a great black spot in the Brazilian horizon; their number already surpasses that of the whites. It might be feared, perhaps, that when they should have counted their numbers, they might be taken by terrible revenge, and that the future would avenge the past. Let us hope, however, that Brazil will not have its San Domingo."[34] In the same vein, Walsh commented, "The number of blacks, and mulatto offspring of blacks, in the country, is now estimated at 2,500,000, while the whites are but 850,000, so that the former exceed the latter in the proportion of three to one. From this great superiority, serious apprehensions have long been entertained, that some time or other, in the present diffusion of revolutionary doctrines on this continent, they will discover their own strength, assert independence for themselves, and Brazil will become a second St. Domingo."[35]

Anxieties over insurrection were well founded. Throughout the history of slavery in Brazil enslaved people actively resisted and fought for their freedom and against Portuguese colonialism. Slave resistance took many forms, including the formation of *quilombos* (fugitive slave communities) and slave revolts. The 1798 revolt of the Alfaiates, also known as the Revolt of the Tailors, was initiated by a group of free and enslaved blacks, mulattos, and whites in Bahia who founded a revolutionary movement for independence. Highly influenced by the French revolution, they wanted, among other demands, the independence of the territory of Bahia and the emancipation of slaves. Among the rebels were four black men between the ages of twenty-four and thirty-six: Luis Gonzaga da Virgens, Lucas Dantas, João de Deus Nascimento, and Manuel Faustino dos Santos Lira. They were hanged and quartered and their bodies displayed in public.[36]

In 1839 in Maranhão, Preto Cosme and Manuel Balaio commanded slaves in a guerrilla struggle involving more than three thousand quilombo inhabitants in collaboration with Bem-te-vis, a predominantly white group opposing the imperial government. This revolt was eventually suppressed, leaving many mortally wounded on both sides. Preto Cosme was hung in São Luis in 1842, and soon after the group that had allied with the slaves against the imperial forces signed a surrender pact in which they agreed to murder the participating slaves.[37]

The enslaved also used the law and the Catholic Church, as we've seen in the inquisitional slave testimonies, as a space to denounce the abuses inflicted on them. Since the colonial period free blacks, with the assistance of the Catholic Church, had also founded their own religious brotherhoods. The church supported these organizations, first because doing so kept blacks from joining white religious brotherhoods, but also as a mechanism of containment to secure the loyalty of the free blacks against the enslaved population. Some of these organizations, however, supported slave insurrections, aided runaway slaves, and worked with the abolitionist movement.[38]

To prevent the unification of blacks and potential revolt, it was crucial for white Brazilians to keep blacks divided and to maintain the loyalty of the socially white. Charles Expilly wrote that white Brazilians were well aware that they were outnumbered and even altered the census data to make themselves the majority. This alteration of census data to make Brazil "whiter" intensified as the nation began its whitening campaigns in the second half of the nineteenth century and lasted well into the twentieth century. Expilly writes, "The fear of revealing to slaves and also to mulattos their immense superiority of numbers explains why the Brazilian government has systematically left this part of the statistics in mysterious obscurity. The oppressors are constrained to conceal their strength from the oppressed; that is logical and expectable."[39]

Passing and social whitening in Brazil affected how blacks saw themselves and each other, and, more importantly, encouraged socially white blacks to see themselves as others and to see other blacks as a group with which they shared no connection. As a result, race offered no presumption of affiliation, and several educated blacks who could have represented the black struggle for equality in many instances failed to do so.[40]

Performing Whiteness

How did socially white Brazilians of African descent assert their whiteness when the vast majority of the population that looked like them was still in slavery? The idea of social whiteness puzzled European travelers of the nineteenth century, and their writings reveal how it appeared to outsiders. Charles Expilly came face-to-face with the complexities surrounding the performance of this unique brand of whiteness throughout his stay in Brazil. He termed social whiteness a "legal fiction" and a "flat denial of one's physiology."[41] He and other Europeans likened social whiteness to an odd game of make believe that somehow had legal credence. One of Expilly's encounters with social whiteness might appear to readers as having been extracted from the pages of a history of the US civil rights movement. On one occasion Expilly was returning a slave woman by the name of Julia, whom he had rented to do work in his house, to her master.[42] As Julia and Expilly started to get on a bus to undertake their voyage, they were confronted with the hostile protests of two socially white mulatto passengers who refused to ride on the same bus with a black slave woman. This story reveals the ludicrous mechanisms of social whiteness and how it was sustained by both mulattos and whites, to the detriment of slaves:

> [Julia] started to go up the steps when two *senhores* shouted indignantly from inside the bus and formally declared their opposition to allowing a slave woman in the same vehicle that transported them. One of these *senhores* was of a dubious white color; the other one looked like a mulatto to me, or at least a quadroon. This irritable sensitivity, which occurred so impudently in the presence of an authentic white person, seemed ridiculous to me, if not foolish, on the part of individuals who most certainly had mixed blood in their veins. I answered that my slave would sit next to me because having paid her fare, she had the same rights as the other passengers. The less white of the two threatened to throw this bitch off the bus if she persisted in remaining on the step; and in effect he began to rush forward. I stopped him with my arm and told him coldly that if he touched my slave he would have to deal with me. The firmness of this language impressed the *senhores*. Changing their strategy, they told the

driver that they would get off the bus if the slave woman got on. With that the situation changed: I could . . . do without the honor of such distinguished company. Upon my authoritative order, Julia sat on the cushioned seat. Not wanting to be caught contradicting themselves, my two suspicious noblemen—probably dried meat merchants—hurried off the bus, complaining loudly about my lack of manners, which they attributed to the bad education received in France.

Risum teneatis! [You can't help but laugh.] I saluted the most illustrious *senhores* ceremoniously and the vehicle, lightened of its burden, went on its way.[43]

Julia's mistress received word of what occurred and was so "indignant about the impudence of one of her slaves toward a white man" that she "whipped her until she bled," giving her fifty lashes. What is astonishing here is that the two "white men" whose honor was so cruelly defended by the mistress were obviously mulattos. The white mistress clearly felt she had some stake in protecting their "whiteness." This episode illustrates how two socially white mulattos asserted their whiteness through violence and discrimination against a black slave. It also reveals that they were very insecure and never entirely comfortable in their whiteness. The two mulattos use the presence of a black slave to assert their whiteness and to detract attention from their own "dubious color." Had they remained on the bus, their color would have stood out starkly in relation to both the slave and the white man. They feared that they would be seen as associated with Julia and separate from Expilly by color—in the eyes of society, more black than white. They were forced to get off the bus to retain their whiteness and their white privilege, as to be associated with Julia would mean being construed as equal to her in color and status. And yet even as they assert their whiteness, they unwittingly cede to the authority of the "authentic white man," proving the ultimate failure of their whiteness in the face of Expilly's exercise of white power. While it is important to acknowledge that Brazilian blacks and mulattos accepted in the ranks of whites did suffer and had to deny their origins, many saw the escape hatch as precisely that, an escape from the confines of race, and sought to protect their privilege and social status at all costs, which often resulted in cruelty toward other blacks.

Throughout the course of Brazilian slavery some free blacks and mulattos were able to whiten themselves through certain professions. Expilly noted, "In Brazil profession determines skin color. Merely by granting employment to an individual, the State assimilates this individual as white, regardless of the color of the person's skin."[44] Blacks and mulattos like Machado de Assis, if they managed to become writers, lawyers, doctors, or politicians, would all be socially classified as white. Data collected during Brazilian slavery shows that free blacks were found in a number of different professions throughout Brazil. They worked as artisans, merchants, farm workers, notaries, and clerks, and in service occupations. But they were barred from holding public office or rising beyond a certain level in the clergy or government and could only attain a certain degree of education. Many did rise to high levels of success, contingent on the support of white patrons.[45]

Free blacks also played a critical role in the civilian militia. Because they outnumbered whites, they were seen as allies against slaves. Many free blacks worked actively as informants to white slaveholders and helped suppress slave uprisings, destroy quilombos and return fugitive slaves. This also happened in the United States. The enlistment of free blacks against the slave masses, as G. Reginald Daniel argues, "contributed as much to [free blacks'] own circumscribed status as to the super-ordinate position of whites."[46]

There were also less illustrious professions through which blacks and mulattos could lay claim to a white identity. Bahian mulatto abolitionist Luiz Anselmo da Fonseca maintained in 1887 that the three important roles in slavery were the overseer (*feitor das fazendas* or *intendente*), the slave catcher who retrieved runaways (*capitão do mato*), and the slave punisher and torturer (*corretor de escravos*). These positions, which were mostly occupied by white men in other slave societies, were held almost exclusively by free and formerly enslaved black men in Brazil. Fonseca writes, "Certainly two-thirds of the individuals who descend to such ignoble tasks are, in this province [Bahia], and probably in the whole country, black men or of color."[47] These positions allowed them to become white and integrated, as well as intimately tied to the violence of slavery. The position of the slave catcher was formally initiated in Brazil in 1722 after a series of slave uprisings in the state of Minas Gerais necessitated retrieving slaves who escaped during the chaos of the rebellions.[48] Slaves feared slave catchers, as they often beat and abused the slaves in their custody.

Englishman Henry Koster discovered this racial transformation firsthand and wrote, "In conversing on one occasion with a man of colour who was in my service I asked him if a certain Capitam-mor[49] was not a mulatto man; he answered, 'he was, but is not now.' I begged him to explain, when he added, 'Can a Capitam-mor be a mulatto man?'"[50]

These fluid racial mutations varied depending on how it was to an individual's benefit to be perceived by and to perceive others. Expilly recounts an example of a black woman who became white in a matter of minutes.[51] Traveling with two mulatto slave catchers, Expilly invited them to take a meal at the home of his

FIGURE 4.1
A black slave
catcher returns a
captured runaway
slave to his master.
Capitão do mato,
lithograph by
Johann Mortiz
Rugendas, 1823.

friend Justino Fruchot, a white Frenchman, who was also entertaining his companion, Manuela, a free black woman. The slave catchers were perplexed when they were served by Fruchot rather than Manuela, who was seated at the table, and they registered their strong protest, saying, "It is impossible for us to allow a slave woman to sit in our company." Fruchot replied just as forcefully that Manuela was not a slave but a free woman and that the slave catchers could sit with her or leave. Trying to calm the situation, Expilly offered that if whites were willing to have blacks as their guests, then surely mulattos could do the same "without lowering themselves." His observation only further inflamed the situation:

> "Sir, you have insulted us!" shouted Valcoreal....
>
> "If you were aware of our habits and customs you would know that we are not mulattos."
>
> . . .
>
> "We have the honor of being slave catchers; therefore we cannot be mulattos," said Valcoreal with impudent arrogance.

Here the slave catcher makes the claim, supported by Brazilian law and social custom, that his profession rather than his skin determines his color. In an effort to remedy the situation, Expilly plays with the boundaries of social whiteness and exposes its superficiality. He invents a story that the elaborate dinner was purchased by Manuela, who is "extremely rich" and whose father "is the officer of the wardrobe of the Emperor Dom Pedro II. In Europe such a post could only belong to a prince by blood." Suddenly the slave catchers show a newfound respect for Manuela, as they recognize instantly that her father is white by profession, though of course he is pure black. To make Manuela's racial transformation more explicit, Expilly states of her father that this "officer of His Majesty the Emperor, despite being black, entered into the class of whites, authentic whites." The slave catchers gladly accede to this magical shift from black to white as Expilly, using the same logic that whitens the slave catchers, claims that "Senhora Manuela, despite the color of her skin, is therefore white like her father."

In addition to the black and mulatto slave catchers, Koster relates that the position of overseer was mostly given to a free mulatto, a creole (native-born black Brazilian), or an African slave. Koster shows that upon the enslaved overseer "more reliance is to be placed than upon a free person of colour, for the slave *feitor* becomes responsible to his master for the work which is to be executed, and is therefore careful that every one should do his duty." The overseer's allegiance to his master and authority over his fellow slaves were often exacted in the form of even more extreme cruelty toward other slaves than that perpetrated by whites or free blacks, and the overseers had to be "watched, that they may be prevented from being too rigorous towards those whom they are appointed to command; their behavior is usually more overbearing than that of free men."[52]

The position in which black Brazilian passers found themselves in the wake of abolition was essentially a choice between black and white, between slavery and freedom. But on some level, we can see that positions assumed by free and socially white blacks and mulattos—such as capitães de mato, overseers, and public slave whippers—through which they inflicted violence upon other blacks, were a way of disassociating themselves from blacks and performing whiteness, and also of performing freedom intraracially. It was not only important to be accepted into the ranks of whites; to solidify one's identity as an intraracial other, it was equally important to also be seen by blacks as an other.

Johann Moritz Rugendas's lithograph *Punitions publiques sur la Place Ste. Anne* (figure 4.2) depicts a black male slave who has been disrobed and tied to a post and is being savagely beaten by a black slave whipper, most likely a former slave himself. At the right sits another slave, who is visibly weakened from

FIGURE 4.2 Slave being beaten publicly by black slave whipper in Rio de Janeiro. *Punitions publiques sur la Place Ste. Anne (Public Punishments in Saint Anne Square), lithograph by* Johann Moritz Rugendas, *1835.*

having been beaten and is being helped up by a black woman. This violent scene of slave torture is a public spectacle. Well-dressed white men, possibly slave masters, sit in front of the crowd and watch with fascination and anticipation as the slave whipper tortures the slave for their pleasure. The slave whipper, well aware that he is an essential part of the spectacle, dramatically raises his hand to inflict an exacting blow to the body of the fettered slave. In the following passage Expilly describes the torture of slaves by black slave whippers: "The victim is laid between two planks. Ropes . . . are used to tie him by the feet, hands, and torso. The whipper—always a free African—takes the whip. This instrument is composed of five small woven strips a foot and a half long attached to a wooden handle. The African whips the slave's back until the overseer orders him to stop. Then the victim's wounds are bathed with a mixture of water, salt, and vinegar and it's over. The tormentor can start again a few days later when the slave has healed."[53] Here we note the cynical care given to the slave's wounds to prepare him for his next whipping.

Upon receiving freedom the formerly enslaved had no control over how they were integrated or the extent to which they would be included in Brazilian society. Many paintings, novels, and travel journals produced during the period document the use of free blacks as agents of torture and violence against the enslaved. White supremacy dictated how black freedom would be registered and archived, allowing the white elite to also control how they themselves would be depicted for posterity in relation to slavery. The integration of free blacks into white society via the creation of occupations such as public slave whippers and capitães de mato was calculated to serve whites while sustaining black oppression. Black freedom became paradoxically entrenched in maintaining slavery, and the assertion of black freedom became intimately tied to reproducing white supremacy. In turn, the comportment of free blacks toward slaves affected how the enslaved viewed those who had been freed and what it meant to be free.

By doing the "dirty work" of the white masters, these black torturers became hypervisible and in this moment they came to take on the face of slavery, of both its violence and criminality, in the place of the white slaveholder. This dynamic calls attention to the spectacularity of black freedom while camouflaging the role of the white master in slave torture. The so-called fluid racial basis of Brazilian slavery was maintained by white control over violence toward blacks: when and which forms of violence were used and became visible and documented, and when it was hidden or erased.

Within social whiteness there was a hierarchy that was rooted in class. Doctors, politicians, and writers were at the top of the whiteness scale, and slave catchers and slave whippers were at the bottom. The profession of slave catcher, though it offered transcendence into whiteness, diminished substantially in prestige in the second half of the nineteenth century as Brazil neared abolition. As abolitionist sentiment began to grow, slave catchers were paradoxically looked upon with scorn by the whites whom they served, and as slavery came to an end their profession was considered shameful, leading many to abandon it.

Historian David Roediger defines whiteness as "the empty and therefore terrifying attempt to build an identity on what one isn't and on whom one can hold back."[54] Because the distinction between bondage and freedom was black and white, in order to solidify a socially white identity, it was essential for free blacks to separate themselves from the enslaved condition, often by asserting domination over slaves. Black participation in slavery made it more difficult to establish an exclusive correlation between whites and the institution of slavery, which complicated the racial terms of Brazilian abolition much more than in the United States.[55] Passing and social whitening allowed free blacks and mulattos, if they so desired, to rewrite themselves in relation to the narrative of slavery by entering into it not as the oppressed but as the oppressor.

The relationship between free blacks and poor whites was equally complex. During slavery and after emancipation poverty was very prevalent among both free blacks and whites.[56] Vidal Luna and Herbert S. Klein have argued that poor whites and free blacks were on approximately equal social footing in terms of distinguishing social factors, such as occupation, meaning that whiteness was not an advantage for the poor and freedom did not elevate blacks above poor whites economically.[57] However, poor whites did enjoy other markers of white racial privilege compared to free and enslaved blacks. Poverty did not necessarily create any form of solidarity between poor whites and blacks that transcended race. As we saw in chapter 3, between white mistresses and enslaved women, gender and the effects of white male supremacy by no means softened slaveholding women's attitudes or actions toward slave women. Reginald Daniel explains that even as free blacks strived to be treated as first-class citizens, they were never totally considered white, and at "any time could be treated as 'inferiors' by even the most socially and culturally 'inferior' whites."[58] While some free blacks may have been on par with whites economically, this factor did not undo the white racial privilege that poor whites held in relation to people of African descent.

The divide between poor whites and free and enslaved blacks appears frequently in the literature of the late nineteenth century. In Aluísio Azevedo's novel *The Slum*, a number of poor white characters actively exploit and even murder black characters. The lead protagonist, João Romão, exploits the labor of his runaway slave girlfriend, Bertholeza, to amass a fortune; lies to her by telling her he purchased her freedom; and at the end of the novel when he grows tired of her, he contacts the son of her former master to return her to slavery. In Azevedo's 1881 novel *The Mulatto*, a wealthy mulatto, Raimundo, passes as white without knowing that his mother is black. He is referred to as an "uppity nigger" or "negro of boastful airs" by both rich and poor whites.

Machado de Assis also depicted poor whites' attitudes toward slaves in his famous short story "Pai contra mãe" (Father Versus Mother), published in 1906 but reputed to have been written prior to abolition in 1888, about a white man, Cândido Neves, who after being unsuccessful at a number of jobs resorts to becoming a slave catcher to support his wife and child. Already struggling financially, he learns that his wife is expecting another child and faces the prospect of leaving his newborn at an orphanage. He receives a lead on a high-reward runaway mulatta slave woman named Arminda, whom he finds by chance. In the initial confrontation between them, as he ties her up, she implores him, "I am pregnant, Sir! . . . If my Lord has a son, I beg you for the love of your own son to let me go; I will be your slave, I will serve you as long as you want; please let me go, young master!" Faced with the cruel dilemma of whether to return the woman and her unborn child to slavery, or forfeit the reward money, he ultimately chooses the money and returns the slave to her master, after which she has a miscarriage. The story illustrates that commonalities such as parents trying to protect their children did not create any form of empathy or solidarity between poor whites and slaves, and that poor whites, despite their poverty, still benefited from white privilege.

Black Resistance to Slavery

Not all free blacks denied their black heritage or eschewed connection with slaves. Some did in fact use their privilege to fight against slavery and help enslaved people. Such was the case of famed Bahian mulatto abolitionist, lawyer, and journalist Luiz Gonzaga Pinto da Gama (1830–1882). Gama was born to a white father and a free African woman, Luíza Mahin, who was purportedly a famous rebel leader in the Bahian Malê revolt of 1835. He was sold illegally into slavery by his father to settle a debt. There is much speculation about whether Mahin actually existed or was a mythical figure created by Gama for personal and political purposes. Historian João Reis refers to Mahin as a "personage" who is the result of a "mixture of a possible reality, fiction, and myth."[59]

Gama spent most of his youth in slavery but later proved that he had been illegally enslaved and won his freedom through the courts. A self-taught lawyer, Gama successfully defended more than five hundred legal cases for other slaves who had been illegally sold into slavery, for which he garnered the title "the Black Apostle of Abolition." Of this time period Gama is the closest to what might be considered a black radical. His biography has several compelling parallels with the life of Frederick Douglass. Gama was most noted for saying during a trial, "The slave that kills his master, in whatever circumstance it may be, always kills as a form of legitimate self-defense." In 1859 Gama published a poem titled "Sortimento de gorras para a gente do grande tom" (Assortment of Hats for People of High Style) in which he vehemently criticized mulattos who discriminated against blacks and denied their black ancestry to pass as white:

All the socially white nobles of this country,
Whose real ancestors are buried in Guinea;
Obsessed with lineage or driven by some hard addiction,

FIGURE 4.3
Luiz Gama ca.
1863. Casa da
Cultura, Bahia,
Brazil.

forget all about their black brethren, their patricians;
Mulattos of whitened color
Deem themselves to be of illustrious origin
Oppressed by the madness that dominates them,
despise their own grandmother, an African woman from the Gold
    Coast:
Oh dear reader, don't be shocked by such news
Because everything in Brazil is a rarity![60]

Black Slaveholders

One of the most distinctive characteristics of slavery in Brazil (as well as in the Caribbean, notably in Haiti) was the existence of numerous free black and mulatto slaveholders.[61] Many prominent blacks descended from free slaveholding families, and some blacks and mulattos, upon being manumitted, purchased slaves to serve in their households. German traveler Wilhelm von Eschwege noted, "The free mulatto also possesses slaves. He lives with arms crossed and considers work an undignified thing."[62] Maria Graham echoed von Eschwege and explained that the free blacks, "when they can afford to purchase a negro, sit down exempt from further care. They make the negro work for them, or beg for them, and so long as they may eat their bread in quiet, care little how it is obtained."[63]

Slave ownership was a possibility for all people, but only a minority of the black population could afford slaves. However, a number of sources indicate that slave ownership extended beyond class lines, and was not merely relegated to the extremely wealthy, even allowing those who were technically enslaved to own slaves of their own. Luna and Klein, in their study of free black populations in the states of São Paulo and Minas Gerais, found that 6 percent of slaveholders in São Paulo were black, and in Minas Gerais, 14 percent. In São Paulo state, 633 free blacks owned slaves in forty-one counties. A total of 1,803 free blacks owned slaves in Sabará, with an average of three slaves per household. In terms of color, pardos comprised 94 percent of slaveholders, roughly 595 families, in contrast to the 39 preto families. Pardos overall owned more slaves than pretos.[64]

Joaquim Nabuco went so far as to argue that the existence of black slaveholders was yet another proof of racial equality in Brazilian society. He remarked that a black "even in the darkness of slavery could buy slaves, perhaps even, who knows, a son of his former master."[65] This fact, according to Nabuco, proved "the fluidity of the classes and individuals, and the unlimited extent of the exchanges between slaves and free men [who] constitute the majority of Brazilian citizens."[66]

African slave Mahommah Gardo Baquaqua wrote of his experience, upon arriving in Rio de Janeiro to be sold at auction, of almost being sold to a man of color: "There was a colored man there who wanted to buy me, but for some reason or other he did not complete the purchase. I merely mention this fact to illustrate that slaveholding is generated in power, and anyone having the means of buying his fellow creature with the paltry dross can become a slave owner, no matter his color, his creed, or country, and that the colored man would as soon enslave his fellow man as the white man, had he the power."[67] Baquaqua's recollection illustrates that slaveholding was fundamentally a question of power and economics, and that being black offered no presupposition of antislavery sentiment or racial kinship.

Even more striking is the story of a mulatto slave by the name of Nicolau whom Koster encountered while staying on a plantation owned by monks in

Jaguaribe, Ceará. Nicolau had worked on the plantation for several years and had gained the trust of the monks. He lived in a state of quasifreedom, suspended between enslavement and social whiteness. The monks allowed him to purchase freedom for his wife and children in addition to purchasing two African slaves of his own, even as Nicolau was obliged to continue in servitude to the monks. He offered to exchange his two slaves for his own freedom but the monks refused to release him. Paradoxically, the slaveholder Nicolau was unable to secure his own freedom.[68]

The story of Nicolau is an account of a man who understands the value and meaning of freedom and laments his own position as a slave, yet purchases two slaves of his own, illustrating the Brazilian slave's extremely individualistic perception of slavery and freedom. Nicolau's own experience with the indignities of slavery did not prevent him from participating in slavery and enslaving other blacks, nor did it engender any antislavery sentiment. Historian John Hope Franklin, in his study of free blacks in North Carolina, has documented the existence of black slaveholders in the United States. He writes, "Without doubt, there were those who possessed slaves for the purpose of advancing their [own] well-being. . . . These Negro slaveholders were more interested in making their farms or carpenter-shops 'pay' than they were in treating their slaves humanely."[69] Some, he noted, would purchase slaves in order to later free them: "It seems that by far the larger portion of free Negro owners of slaves were the possessors of this human chattel for benevolent reason. There are numerous examples of free Negros having purchased relatives or friends to ease their lot. Many manumitted such slaves, while others held title to slaves who were virtually free."[70] However, others, like black slaveholders, were much more interested in their own profit and social position and amply exploited the labor of enslaved men and women. Franklin writes, "There was some effort to conform to the pattern established by the dominant slaveholding group within the State in the effort to elevate themselves to a position of respect and privilege."[71]

Koster also relates that blacks' experiences of having suffered enslavement did not necessarily temper their treatment of slaves; rather, they sometimes proved to be even more violent than the white master: "It is likewise frequently observed that even manumitted Africans who become possessed of slaves, which occasionally occurs, treat them in a severe and unfeeling manner, that is nothing softened, but rather rendered more violent, by a remembrance of their own sufferings."[72] Likewise, Expilly wrote of a formerly enslaved African woman that in "cruelty she surpasses that of whites, and she becomes a merciless mistress for the slaves she owns."[73]

The existence of black slaveholders and their treatment of their slaves expose sharp divisions among blacks throughout the history of Brazilian slavery. Koster observed that slave and slaveholder were irrevocably divided regardless of race: "The consideration with which the free persons of mixed castes are treated, tends to increase the discontent of their brothers who are in slavery. The Africans do not feel this, for they are considered by their creole brethren in colour, as being so completely inferior, that the line which by public opinion has been drawn between them, makes the imported slave feel towards the creoles as if they had not been originally from the same stock."[74] Lacking any feeling of unity with blacks as a whole, and seeing the opportunity to access white privilege, free blacks willingly took on the role of cruel slaveholder: disidentification bred contempt.

Scholarship on slavery in the Americas has examined at length the role of the slave in the construction of white master identity and the participation of Africans in the trans-Atlantic slave trade, but the existence of black slaveholders poses a more complicated question: What purpose and meaning did the slave hold for the formerly enslaved turned master?[75] How did black masters assert their authority over people of their own race when the line distinguishing them from their slaves was so tenuous, when skin color did not readily distinguish them as free or enslaved? Brazilian historian Júnia Furtado in her notable study of eighteenth-century slave woman Chica da Silva, who owned a significant number of slaves, has noted that slave ownership for emancipated and free blacks was "an essential mechanism in the pursuit of insertion into the world of the free where disdain for work and for living by one's own graft reigned supreme."[76] Moreover, Furtado maintains, for free blacks "their only chance of diminishing the social exclusion and stigma of their origins was to avail of precisely the mechanisms the whites used for their survival and promotion."[77]

Machado de Assis's novel *Memórias póstumas de Brás Cubas* (The Posthumous Memoirs of Brás Cubas, 1881) dedicates a chapter to exposing the relationship between slaves and formerly enslaved black slaveholders. Though brief, Machado's is one of the few novels of the period to directly depict the violence of black slaveholders toward their slaves. In a short chapter titled "The Whipper," the main character, Brás Cubas, a wealthy white man from a slaveholding family, is taking a walk on Valongo Street (the site of Rio's largest slave market) when he hears a commotion and sees a crowd forming. To his surprise, he discovers that the man causing this scene is his former slave, Prudêncio, whom he has not seen in several years. Prudêncio is now a slaveholder and he is reprimanding and whipping his own slave for being a drunkard, calling him a "bum," "devil," and "animal" in front of a crowd of onlookers. Brás Cubas tells Prudêncio to forgive the slave and Prudêncio complies. Brás Cubas explains the incident in these words:

It was the way Prudêncio had to rid himself of the beatings he'd received by transmitting them to someone else. As a child I used to ride on his back, put a bit into his mouth, and whip him mercilessly. He would moan and suffer. Now that he was free, however, he had the free use of himself, his arms, his legs, he could work, rest, sleep unfettered by his previous status. Now he could make up for everything. He bought a slave and was paying him back with high interest the amount he'd received from me.[78]

This depiction of a formerly enslaved slaveholder, written by a socially white mulatto author, provides critical insight into how Machado himself and the white elite that he depicted in his works viewed black slaveholders and their relationship to the enslaved. The above scene shows how public physical violence served as a means to distinguish the conditions of freedom and enslavement. The narrator interprets Prudêncio's violent behavior toward his slave as meaning that he was somehow dealing with his own pain and trauma. This description, as well as Henry Koster's observations of black slaveholders, suggests that the racial trauma of black slaveholders as part of a multiracial society was dealt with and released intraracially, through violence, and that this violence against slaves constituted a form of catharsis. This phenomenon recalls how a number of white mistresses took out their revenge against enslaved women for the abuses their husbands inflicted upon them. In both instances, the actual target—white male supremacy, and for free blacks, slavery and racial discrimination—cannot be attacked directly, one's pain and trauma is meted out interstitially.

In beating and humiliating his slave in public, Prudêncio calls attention to himself, showing the gathering crowd that he is a property owner, a master. Part of the logic of the performance that is inherent to social whiteness is the public recognition by whites (as we saw upon Machado's death) that confirms this illusory difference between Prudêncio and his slave. Black freedom and social whiteness, in order to be legitimated, depend on a public show of violence toward other blacks that must be visually recognized by whites.

In this chapter Machado reflects the attitudes of white slaveholders and the Brazilian elite who might have seen former slaves' "happy ending" in their ability to become masters and inflict their own pain on slaves. This scene recalls Joaquim Nabuco's comments that the possibility of blacks owning slaves was proof of the absence of racism in Brazil. The hypervisibility of intraracial violence in the context of slavery (and arguably beyond) came to obscure the white supremacist mechanisms that structured it. Even though white supremacy was the basis of slavery and was a system built by whites for their benefit, they were able to distance themselves, if not remove themselves entirely, from being the creators of the conditions under which this particular form of violence came into existence. "Black-on-black" violence and conflict between free and enslaved blacks became intimately linked to how elite white Brazilians substantiated their benevolent position toward slaves as part of the myth of Brazil's exceptional slavery. With this logic, white slaveholders exculpated themselves of the heinous acts committed against blacks under slavery. Their crimes became overshadowed by the hypervisibility of black people perpetrating acts of violence against one another.

Black Opposition to Abolition and Individual Transcendence of Race

As the abolitionist movement gained momentum in Brazil, some free blacks and mulattos showed little interest in slave emancipation, and in some cases they actively participated in proslavery campaigns, working in league with whites to suppress slave revolts by serving as informants or spies, or informing masters of the plans or whereabouts of fugitive slaves. Others, such as Henrique Dias, born in the state of Pernambuco to manumitted African slaves, participated in the suppression of quilombos in Bahia.[79] In 1887 Anselmo Fonseca described free blacks and mulattos as the "principal adversaries" of slaves and as constituting a "contrary force to civil liberty."[80] Fonseca saw many free blacks and mulattos as deserting their own race in order to gain white acceptance and social recognition. "How can slavery be abolished in Brazil," he asked, "if the free men of color . . . [play] the role of traitors, executioners, and persecutors of their own brothers, while they flatter the whites and are subservient to the latter's criminal interests . . . [thereby becoming] even more deserving of their disdain?"[81] Fonseca was especially critical of counselor Domingos da Silva: "In 1884 nearly thirty people presented their candidacy for posts as general deputies to the Bahian state legislature. Among them there was only one man of color, Counselor Domingos da Silva, former professor of the School of Medicine of that province. He was the only one who in a written public document had the courage to ask for votes in support of slavery. And, together with Sr. Pedro Moniz, who represented the sugar mills of Santo Amaro, and Srs. Lacerda Werneck and Coelho Rodrigues, he voted against the abolition of flogging."[82] The following year, another free man of color, who Fonseca says was known for being "one of the most intolerant slavocrats in Bahia,"[83] resigned from his position at the *Diário da Bahia* because the newspaper refused to publish an announcement for a runaway *ingênuo* (a black child who was born free after passage of the Law of the Free Womb).

It is quite reasonable to surmise that many free and socially white blacks and mulattos, like the Brazilian white elite, saw abolition as a threat to a social order that benefited them and feared that abolition could ultimately undo their privilege. Though many did experience racism and prejudice, their favored position in relation to the enslaved caused many of them to be silent. Their silence, however, as poet Audre Lorde warned, "did not protect them,"[84] but, according to G. Reginald Daniel, held them in a position of "second-class citizenship during slavery, and would hold the African Brazilian masses at the bottom of the social hierarchy long after abolition."[85]

Though some blacks and mulattos did use their privilege to support abolition and help the black masses, they did not constitute the majority. Joaquim Nabuco remarked in 1884,

> Unfortunately, gentlemen, we fight against the indifference that our cause [slave emancipation] inspires in the same people who should be our allies and whom slavery reduces to the most miserable state of dependence. It is sad to say it, but the truth of the matter is that wouldn't the men of color, the grandchildren of slaves, who wear on their faces the martyrdom of their race adhere to our cause with dedication and loyalty as one would expect from the inheritors of such suffering? No, they don't dare to join forces with the abolitionists and many are found on the other side.[86]

Abolitionist Antônio Bento of São Paulo, like Fonseca and Nabuco, saw the divisions between free blacks, mulattos, and slaves as a substantial barrier to slave emancipation and admonished them to unite. In an article written in the *Correio Paulistano* in 1883 he illustrated the attitudes of free blacks, protective of their own interests, who voted for white proslavery candidates over the abolitionists: "It appears that some black and mulatto voters, instead of voting for the abolitionist candidate who in the Assembly comes to be the representative of that unfortunate and outcast race, vote for the white candidates. . . . They do not even think that at the very moment that they are electing the whites, countless blacks and mulattos shackled with iron are groaning under the whip. Take courage, blacks and mulattos, and remember that your union can bring triumph to the cause of liberty. Have some shame and be men."[87]

Despite the existence of social whiteness, which they themselves supported, white abolitionists attempted to shame free blacks and mulattos for having no allegiance to their race, even calling them traitors. Brazilian slavery and the practice of social whitening attempted to break the bonds of solidarity among blacks. Although white Brazilians were complicit in the whitening of free blacks and mulattos, as the abolitionist movement began, the idea of free and formerly enslaved black people advocating for the maintenance of slavery seemed peculiar even to whites. Even Nabuco, who rushed to spare Machado de Assis from being called a mulatto, was not race blind when it came to formerly enslaved blacks and mulattos campaigning against abolition. Yet because abolition was heralded as a form of national redemption, a movement in which elite white Brazilians felt that they themselves were being freed from slaves and that benefited them and the nation's image, they advocated for racial solidarity among blacks and mulattos—as long as whites could control it and it was in line with their own political interests.

The history of what legal scholar Randall Kennedy has termed "racial betrayal" was by no means unique to Brazil but was found in other parts of the Americas.[88] It was a significant impediment to collective black resistance and progress during and after slavery.[89] In 1923 Jamaican-born black radical Marcus Garvey proffered that with respect to "intra-racial treason," people of African descent were "more encumbered in this way than any other race in the world."[90]

David Walker, an African American born in 1785 to a free mother and an enslaved father, lived in Boston and fought against British colonization and slavery in the United States. In 1829 he wrote *Appeal to the Colored Citizens of the World but in Particular, and Very Expressly, to Those of the United States of America*, in which he attacked the institution of slavery and the discrimination suffered by blacks in the North and in the South. As with Luiz Gama, one of Walker's primary subjects of critique was free and enslaved blacks who betrayed people of their race by serving as allies to white slaveholders and actively promoting white supremacy to support their own interests and advancement. Walker bemoaned the fact that while a number of whites were working toward slave emancipation, "black people are, by our treachery, wickedness, and deceit, working against ourselves and our children."[91] Walker saw the participation of blacks in the institution of slavery as the ultimate contradiction and betrayal, and berated them, referring to them as "ignorant and treacherous creatures" who were "in league with tyrants, and who receive a great portion of their daily bread, of the moneys which they acquire from the blood and tears of their more miserable brethren, whom they scandalously delivered into the hands of our *natural enemies!!!!!*" Walker also attacked the free blacks in the large cities of Boston, New York, Philadelphia, and Baltimore who went around to black communities in search of fugitive slaves in the guise of helping them flee or of being in solidarity but with the real intention of "selling their own brethren into *hell upon earth*, not dissimilar to the exhibitions in Africa, but in a more secret, servile and abject manner."[92]

Black complicity and participation in slavery adds another dimension to understanding the longevity of Brazilian slavery. It became very difficult to argue against an institution that oppressed blacks when blacks themselves were actively participating in the oppression of other blacks. This greatly complicated Brazilian slavery and nineteenth-century race relations, perhaps even more than in the United States, and it helps to explain some of the contemporary challenges to Brazilian race relations and Afro-Brazilian identity politics that are direct results of slavery, social whitening, and black participation in slavery.

This division between Afro-Brazilians over the course of Brazilian history has helped to produce complex forms of institutional and interpersonal violence. João Costa Vargas and Jaime Ampara Alves, in their intersectional analysis of contemporary police brutality in São Paulo, have shown how the large percentage of black Brazilians employed in the police force has functioned as an excuse to deny the strategic and institutionally racialized contours of police brutality. Afro-Brazilians' participation in these acts of violence, Vargas and Alves maintain, "complicates, rather than contradicts, the racialized aspects of policing strategies."[93] The authors further suggest that these Afro-Brazilian police officers who inflict violence on predominately black communities function as part of an "institutional framework" that is "itself immersed in and reproducing non-citizenship, that cannot be reduced by or separated from individual members of that framework."[94]

Here we can see a genealogy from slavery to the present that repeats throughout Brazilian history, whereby inclusion of blacks in institutional frameworks, or the miscegenation of oppression, has strategically functioned to distort and solidify institutional forms of antiblack domination. Thus, much like the socially white, the slave catcher, or the public slave whipper working within the framework of slavery, the Afro-Brazilian police officer, in his position of relative power and privilege in relation to the poor black favela inhabitants, finds himself caught between racial identification and the power and privilege of institutional allegiance.

The Brazilian racial system took an individualistic slant, opening spaces of privilege for individual free blacks and mulattos and making possible the realization of individuality and individual identity (real or imagined) independent of racial heritage. Social whitening propagated the notion of individual transcendence of race and encouraged blacks to see themselves as individuals separate from a racial collective. Self-interest and personal empowerment took precedence over any goal of uplifting blacks as a racial group. Though there are exceptions, most free blacks and mulattos in Brazil were concerned about enjoying and maintaining their privilege, not extending that privilege to other blacks and mulattos. Many had no affective tie to race, as one's race alone did not create a homogeneous racial experience. Solidarity or affective bonds among people of African descent were often formed on the basis of origin, such as one's region, African tribe, country, religion, or class. Many of the slave revolts that occurred in the nineteenth century, such as the Malê Revolt in 1835, were mobilized on the basis of religion or common African origin, not skin color.[95]

The diversity of slaves and formerly enslaved people of African descent during Brazilian slavery also had a profound impact on how they viewed and experienced freedom. The condition of freedom was not experienced and performed in the same way by all freed slaves. Freedom was experienced in very individualistic and personal ways in relation to race. Freedom fundamentally offered the possibility of the emergence of blacks as individuals and the transcendence of an imposed racial identity that was rooted in enslavement. During slavery "black identity" was "slave identity," and part of being free and socially white was determining how one would identify with slavery, the enslaved, and race.

One of the fundamental differences between the United States and Brazil is that in Brazil freedom offered an illusory form of deracialization, in which racial identification became a choice rather than an imposition. Though the socially white and the emancipated were clearly physically read as being of African descent, it was in no way socially advantageous for them to identify as black. As a result, many did not want to be seen as part of a black collective, which became central to how they embodied their own individual freedom. An important factor that greatly contributed to the longevity of Brazilian slavery was that freedom allowed former slaves to believe that they could benefit from slavery and white supremacy as whites did—and many did.

Conversely, in the United States the one-drop rule and binary racial categorization made individual desire, strivings, and identity virtually impossible to conceive of independent of race, as the individual always had a direct relationship to blackness. This difference between the United States and Brazil is crucial: the power of the possibility of individual desire as a function of social whiteness informed how black Brazilians saw race and themselves, and also their notions of national citizenship.

This distinction also adds important complications to our contemporary understanding of what constituted black identity until the twentieth century, and our tendency to label or categorize period Brazilian writers, politicians, artists, and musicians of African descent as strictly black or Afro-Brazilian. Today we may tend to attribute to nineteenth-century men and women of African ancestry a black identity that they themselves did not assume during their lifetime or might not have wanted. Debates about whether Machado de Assis did or did not embrace his black heritage, for example, are still underway, but the understanding of individuality and individual desire as a reality of social whiteness forces us to grapple with the question of whether people are defined by their racial ancestry or by the identity or race that they themselves choose.

What are we to make of the reality that for many slaves, part of imagining freedom was the hope that they might one day own slaves of their own, and that for some of the formerly enslaved, the assertion of individual freedom and personhood was made manifest through the dehumanization of other blacks? Neither race nor common condition of enslavement or suffering offered any presumption of kinship or attitudes that were different from those of white slaveholders. Black slave ownership and intraracial violence as part of slavery disrupts many of the common assumptions that we hold about slavery. For many people, it seems inconceivable or a violent contradiction that a former slave would take on the profession of a slave whipper who mercilessly tortures slaves in public plazas, or of a slave catcher who goes in search of runaway slaves to bring them back to their master for payment, or that formerly brutalized slaves would purchase slaves only to subject them to the same forms of violence that the former themselves had endured. These illegible contradictions, which perhaps don't make sense to us today, force us to examine how black people participated (or participate) in reproducing a system of white supremacy, and the fundamental role that intraracial violence played in manifesting the freedom and citizenship of the socially white and the formerly enslaved. This interstitial violence, like the social whitening of free blacks and mulattos, ultimately supported an insidious system of oppression while feigning to represent a new social order.

Reverse Miscegenation and the Loss of White Privilege

Though miscegenation was heralded as the foundation of Brazilian racial and national exceptionalism and national identity, ultimately social whiteness came with sexual restrictions. As Zita Nunes argues, both sex and reproduction in the making of the Brazilian nation were a "project by and for white men," and the "father of the nation is thus the white man, the only appropriate sexual partner for both white women and women of color."[96] Reverse miscegenation, or sex between black men, free or enslaved, and white women, contradicted that canon of slave society that had to be maintained in spite of any demographic or political changes. These liaisons were inevitable, and they might have validated the notion of an egalitarian society, but in fact the intolerance and violence that ensued from relationships between free black men and white women belied Brazil's benevolent race relations. Socially white black men could own slaves, participate in proslavery campaigns, and rise through the ranks to become prominent members of Brazilian society, but sex with or marriage to white women was met with strong opposition and was grounds for revoking their "honorary white cards."

Why, in a mixed-race society rooted in interracial sex, would reverse miscegenation prove so problematic? The antagonism against black men as sexual partners of white women relates to the need to continue the production of slave children, limit births of free black children, and maintain white male power. In Brazil and throughout the Americas, slavery, freedom, and race were reproduced through black and white women. The law in slave societies in the Americas stipulated that children received the status of their mother, whether free or enslaved. With this law the children of white fathers and black mothers were born legally enslaved, allowing white masters to enslave their own progeny. While sex between white masters and slave women perpetuated slavery, sex between free black men and white women threatened the continuity of slavery and white male domination by producing free mulatto children. These children contradicted the legal and social definitions of slavery and freedom as well as the position of white men , all aspects necessary for enforcing the racial hierarchy.[97]

As the reality of abolition approached, white males sought to retain control over all women's bodies (as well as black men's) to maintain their supremacy, which meant also having exclusive access to white women. Free blacks could access many other aspects of white society (subject to control by whites), but not white women. White men secured their exclusive control over miscegenation by enacting strong social measures to prevent black and mulatto men from having sex with or marrying white women. These relations were policed with extreme brutality, with black men receiving the brunt of the punishment, while sex and rape between white men and black women was normalized and became woven into a twisted national tale of love between the races.

It was critical for white men to control the race and legitimacy of their children and grandchildren in part because legitimacy was tied to the distribution of inheritances. A marriage between a free black man and a white woman meant that their mulatto children could possibly share in the division of the estate of their white grandfather. Throughout the Americas interracial marriage has been a source of anxiety and violence over the centuries, especially between black men and white women. In the United States forty-one states had laws prohibiting interracial marriage at some point in their history. Antimiscegenation statutes remained in force throughout the South until the 1967 Supreme Court ruling in *Loving v. State of Virginia*. In 1885 W. C. Benet, a judge and state representative from South Carolina, wrote in the Augusta *Chronicle*, "The proud race whose blood flows in our veins will never stoop to marriage with the negro, nor with any colored race. . . . Race fusion is so abhorrent to our race instincts and so out of accord with the history of our race that we can smile at the absurd suggestion. . . . There may be isolated cases of intermarriage, but they will never betoken a movement."[98] In 1867 Buckner H. Payne, a Nashville publisher, argued that interracial marriage was a sin and those who dared it risked reaping the wrath of God: "The states and people that favor this equality and amalgamation of the white and black races, *God will exterminate*. A man cannot commit so great an offense against his race, against his country, against God, . . . as to give his daughter in marriage to a negro—a *beast*."[99] In Brazil marriage between black men and white women was never illegal, but societal opposition to these unions was pervasive. Maria Graham noted that whites were "extremely anxious to avoid inter-marriage" and would "prefer giving their daughters and fortunes to the meanest clerk of European birth" rather than to the "richest or [most] meritorious" black man.[100] Expilly agreed with Graham and wrote, "No one in Brazil has ever seen a *white man* marry a negress. For even stronger reasons, a *white woman*, has never dared to legally consent to unite her destiny with that of a *black man*."[101] No amount of money could make a socially white, free black man white enough to marry into a white family. While white men may have been color-blind when it came to the employment of socially white blacks and social interactions with them, they drew a color line at including black men in their families.

As many observers noted, these restrictions were not immediately recognizable. The visibility of free blacks in high social positions and the social interactions between the races during Brazilian slavery stood out as anomalies, especially in comparison to other slave societies in the Americas, leading many to believe that Brazilian race relations were an exception to the rule. But there was a distinct disconnect between the so-called equality in the law and the true status of blacks in Brazilian society. Regardless of any legal freedoms that blacks and mulattos may have gained, barriers were constructed socially to retain their loyalty, contain them within specific roles, and keep them out of white families.

Expilly noted this difference between Brazilian law and white attitudes and social customs:

> The law and prejudice are two very distinct powers that must not be confused. The constitution may well proclaim the equality of all citizens; prejudice is stronger than the constitution and it erects an insurmountable barrier. . . . Epaulets, decorations, and titles are given to mulattos; but no alliances are formed with them. . . . Under the law, men of color can

become generals, barons, deputies, commanders, but prejudice declares them unworthy of alliance with white families. . . . A high functionary, the minister of the empire if you wish, will receive a mulatto adorned with military decorations at his home; he will invite him to dinner, and at an evening ball he will order his wife to overcome her repugnance and dance with him. But never, I repeat never—even if the mulatto is as rich as all the Rothschilds together—will the high functionary give him his daughter's hand.[102]

Marriage to white women was more than symbolic. For the socially white black man, interracial marriage was a means of solidifying class identity, social ascension, and belonging for both themselves and their lighter-skinned progeny.[103]

Thus white women had to be guarded from relations with black men for two reasons: white women reproduced free children, and they offered social and legal legitimacy to blacks and their children, further upsetting the growing demographic imbalance between blacks and whites. Though there are several documented marriages of mulattos and black men to white women—Machado de Assis married a white woman, as did Frederick Douglass—the general attitude toward mixed-race unions was undeniably hostile. Historians in the United States have argued that the most severe and violent policing of interracial unions between black men and white women began immediately following abolition, which engendered a crisis over racial and sexual equality.[104] In the patriarchal Brazilian family structure, unions between black men and white women threatened a reconfiguration of the family and nation by potentially replacing the white patriarch with a black one. As Robyn Wiegman points out, the black man's "threat to masculine power arises not simply from a perceived racial difference, but from the potential for a masculine sameness."[105] The possibility of equality between white and black men would negate racial difference and its social meaning. A black man who takes a white wife is no longer simulating white masculinity in the game of social whiteness but performing independently willed, transgressive black masculinity. Both races understood that social whiteness was never intended to bring about true equality; it was an artifice meant to preserve the remaining shreds of the old social order as slavery was dismantled. It could not be carried to the point of allowing free blacks to replace white men as reproducers, heads of families, and husbands of white women.

The following excerpt from the memoir of writer Graça Aranha from the northeastern state of Maranhão illustrates the extreme prejudice against interracial unions across socioeconomic classes and his family's heavy investment in white racial purity:

In the family of my paternal grandfather the preconception against blacks and mestizos was aggressive. They sought purity of race with furious zeal. The Maceis Parentes and the Aranha families never mixed with Indians. Mating with *negros* and mulattos would have been an abominable thing. In the interior of the province I often met these relatives of mine, in extreme poverty, barefoot, simple workers, employees on the *fazendas* [farms], but totally preserving the purity of the white blood. They were generally blond with blue eyes, with the same features that one could find in most of my father's sons and also in two of my brothers. My paternal aunts, like hunting animals, sniffed and discovered the mestizo elements no matter how one tried to hide it. Tireless fanatics in the name of this prejudice, if they knew of some relative's marriage plan, they started to investigate the entire pedigree of the suitor and if they discovered even the smallest drop of negro or Indian blood, they would not give up until they saw the unhappy alliance destroyed.[106]

Regardless of the prestige, money, or social whiteness of her black suitor, a white woman would risk becoming a social pariah if she contemplated marrying a black man. As Expilly wrote, she "would immediately be rejected by everyone of pure race; she would be held in contempt, pointed at, and mercilessly excluded from the social circles where she was previously an ornament and a source of pride."[107]

Noted eighteenth-century Afro-Brazilian slave woman Chica da Silva, through her relationship with João Fernandes de Oliveira, who was at the time the richest man in the Brazilian empire, was able to obtain her freedom and assimilate into white society to a certain degree. In her biography of Chica da Silva, Júnia Ferreira Furtado recounts that the former slave was allowed to attend white social events and even owned slaves herself, but she was nevertheless regarded with contempt by the white elite. Their mulatto son, João Fernandes de Oliveira Grijó, learned that despite his wealth he was not worthy to marry into a white family. As the firstborn son, Grijó was the inheritor of a substantial fortune, and as a result he became socially white. João Fernandes expected that his children would attain his own level of wealth and prestige. With the intent of maintaining the family's money and prominence, in his will João Fernandes prohibited his descendants from marrying below their station. The institution of marriage at this time was extremely strategic, especially for those who had the stain of mixed blood in their family lineage.[108] In this sense, marriage was used as a mechanism for whitening. If João Fernandes's children married outside the white race, they would perpetuate the stigma that already marked their lineage through Chica da Silva.

Grijó complained that it was virtually impossible for him to meet the requirement of marrying a woman equal to his station, as strong prejudice against interracial marriage made it very difficult to "find anyone among the nobility willing to grant him a daughter's hand in marriage and call him son-in-law."[109] Though his inheritance and substantial fortune were well known, he had never received a marriage proposal. He is quoted as saying that he believed that the white elite "would rather see their daughters live in mediocre decency than allow into their families a blemish so patent to the eyes of all."[110] Ultimately, Grijó's inheritance from his mother—her color and her status as an ex-slave—proved impossible to overcome. Grijó, like many Brazilian blacks who passed, distanced himself from his mother and spent his entire life trying to rid himself of the stigma of his birth.

The story of the son of Chica da Silva, a slaveholder in her own right, illustrates how the black mother and her connection to slavery and illegitimacy haunted the socially white mulatto. There was no way that he could be dissociated from her. Ultimately white men who had relations with slave women had full control over legitimacy, and their mulatto children were cast out by the white families that would not have them as husbands to their daughters. Their black mothers, as the incarnation of both captivity and illegitimacy, rendered them permanently illegitimate in the social realm. During slavery elite white Brazilians believed that free blacks and mulattos, due to their partial or full African heritage, were undeserving of the freedoms and privileges afforded to whites.

The social barrier against black men marrying white women continued in Brazil well beyond the nineteenth century. In 1953 North American anthropologist Ralph Beals noted that the black man in Brazil "seems to be 'deprived' only of free access to those social contacts that normally lead to courtship and marriage with the white girls of that class. This is the common denominator of the racial situation in Brazil."[111] In the same year, Thales de Azevedo, in his study in Bahia, the most culturally and racially African state in Brazil, explained that whites were deeply invested in retaining the purity of their families and "justify their opposition to interracial marriage not only based on ideologies concerning the mental and moral inferiority of blacks, but also an 'instinctive' repulsion for certain organic characteristics of Africans and their close descendants." Citing a mulatto who was raised among whites in Bahia, he refers to the "instinctive repulsion that the white race has for the defects of the sister race, because they are pure or almost pure."[112]

Social Hostility against Depictions of Black Men
with White Women

The Brazilian public, like most societies throughout the Americas in the nineteenth century, was not only against reverse miscegenation, it was even opposed to fictional depictions of it. Aluísio Azevedo's 1881 novel *O mulato* (The Mulatto), published seven years prior to the abolition of slavery, marked the inauguration of the Brazilian naturalist movement. The novel is perhaps the most accurate portrait of the social realities facing mulatto men, and the picture it paints is confirmed by several other observers of the period. Upon publication the novel caused such a hostile uproar that Azevedo was forced to leave his hometown and settle in Rio.[113] The public was outraged by the novel's depiction of a mulatto impregnating and trying to marry a white woman. The reception of the novel in many ways mirrored the actual social climate depicted in the novel surrounding marriage between black men and white women.

O mulato is an exposition of the social prejudice facing the male mulatto. The novel recounts the story of Raimundo, the son of a Portuguese slaveholder and his mistress. As a young child Raimundo witnesses his father's wife brutally torture his mother. Due to his fair skin and white features, he grows up unaware of his blackness and that he is the child of a slave. The plot is constructed around his search to reconstruct his past and uncover the identity of his mother. After completing law school in Portugal, Raimundo returns to Brazil to settle the estate he inherited from his deceased father. He falls in love with his cousin, Ana Rosa, and asks for permission to marry her. At this point the secret of his racial identity is revealed to him and he is denied Ana Rosa's hand. He continues to pursue her amid great racial prejudice. Incensed by the possibility of this interracial union, the parish priest and Ana Rosa's former suitor conspire to kill Raimundo. The novel paradoxically culminates in his tragic murder and with Ana Rosa happily married to the suitor, the man she once despised.

The prejudice against marriage between black men and white women was so deep-seated that Raimundo is not even allowed to marry into his own family. In the following scene Raimundo is told by his uncle that his social whiteness does not make him white enough to marry his cousin:

> "I denied you my daughter's hand because you are . . . you are the son of a slave woman."
>
> "I!"
>
> "You're a colored man! . . . And that, unfortunately, is the truth. . . . My wife's family was always quite scrupulous in that regard, and all of Maran-

hão is like them. . . . You can't imagine how deep the prejudice against mulattoes is around here! They'd never forgive me for such a marriage; besides, in order to carry it out, I'd have to break the promise I made to my mother-in-law not to give her granddaughter to anyone other than a proper white man, either Portuguese or the direct descendent of Portuguese. You're a very worthy young man and quite deserving of esteem, but you were freed at your baptism, and everyone here is aware of it."[114]

Raimundo's reply to his uncle expresses his frustration with these social norms that prioritized biological whiteness over social whiteness and created insurmountable barriers to intimacy:

"Just because it happens that my mother was not white. . . . What good is it for me to have so diligently pursued an education? What good are my exemplary conduct and moral integrity? . . . Why have I kept myself undefiled? Why the devil have I aspired to become a useful and honest man? . . . For, no matter how high my ideals, everyone here has avoided me, simply because my wretched mother was black and had been a slave. But, what fault is it of mine for not being white and not being born free? . . . They won't allow me to marry a white girl?"[115]

When Ana Rosa reveals the news of her pregnancy, her grandmother inveighs to Raimundo, "Pregnant? So be it! But I'd rather have her dead or a prostitute. . . . A nigger! . . . You're the son of [a slave woman]! Freed at baptism! You're a half-breed, a mulatto!"[116] In spite of the elaborate ruse of social whiteness and the benefits it conveyed to a limited number of free blacks, the facts of one's birth could never be transcended, neither by individuals nor by the black race as a whole, not even if one had been freed at birth and lived as a free person one's entire life. Black freedom was always conditional and subject to white male supremacy. Freedom never erased color, memory, or the past rooted in enslavement.

FIVE

O Diabo Preto (The Negro Devil): *The Myth of the Black Homosexual Predator in the Age of Social Hygiene*

The Brazilian Social-Hygiene Movement

In 1916 medical doctor Miguel Pereira, professor and distinguished member of the National Academy of Medicine, famously declared during a speech at the Faculty of Medicine in Rio de Janeiro, "Brazil is one big hospital."[1] This curious phrase came to characterize late nineteenth- and early twentieth-century Brazil: a nation that saw itself ridden with sick citizens, and an abundance of doctors and politicians with pseudoscientific theories and prescriptions to cure them. Transgressive acts that had for centuries been considered simply sinful or unnatural by the Catholic Church and society at large now became sicknesses that the nation had to somehow cure itself of. The preoccupation with illness that became pervasive throughout Brazilian society, medicine, public policy, and culture gave rise to a "social-hygiene" movement to cleanse the nation.

Led by doctors, politicians, and writers, the movement began in the second half of the nineteenth century shortly after independence, while slave emancipation was still being hotly debated, and lasted into the early twentieth century. Although the movement was primarily concerned with issues of public health and sanitation, its reach extended to several other areas of Brazilian society. It attempted to study the nation's social problems—what the inquisitors had previously considered heresies and crimes against God—and find solutions to them through science and medicine. Among these problems were promiscuity, prostitution, sexually transmitted infections such as syphilis, male and female homosexuality, alcoholism, and mental illness.

Scientific studies and interventions, doctors and politicians claimed, were carried out in the name of national progress. The social-hygiene movement proliferated a discourse of "healthy body, healthy nation," arguing that Brazilians' physical health had a direct impact on the nation's political and economic well-being. But, inevitably, the social-hygiene movement was entrenched in preexisting attitudes about race, gender, sexuality, and socioeconomic status and invested in maintaining white male supremacy over the nation. The movement created its own victims by forcing "hygiene" and definitions of illness on Brazilians according to their perceived social status, all under the protective guise of science and medicine.

The leaders of the social-hygiene movement were especially bent on showing the degeneracy and deviancy of black Brazilians and the poor, which undermined their program of national cleansing. Blacks and the poor were believed to be genetically predisposed to mental illness, vagrancy, prostitution, and homosexuality. Their inborn degeneracy—especially sexual—was contagious and a threat to the white elite and the nation. It was during this period that doctors and writers alike most clearly articulated the connection between sex, sexuality, and race and their centrality to Brazilian national identity. Medical literature, like abolitionist discourse of the period, viewed blacks and mulattos and the poor as immoral and prone to sexual excess, with no control over their animal instincts. Sander Gilman has shown that discourses of racial, gender, and sexual pathology proliferated in the late nineteenth century out of a need to "distinguish the healer from the patient as well as the 'healthy' from the 'sick.'"[2] The rhetoric of contamination central to antislavery and abolitionist discourse, which argued that slavery was harmful to whites because it brought them in contact with the immorality of slaves, took on a less moralistic posture among the social hygienists. Armed with the tools of medicine, they instead sought to scientifically prove, diagnose, and cure degeneracy while marginalizing those who they thought were responsible for the nation's ills.

The Syphilis Epidemic

The social-hygiene movement stemmed in part from a syphilis epidemic. Doctors were alarmed by the high rate of syphilis and other sexually transmitted diseases that had infected a significant portion of the population. The cause and first cure for syphilis were not discovered until the first decade of the twentieth century. Before then, myths and stereotypes about the causes of the disease and ignorance of its transmission and repercussions abounded. Those myths led to equally peculiar notions about hetero- and homosexuality and about race and sex.

Syphilis had had a long history on Brazilian soil. According to Gilberto Freyre, Brazilian civilization and syphilis went "hand in hand": "Brazil would appear to have been syphilized before it was civilized,"[3] he wrote. Prior to the social-hygiene movement, national attitudes about the disease varied greatly. Syphilis was common throughout cities and on the plantations. In 1845 medical doctor Herculano Augusto Lassance Cunha of Rio de Janeiro wrote a dissertation in which he observed that syphilis in Brazil was "near to being hereditary and so common that the people do not look upon it as a scourge, nor do they stand in fear of it."[4] In 1878, while traveling in the Brazilian northeast, Frenchman Émile Béringer was appalled by Brazilians' lax attitudes toward the disease and wrote, "Syphilis wreaks great havoc. The major portion of the inhabitants do not look upon it as a shameful disease and do not pay much attention to it. Aside from its influence on the development of numerous special afflictions, it accounts for ten deaths in every thousand."[5]

In the early nineteenth century King Maximilian I of Bavaria sent a scientific expedition to Brazil. Biologist Johann Baptist von Spix and botanist Carl Friedrich Philipp von Martius were among the expedition. They traveled extensively throughout Brazil from 1817 to 1820, reaching Rio de Janeiro, the southern and eastern provinces, and the Amazon. Their explorations of the interior of the country were among the most important scientific expeditions of the nineteenth century.

Spix and Martius were both physicians and wrote in great detail about the diseases they encountered among the Brazilian population, noting specifically "the incredible extent of syphilis, and its incalculably fatal consequences to the health and morals of the inhabitants."[6] They were disturbed to note that syphilis was for some men a badge of honor: "Not only does the universality of the contagion most seriously tend to diminish the population, but the unblushing openness with which it is spoken of destroys all moral feeling."[7] They referred to this attitude toward syphilis as the "darkest side in the picture of the Brazilian character" and proof of the extent to which white slaveholders "degrade themselves."[8]

Syphilis was popularly referred to throughout the nineteenth century as a *doença de homem*, a "manly man's disease." Slave masters' young sons would proudly display their syphilis scars, as they were considered a young man's badge of honor—a testament to his virility and sexual prowess. In fact, if a young master did not have syphilis scars by a certain age he would be subjected to ridicule by his friends.[9]

Virgin slave girls as young as twelve years old would be given to white men "rotting with syphilis," as it was believed that taking a girl's virginity would cure the disease.[10] This was also the case with other sexually transmitted diseases, such as gonorrhea. Dr. João Álvares de Macedo Junior wrote in 1869 that it was a common belief that having sex with a girl at the age of puberty could cure a man of gonorrhea. "The inoculation of a pubescent female with this virus," he writes, "is the surest means of extinguishing it in oneself."[11]

Social Hygiene and Sex

As during the Inquisition, sex was spectacularly salient in the social-hygiene movement and marked by a lack of knowledge and prejudices that strike us as farcical today. Science, medicine, and culture became greatly intrigued by sex and sexual deviance. This intrigue bordered on national obsession, driven by a fascination with, as Robert Young puts it, "people having sex—interminable, adulterating, aleatory, illicit, inter-racial sex."[12]

While during the Inquisition sex was defined in vague, simplistic terms and considered merely sinful and heretical in the eyes of God and the Catholic Church, nineteenth-century doctors developed new ways of designating and classifying sexual behaviors based on notions of illness and perversion. Unlike the inquisitors, medical doctors and sexologists of the late nineteenth and early twentieth centuries concerned themselves with asking why people engaged in sexual deviance and grouping these individuals into categories based on the nature of these acts, pathologizing the acts rather than condemning them as sinful. The social-hygiene movement meddled its way into Brazilian bedrooms and brothels, attempting to scrutinize and regulate the bodily functions and sexual practices of the nation's citizens. Individuals who engaged in deviant sexual behaviors would be placed under a microscope and observed with intense curiosity—and contempt—by the nation's doctors. When it came to people of color and the poor, these scientific endeavors were guided by unspoken theories of race that automatically placed blacks in deviant sexual categories while elevating the sexual behaviors of white males to the status of promoting national progress.

National Progress and White Male Sexual Supremacy

In 1869 Dr. José Ricardo Pires de Almeida lamented that Brazil did not "possess the same virility" as other nations and that it had suffered a "significant decline in male potency."[13] Fourteen years later, in 1883, Joaquim Nabuco expressed agreement with Almeida's sentiments and also decried Brazil's effeminacy. He saw the Portuguese as the culprits, arguing that "had the Portuguese had the intuition in the sixteenth century to know that slavery is always a mistake, Brazil would not have turned into what it is today." Were it not for the Portuguese importing millions of Africans and having sex with them, Brazil would be a manlier nation, "healthy, strong, and virile like Canada and Australia."[14]

Many period thinkers were convinced that Portuguese colonialism, and more particularly slavery, had tarnished the nation's sexuality and had left behind a legacy of perversion and debauchery that had rendered Brazil an unmanly and impotent nation. "From the beginning of our colonization," wrote Joaquim Nabuco, "Portugal unloaded in our territory its criminals, its whorish women, and every last bit of their social dung. . . . And this is how Brazil became what it was until yesterday, the Congo."[15] Once again the white elite saw themselves as the victims of slavery and of blacks who had corrupted their morality, language, food, and race. Sex in late nineteenth-century Brazil and within the hygienic purview came to occupy physical and political extremes, and as was the case throughout Brazilian history, it was imbued with concrete political meaning. It was during this period according to Brazilian anthropologist Sérgio Luís Carrara that the "question of responsibility and consequently, self-control/restraint, appear specifically around sex and its relation to will."[16] Sex was a slippery slope that on the one hand was necessary for personal health and national vitality, while on the other hand, if practiced incorrectly, represented the ultimate form of illness and national destruction.

For several period doctors, intellectuals, and politicians, the vision of the Brazilian national body and the Brazilian citizen were both white and male, and as a result the nation's future greatly depended on the bodily functions of white men.[17] This conflation of the nation with the white male body and sexual and national politics is rooted in what Sérgio Buarque de Holanda articulates as the proverbial confusion between the public and private spheres that he argues was a hallmark of Brazilian civilization.[18] This vision of the nation as white and male is in contrast to that of the United States and other countries that conflated the nation with the image of the virtuous white woman. Until well into the late twentieth century many authors, when writing of "the Brazilian citizen," referred almost exclusively to elite white men to the exclusion of black and white women and black men. When black and white women and black men were mentioned in period literature, they were not included as part of the collective body politic or the national vision of what constituted a citizen.[19] As Brazilian literary critic Richard Miskolci points out, the national obsession with sexuality in the late nineteenth and early twentieth centuries emerged through "political, scientific, and literary discourses" that had a primary aim to "civilize" the Brazilian nation through practices that were overtly prejudiced, and policing intimate relationships conformed to the heterosexual reproductive ideal, construed as white and virile."[20]

Medical literature viewed the nation's progress as rooted in the promotion of white male racial and sexual supremacy and heterosexuality. Medical studies on sex and sexual perversion grew out of a desire to examine how they harmed the white body and white sexuality, and by extension the nation. This focus was not, however, to the exclusion of white women, whose bodies, heterosexuality, and exclusive sexual desire toward white men were crucial to the reproduction of the white family. The social-hygiene movement attempted to do damage control by actively warning males against promiscuity and deviant sexual behavior. For period doctors, sexual promiscuity was much more perilous than a simple question of tainted morality. Promiscuity, wrote Dr. João Alvares de Azevedo Macedo Júnior in his 1869 medical thesis, enfeebled the body and the nation and caused an array of serious physical ailments that included "weak fevers, fainting spells, paralysis, apoplexies, convulsions, dementia, gout, and excessive loss of semen."[21] And yet doctors and medical literature also agreed that celibacy or being unmarried were equally pernicious to a man's health. Dr. Antônio da Fonseca Vianna, years earlier, issued a caution in his 1842 medical thesis to celibate and unmarried men that "a life in isolation, the burden of vexations without a female companion to console and relieve sorrows, almost always causes hypochondria, tuberculosis, and many other illnesses."[22]

Though many were convinced that the licentious atmosphere of slavery had perverted white sexuality and was the cause of many national ills, the new nation also held fast to sexual ideologies that had been the foundation of Portuguese colonialism and Brazilian slave society. As during slavery and throughout the course of the nineteenth century, families were deeply invested in white male heterosexuality, and virility and sexual prowess were prized commodities.

As Freyre has noted, during slavery, no plantation owner or slave mistress "wanted an effeminate son." Young white boys who were virginal and not sexually active were deemed "ladylike" and shamelessly ridiculed. Plantation families wanted a sexually dominant, macho son, or, per Freyre, a real "woman-chaser," a "ladies-man," the ultimate "deflowerer of maidens" who wasted no time in ravaging the slave women of the plantation so that he might "increase the herd and the paternal capital."[23] Slave masters wanted their sons to become sexually active as early as possible, and some mothers would "thrust into the arms of their bashful and virginal sons young Negro and mulatto girls who were capable of awakening them from their apparent coldness or sexual indifference."[24] But before indulging in what Freyre calls the "great mire of flesh"—the slave woman or raping young slave boys—the young white master honed his sexual prowess through a host of masturbatory practices that included bestiality (penetrating cows, nanny-goats, ewes, hens, and other domestic animals), along with various fruits, including bananas, watermelon, and *mandacarú*, in "an effort to satisfy that fury with which the sexual instinct dawns in them."[25] Both Freyre and the young white master appeared to have been particularly fond of the mandacarú fruit, for he describes it bizarrely, as if writing from personal experience, as having a "clinging quality that is almost like that of human flesh."[26] These sexual practices were continued through adolescence until the master was married, and served as a way for him to relieve himself when "nurses, mulatto girls, slave boys, [or] public women" weren't at his immediate disposal.[27]

According to historian Jeffrey Needell, much of Freyre's work, particularly as it relates to slavery, is fundamentally linked to his own self-image and self-exploration. This focus, according to Needell, led Freyre to "portray Brazilians, by which he implicitly meant Brazilians who were white elite males, as driven by their libidos and the sensual ambiance of the tropics to a predatory, unceasing search for penetration. Initially, any orifice reminiscent (however vaguely) of a woman's vagina would do."[28] In Freyre's work, as in the male rape cases examined in chapter 2, we see the connection between penetration and property, and pleasure and penetration as a right or rite and consummation of ownership. In this sense the master's penetration or sexual abuse of the slave boy should not be viewed as a homosexual act—the slave child was a penetrable orifice, just as fruits, animals, and women were all at his disposal.

For period doctors white men's orgasms were serious business and of great national and medical concern. In a discourse that can only appear comical today, doctors argued that the regularity of white men's orgasms had a direct impact on all aspects of the nation. Pires de Almeida fervently informed the Brazilian public, "No one can ignore the impact of the genital apparatus on the rest of the economy. . . . When citizens don't orgasm, as it were, with all their might, the army can't summon its bravery. . . . The profusion of sperm debases the male body and hinders a more masculine spirit. . . . That conserved semen, reabsorbed in our own economy, will make us virile, agile, and fearless."[29]

Brazilian social hygienists and medical officials still wanted, or in fact needed, male citizens to have copious amounts of sex, but they were greatly concerned with how and with whom this was done. Instead of promiscuous liaisons, they actively promoted monogamy and marriage so that men could have regular sex and plentiful, "healthy orgasms" with honest women in the name of national progress. It was very important, however, that these crucial national orgasms not be masturbatory, because period doctors warned that excessive masturbation could turn a man into a homosexual.

Early Studies of Homosexuality in Brazilian Medicine

In a disquieting tone Paulistano coroner Dr. Viriato Fernandes Nunes urgently alerted Brazilian medical officials and intellectuals that "all sexual perversions violently attack the norms of society." For Nunes, sexual perversions included masturbation, bestiality, sadomasochism, and homosexuality, all of which he saw as fundamentally interrelated. He warned, "Homosexuality is the destruction of society, it is the decay of countries; if it were the norm, the world would end in no time."[30]

The first medical studies of homosexuality in Brazil were produced in the second half of the nineteenth century. They were largely based on the work of European doctors and sexologists such as Austrian doctor Karl-Maria Kertbeny, French doctor Julien Chevalier, and German sexologists Albert Moll and Richard von Krafft-Ebing. Though Brazilian doctors drew extensively from these works, they uniquely altered them to fit the Brazilian context. Previously sodomy and sexual acts between persons of the same gender had been viewed by society and the Catholic Church as sinful and unnatural, but not as bearing a connection to sexual orientation. With the emergence of homosexuality as a sexual category in the late nineteenth century, the sodomite was no longer simply a sinner but became, according to Foucault, a "personage, a past, a case history, and a childhood, in addition to being a type of life, a life form, and a morphology with an indiscreet anatomy and possibly mysterious physiology." According to Foucault, sodomy shifted from a "habitual sin" to a desire that was part of a person's nature.[31] Medical doctors were no less prying or voyeuristic than the inquisitors, nor were their "scientific" studies any less moralistic or judgmental. As during the Inquisition, it was heterosexual white men who defined same-sex relations according to their own values and needs. This time, instead of deciding who needed to repent or be fined for their transgressions against God, medical professionals were determining who was sick and needed to be cured. This diagnostic process neither benefited nor accurately represented those who engaged in same-sex sexual acts. In addition to classifying sodomites as homosexual and noting the potential causes behind their behaviors, doctors sought to develop a specific language to describe the sodomite pathologically. The Brazilian homosexual's "singular nature" became a source of both intrigue and national disquiet, and homosexuality, as doctor Leonídio Ribeiro wrote, became a "social problem to be resolved through medicine."[32]

In 1872 Francisco Ferraz de Macedo, a medical doctor and pharmacologist, published one of the earliest studies on homosexuality, titled "About Prostitution in General and Particularly in Rio de Janeiro." Macedo's intent was to document and analyze the pervasiveness of prostitution in order to develop public health measures to contain the spread of syphilis. At the time doctors believed that female prostitutes were the primary carriers of syphilis and other sexually transmitted infections. In fact they believed that only women could spread sexually transmitted diseases, and as a result, some men, according to Macedo, preferred to have sex with other men or male prostitutes due to their fear of contracting syphilis (and also because male prostitutes were substantially cheaper than women).[33] Macedo argued that the absence of clean women and proper heterosexual outlets were among the primary social causes of homosexuality.

Period medical literature recognized various types of homosexual activity, with the active partner (the penetrator), as during the Inquisition, being more acceptable than the passive (the penetrated) because he maintained his gender integrity and masculinity. As historian James Green has noted, this bias shielded those taking the active role from the gaze of the physicians, lawyers, and other voyeurs who produced most of the literature on Brazilian homosexuality at the end of the nineteenth century.[34] Macedo found that soldiers, businessmen, and artists made up the greatest portion of active pederasts. He argues that sodomy was pervasive in the military, "due to soldiers' time restraints and lack of other means" and asserts that many low-ranking officers were victims of sexual abuse and rape by their superiors.

Throughout his study however, Macedo stresses that homosexuality was not natural but rather the direct consequence of specific environmental circumstances, especially extreme poverty and improper moral upbringing. He notes, "A boy who has received paternal virtues and advice, corroborated by his teachers who educate his spirit . . . will never turn toward the black sin; he will never be interested in or confused by the whirlwind of sodomites; he will never be found in Rio de Janeiro mixed up in the multitude of male prostitutes."[35]

Macedo additionally included in his treatise male prostitutes and occasional hustlers who, although they did not consider themselves homosexual, sustained themselves by selling sexual favors to men in exchange for money, food, or a place to stay. Several upper-class white men exploited the extreme poverty that many blacks and poor people of color endured as a means of satisfying their sexual desires.

Dr. Pires de Almeida, writing in 1902, notes that although male prostitution existed in countries around the world, "until fifty years ago, it was nowhere more ostensibly common than in Rio de Janeiro."[36] He goes on to state that men "engaged in lascivious pleasures in boardinghouses, establishments that rented rooms by the hour, and private homes. . . . All of these *rendez-vous* were generally known by police, who tolerated this masculine practice that took place in the light of day and the dark of night."[37] He asserts that male prostitution diminished by the turn of the century after the abolition of slavery due to the increase of female prostitutes, especially among the newly arrived immigrant women.[38]

Macedo believed that the problem of homosexuality needed to be actively combated in the men and women of the demimonde, who he believed to be the greatest practitioners of the "nefarious act." Mirroring the language of the Inquisition, he observes that "rarely does one find among the groups of proponents of the nefarious sin any illustrious man of careful upbringing."[39]

Talisman Ford has shown that unlike European sexologists, who considered any man who engaged in sex with another man, regardless of his active or passive position, to be homosexual, Brazilian sexologists placed emphasis on sexual position and the degree of the individual's masculinity or effeminacy. Unlike the Europeans, Brazilian doctors conflated male homosexuality with effeminacy and passivity during sex, and accordingly passive and effeminate men became the central focus of Brazilian medical research on homosexuality.[40] James Green writes that according to period doctors, the active male "possessed masculine characteristics and therefore did not have the same fixed homosexual essence typical of the effeminate man."[41] This variation shows how the Brazilian construction of male homosexuality may have been significantly impacted by the history of same-sex sexual practices during Brazilian slavery and during the colonial period as evidenced in the archives of the Inquisition. Though on the surface it would appear that there was a shift in how period doctors treated sex between persons of the same gender relative to how it was treated by the Catholic Church and the Inquisition, we see that in addition the history of slavery framed how Brazilian medical doctors conceived the gender and racial meanings of sexual penetrability and passivity. The rape and sexual abuse of enslaved black men and their supposed inherently perverse and degenerate natures and passivity came to influence their hypervisibility in medical literature on homosexuality. It may have been problematic for period doctors to place emphasis on the active man in medical literature on homosexuality, since historically in many instances during slavery the active penetrator was the white master. Many of these doctors came from slaveholding families. Is it possible that they themselves had engaged in sexual relations with enslaved men? At the very least it seems that they, like Freyre, must have been aware of the existence of sex between white slaveholding men and male slaves.

The medical literature produced during the late nineteenth and early twentieth centuries in Brazil posited that homosexuality was caused by physiological disorders and mental illness. Doctor Francisco José Viveiros de Castro also cited masturbation, hereditary defects in glandular development, alcoholism, unhealthy living, stays in prison, old age, and impotence as causes of homosexuality. More importantly, Viveiros de Castro reported that the male homosexual suffered from a severe psychological disorder called "effeminization" that affected every area of his life:

> Like women they have a passion for grooming themselves, ornaments, flashy colors, lace and perfumes. . . . They carefully shave themselves. . . . They give themselves feminine names—Maintenon, Princess Salomé, Foedora, Adriana Lecouvrer, Cora Pearl, etc. They are capricious, envious, and vindictive. . . . They go quickly from ferocious egotism to tearful sensitivity. They are prone to lying, making false accusations, cowardice, and the obliteration of moral sense. The anonymous love letter is the most exact expression of their courage. They do not enter professions that require manly qualities, but prefer to be tailors, dressmakers, launderers, starchers, hairdressers, florists, etc.[42]

Yet, more than their apparent lack of masculinity and their feminine manner, male homosexuals, according to Viveiros de Castro, were violent and prone to fits of jealousy and rage: "Their jealousy is a mixture of endangered sensuality and wounded self-esteem. There are known instances of pederasts who, in fits of jealous rage, have torn their companions' belly or ripped the skin from his scrotum and penis with their teeth."[43] Leonídio Ribeiro also saw effeminate homosexual men as violent and noted that "the known cases of sadism do not occur among excessively masculine individuals, as is the popular notion, but rather among the effeminate [types], such as the Marquis de Sade."[44] This particular observation is a gross misstatement given the history of masters raping enslaved men.

The work of Francisco Pires de Almeida, mentioned earlier, challenged several of the social and class arguments made in period studies on homosexuality. In his study *Homosexualismo: A libertinagem no Rio de Janeiro: Estudos sobre as perversões do instinto genital* (Homosexuality: Libertinage in Rio de Janeiro: A Study of the Perversions of Genital Instincts), though he associated homosexuality with prostitution, he argued that this "moral perversion" was not solely found among the city's poor but had also infected Rio's elite and prominent men, including clergymen, public officials, judges, and high-ranking navy officials. To prove his point, throughout the text Pires de Almeida "outs" several men who despite their social position and prestige engaged in sex with other men. He writes, for example, of a "reputable lawyer" in Rio de Janeiro in the 1860s "who despite being married . . . sought out unnatural pleasures even with the most repulsive individuals. It is said that he frequently sought out a big, black, muscular African man, with large, ugly features to share a bed under his own roof, showing no concern for the tears of his unhappy and abandoned wife."[45] This case study shows how interracial homosexuality was thought to infiltrate the home (in a literal sense, and as a metaphor for the nation) and destroy white marriages. The difference here is that Pires de Almeida, unlike other period doctors, points out that it was the "reputable" lawyer who sought out black men for sex. Pires de Almeida offered clues for identifying homosexual men: they had a penchant for wearing the color red, and passive male homosexuals were unable to whistle due to the "uncomfortable convulsions that it produces in their rectum."[46]

Constructing the Black Homosexual

During the late nineteenth century, as Siobhan Somerville has argued, studies of homosexuality were conceived around the same ideologies of white racial superiority that underlay so-called scientific studies of race.[47] The debate surrounding definitions of hetero- and homosexuality throughout the Americas had a direct connection to the debate around the divisions between black and white as racial boundaries were increasingly blurred.[48] The sin of sodomy, same-sex desire, and blackness were interrelated, and although white men and women predominated as perpetrators in the inquisitional sodomy cases, black men and women were seen as the cause of whites' perversion during and after slavery. Though homosexuality as a sexual category did not exist at the time of the Inquisition, the history of male rape and intragender sexual relations under slavery had a profound impact on the construction of racialized homosexuality in Brazilian medicine.

The emergence of studies on homosexuality came at a critical moment in Brazilian history, at the confluence of independence, the emancipation debate, and the beginning of the nation's whitening projects. These historical moments framed how homosexuals were defined in the Brazilian context, and the specific racial, sexual, and political meanings and anxieties that would be projected onto them. The rhetoric of contamination and the discourse of white victimhood that argued that slavery was bad for whites because it brought them into contact with perverse blacks also fueled studies of homosexuality in Brazil.

In the aftermath of colonialism the process of defining Brazilian national identity was carried out through a strategic process of "antithesizing," that is, defining what the Brazilian nation was by identifying what it was not. Brazilian politicians in the wake of abolition undertook a total cost accounting, pinpointing the collateral damages of slavery and Portuguese colonialism in an attempt to rectify them. Medicine and science played a major role in this process. The hygienic and scientific focus on the homosexual and on social deviancy was about curing, reforming, and obliterating what did not fit the national ideal. In the national and medical imaginary, blackness, disease, and homosexuality became intimately connected. Homosexuality and homosexuals, like blacks and blackness, came to be seen as a threat, a transmittable disease that could potentially destroy white male supremacy and the white family. Homosexuality in period literature (medical and fiction) was written about in the same fashion as sexually transmitted diseases. As doctors studied the effects of STDs such as syphilis and the "fatal effects" of homosexuality and what they termed the "black stain" of miscegenation, virtually all used the same pathological rhetoric of contact, contagion, and contamination. As Joaquim Nabuco wrote in his famous *O abolicionismo* (Abolitionism, 1883), "Between us there is no dividing line. . . . The contact between the two races is synonymous with contagion."[49]

With a complex legacy of miscegenation, white racial purity and heterosexuality were intimately interconnected in postindependence Brazil. Period scientific discourse shows the convergence of national, racial, and sexual anxieties that attempted to create a hierarchy of sexualities (as they did with race), with heterosexuality, particularly white male heterosexuality, being the only possible and real sexuality. The predominating political view of Brazil as a white patriarchal family was the foundation of the crisis over white male heterosexuality and sexual supremacy that undergirded studies of male homosexuality. The future of the nation depended on the morally and sexually strong white man, the all-powerful white father, and anything that threatened his sexual and gender integrity imperiled the future of the nation.

Medical literature after abolition conflated race and class, neatly substituting the image of the criminal and pathological poor black for the criminal and pathological slave. After emancipation, many former slaves migrated to large cities in search of economic opportunity. Due to racial discrimination, blacks and mulattos were pushed to the margins of society and became the target of these ill-conceived scientific studies. As James Green has shown, a connection between race and homosexuality was consistently "embedded in the underlying themes of the text" of medical studies on homosexuality. This correlation was often established by using blacks' bodies to "symbolize the excesses of the 'perversion.'" These studies, according to Green, "relied on pejorative cultural stereotypes about nonwhite Brazilians held by many in the medicolegal profession as well as among sectors of the intellectual elite in general."[50] Brazilian medical and legal discourse saw these sick and contagious individuals as a threat to national progress and a severe social problem to be suppressed or cured as part of a national process of cleansing. This nationalist agenda maintained that by curing them, the nation might also be cured.

Protecting Society: Curing and Creating Asylums for Homosexuals

As sex between people of the same gender had been criminalized and condemned for centuries, period doctors sought to decriminalize homosexuality. Prior to independence the law had prescribed (in theory) severe punishments, including prison, for men who engaged in sodomy. Aside from the small faction of men who ostensibly engaged in sex with other men to avoid contracting syphilis or to save money on female prostitutes, doctors considered the majority of homosexuals to be sick individuals who could not control themselves. According to Ribeiro they "manifested clear pathological tendencies, whether psychological or somatic, all in need of medical or psychiatric care or intervention."[51] Doctors began to push for officials and the law to recognize homosexuals and pederasts as mentally ill and encouraged medical treatment and the construction of facilities where they could be cured.

The decriminalization of deviant behavior now deemed by medical doctors as "illness" became integrated into the law. The new Imperial Penal Code, drafted in 1830 after independence, considered both the mentally ill and minors as inherently "irresponsible," and it was left to the discretion of the courts to determine if these sick individuals should be placed in "houses destined for them."[52] Mulatto writer Lima Barreto wrote about these asylums, which he referred to as the *cemetério dos vivos*, the cemetery of the living, where he was committed several times for alcoholism and mental illness.[53] These facilities were designed for people suffering from alcoholism, homosexuality, vagrancy, drug addiction, or any kind of deviant behavior condemned by Brazilian officials. The legislation of 1830 also eliminated previous direct references and punishments related to sodomy found in the Filipine Code and decriminalized most sexual acts between consenting adults. The law did, however, punish what was termed "public affronts on decency."[54] This ambiguous phrase, like "female honesty" in rape law, left many individuals vulnerable to the abuses of police and public officials, who determined in ways that benefited themselves what exactly constituted "public assaults on decency." James Green has shown that the ambiguity of this term in some instances allowed police to blackmail citizens by extorting money from them under threat of arrest.[55]

The poor and black Brazilians were consistently targeted for arrest for homosexuality, vagrancy, prostitution, and public indecency, which meant that they were forced into these special houses much more often than white middle- and upper-class Brazilians. Foucault notes that in the nineteenth century psychiatry and medicine gave birth to a particular kind of racism, a "racism against the abnormal" motivated by a fear of hereditary transmission of defects.[56] This racism rooted in sexuality became projected toward anything that veered from whiteness and the heteronormative.

In the case of pederasts, criminologist Aldo Sinisgalli remarked that it was simply "not fair that society be exposed to the dangers of their morbid tendencies."[57] Viveiros de Castro and Sinisgalli believed that the most severe legal punishments should be applied to homosexuals who were too debauched and corrupted to be treated, especially if they attempted to corrupt a minor. Sinisgalli wrote that the homosexual who "seeks to seduce minors undermines public decency, and infringes upon individual and social rights."[58] Though the ostensible motive of this belief was the protection of children, in the case of José Augusto do Amaral, the "Black Devil," presented below, it would be applied to criminalize race rather than sexual predation.

Gilberto Freyre and the Deheterosexualization of Black and Indigenous Men

National discourses of white male racial and sexual supremacy also carried with them discourses that outwardly emasculated and deheterosexualized men of African and indigenous descent. These discourses were most directly articulated in the work of Gilberto Freyre in the early twentieth century. Freyre most pointedly articulates Brazil's racial and national exceptionalism through sex.

Sander Gilman has argued, "Any attempt to establish that races were inherently different rested to no little extent on the sexual difference of the black."[59] An essential part of constructing white male (sexual) supremacy and difference in Freyre's work was constructing historical, racial, and sexual discourses around the relationship between black, indigenous, and white men. Accordingly, most notably in *The Masters and the Slaves* and *The Mansions and the Shanties*, Freyre describes at great length the construction and evolution of white, black, and indigenous masculinities under Brazilian slavery through sex and sexuality.

Freyre employs heterosexuality and homosexuality to describe racial difference. Homosexuality and its racialization became a framework for historicizing the power dynamics and sexual relationship between black, indigenous, and white men under slavery and colonial society. The connection between the penetrator and the penetrability of enslaved bodies, domination, and submission under slavery and Portuguese colonialism frames the heterosexual supremacy of white men and the effeminate, passive homosexuality of black and indigenous men in relation to them. Freyre construes white male heterosexuality as the only national heterosexuality, and black and indigenous men as the consummate male other and inferior in Brazilian history.

Freyre's depiction of the nation's black and indigenous men in his early works written in the twentieth century is notably influenced by turn-of-the-century studies of homosexuality. As Zita Nunes has argued in her analysis of Freyre's work, in his descriptions of black and indigenous men he "goes to great length to prove their disinterest in women and their inability to be productive as fathers."[60] Freyre's national miscegenation narrative between white men and black and Amerindian women is dependent on a narrative of racialized male homosexuality. Literary critic Idelber Avelar points out that Freyre's interpretation of the Brazilian nation is both "sexual" and "presumably heterosexual," but also undeniably "haunted by homosexuality."[61] Freyre uses homosexuality to historicize black, mulatto, and indigenous men's participation, or lack thereof, in the nation's miscegenation narrative. In many instances, he openly uses the terms *bisexual/ity, effeminate, invert, pederasty,* and *homosexual* in both *The Masters and the Slaves* and *The Mansions and the Shanties* to describe the nation's black and indigenous men, their relationship to women of their race, and especially the difference between black and indigenous men and white men, and black and indigenous men's relationship to white men. Freyre also contributes to the literature on homosexuality by historicizing the nation's black and indigenous men through the lens of homosexuality, and in doing so, contributes to the pathological conflation of nonwhite men and homosexuality.

Freyre's work in the twentieth century came at a time when studies of homosexuality and eugenics were being conducted throughout Brazil and the nation was still heavily invested in asserting its "active masculinity." His historical project was both a continuation of and a deviation from the hygienists. It countered the pessimism of the hygienists, who lamented the nation's effeminacy and loss of male potency, by showing them that the hyperheterosexual virility that they so much desired for the nation was already an essential part of Brazilian history and the national character, as proven by miscegenation between white men and black and indigenous women. Freyre converted Brazil's interracial sexual history into a source of pride by sanitizing the history of rape and sexual violence and turning it into a story of intimacy between the races and proof of white male sexual prowess.

Needell has suggested that in writing *The Masters and the Slaves* and *The Mansions and the Shanties* Freyre's hyperheterosexual narrative of the nation may have been much more personal than historical in that he may have been working out anxieties around his own ambiguous heterosexuality and long-standing sexual desire for mulatto women that he experienced as an adolescent.[62] In 1980 Freyre, then eighty years old, granted an interview that was published in the Brazilian edition of *Playboy* to journalist Ricardo Noblat, in which he openly discussed his life, work, and personal experiences. After recounting losing his virginity at age fifteen to a domestic servant, he says that he never had homosexual experiences during his childhood and remarks that this perhaps led him to do so later on in his twenties while traveling in Europe:

> FREYRE: Well, you can imagine someone like me who is interested in everything pertaining to the human experience, I was curious to see what nonheterosexual love was like. I had a few unpleasurable homosexual adventures....
>
> PLAYBOY: Where did they happen?
>
> FREYRE: In Europe. But they were causal, unpleasurable experiences. Because none of them turned me into a homosexual. If they had been pleasurable, I probably would have said, homosexuality is the greatest sexual experience![63]

Here we note that Freyre's admission that he engaged in homosexual sex is tempered by strong denials that he enjoyed it.

In *The Masters and the Slaves* Freyre attempts to disprove the stereotype, commonly asserted throughout Brazilian slavery and throughout the Americas, that black men were hypersexual and had uncontrollable sex drives. He makes his point by desexualizing them, arguing that they have abnormally low sex drives and that they need "constant excitation and sharp stimuli. Aphrodisiac dances. A phallic cult. Orgies." Moreover, the "orgiastic character of their festivals create[s] the illusion of an unbridled eroticism."[64] He makes similar claims about Amerindian men: "The sexual impulse in the American savage was relatively weak. At least in the man—the more sedentary and regular life of the woman endowing her with a sexuality superior to that of the male, to so disproportionate a degree as will perhaps explain the [constant arousal] of many women toward white men."[65] The message is clear: only white men can sexually satisfy their women. This centers white male desirability, naturalizes the attraction and eventual sexual contact between white men and indigenous women, and frames it as logically consensual.

In *The Mansion and the Shanties*, Freyre continues his thesis, arguing that black men are like women in their manner. Their resistance to white men is always "mellifluous" and they defend themselves against dominant white men "subtly and effeminately."[66] Black men possess a "set of exclusively sweet and graceful qualities that one would suppose resulted, absolutely, from the [female sex]." These qualities found in women "were like the same set of passive and inferior traits of black men, which were equally attributed to them—under the patriarchal slave regime and even today—on a physical and biological basis of the [black] race."[67]

For Freyre, historically, the indigenous man was effeminate and often bisexual or homosexual. Freyre informs his readers that "among the Amerindians, pederasty was not practiced because the men were deprived of women or because women were scarce," but because they enjoyed it.[68] Moreover, the indigenous man "prefers the regular and domestic life of the woman to that of movement and warfare which the man leads." Drawing directly from studies of homosexuality Freyre notes specifically that indigenous healers were always either homosexuals or of the "effeminate and invert type." This tendency was either "congenital or an acquired perversion."[69]

In contrast, the hypersexuality that was commonly ascribed to black men in other American slave societies Freyre attributes to white men, whose "sexual appetite is ordinarily excited without great provocation. Without effort."[70] White masters were alpha males, voracious, active penetrators, penetrating animals, fruits, and black, white, and indigenous women and men, all to satisfy their insatiable sexual appetites. Alluding to "scientific terms," Freyre states that like domesticated animals, white men's "sexual system is found to be more highly developed" than that of black men, whom he likens to "wild animals." Because white men did not have to work, their "reproductive glands absorb a major quantity of nourishment." With their ultranourished reproductive glands and leisure time they inevitably had more time to think about sex—a "greater preoccupation with sexual matters, a greater degree of erotic mania, and more amorous refinements" compared to black men, whose sexual energies were spent in labor.[71]

According to Freyre, men of African descent were too lazy to have sex with black women and they had a hard time achieving and sustaining erections, relying on erotic dances and orgiastic practices to arrive at "a state of excitation and erection such as is readily accomplished by the civilized." White men,

Freyre states, are "always ready for coitus," whereas "savages practice it only when pricked by sexual hunger."[72] The white slave master was so preoccupied with sex that according to Freyre his body became "little more" than a walking "membrum virile" (male member).[73] It was not unusual, Freyre remarks, to walk through the plantation and encounter a "squeaking hammock, with the master copulating in it."[74]

Freyre reproduces the active/passive, penetrator/penetrated dyad between white and black men. The inherently passive nature of black and indigenous men is in direct contrast to white men's hyperactive nature—a not-so-veiled allusion to the conflation of homosexuality and passivity made in the medical studies on homosexuality. Freyre argues that although white masters typically possessed smaller bodies than black men, their small frame did not account for their large and "arrogantly virile" penises,[75] in contrast to black men, "for so many of those enormous [black] giants had the penis of a small boy."[76] He states that masters had to thoroughly inspect black slaves' penises before buying them because so many of them were "underdeveloped or ill-shaped," such that they would "prove bad procreators" and not able to perform sexually and reproduce slaves.[77] Freyre also lets us know that almost all indigenous men had small penises and, as a result of this, practiced a number of different methods to make them larger—proof of the "necessity that the natives felt of making up for a physical or psychic deficiency with regard to the generative function."[78] In fact he asserts confidently that it is "indeed a known fact that among primitive peoples the sexual organs are generally less developed than among the civilized [white men]."[79] Thus civilization is conflated with large penises, high sex drives, and racial and sexual supremacy. The overall inferiority and primitive nature of black and indigenous men are evidenced in their small penises, impotence, and homosexual tendencies.

Freyre also distinguishes black men from mulattos, considering the latter to be counterfeit white men both sexually and in terms of intelligence. The mulatto is a boy in contrast to the white man. In the following passage, Freyre makes us aware of the effeminate, lustful, homosexual fawning of mulattos toward white men:

> The mulatto's eagerness to please [white men], it is true, reaches the limits of *molície*—certain girlish tenderness, certain gestures of sweetness, gestures almost of a woman pleasing a man, when around the socially dominant white male. Something resembling the adolescent in the presence of the socially and sexually mature man, the complete and triumphant man whom the adolescent, intimately, seeks to surpass; whom the ado-

lescent imitates, exaggerating his adult characteristics—the thick voice, the strength, the intellectual and physical superiority; and in whose proximity he endeavors and strains to flatter and stroke in praise, in desiring intimacy. Socially incomplete, the mulatto seeks to complete himself through that sweet, oleaginous, and somewhat feminine effort.[80]

Here Freyre employs homosexuality and its period conflation with effeminacy to describe the way the mulatto attempts to socially ingratiate himself and gain the acceptance of white men. The mulatto, in Freyre's view, eroticizes, fetishizes, and covets the white man's social power and sexuality, regarding him with both envy and sexual desire. Freyre uses the term *molície* to describe the mulatto's interaction with white men. *Molície* was used during the Inquisition to refer to nonpenetrative sexual acts between men, such as oral sex and masturbation. Here, it means effeminate, delicate, and having homosexual tendencies in relation to the socially, sexually, and intellectually dominant heterosexual white man. This "intimacy" that Freyre claims the mulatto covets is a desire to both be that which he is not—white and male—and to be sexually intimate with the white man.

The white man is the father that the mulatto adolescent attempts to emulate, the embodiment of everything he wishes to be, but inevitably the mulatto falls short. Freyre uses the historical narrative of social illegitimacy attached to the mulatto to illustrate the mulatto's inferiority to white men. The mulatto will always be the bastard son, never to be accepted by nor equal to the white father. Freyre consistently describes black and mulatto men as boys, with small penises and prepubescent sex drives. As Zita Nunes has remarked, they are "so desexualized in Freyre's work as to be barely capable of engendering children."[81] Freyre's writing coincides with the belief of the late nineteenth and early twentieth century that mulattos were sterile and could not reproduce.

In his footnotes, to provide evidence of the homosexuality of indigenous men, Freyre draws attention to the number of indigenous men brought before the Inquisition for sodomy, but neglects to mention that white men predominated in these cases. He reports that during the Inquisition indigenous men confessed to engaging in sodomy "with so much candor" that for them it was "nothing more than a peccadillo [a minor sin]." He lets us know that this caused the Portuguese to quickly identify indigenous men "with the practice of pederasty, a practice that to Christians was so abominable a one."[82] He cites a case involving an indigenous man by the name of Acahuy and an older white man named Balthazar da Lomba denounced in Pernambuco for sodomy. Freyre's choice of this particular case is of interest, as it brings his central thesis into question. His focus is on proving the homosexuality of indigenous men, but the denunciation was brought against Balthazar da Lomba, an unmarried white man whom the documents describe effeminately as a man "fifty years of age and who regularly sewed, wove, and kneaded bread like a woman." He was accused of being penetrated by several indigenous and black men. According to testimony, "three or four years ago, a slave woman saw Balthazar with a black man, being penetrated on the grass outside the house." Another denouncer testified that "in the dark, he placed his ear on an opening in the door, and heard in Balthazar's room an indigenous man by the name of Acahuy, age 20, and saw that they were both in a hammock and felt it rocking and the two of them moaning as if they were engaged in the nefarious act; he also heard the Indian say some words in his language to Balthazar, that meant 'Do you want some more?'"[83]

Freyre cites this particular case as evidence of indigenous homosexuality and neglects to consider the involvement of the white male who was caught being penetrated. The documents and testimony describe Balthazar da Lomba with the same pejorative stereotypes of effeminacy and sexual passivity that according to Freyre are inherent to indigenous men. Historian Luiz Mott, in his research on male sodomy during the Portuguese Inquisition in Brazil, found only three documented cases of indigenous men reported for sodomy, two serving as active and the other as passive, in contrast to six times the number of white men.[84]

Freyre's contribution to the historicization of race and homosexuality is that, writing in the twentieth century amid the proliferation of studies of homosexuality, he analyzes the same-sex sexual practices during slavery and the colonial period that we have examined previously through the lens of pathological views of homosexuality prevalent at the time. By emphasizing his effeminacy and especially his passivity, the man of color is neatly placed in the contemporary pathological prototype of the homosexual, which is but a logical historical evolution.

Postabolition Penis Envy

Freyre's constant discussion of men's penises is by no means accidental. We could read this as a bizarre scholarly sexual competition between white, black, and indigenous men, but Freyre's emasculation and homosexualization of black and indigenous men evinces what could be called, after Freud, postabolition penis envy.

Freud's theories of penis envy and female sexuality, like Freyre's narrative of nation, are inherently phallocentric. The first articulation of this concept appears in Freud's 1908 essay *On the Sexual Theories of Children* and subsequently in his 1913 *Observations and Analyses Drawn from Analytical Practice,* twenty years before the publication of *The Masters and the Slaves.* In Freyre's work black and indigenous men function as subaltern male figures in terms of race, gender, and sexuality, which leads Freyre to emphasize their effeminacy and homosexuality in relation to white men. Freud argued that when girls realize that boys have penises, they immediately begin to compare their own genitalia to the penis and arrive at the conclusion that the vagina is inferior. Freud does not mean that the female child would prefer to be a boy, only that she wishes to possess the male organ itself. As a result of this comparison, females are left perpetually with "penis envy."[85] According to Freud, the penis-envy stage begins the transition from attachment to the mother to competition with the mother for the attention of the father.[86] It is important to underscore that this void, or envy, that women feel in relation to their genitalia is permanent, along with their subsequent feelings of inferiority and inadequacy.

This concept, though gender specific and highly problematic in myriad ways, provides critical insight into how Freyre conceives of white male supremacy in the phallic and racial senses. Freyre's emphasis on penis size—the large penis size and hypervirility of white men, and the small penises and effeminate passivity (almost like women) of black and indigenous men—sets up this contrast between male and female genitalia found in Freud's theory of penis envy. In Freud, the desire for what the woman will never possess—the penis that is the source of her inferiority—is equally important. With this feeling of inferiority comes desire for the father and competition with the mother for his affection. This is also the case in Freyre's work with black and indigenous men, who have feelings of inferiority and envy but also homosexual desire for white men, and are drawn into competition with women of their own race for white men's attention.

Even though Freud is referring specifically to women, we can apply his theory to Freyre in the sense that Freyre places this penis envy in a racialized same-sex context in which homosexuality is used to feminize the nation's black and indigenous men and to symbolically castrate them, thereby rendering their relationship to white men as one of desire, envy, and racial and physical inferiority, which, as Freud argues, is never entirely resolved by the individual.

To establish the difference between white men and black and indigenous men as well as construct them as inherently inferior to white men, Freyre diminished their penis size and undermined their physical relationship not only to women of their own race but to all women. Postabolition racial and sexual anxieties are worked out on the genital level.

Frantz Fanon tells us that for the black male, "everything takes place at the genital level," and "not only must the black man be black; he must be black in relation to the white man."[87] This is key to understanding Freyre's historicization of white, black, and indigenous masculinities under slavery. As with the nation in the twentieth century, Freyre sets up this necessary antithetical relationship between men to bolster white male supremacy. Taking Fanon's assertion into account, in the context of slavery and after abolition, black men and black masculinity cannot exist independently but must also maintain a relational and antithetical relationship to white men and to white masculinity. As postemancipation Brazil was defining what it was by defining what it was not, Freyre in essence did the same thing in the sexual narrative of nation, defining white men and white masculinity as the antithesis of black and indigenous men. Yet without black and indigenous men, white men could not exist, as they add a necessary counterpoint.

Applying the theory of penis envy in the postabolition context, here the white man becomes the object both racially and physically that black and indigenous men will always envy but never equal. In the United States, thousands of black men were lynched and castrated during slavery and throughout the twentieth century. In both contexts—the actual physical castration of the black man in the United States and the historical castration of the man of color in Freyre's work—the aim is the same: nonwhite (hetero)sexuality and generative capabilities become threats to white male supremacy in the past and the present in which Freyre is writing, and must be dealt with at the genital level. This castration in discourse works toward the same goal of erasing black and indigenous men from the miscegenation narrative.

Fanon draws connections between racism, or what he termed "negrophobia," sexual desire, and homosexuality. "Still on the genital level," he writes, "when a white man hates black men, is he not yielding to a feeling of impotence or of sexual inferiority? Since his ideal is an infinite virility, is there not a phenomenon of diminution in relation to the Negro, who is viewed as a penis symbol?"[88] Like many white men in the United States in the era, Freyre notably abhors the idea of black men having sex with white women despite its existence throughout Brazilian history. As Zita Nunes points out, for Freyre in *The Masters and the Slaves*, the "idea that white women could bear miscegenated children is so threatening, however, that he rejects it as preposterous, as so much unfounded and malicious gossip."[89]

Could we also consider Freyre's castration of black and indigenous men and his insistence on their effeminacy and lack of virility—when he does not outwardly suggest that they are homosexuals or bisexuals—a way of working through the history of male rape and same-sex sexual relations under slavery? If we recall his description of the sexual initiation of the master's son, we can see how he develops white male racial and sexual supremacy and the passivity of black and indigenous men from childhood.

Freyre's phallic narratives of nation and white male racial and sexual supremacy are constructed through the impenetrability of the white male body and the hyperpenetrability, submission, and passivity of the nation's subaltern bodies: Brazil's women—white, indigenous, black, and mulatto—and indigenous, black, and mulatto men. By endowing black, mulatto, and indigenous men with small penises, low sex drives, and difficulty achieving erections, and rendering their sexuality nongenerative, Freyre is able to thwart their reproductive capabilities and castrate them metaphorically. As such, black and indigenous men are no longer a threat to Brazilian women and would not obstruct Brazil's whitening efforts, as they would not reproduce nonwhite children.

In this way Freyre displaces the nation's black and indigenous men from the realm of heteronormativity as their inherent defects confine them to nongenerative sexuality. In order for the white man to be the father of the nation and have control over the nation's procreation, both in the past and the present, during attempts to whiten the country and erase the black race through European immigration, the man of color must be prevented from procreating and constructed as homosexual.

Brazilian Naturalism and Homosexuality

The Brazilian hygiene movement coincided with the arrival of the naturalist movement in literature, and both trends produced portrayals of homosexuality. Unlike romanticism, which created highly symbolic and idealized depictions of Brazilian society, naturalists found their subject matter in the darker side of day-to-day life and in the men and women of the demimonde. The naturalists and the literature they produced were heavily influenced by Charles Darwin's theory of evolution. They believed that people were determined by the forces of heredity, history, the environment, and the time in which they lived. The will of the individual could not resist the pull of these forces. Brazilian naturalism is distinguished by its pronounced focus on the physical body and sexuality. For the naturalist, physical desire was the result of environment, social conditions, and biology. As Sônia Breyner observes, the body in naturalist literature comes to stand as a metaphor for Brazilian history and society.[90]

Naturalist literature was particularly invested in situating the body and physical desire in relation to the nation's social problems. It was heavily influenced by the medical discourse of the period, and the doctor-novelist, best exemplified in Júlio Ribeiro's novel *A carne* (The Flesh, 1888), emerges at this time. The contact of the main character, Lenita, with the degeneracies of slave life on a Brazilian plantation leads her to a sexual awakening that ultimately causes her fall from grace when she engages in premarital sex and bears a child out of wedlock. Authors such as Ribeiro employed literature to realistically represent medical theories of contagion and degeneracy. Naturalist literature did not merely function as a form of artistic expression but aimed to serve public health.

Both medical discourse and naturalist literature often described cases that doctors reported about their patients, differing only in that naturalist novels were about fictional characters. Authors and doctors depicted homosexuals and lesbians' lives as always complicated, and their behaviors as immoral and decadent, ultimately ending in tragedy. For the naturalist deeply invested in promoting bourgeois notions of normality, the message was clear: wayward lives end badly, and as Carlos Figari observes, "The framework is closed, there is no other way to live than the 'correct' way."[91]

The literary narratives produced during this period in the spirit of national progress, like the medical literature, attempted to diagnose and cure perversities. In exploring these questions, naturalist literature performed a national diagnostic as well. The body and its deviant conflicting desires and behaviors became a terrain of literary and scientific inquiry. Amid the influence of social Darwinism, these narratives tended to describe reality not necessarily as it was, but rather presented an idealized version of how they wished it to be. As Richard Miskolci shows, period intellectuals and politicians put forth theories that aided them in "diagnosing their present reality in a negative light under the imperialist vision of the world, which inevitably led them to develop prescriptive analyses of what Brazil *should be*."[92] In the work of the naturalist writers and medical studies, homosexuality comes to represent the synthesis of interlocking questions of national sexuality in which racial prejudice and homophobia work in tandem under the banner of national progress and public health.

Bom-Crioulo: Brazil's First "Black Homosexual" Novel

Adolfo Caminha's 1895 novel *Bom-Crioulo* (The Black Man and the Cabin Boy), a product of Brazilian naturalism, was the first novel in Latin America to overtly depict homosexuality—in this case between a former slave and an adolescent white boy—and was the first Brazilian novel to have a black man as the lead protagonist.

Adolfo Caminha, born in the northeastern state of Ceará in 1867, had a short, scandalous, and tragic life. He was orphaned at an early age and was taken to Rio de Janeiro by an uncle, who enrolled him in the naval academy. He became a midshipman and traveled to the Caribbean and the United States. Returning to Ceará in 1887 as a second lieutenant, he engrossed himself in the intellectual and political life of the state and a year later embarked on an ardent love affair with Isabel Jutaí de Paula Barros, the wife of an army officer who ended up leaving her husband for Caminha. The ensuing scandal led to his resignation from the navy. He returned to Rio de Janeiro in 1892 with his paramour and worked as a low-level clerk to support his literary career. He died of tuberculosis in 1897, at the age of twenty-nine.

Bom-Crioulo is a complex novel that explores the connections between race, homosexuality, and postcoloniality in late nineteenth-century Brazil. It tells the story of Amaro, a black slave who escapes from a Brazilian plantation in search of freedom. He enlists as a sailor in the navy, where he later receives the name Bom-Crioulo (Good Negro). While stationed in southern Brazil he takes a liking to a fifteen-year-old white ship boy, Aleixo. Bom-Crioulo later seduces Aleixo after taking a flogging on his behalf. When the ship arrives in Rio de Janeiro, Bom-Crioulo rents a room in a boarding house belonging to his long-time friend Dona Carolina, a Portuguese washerwoman and prostitute. Here Bom-Crioulo and Aleixo spend their time on shore. Their relationship comes to a halt when Bom-Crioulo is transferred to another ship. Left alone in the boarding house, Aleixo comes to resent his previous sexual relationship with Bom-Crioulo and soon falls prey to the seductions of Carolina and starts a sexual relationship with her. Bom-Crioulo learns of the relationship and, enraged, sets out to exact his revenge on Aleixo. He encounters Aleixo on a crowded street, seizes him, and slashes his throat with a razor. The novel culminates with Bom-Crioulo being taken away by the police while a crowd feverishly gathers to see Aleixo's corpse.

This novel, like most Brazilian naturalist works, belonged to a strand of literature that was referred to at the time as *literatura para homens* (literature for men), which was marketed primarily to a literate elite white male readership. These novels in many cases bordered on, and in some cases were, pornography. Replete with scandalous sex scenes and no shortage of detail, these novels delved into every imaginable taboo: adultery, incest, male and female homosexuality, masturbation, voyeurism, and prostitution. These books, as literary critic Alessandra El Far points out, sold the most copies toward the end of slavery in the late nineteenth century and the beginning of the twentieth century, especially in major city centers such as Rio de Janeiro.[93] Caminha was well aware that literatura para homens was what sold the most copies, and he wrote a novel that fully embodied the genre. However, to his chagrin, *Bom-Crioulo* was received pugnaciously by his elite white male readership, who were used to reading more favorable portraits of themselves. Caminha's explicit depictions of homosexuality, particularly between a former slave and a white adolescent, scandalized readers and gave rise to a great deal of speculation regarding the author's sexuality.

But more than the depiction of homosexuality, in the wake of emancipation, white male readers were most enraged by the fact that Caminha had dared to write a novel in which a white man was depicted effeminately and as sexually passive to a former slave. Indeed, Caminha did not write favorably of white men, in whom Brazilians had "deposited their future hopes of the nation."[94] Published only seven years after the abolition of slavery, the novel emerged just as Brazil was grappling with the reality of black freedom while attempting to solidify white male supremacy. Given the importance of promoting white male heterosexuality, sexual dominance, and virility, readers were disturbed by the potential political meanings of these homosexual images, perceiving them as a sinister omen of national destruction.

Valentim Magalhães, founder of the Brazilian Academy of Letters and one of the foremost literary critics of the time, wrote a scathing review in the newspaper *A Notícia* in November 1895 fervently condemning the novel:

> Well *Bom-Crioulo* exceeds everything that one can imagine in the way of gross filth. . . . It is not a mischievous, cheerful, playful book, recounting bedroom or brothel scenes, or lovers' frolics among the grass, blessed by the good Lord, as in [Émile Zola's novel] *Germinal* . . . none of that. It is a foul book, because it explores—the first to do so as far as I know—a branch of pornography which has so far been unpublished because it was unmentionable, against nature and ignoble. It is not just a spicy book: it is a rotten book; it is a sick novel, a dung-novel, a pus-novel. . . . This young man is unaware of what he is doing, either through literary obsession or moral perversion. Only thus can one explain the fact that he could find such a subject literary and think that the story of the bestial vices of an uncouth Negro sailor could be interesting literature.[95]

Magalhães ended his review by informing his readers that after reading *Bom-Crioulo* he was so repulsed that he threw it in the trash. Noted literary critic José Veríssimo was equally disgusted by the novel and declared that it appeared to him to be more autobiographical than fictional or literary: "Mr. Caminha . . . was a ship boy just like his little blonde boy Aleixo. . . . How does Mr. Adolfo

Caminha expect a man to be respected and esteemed if, without any social utility, he has spent long days analyzing and discussing the unlikely psychology of nauseating crimes against nature and afterwards trying to awaken in us a shudder of impure and morbid curiosity?"[96] Despite the harsh reactions of its critics, *Bom-Crioulo* sold a significant number of copies and was considered a best seller. The incendiary reactions to the novel, however, provoked Caminha to write a response to his critics a year later. In "Um livro condenado" (A Condemned Book), which appeared in the literary magazine *A Nova Revista*, he attacked the hypocrisy of Rio de Janeiro intellectuals who lauded the writings of European naturalist novelists such as Gustave Flaubert, Guy de Maupassant, Eça de Queiroz, and Émile Zola, whose novels depicted instances of moral depravity, adultery, incest, and prostitution, yet they condemned *Bom-Crioulo*. Caminha asked, "Which is more pernicious: *Bom-Crioulo*, in which homosexuality is studied and condemned, or those pages which are in circulation preaching in a philosophical tone the break-up of the family, concubinage, free love, and all sorts of social immorality?"[97] Though not a medical doctor, Caminha appears to have been fairly well versed in period studies on homosexuality, and he argued that *Bom-Crioulo*, more than a fictional account or a figment of his perverse imagination, was an accurate medical case study detailing the tragic realities and devastating effects of the "sexual inversion" of a degenerate black man, confirmed in the works of some of the most prominent European sexologists of the period. Caminha added that while in the navy he had personally witnessed several of the events described in the novel. He asked his critics, "After all, what is *Bom-Crioulo*? Nothing more than a case of sexual inversion studied in Krafft-Ebing, Moll, and in Tardieu and in the books of legal medicine. A crude sailor, of slave origin, uneducated, without any sense of sociability, in a fatal moment obeys the homosexual tendencies of his organism and practices a vile act: he is an innate degenerate, an irresponsible man proven by the lowly acts he commits such as murdering his friend; he is a victim of his instincts."[98]

Although most criticism of *Bom-Crioulo* has traditionally tended to focus on the novel's overt depiction of homosexuality, a more important question is why Caminha wrote a novel about homosexuality between, specifically, an ex-slave and a fifteen-year-old white boy, and the meaning of their story in relation to Brazil's history of male rape during slavery and the national preoccupation with white male heterosexuality. Caminha, in other words, like the medical doctors of the period, was attempting to prove a scientific thesis through literature, and considering his choice of characters is essential to understanding his overall project. Caminha could easily have written a novel about two white homosexuals, but rather interestingly chose a former black male slave in his thirties and a virginal adolescent white boy. With this choice, Caminha created an "innate degenerate" who was black, homosexual, and mentally ill, a danger to himself and highly contagious to the white man and to society at large.

Bom-Crioulo engages in what is now termed the "grooming" of young victims by pedophiles, acting as a father figure to Aleixo, protecting him, and slowly gaining his confidence. Aleixo soon submits to him sexually, giving him what Bom-Crioulo refers to as the "greatest proof of friendship of all . . . sleeping under the same blanket in the prow of the corvette, in each other's arms, like a pair of newly-weds in the throes of passion of their first coupling"[99]

As Caminha explained in response to the haranguing of his critics, the novel was greatly influenced by late nineteenth-century medical literature on homosexuality, and perhaps to show off his knowledge, he sprinkles the symptoms described in these studies throughout the text to medically confirm Bom-Crioulo's homosexuality. He writes of Bom-Crioulo, "It had been hard enough as it was for him to remain a virgin till the age of thirty, enduring embarrassments that no one would believe, and being obliged often to commit excesses which medical science condemns" (63). In accordance with period medical studies, Caminha lets us know that until he had sex with Aleixo, Bom-Crioulo frequently masturbated, further proof of his homosexuality.

Caminha informs the reader that Bom-Crioulo was a failed heterosexual, as women "left him impotent for the act of love" (62). When he was twenty years old he was "unexpectedly forced to sleep with a girl in Angra dos Reis," and "his performance as a man on that occasion had, incidentally, left a great deal to be desired." He attempted to have sex with a French prostitute and again ended up being "quite ashamed of himself" and swore "never again to have anything to do with 'those things'" (49). Caminha's descriptions of Bom-Crioulo's poor sexual performance with both a woman of his own race and a white woman would seem to corroborate Freyre's claims decades later about the sexual insufficiency of men of African descent. Looking at this literary account in relation to Freyre, we can see a genealogy of postabolition rhetoric surrounding the deheterosexualization of black men.

Interestingly, although Bom-Crioulo had sex with two women in his twenties, he considers that he only lost his virginity at the age of thirty, when he has sex with Aleixo, making Bom-Crioulo even more of an anomaly. Beyond medicine, however, Caminha's view of Bom-Crioulo's homosexuality is a fusion of the medical and the religious. Caminha, like the inquisitors, employs the religious view of blacks as inherently sinful and morally predisposed to unnatural vices such as sodomy to affirm the connection between blackness and homosexuality. Bom-Crioulo's homosexuality, as Caminha writes, was "a punishment for his sins, no doubt" and it was "nature herself who was imposing this punishment on him" (64). Even though Caminha admits throughout the novel that white men engaged in homosexuality, he claims that black men "were even more likely to!" (64).

Caminha attempts to make a distinction between sodomy and homosexuality through race. Bom-Crioulo's homosexuality is an inborn degeneracy that he cannot understand or resist. Because of his innate sickness he desires "vulgar intercourse"; he initiates it, and he does not regret it. In contrast, Aleixo, the virginal adolescent white boy, is a victim of the black male's uncontrollable homosexual impulses.

Consistent with the medical literature, Caminha sets off a difference between curable and incurable homosexuality, now based on race. Here the white man, Aleixo, although succumbing under pressure to the black man, never expresses any homosexual desire and ultimately proves his heterosexuality with women. The black man, Bom-Crioulo, persists with his homosexual desire until his innate depravity leads him to murder his victim. For Bom-Crioulo, there is no cure or salvation.

As with blacks in period medical studies, this first novel to have a black man as the leading protagonist also serves as the face of homosexuality. *Bom-Crioulo* warns white Brazilians about the connection between blackness and homosexuality and their dangers for white men and the nation. Here again we see whites' anxieties that they could be subjugated by blacks, as in this scene in which Bom-Crioulo creates a virtual prison for Aleixo as his sexual slave in their boardinghouse room:

> Only one thing vexed the cabin-boy—the black man's sexual whims. Because Bom-Crioulo was not satisfied merely with possessing him sexually at any hour of the day or night. He wanted much more; he obliged the boy to go to extremes, he made a slave, a whore of him, suggesting to him that they perform every extravagant act that came into his mind. The very first night he wanted Aleixo to strip, to strip right down to the buff: he wanted to see his body. Aleixo replied sulkily that that wasn't something you asked a man to do! Anything but *that*. But the black man insisted. . . . And the boy, obedient and afraid, slowly unbuttoned his flannel shirt and then his trousers. He was standing, and he placed his clothes on the bed, item by item. Bom-Crioulo's desire was satisfied. Aleixo appeared before him now in full, exuberant nudity, his skin very white, and his curvaceous buttocks standing out in the voluptuous semi-darkness of the room. . . . Bom-Crioulo was in ecstasy! . . . He had never seen such a

beautifully rounded male body, such arms, such firm, fleshy hips. With breasts, Aleixo would be a real woman! . . . "That's enough!" implored Aleixo. "No, no! just a little bit longer." Bom-Crioulo took up the candle, trembling, and, coming closer, continued his detailed examination of the cabin-boy, feeling his flesh, praising the perfume of his skin, at the peak of lustfulness, at the extremity of desire, his eyes darting sparks of pleasure. "That's all!" said Aleixo suddenly, impatient by now, and blew out the candle. There followed then, in the darkness, a slight skirmish of whispered words and groans. And when Bom-Crioulo, once more triumphant, lit a match, he could hardly stand on his own two feet. These were the "vexations" that Aleixo had to bear. (75–76)

Bom-Crioulo, to the horror of readers, emasculates, feminizes, and sexually humiliates Aleixo for his pleasure. This scene could also be read as a reversal and dramatization of the history of male rape and sexual violence against enslaved men. Aleixo's humiliation appears to intensify Bom-Crioulo's desire, suggesting racial revenge and also the sadism that doctors such as Viveiros de Castro attached to male homosexuality.

As the novel progresses, Aleixo unabashedly discloses that he is repulsed by Bom-Crioulo, by "having to put up with his whims, his nigger smell, his bullish instincts." Moreover, "He had ended up despising the black man, almost hating him, full of aversion, full of disgust for that animal in the form of a man, who said he was his friend in order to enjoy him sexually" (103). Their encounters are always characterized by coercion, violence, and fear, blurring the line between rape and consensual sex. In fact most homosexual scenes in late nineteenth- and early twentieth-century Brazilian literature carry strong connotations of rape or coercion, which are used to illustrate the unnaturalness of homosexuality, its inherently perverse and pathological nature, and its tragic effects. In this period there is almost always a direct connection to prostitution to illustrate the racial and class conflations of homosexuality as well as its violence, unnaturalness, and pathology. Bom-Crioulo, as a perverse ex-slave predator, is intent upon corrupting and destroying an innocent white boy representing the Brazilian nation, confirming doctors' fears about the effeminization of its men.

Homosexuality in period literature (medical and fiction) was described in many instances in the same fashion as STDs. Homosexuality, as Viveiros de Castro affirmed, was "always acquired," transmitted through sex.[100] At the same time that doctors were studying both the effects of STDs such as syphilis and the "fatal effects" of homosexuality, abolitionists Joaquim Nabuco and others claimed that the moral depravity of blacks had been transmitted through interracial sex throughout the history of Brazilian slavery. Naturalist and medical literature show that the pleasure and perversion of homosexuality was not just in engaging in homosexual sex but also in corrupting others who were not homosexual through sex. Homosexuality, like blackness, was about getting access to and destroying through sex what blacks were not and what they would never possess.

The metaphor of the relationship between Bom-Crioulo and Aleixo extends beyond the emasculation of Brazilian white men to the place of Brazil in the world. In order for Brazil to assert itself as a nation and avoid being dominated by Europe and the Americas, it needed to define itself as dominant and heterosexual. The grave dangers to Brazil of black homosexuals are driven home in the final scene of the book, in which Bom-Crioulo violently exacts his revenge. At the very moment when Aleixo attempts to assert his heterosexuality, he is savagely murdered. *Bom-Crioulo* is not an interracial homosexual love story gone wrong but a cautionary tale for the nation to open its eyes to what José de Alencar called *o demônio familiar*, a demon that is both familiar and a threat to the Brazilian family. Historical proof of the torture and rape of slave men was cast aside as these men took on the roles of homosexuals, rapists, pedophiles, and murderers bent on destroying the nation and its hopes of progress embodied in the heterosexual white male.

O Diabo Preto (The Negro Devil)

The themes of disease, anxiety, and domination found their perfect expression in the fabricated image of the black male homosexual, who came to represent all that many white Brazilians hated and feared while deflecting attention away from how they had created the "diseased" social system that was now overwhelming them. Thirty-one years after the publication of *Bom-Crioulo*, the main character of the novel came to life—at least, in the minds of many white Brazilians—in the city of São Paulo in 1926. The case of José Augusto do Amaral, or, as he came to be called in the São Paulo press and media, Preto (Black) Amaral, became infamously known throughout Brazil. To this day Amaral is remembered as Brazil's first serial killer. For many of the nation's citizens, a serial killer was necessarily poor, black, and homosexual.

Amaral was born a slave on a plantation in Conquista, in the state of Minas Gerais in 1871. In 1888, at the age of seventeen, he was freed by the Golden Law that abolished slavery, and he enlisted in the army. After leaving the army he settled in São Paulo, where he lived in virtual poverty, working at odd jobs to survive. Like many poor and homeless Afro-Brazilian men in the cities, he was imprisoned three times on charges of vagrancy. Historians George Reid Andrews and Kim Butler, as well as sociologist Florestan Fernandes, have documented the extreme prejudice that blacks of the time encountered in São Paulo, where they were in the minority.[101] After the abolition of slavery, article 399 of the 1890 penal code was used to imprison jobless, homeless Afro-Brazilians for "failing to exercise an official profession or job to earn a living, or not possessing a means of subsistence and a proper home in which to live."[102]

In a word, Amaral was guilty of the crimes of being black and in extreme poverty. He joined the ranks of thousands of former slaves who left the plantations and migrated to the cities in search of jobs but were unable to find work due to racism thereby becoming destitute. The São Paulo *Gazeta* described Amaral in an article published on June 1, 1927, as a "vagrant, with no profession nor any will to work." As a former slave and a poor person, he was already a criminal in the eyes of the police and society.

In January 1926 the body of a fifteen-year-old white boy was found in the vicinity of the Campo de Marte airport. It was reported to the police that the victim had last been seen in the area in the company of a tall black man. Amaral was among the scores of "tall black men" who were rounded up by the police for questioning and he was pegged as the main suspect. Whites in São Paulo were outraged and called for his lynching. The headlines referred to him as the "Monstro Negro" (Black Monster), "Besta-Fera" (Wild Beast), and "O Diabo Preto" (The Negro Devil).

As reports about Amaral inundated the newspapers, parents of other missing boys came forth and accused him. Ultimately Amaral was charged with three homicides. The medical examiner concluded that the killer had strangled the victims to death with a belt and then engaged in anal intercourse with them.

After his arrest Amaral was given medical and psychiatric evaluations. The doctors noted that he possessed abnormally large genitalia, which was believed to be an indicator of homosexuality and a propensity for sexual crimes. Noted psychiatrist Antônio Carlos Pacheco e Silva, a professor at the Faculty of Medicine at the University of São Paulo, declared in his report:

[Amaral's case] is a matter of, in our opinion, a sadistic criminal and necrophiliac, whose perversion is further complicated by pedophilia, in which the child is the special and exclusive object of his pathological disposition. . . . Amaral fits within the group of sexual perverts characterized by a permanent state of sexual hyperexcitation and who, under the influence of that excitement, which is continuous and lethal, are driven

FIGURE 5.1
José Augusto do Amaral. "Preto Amaral," Museu de Crime São Paulo.

to the act, more or less automatically, without having the ability to think and to judge the act impulsive. The crimes of the sadistic-necrophiliacs are executed with relative calm, with prudence, and by ambush, and the criminal acts as if he were practicing a normal action.[103]

In his deposition Amaral swore his innocence and that he had not previously known any of the victims.[104] However, the police claimed that he had confessed to all of the crimes. Like the fictional character Bom-Crioulo, Amaral had no previous history of sexual crimes, homosexuality, pederasty, or other crimes in his fifty-six years, with the exception of his arrests for vagrancy. Historian Paulo Fernando de Souza Campos has argued that Amaral was tortured and made to confess to crimes that he did not commit.[105] The police never produced any concrete evidence linking Amaral to any of the crimes—their only evidence was the examination of his genitalia and the psychiatric report. While he was in prison several other children went missing in São Paulo. Amaral was never tried, as he died in prison of tuberculosis in 1927.

Though he was never found guilty, Amaral was sufficiently guilty in people's minds that he remains known today as Brazil's first serial killer and his case is displayed in the Museum of Crime in São Paulo in an area designated for sexual criminals. He came to embody a panoply of perversions, pathologies, and crimes that the nation was trying to cure: homosexuality, rape, vagrancy, pedophilia, necrophilia, murder, and sadism. He took his place in a postabolition criminal imaginary that emerged throughout the Americas. Like the invented character of Bom-Crioulo, the true story of Preto Amaral, the Negro Devil, tragically illustrates the conflation of blackness, homosexuality, pathology, and criminality that emerged in Brazil after slavery.

The Elimination of Black Men from Reproduction and the Whitening Project

The criminalization of black homosexuals was intimately related to Brazil's plan to whiten the country by replacing blacks with European immigrant workers. An image was created of emancipated blacks as predatory sexual criminals, which, in addition to their extreme social and economic marginalization, justified incarcerating and institutionalizing Afro-Brazilians, with the ultimate goal of wiping them out.

Postabolition societies across the Americas fabricated black monsters and devils who, once they were no longer under white control, sought to destroy white society. These images illustrate the historical connection between racial domination and sex, from slavery to postemancipation. Criminality became another mechanism of white domination, and through the creation of these images whites were able to control blacks by criminalizing black freedom.

In the United States, the parallel to Brazil's black homicidal pederast was the black male rapist who preyed on white women. The creation of this myth, according to historian Winthrop Jordan, was both an inversion and a projection of the white male/master rapist.[106] Ellen Barret Ligon, a doctor in Mobile, Alabama, in a 1903 article in *Good Housekeeping*, expressed the widespread paranoia of black male lust for white women that plagued the minds of many whites: "The white woman is the coveted desire of the negro man. The despoiling of the white woman is his chosen vengeance. . . . The white woman must be saved."[107] This myth resulted in thousands of false accusations leading to the heinous lynchings, torture, castration, and deaths of black men across the United States.

Whereas in the United States white men were supposedly protecting white supremacy and the nation, as embodied in white women, from black men, Brazil went to great lengths to protect its masculinity and heterosexuality from black men. The invented image of the black homosexual rapist replaced the white master who actually raped enslaved men throughout Brazilian slavery. In Brazil the black homosexual predator was dangerous because of his masculinity and lack of passivity, embodying the postabolition anxiety over the sexual freedom of emancipated slaves. The black homosexual's lack of stereotypical effeminate passivity that whites attributed to homosexuals made him difficult to detect and therefore more dangerous. Many whites feared that active homosexuals like Bom Crioulo and Amaral (though there is no evidence at all that Amaral was a homosexual) would emasculate white men and turn them into effeminate homosexuals.

Laura Moutinho has shown in her research on interracial couples in twentieth-century Brazil that amid discourses of white male racial and sexual supremacy, the high percentage of interracial marriages between black men and white women is evidence that black men were not completely desexualized on a national level.[108] While this perspective is certainly valid, the postabolition myth and fictions of the black male homosexual predator show that this eroticization in relation to the discourses of white male racial and sexual supremacy occurred through the pathological lens of homosexuality. Bom-Crioulo and Preto Amaral are both eroticized, but through pathology: homosexuality, pedophilia, sadism, necrophilia, and rape. Their eroticization shows the danger of their very existence for the nation. Black men and black male sexuality became a problem in postabolition Brazil because they imperiled the future of the nation. Black male reproduction with black or white women would further increase the black population, which the nation was desperately trying to exterminate through European immigration. The deheterosexualization of black men, the elimination of their generative capabilities, was a way of displacing them from the future of the nation. The homosexualization of the black man was a way of erasing him from the generative myth of nation as Brazil sought to whiten itself and assert itself as a white nation. But by the proliferation of this myth, white male heterosexuality was paradoxically placed in peril.

These examples of different sexual perversions—heterosexual, homosexual, necrophiliac, and so on—show that what was significant was not only the nature of the perversion but, more specifically, the image of blacks that was constructed in the white imagination. These stories are intentionally spectacular in order to draw attention to black perversion and criminality, while concealing the equally spectacular but real historical conduct of whites toward blacks. The stories of the black rapist, murderer, homosexual, pedophile, and necrophiliac were merely a turn-of-the century extension of the image of blacks that had existed since the beginning of slavery.[109] Blacks needed to be demonized, whether to enslave them, incarcerate them, or eradicate them, and these myths of the black menace to white society endure in modern Brazil and the United States today.

Seeing the Unseen:
The Life and Afterlives of Ch/Xica da Silva

Throughout this book we have explored aspects of Brazilian slavery that have been silenced, misnamed, and concealed. In the last pages, drawing from the biography and modern-day visual representations of the life of eighteenth-century slave woman Chica da Silva, we will examine how her life story has been used as a conduit to create visual archives in the contemporary rendering of Brazil's histories of miscegenation and same-sex sexual violence. We will explore more specifically how the contemporary visual narratives of film and the telenovela, or soap opera, create new archives rooted in the old and continue to reinforce the exceptionality of Brazilian slavery, sanitize the country's history of sexual violence, and bolster the myth of racial democracy.

Chica da Silva: The Woman

Chica da Silva was born Francisca da Silva da Oliveira between 1731 and 1735 in the region of Minas Gerais. She was a product of miscegenation. Her father was a white man named Antônio Caetano de Sá, and her mother, María da Silva, was his slave born in Africa. From childhood to adolescence Chica had a number of different masters; she bore her first child, Simão, with her second master, Manuel Pires Sardinha, in 1751. As is the case with the details surrounding her own birth, the historical record cannot confirm whether these children were the product of rape or sexual abuse. Chica eventually began a relationship with one of the wealthiest men in colonial Brazil, a white Portuguese diamond-mine owner, João Fernandes de Oliveira. Through her relationship with Fernandes, Chica was able to obtain a measure of social mobility at that time and was even manumitted by Fernandes. She lived as his concubine for fifteen years and gave birth to thirteen children, whom Fernandes formally recognized and educated. By the time of her death, Chica had become a prominent member of society and belonged to a number of elite social clubs, several of which were open exclusively to white members. Upon her death she was buried in a cemetery reserved for the white colonial elite.

Chica's rags-to-riches story has captured the Brazilian historical, literary, and filmic imagination. As a result, Chica da Silva has come to be one of the most prominent and controversial historical figures in Brazil. Her story has been represented in various forms of popular culture. Directors, musicians, actors, and historians alike have portrayed what they believe Chica da Silva embodied. Through film, telenovelas, and a multitude of ballads evoking her name, Chica and what people perceive her to represent remain relevant in the study of race, gender, and sexuality in Brazil from slavery to the present.

Chica da Silva's first incarnation came in 1896, a century after her death, with the publication of *Memórias do Distrito Diamantino* (Memories from the Diamond District) by Brazilian Joaquim Felício dos Santos.[1] Dos Santos came across Chica's story while in the region and published one of the first accounts—arguably the most influential—of Chica's life. It would come to shape subsequent representations of her life and legacy a century later. Dos Santos rendered Chica as little more than a caricature based in period stereotypes of enslaved women, as a conniving seductress who used sex and her hypersexual nature to seduce, manipulate, and gain influence over one of the richest men in colonial Brazil and thereby climb the colonial social ladder, earning her the nickname of "Chica-que-Manda" (Chica the Boss).

Italian Jesuit priest André João Antonil, who lived and worked in Brazil in the late seventeenth century, wrote in 1710, roughly twenty years before Chica's birth, that the money that slave women used to purchase their freedom "rarely comes out of any other mines than their bodies, with repeated sins; and after they are freed, they continue to be the ruination of many."[2] Antonil mirrored the prevailing view that slave women used sex and their bodies not only to secure their freedom from white men but also to ruin those men morally and financially. Here again, as we have seen throughout this book, white men become the victims of black sexuality. Sex, in the view of many, was black women's sole commodity and their most influential asset. In fact, sex did gain some slave women their freedom. The exchange of sex (extended informal relationships, concubinage, prostitution) for freedom, again, overshadowed the conditions that often drove enslaved women to willingly or unwillingly engage in these relationships. This functioned in some ways as an equalizer and as a form of erasure. The sexual agency that some enslaved women used to secure their freedom concealed the victimization and sexual abuse they suffered. As we have seen in this book, there is an inability to reconcile the entirety of enslaved men and women's lives and experiences, both the physical and sexual violence they suffered and the agency that they exercised to escape it. Black women's sexual agency, the exchange of sex for freedom, came to obscure the conditions that placed them in this position and that were a critical fundaments to the national miscegenation narrative and the myth of racial democracy.

Dos Santos did little to alter this view of black women that had been ingrained in the culture of slavery and continues to haunt contemporary depictions of Chica da Silva. As historical research has shown, particularly in the notable work of historian Júnia Furtado,[3] the fictions and myths of Chica da Silva that emerged after her death have come to overshadow and further complicate the reality of her already complex life.

Xica da Silva: 1976

In 1976, nine years prior to the end of the military dictatorship that had ruled Brazil since 1964, the feature film *Xica da Silva* was released. Starring Afro-Brazilian actress Zezé Motta and produced by Carlos Diegues—one of the architects of the Cinema Novo movement that emerged to grapple with questions of social inequality during the unrest of the 1960s and 1970s—*Xica da Silva* was a sort of blaxploitation film typical in the 1970s throughout the Americas. It was based on dos Santos's novel. The film received rave reviews and was selected to represent Brazil at the Academy Awards in the category of Best Foreign Language Film, but ultimately it did not receive a nomination. The film embodies the complexities of the 1970s: repression by a military dictatorship, free love, the simultaneous celebration and debunking of the myth of racial democracy, and the emergence of a black pride movement in Brazil. The importance of this film beyond its popularity is its packaging of Chica, changing the spelling of her name to "Xica" to express the supposed hypersexual nature of this important historical figure. The depiction of Chica's sexual relationship with her white masters reproduces the narrative of genteel miscegenation, suggesting that Xica and other enslaved women were in control, and erases the reality that many enslaved women did not choose whom they had sex with but were forcibly raped.

In the opening scene of the film Xica is found working in her master's house when his son uses an animal call to summon her to have sex and she replies, "No, not today." The young master grabs her from behind and exclaims, "Yes, today and every day." Xica exclaims, "Let me go!" and he replies, "Come here, my ugly little negress" and rips off her blouse, exposing her breasts. Xica covers her chest, feigning shame, and then smirks and runs into the house, where they proceed to have sex. Some moaning is heard coming from the house and the young master begins to protest, "Xica, wait." She asks him, "Is that not what you wanted?" He replies, "Not that, Xica." "Yes, this," she insists and finally he lets out a loud scream. The viewer does not see them having sex. What is key in this scene is this reversal of sexual coercion. Rape and sexual coercion by the master's son and Xica's initial refusal to have sex are depicted as foreplay, or Xica playing hard to get. When she gives in and they move offscreen, inside the house, the film reverses the rape by making the slave woman the aggressor and the white man her victim. It is the young white master who then protests and exclaims, "No, Xica!" and becomes victim to whatever sexual act she is forcing upon him that the viewer is not privy to see. All sex scenes involving Xica and white men replicate this same dynamic, in which Xica is the predator and the white men are her prey. But the film does not reveal the fact that Manuel Pires Sardinha, Chica's second master, purchased her as an adolescent and impregnated her three times. Their illicit sexual relationship even ended up in the hands of the Inquisition. Portuguese Manuel Vieira Couto brought forth a denunciation for concubinage and told the inquisitors that Chica's master had purchased her "for this express purpose."[4] The film, like many of the stories recounted throughout this book, denies the power dynamic between white masters and enslaved women.

After this scene the film shifts to the first meeting between Xica and João Fernandes de Oliveira. Xica learns of his arrival and his vast wealth and goes out of her way to meet him. In the scene from the film below Xica is displaying her naked body to João Fernandes and her current master in an effort to get herself sold to Fernandes. She exclaims to him, "The worst part, Master, is that he abuses and beats me. . . . Why just now he hurt me here. For this reason I came running here to show you. . . . Every day he beats me. . . . My whole body is burning." While demonstrating to João Fernandes each place on her body where her master has injured her, she rips off her dress piece by piece until she is standing completely naked before him, smiling. The scene turns what is initially presented as the entreaty of an enslaved woman to be released from her master because of his abuse into a sexualized spectacle. Sexual and physical violence are

FIGURE A.1 Xica da Silva stands naked before João Fernandes
(*Xica da Silva* film, 1976).

eroticized. Her striptease seemingly nullifies her claims of abuse and renders them unbelievable. Sex and the claims of abuse are presented as devious tactics by which Xica and other enslaved women manipulate white men into giving them what they want and climb the social ladder.

At no point in the film is Xica or other enslaved women's abuse or vulnerability at the hands of white masters acknowledged or depicted. In the film, as we have seen throughout this book, interracial sex and sexual violence were integral parts of the lives of enslaved men and women and the history of Brazilian slavery. The way that those stories were represented after they occurred and how they were integrated into or discarded from the national narrative continues to impact our knowledge of the unseen lives of the enslaved. The film merely reproduces the interracial sexual narrative of the myth of racial democracy and the exceptional narrative of Brazilian slavery. Here the enslaved woman is a sexual predator seeking to seduce, corrupt, and manipulate white men with sex for her gain. The film embodies the problem at the heart of the sexual narrative in the myth of racial democracy: interracial sex was a fundamental part of creating racial fluidity and supposed racial harmony, but sexual violence and racial equality through sex are fundamentally incompatible. The narrative of consensual interracial sex overshadows the reality of rape and sexual violence.

1996: Same-Sex Relations and Slavery in the Telenovela

Twenty years after *Xica da Silva* was produced, in 1996 the Brazilian television network Rede Manchete adapted the film into a telenovela by the same name, written by Walcyr Carrasco and directed by Walter Avancini. The program was a great success and broke barriers by casting Afro-Brazilian actress Taís Araújo in the role of Xica da Silva, the first Afro-Brazilian to lead in a Brazilian telenovela. Xica's mother was played by Zezé Motta, the same actress who played Xica in Diegues's film. Though the telenovela drew inspiration from Diegues's film, its storyline went in an entirely different direction. One particular inclusion of interest is the depiction of a same-sex relationship between an effeminate white master, José Maria, also referred to as Zé Mulher (Joe Woman), played by Guilherme Piva; and a black male slave, Paulo, played by Déo Garcez. Their sexual relationship is complicated by the presence of José Maria's wife, Elvira (Giovanna Antonelli). José Maria is a friend and personal confidant of Xica da Silva. He continually denies his homosexuality though it is widely known. In order to receive his familial inheritance, José Maria must marry and produce heirs. He marries the prostitute Elvira but is unable to consummate the marriage because he is not attracted to her. The same-sex relationship is first revealed to the viewer in episode 15 when a white slave trader arrives at Xica's home while she is meeting with José Maria and announces that he has procured the slave that Xica has been looking for. Xica had asked the slave trader to find an attractive male slave to give as a gift to her homosexual friend. Xica presents Paulo to José Maria and says that he is to be used for "anything and everything that you may need." When José Maria asks her to clarify how the slave is to be used, she replies, "What do you think? For you to enjoy him!" She continues, "Take that slave and take advantage of him." José Maria asks, "And what if someone finds out, and what if [the slave] doesn't like it?" Xica replies, "Do as I do with my man. Teach him. Teach him your art."

Though this story of homosexuality has no historical basis in the actual biography of Chica da Silva, it is curious that the writers of the soap opera chose to include it and also curious how they chose to portray it. This relationship brings to viewers two critical themes that we have examined: the rape and sexual abuse of enslaved men by white masters presented in the archives of the Inquisition, and the complicity of free blacks in the enslavement and violence inflicted on people of their own race. Xica, in the telenovela, a former slave turned slaveholder who likely suffered sexual violence herself, purchases a male slave exclusively for her friend to use sexually for his pleasure. When Paulo is es-

FIGURE A.2 José Maria examines Paulo (*Xica da Silva* telenovela, 1997).

corted outdoors, a group of slave women flirt with him, remarking how attractive he is. When they learn that he has been purchased as José Maria's personal slave, they taunt him for his impending sexual abuse.

Upon Paulo's arrival at José Maria's home, José Maria immediately begins to seduce him, making him sleep in his bed to protect him, touching him, and making Paulo bathe him in the nude. The viewer never actually sees them having sex; it is only alluded to. José Maria frames the sexual abuse that he inflicts on Paulo as a means of helping José Maria become aroused so that he might be able to consummate his marriage with Elvira and conceive an heir. Paulo (representing José Maria's homosexuality) is presented as an interstice between himself and Elvira (who represents social heterosexuality). As we saw in chapter 2, same-sex sexual acts such as the sexual initiation of the master's son and the rape of male slaves functioned in tandem with heteronormativity. The sexual abuse of a male slave in the telenovela is depicted as a vehicle for solidifying José Maria's heteronormative social persona.

At first Paulo abhors the prospect of being the sexual object of his new master, but as the story progresses, he capitulates to José Maria's desires. The ménage à trois between Paulo, José Maria, and Elvira is further complicated by

FIGURE A.3 Paulo bathes José Maria (*Xica da Silva* telenovela, 1997).

the fact that Paulo is forced to have sex with Elvira as well, and at times with both of them at the same time. Both film and telenovela reproduce the historical unrapability of enslaved men and women by the exclusive representation of sex between masters and slaves as always consensual, and enslaved resistance to sexual abuse as disingenuous. In the final episode of the telenovela José Maria presents his family to Xica's son. The result of this bisexual relationship is a mixed-race family with seven children, some of them black and fathered by Paulo, and the others white, ostensibly José Maria's progeny.

The triangular relationship between Paulo, José Maria, and Elvira, their resulting mixed-race family, and the black slaveholder (Xica da Silva) who brought them together remind us that the sexual and racial history of Brazilian slavery is neither black and white nor simply heteronormative. The racial and sexual fluidity that worked hand in hand under slavery had a profound impact on every area of Brazilian society, especially on constructions of race, gender, and sexuality and how the nation would be imagined both during slavery and in its aftermath.

FIGURE A.4 José Maria, Elvira, and Paulo's blended mixed-race family (*Xica da Silva* telenovela, 1997).

The Mulatta Writes Back

In 2002 Afro-Brazilian actress, poet, and performance artist Elisa Lucinda, in her collection of poetry *O semelhante* (The Semblance), published a poem called "Mulata exportação" (Exportation Mulatta). Written in the first person, Lucinda's poem boldly challenges the historical conflation of interracial sex and antiracism from slavery to the present that has been discussed throughout this book. Performed on a number of Brazilian television shows and at poetry and literary festivals, the poem shows how Afro-Brazilian women through the arts and performance are actively combatting the racial and sexual mythologies that continue to prevail in Brazilian society and culture. The poem is narrated as an exchange between a white Brazilian intellectual and the poet in the present, but shifts to the white man as a white slave master and Lucinda as a slave, blending time to illustrate continuity. The poem opens with the white intellectual / slave master: "What a beautiful little negress. . . . Come, baby, come be my apology. . . . Come be my alibi, my good conduct. . . . I'll put you up in a house, but no one can know about it, understand sweetie? . . . With me you will forget chores, slums, slave quarters, nothing will hurt you anymore."[5] The poem replicates the illicit relationship between a white man and a mulatta, much like the representations of Chica da Silva. The mulatta is used for sex both in the past and in the present, but in the white man's imagination, sex represents a means of transcending race and racism and the history of slavery. Lucinda powerfully ends the poem by declaring boldly to the white intellectual/master, "It doesn't work! Oppression, barbarity, genocide, none of this is resolved by screwing a black woman. To cease being racist, my love, is not fucking a mulata!" She makes plain that Brazil's history of racial and sexual violence and conflict cannot be resolved, eradicated, or merely forgotten through contemporary sex or sexual desire, but must come about through a change of consciousness and coming to terms with the violent realties of sexual exploitation during slavery.

The unseen, unspeakable, uncomfortable narratives of slavery—male rape, sex between enslaved women and white mistresses, the prostitution of enslaved women by white women, formerly enslaved people who knew what it was like to be enslaved and yet subjected others to enslavement and cruelty, the discourses of emasculation and pathological constructions of male homosexuality rooted in the history of same-sex sexual relations under slavery: all of these challenge our commonplace assumptions about slavery and how it worked. These stories that somehow don't fit neatly into the story that we know or tell about slavery reveal that slaves, as Sojourner Truth cautioned, "despite our looking" took some secrets to the grave that defied logic, normalcy, and language. Slavery—its violence and its legacies—reproduced itself in complex ways through intimacy, through sameness, through ambiguities, and through irreconcilable contradictions. The unseen of slavery lies not only in the acts, sins, and innominate crimes that occurred between masters and slaves but also in the traumas and scars left in its wake. Just as we will never know all of slavery's secrets, neither will we know the full extent of these traumas. The stories of the exploitation of enslaved and free Afro-Brazilian women and men have been presented here so that their voices may be heard today by the ancestors of slaves and slaveholders alike, and by everyone whose fate in Brazil today, whether good or bad, rests on the history of slavery and the country's iniquitous attempts to come to terms with it while maintaining the fundamental power relations of white supremacy.

INTRODUCTION

1. Anthropologist Peter Fry has argued that "the myth of racial democracy coexists with the myth of the inferiority of the black." Peter Fry, "Estética e política: Relações entre 'raça,' publicidade e produção da beleza no Brasil," in *Nu e vestido: Dez antropólogos revelam a cultura do corpo carioca*, ed. Mirian Goldenberg (Rio de Janeiro: Editora Record, 2002), 304. Similarly, Peter Wade has asserted that it is in miscegenation "that racism and racial democracy coexist." Peter Wade, *Race and Sex in Latin America* (London: Pluto Press, 2009), 175.

2. James H. Sweet, *Domingos Álvares, African Healing, and the Intellectual History of the Atlantic World* (Chapel Hill: University of North Carolina Press, 2013); James H. Sweet, *Recreating Africa: Culture, Kinship, and Religion in the African-Portuguese World, 1441–1770* (Chapel Hill: University of North Carolina Press, 2003); Wade, *Race and Sex*; Nicole von Germeten, *Violent Delights, Violent Ends: Sex, Race, and Honor in Colonial Cartagena de Indias* (Albuquerque: University of New Mexico Press, 2013); François Soyer, *Ambiguous Gender in Early Modern Spain and Portugal: Inquisitors, Doctors, and the Transgression of Gender Norms* (Leiden: Brill Press, 2012); Laura de Mello e Souza, *The Devil and the Land of the Holy Cross: Witchcraft, Slavery, and Popular Religion in Colonial Brazil* (Austin: University of Texas Press, 2004); Ronaldo Vainfas, *Trópico dos pecados: Moral, sexualidade, e Inquisição no Brasil* (Rio de Janeiro: Editora Nova Fronteira, 1997); Luiz Mott, *Escravidão, homossexualidade, e demonologia* (São Paulo: Editora Ícone, 1988); João Silvério Trevisan, *Devassos no paraíso: A homossexualidade no Brasil, da colônia à atualidade* (Rio de Janeiro: Editora Record, 2007); and Amílcar Torrão Filho, *Tríbades galantes, fanchonos militantes: Homossexuais que fizeram história* (São Paulo: Edições GLS, 2000).

3. For criticism of inquisitional trials as historical sources of evidence see Renato Rosaldo, "From the Door of His Tent: The Fieldworker and the Inquisitor," in *Writing Culture: The Poetics and Politics of Ethnography*, ed. James Clifford and G. E. Marcus (Berkeley: University of California Press, 1986); Edward Muir, book reviews of *Trent 1475: Stories of Ritual Murder Trial*, by R. Po-Chia Hisia, and *From Bishop to Witch: The System of the Sacred in Early Modern Terra d'Otranto*, by David Gentilcore, *Journal of Modern History* 67, no. 1 (March 1995): 182–85. Also see Martin G. Peggs, "Historians

and Inquisitors: Testimonies from the Early Inquisition into Heretical Depravity," in *Understanding Medieval Primary Sources: Using Sources to Discover Medieval Europe*, ed. Joel T. Rosenthal (New York: Routledge, 2014); and Carlo Ginzburg, "The Inquisitor as Anthropologist," in *Clues, Myths, and the Historical Method*, trans. John Tedesechi and Anne C. Tedesechi (Baltimore: The Johns Hopkins University Press, 1980).

4. Historian David Higgs offers a brief discussion of some of the problems posed by Inquisition documents as historical evidence as they relate to sodomy cases during the Inquisition in Portugal and Brazil. "Tales of Two Carmelites: Inquisition Narratives from Portugal and Brazil," in *Infamous Desire: Male Homosexuality in Colonial Latin America*, ed. Pete Sigal (Chicago: University of Chicago Press, 2003). Also see Ronaldo Vainfas, Bruno Feitler, and Lana Lage da Gama Lima, eds., *A Inquisição em xeque: Temas, controvérsias, estudos de caso* (Rio de Janeiro: Editora UERJ, 2006); and Gilberto de Abreu Sodré Carvalho, *A Inquisição no Rio de Janeiro no começo do século XVII* (Rio de Janeiro: Imago, 2008).

5. Antoinette Burton, *Dwelling in the Archive: Women Writing House, Home, and History in Late Colonial India* (New York: Oxford University Press, 2006), 26. Also see her edited volume *Archive Stories: Facts, Fictions, and the Writing of History* (Durham, NC: Duke University Press: 2006).

6. John Arnold, "The Historian as Inquisitor: The Ethics of Interrogating Subaltern Voices," *Rethinking History* 2 (1998): 379–86.

7. See Paulina Alberto, *Terms of Inclusion: Black Intellectuals in Twentieth-Century Brazil* (Chapel Hill: University of North Carolina Press, 2011); Kia Lilly Caldwell, *Negras in Brazil: Re-envisioning Black Women, Citizenship, and the Politics of Identity* (New Brunswick, NJ: Rutgers University Press, 2007); Elisa Larkin Nascimento, *The Sorcery of Color: Identity, Race, and Gender in Brazil* (Philadelphia: Temple University Press, 2003); Jerry Dávila, *Diploma of Whiteness: Race and Social Policy in Brazil, 1917–1945* (Durham, NC: Duke University Press, 2003); Jan Hoffman French, *Legalizing Identities: Becoming Black or Indian in Brazil's Northeast* (Chapel Hill: University of North Carolina Press, 2009); Donna M. Goldstein, *Laughter Out of Place: Race, Class, Violence, and Sexuality in a Rio Shantytown* (Berkeley: University of California Press, 2003); Michael Hanchard, *Orpheus and Power: The Movimento Negro of Rio de Janeiro and São Paulo, Brazil, 1945–1988* (Princeton, NJ: Princeton University Press, 1994); Alexandra Isfahani-Hammond, *White Negritude: Race, Writing, and Brazilian Cultural Identity* (New York: Palgrave Macmillan, 2005); Emanuelle Oliveira, *Writing Identity: The Politics of Afro-Brazilian Literature* (West Lafayette, IN: Purdue University Press, 2007).

8. Michel-Rolph Trouillot, *Silencing the Past: Power and the Production of History* (Boston: Beacon Press, 1995), xix.

ONE. Racial and Sexual Paradoxes

1. Rui Barbosa, *Obras completas de Rui Barbosa*, vol. 17 (Rio de Janeiro: Ministério de Educação e Saúde, 1942), 338–40.

2. Félix Peixoto de Brito, *Considerações geraes sobre a empanicação dos escravos no império do Brasil* (Lisbon: Typographia Portugueza, 1870), 3.

3. Luiz Peixoto de Lacerda Werneck, *Ideas sobre colonizacação precididas de uma succinta exposição dos princípios geraes que regem a população* (Rio de Janeiro: Typographia Universal de Laemert, 1855), 47.

4. Robert Conrad, *The Destruction of Brazilian Slavery, 1850–1888* (Berkeley: University of California Press, 1972), 50.

5. José Thomáz Nabuco de Araújo and José Antônio Pimento Bueno, *Trabalho sôbre a extinção da escravatura no Brasil* (Rio de Janeiro: TYP Nacional, 1868), 68.

6. José Martiniano de Alencar, *Cartas à favor da escravidão* (São Paulo: Hedra, 2008), 105.

7. Thomas E. Skidmore, "The Death of Brazilian Slavery, 1866–68," in *Latin American History: Select Problems, Identity, Integration, and Nationhood*, ed. Frederick Pike (New York: Harcourt, Brace & World, 1968), 143–44.

8. Adèle Toussaint-Samson, *A Parisian in Brazil: The Travel Account of a French Woman in Nineteenth-Century Rio de Janeiro*, trans. Emma Toussaint (Wilmington, DE: Scholarly Resources, 2001), 44.

9. Toussaint-Samson, *A Parisian in Brazil*, 80.

10. Joaquim Nabuco, *O abolicionismo* (London: Abraham Kingdon, 1883; Brasília: Editora UNB, 2003; 1883), 24–25.

11. Alencar, *Cartas à favor da escravidão*, 108. Alencar further asks, "Would it by chance be France? France has no right to raise her voice in this matter. It is not possible. France abolished slavery in its colonies at the end of the last century, at the very moment when they proclaimed before the world the pompous declaration of the rights of man. . . . They retracted slavery years later only to abolish it in 1848. To maintain that a man who was born a slave as such is an institution, to reduce a man to a slave is a crime. . . . England was afraid that the slave trade that they renounced with grief would fall into the hands of another nation. It wanted to force France, Spain, Portugal, and Holland to abruptly change the regime in their colonies, without inquiring as to whether these countries had arrived at the degree of moral preparation in which they could give freedom to the blacks, abandoning on the contrary the property and lives of whites to the grace of God." Alencar, *Cartas à favor da escravidão*, 108.

12. Alencar, *Cartas à favor da escravidão*, 89.

13. Odival Cassiano Gomes, *Manoel Vitorino Perreira: Médico e cirugião* (Rio de Janeiro: Agir, 1953), 161.

14. *Annaes da camâra e senado*, 1871, vol. 3 (Rio de Janeiro: Typographia do Diário do Rio de Janeiro, 1871), 174.

15. Alencar, *Cartas à favor da escravidão*, 69.

16. *Annaes da camâra e senado*, 1875, 4:400.

17. Seymour Drescher, "The Atlantic Slave Trade and the Holocaust: A Comparative Analysis," in *Is the Holocaust Unique? Perspectives on Comparative Genocide*, ed. Alan S. Rosenbaum, 98–99, 2nd ed. (Boulder, CO: Westview Press, 2001).

18. *Polícia: Ofícios e ordens: Registro dos ofícios e ordens expedidos aos juizes do crime dos bairros, 1811–1812*, códice 329, vol. 1, Arquivo Nacional do Rio de Janeiro.

19. *Rio News*, December 15, 1882, quoted in Conrad, *Destruction of Brazilian Slavery*, 25.

20. Jorge Benci, *Economia cristã dos senhores no governo dos escravos: Livro brasileiro de 1700* (São Paulo: Editora Grijalbo, 1977), 379.

21. Benci, *Economia cristã.*

22. James H. Sweet, *Recreating Africa: Culture, Kinship, and Religion in the African-Portuguese World, 1441–1770* (Chapel Hill: University of North Carolina Press, 2003), 61.

23. Robert Edgar Conrad, *The Destruction of Brazilian Slavery, 1850–1888* (Berkeley: University of California Press, 1972), 28. For additional statistics on slave malnutrition and death rates, see Stuart B. Schwartz, *Slaves, Peasants, and Rebels: Reconsidering Brazilian Slavery* (Urbana: University of Illinois Press, 1995), 40–41; Boris Fausto and Sergio Fausto, *A Concise History of Brazil*, 2nd ed. (New York: Cambridge University Press, 2014), 20–21; Herbert S. Klein and Francisco Vidal Luna, *Slavery in Brazil* (New York: Cambridge University Press, 2010), 151–88; Leslie Bethell, *The Abolition of the Brazilian Slave Trade: Britain, Brazil, and the Slave* (New York: Cambridge University Press, 1970), 4–10.

24. Quoted in *Rio News*, June 24, 1884.

25. Thomas Nelson, *Remarks on the Slavery and Slave Trade of the Brazils* (London: J. Halchard and Son, 1846), 29–32.

26. Mahommah Gardo Baquaqua, *The Biography of Mahommah Gardo Baquaqua: His Passage from Slavery to Freedom in Africa and America*, ed. Robin Law and Paul E. Lovejoy (Princeton, NJ: Markus Wiener, 2007), 165–61.

27. Antônio Coelho Rodrigues, *Manual de um subdito fiel ou cartas de um lavrador a sua magestade o imperador sôbre a questão do elemento servil* (Rio de Janeiro: Lith. De Moreira, Maximo, 1884), 10.

28. *Annaes da câmara e senado*, 1880, 4:445–46.

29. *Annaes da câmara e senado*, 1880, 4:136.

30. Herbert H. Smith, *Rio News*, December 15, 1881, 1–2, quoted in Robert Brent Toplin, *The Abolition of Slavery in Brazil* (New York: Atheneum, 1972), 25.

31. Conrad, *Destruction of Brazilian Slavery*, 230.

32. Englishwoman Maria Dundas Graham, also known as Lady Callcott, who traveled throughout Brazil with her husband from 1821 to 1823, described the abject neglect of slaves who were let go because they could no longer work and were left to die: "Here it is not uncommon to give a slave his freedom, when he is too old or too infirm to work; that is, to turn him out of doors to beg or starve. A few days ago, as a party of gentlemen were returning from a *picnic*, they found a poor negro woman lying in a dying state, by the side of the road. The English gentlemen applied to their Portuguese companions to speak to her, and comfort her, as thinking she would understand them better; but they said, 'Oh, 'tis only a black: let us ride on,' and so they did without further notice. The poor creature, who was a dismissed slave, was carried to the English hospital, where she died in two days. Her diseases were age and hunger." Maria Dundas Graham, *Journal of a Voyage to Brazil, and Residence There during Part of the Years 1821, 1822, 1823* (London: Longman, Hurst, Rees, Orme, Brown, and Green, 1824), 144–45.

33. See Idelber Avelar, "Cenas dizíveis e indizíveis: Raça e sexualidade em Gilberto Freyre," *Luso-Brazilian Review* 49, no. 1 (November 2012): 168–86; Jossianna Arroyo,

"Brazilian Homoerotics: Cultural Subjectivity and Representation in the Fiction of Gilberto Freyre," in *Lusosex: Gender and Sexuality in the Portuguese-Speaking World*, ed. Susan Canty Quinlan and Fernando Arenas (Minneapolis: University of Minnesota Press, 2002), 57–83; Joshua Lund and Malcolm McNee, eds., *Gilberto Freyre e os estudos latino-americanos* (Pittsburgh: Instituto Internacional de Literatura Iberoamericana, 2006); Christopher Dunn, "A retomada freyreana," in Lund and McNee, *Gilberto Freyre*, 35–54; Hermano Vianna, "A meta mitológica da democracia racial," in Joaquim Falcão and Rosa Maria Barboza de Araújo, eds., *O imperador das idéias: Gilberto Freyre em questão* (Rio de Janeiro: Fundação Roberto Marinho: Topbooks, 2001), 215–21; Ricardo Benzaquen de Araújo, *Guerra e Paz:* Casa Grande e Senzala *e a obra de Gilberto Freyre nos anos 30* (Rio de Janeiro: Editora 34, 1994).

34. See Antônio Sérgio Alfredo Guimarães, *Classes, raças, e democracia* (São Paulo: Editora 34, 2002), especially the chapter titled "O itinerário da democracia de Roger Bastide," 141–44.

35. Jerry Dávila, *Hotel Trópico: Brazil and the Challenge of African Decolonization* (Durham, NC: Duke University Press, 2010), 18–20.

36. João Batista de Lacerda, "Sur les métis au Brésil," *Premier Congrès Universel des Races* (Paris: Imprimerie Devouge, 1911), 29–30.

37. Joaquim Pedro de Oliveira Martins, quoted in Joaquim Nabuco, *O Brasil e as colônias portuguesas*, 2nd ed. (Lisbon: Parceria A. M. Pereira, 1881), 50.

38. Gilberto Freyre, *The Masters and the Slaves: A Study in the Development of Brazilian Civilization*, trans. Samuel Putnam (Berkeley: University of California Press, 1986), xiv.

39. "Sexualidade e cultura em *Casa Grande e Senzala*," in Gilberto Freyre, *Casa-grande e senzala: Formação da família brasileira sob o regime da economia patriarcal*, ed. Guillermo Giucci et al. (Madrid: Archivos/UNESCO, 2002), 771–85, 781.

40. José do Patrocínio, "O Grande Projeto," *Gazeta da Tarde*, Rio de Janeiro, May 5, 1887.

41. Nabuco, *O abolicionismo*, 195–96.

42. Gerald J. Bender, *Angola under the Portuguese: The Myth and the Reality* (Berkeley: University of California Press, 1978), 4–5.

43. Sérgio Buarque de Holanda, *Roots of Brazil* (Notre Dame, IN: University of Notre Dame Press, 2012), 117.

44. Erica Lorraine Williams, *Sexual Tourism in Bahia: Ambiguous Entanglements* (Urbana: University of Illinois Press, 2013).

45. Ronaldo Vainfas, *Trópico dos pecados: Moral, sexualidade, e Inquisição no Brasil* (Rio de Janeiro: Editora Nova Fronteira, 1997), 72–76.

46. Ann Laura Stoler, *Race and the Education of Desire: Foucault's "History of Sexuality" and the Colonial Order of Things* (Durham, NC: Duke University Press, 1995), 190.

47. Albert Gomes, *Through a Maze of Colour* (Port of Spain, Trinidad: Key Caribbean Publications, 1974), 9–10.

48. See Miguel Vale de Almeida's "Not Quite White: Portuguese People in the Margins of Lusotropicalism, the Luso-Afro-Brazilian Space, and Lusophony," unpublished paper presented at "António Vieira and the Futures of Luso-Afro-Brazilian Studies," Cen-

ter for Portuguese Studies and Culture, University of Massachusetts Dartmouth, May 2–3, 2008, 5.

49. Boaventura de Sousa Santos, "Entre Próspero e Caliban: Colonialismo, pós-colonialismo e inter-identidade," in *Entre ser e estar: Raízes, percursos, e discursos da identidade*, ed. Maria Irene Ramalho and António Sousa Ribeiro (Porto, Portugal: Edições Afrontamento, 2001), 20.

50. Angela Gilliam, "Women's Equality and National Liberation," in *Third World Women and the Politics of Feminism*, ed. Chandra Talpade Mohanty, Ann Russo, and Lourdes Torres (Bloomington: Indiana University Press, 1991), 226–27.

51. Paulina Alberto, *Terms of Inclusion: Black Intellectuals in Twentieth-Century Brazil* (Chapel Hill: University of North Carolina Press, 2011).

52. Donna M. Goldstein, *Laughter Out of Place: Race, Class, Violence, and Sexuality in a Rio Shantytown* (Berkeley: University of California Press, 2003), 127.

53. Frantz Fanon, *Black Skin, White Masks*, trans. Charles Lam Markmann (New York: Grove Press, 1967), 165.

TWO. Illegible Violence

1. Processo 12894, Arquivo Nacional da Torre do Tombo, Lisbon; *Livro da visitação do Santo Ofício da Inquisição ao estado do Grão-Pará, 1763–1769* (Petrópolis, Brazil: Vozes, 1978), 261–65. The source is *Livro da visitação do Santo Ofício.*

2. The Spanish Inquisition established courts in Mexico City, with subsequent courts in Lima, Peru, in 1570 and Cartagena, Colombia, in 1610.

3. See James E. Wadworth's *Agents of Orthodoxy: Honor, Status, and the Inquisition in Colonial Pernambuco, Brazil* (Lanham, MD: Rowman and Littlefield, 2006) and *In Defence of the Faith: Joaquim Marques de Araújo, a Comissário in the Age of Inquisitional Decline* (Montreal: McGill-Queen's University Press, 2013).

4. Heitor Furtado de Mendonça in Bahia and Pernambuco from 1591 to 1595; Marcos Teixeira in Paraíba from 1618 to 1620; and Geraldo José de Abranches in Pará from 1763 to 1769.

5. Anita Waingort Novinsky, *A Inquisição* (São Paulo: Brasilense, 1982), 76–80.

6. Michel Foucault, *The History of Sexuality*, vol. 1, trans. Robert Hurley (New York: Vintage Books, 1990), 101.

7. Katherine Crawford, *The Sexual Culture of the French Renaissance* (New York: Cambridge University Press, 2010), 4.

8. See Ronaldo Vainfas, "Inquisição como fábrica de hereges: Os sodomitas foram Execação?" in *A Inquisição em xeque: Temas, controvérsias, estudos de caso*, ed. Ronaldo Vainfas, Bruno Feitler, and Lana Lage da Gama Lima (Rio de Janeiro: Editora UERJ, 2006), 267.

9. Luiz Mott, *O sexo prohibido: Virgins, gays, e escravos nas garras da Inquisição* (Campinas, Brazil: Pairus, 1988).

10. Carlos Figari, *@s "@utros" Cariocas: Interpelações, experiências, e identidades homoeróticas no Rio de Janeiro: Séculos XVII ao XX* (Belo Horizonte, Brazil: Editora UFMG, 2007), 40.

11. José Henrique Pierangelli, *Códigos penais do Brasil: Evolução histórica* (São Paulo, Brazil: Jalovi, 1980), 26.

12. Luiz Mott, "Pagode Português: A subcultura gay em Portugal nos tempos da Inquisição," *Ciência e Cultura* 40 (February 1980): 121–23.

13. Ronaldo Vainfas, "The Nefarious and the Colony," in *Pelo Vaso Traseiro: Sodomy and Sodomites in Luso-Brazilian History*, ed. Harold Johnson and Francisco A. Dutro (Tucson, AZ: Fenestra Books, 2006), 342.

14. Sônia A. Siquiera, *A Inquisição portuguesa e a sociedade colonial* (São Paulo: Editora Ática, 1978), 237.

15. Ronaldo Vainfas, "Sodomy, Love, and Slavery in Colonial Brazil: A Case Study of Minas Gerais during the Eighteenth Century," in *Sex, Power, and Slavery*, ed. Gwyn Campbell and Elizabeth Elbourne (Athens: Ohio University Press, 2015), 537–38.

16. Vainfas, "Sodomy, Love, and Slavery."

17. Vainfas, "Sodomy, Love, and Slavery," 536.

18. Vainfas, "Sodomy, Love, and Slavery," 538.

19. Vainfas, "Sodomy, Love, and Slavery," 534.

20. Processo 45, *Processos da Inquisição, Inquisição de Lisboa*, Arquivo Nacional da Torre do Tombo, Lisbon.

21. Historian Geoffrey Spurling has argued that the revelation of a man engaging in sodomy could greatly compromise a man's honor and social standing, especially if he was being penetrated. See his "The Changing Face of Honor" in *The Faces of Honor: Sex, Shame, and Violence in Colonial Latin America*, ed. Lynne L. Johnson and Sonya Lipsett-Rivera (Albuquerque: University of New Mexico Press, 1998) and "Under Investigation for the Abominable Sin: Damian de Morales Stands Accused of Attempting to Seduce Anton de Tierra de Congo," in *Colonial Lives: Documents on Latin American History, 1550–1850*, ed. Richard Boyer and Geoffrey Spurling (New York: Oxford University Press, 2000).

22. *Livro da visitação*, processo 12894.

23. Arquivo Nacional da Torre do Tombo, processo 17.759.

24. Arquivo Nacional da Torre do Tombo, processo 11061.

25. Arquivo Nacional da Torre do Tombo, processo 7467.

26. Some slave owners confessed their sins to the Inquisition voluntarily.

27. *Segunda visitação do Santo Ofício as partes do Brasil pelo Inquisidor e visitador o licenciado Marcos Teixeira, Livro das confissões e ratificações da Bahia, 1618–1620*, Anais do Museu Paulista, microfilm call number XVII, 444–46.

28. *Segunda visitação*, 444–46.

29. Arquivo Nacional da Torre do Tombo, Caderno do Nefando, number 20 fl. 439 11/12/1739.

30. *Processos da Inquisição, Inquisição de Lisboa*, processos 4769 and 4230, Arquivo Nacional da Torre do Tombo, Lisbon.

31. Arquivo Nacional da Torre do Tombo, Caderno do Nefando, number 20 fl. 329 10/16/1742; Luiz Mott, "The Misadventures of a Portuguese Man in Seventeenth-Century Brazil," in *Pelo Vaso Traseiro: Sodomy and Sodomites in Luso-Brazilian History*, ed. Harold Johnson and Francis A. Dutra (Tucson, AZ: Fenestra Books, 2007), 298.

32. *Primeira visitação do Santo Ofício às partes do Brasil pelo licenciado Heitor Furtado de Mendonça denunciações de Pernambuco, 1593–1595* (São Paulo: P. Prado, 1929), 399; Arquivo Nacional da Torre do Tombo, Caderno do Nefando, number 20, fl. 329, 1/15/1762.

33. Arquivo Nacional da Torre do Tombo, Caderno do Nefando, number 20 fl. 329 1/15/1762.

34. Arquivo Nacional da Torre do Tombo, processo 10426.

35. Vainfas, "Sodomy, Love, and Slavery," 535.

36. Arquivo Nacional da Torre do Tombo processo 16687.

37. Saidiya V. Hartman, *Scenes of Subjection: Slavery, Terror, and Self-Making in Nineteenth-Century America* (New York: Oxford University Press, 1996), 23.

38. Vainfas, "Sodomy, Love, and Slavery"; Luiz Mott, "O Sex Cativo: Alternativas eroticas dos africanos e seus descendentes no Brasil escravista," in *O sexo proibido: Virgens, gays, e escravos nas garras, Inquisição* (Campinas, Brazil: Papirus, 1988), 44.

39. Arquivo Nacional da Torre do Tombo, Caderno do Nefando, number 20 fl. 360 2/6/1792.

40. Frank Tannenbaum, *Slave and Citizen: The Classic Comparative Study of Race Relations in the Americas* (New York: Alfred A. Knopf, 1946; Boston: Beacon Press, 1992), 97.

41. Tannenbaum, *Slave and Citizen*, 63.

42. James H. Sweet, *Domingos Álvares, African Healing, and the Intellectual History of the Atlantic World* (Chapel Hill: University of North Carolina Press, 2011), 151–52.

43. Sweet, *Domingos Álvares*.

44. Jorge Benci, *Economia cristã dos senhores no governo dos escravos: Livro brasileiro de 1700* (São Paulo: Editora Grijalbo, 1977), 84.

45. See Mott, *O sexo proibido*, 41.

46. João Lúcio de Azevedo, *História de Antônio Vieira* (São Paulo: Alameda, 2008); Alcir Pecora, *Teatro do sacramento*, 2nd ed. (São Paulo/Campinas: Editora da Universidade de São Paulo/Ed. Unicamp, 2008).

47. The New Testament perpetuates the sanctioning of slavery and exhorts slaves to obey their masters, as in Ephesians 6:5 ("Slaves, obey your earthly masters with respect and fear, and with sincerity of heart, just as you would obey Christ") and 1 Timothy 6:1 ("All who are under the yoke of slavery should consider their masters worthy of full respect, so that God's name and our teaching may not be slandered"), indicating to slaves that resisting their condition would be a sin against God and the church. But the Bible in places also admonishes slaveholders to treat their slaves well, as in Colossians 4:1: "Masters, provide your slaves with what is right and fair, because you know that you also have a Master in heaven."

48. António Vieira, *Sermões pregados no Brasil*, vol. 2, *A vida social e moral na colônia* (Lisbon: Agência Geral das Colónias, 1940), 399–400.

49. Vieira, *Sermões pregados no Brasil*, 30–31.

50. It was very common during the early modern period to refer to enslaved people as coming from Ethiopia. Ethiopia came to stand for Africa collectively. Demographic data documenting enslaved countries and regions of origin indicate that none of Brazil's enslaved actually came from Ethiopia.

51. Vieira, *Sermões pregados no Brasil*, 26.

52. José Martiniano de Alencar, *Cartas à favor da escravidão* (São Paulo, Brazil: Hedra, 2008), 105.

53. Cited in E. Bradford Burns, ed., *A Documentary History of Brazil* (New York: Alfred A. Knopf, 1966), 83.

54. Frantz Fanon, *Black Skin, White Masks*, trans. Charles Lam Markmann (New York: Grove Press, 1967), 30.

55. N. L. Stepman, "Race and Gender: The Role of Analogy in Science," *Isis* 77 (1986): 265–66.

56. Sander L. Gilman, *Sexuality* (New York: 1989), 29. In Genesis 9:18–29, Noah planted a vineyard, got drunk on his wine, and retired to his tent, where he lay naked. Ham saw his father naked and reported this to his two brothers. His brothers covered Noah, but the passage specifies that they did this in such a way that they did not see his nakedness, by entering Noah's tent backward. Verse 24 reads, "When Noah awoke from his wine, he knew what his youngest son had done to him" (New American Standard version). One interpretation of this passage is that Ham committed sodomy against Noah, who retaliated by placing the curse of slavery on Ham's son, Canaan. At the very least, the biblical prohibition against the male same-sex gaze is clear.

57. Hartman, *Scenes of Subjection*, 88.

58. Joaquim Augusto de Camargo, *Direito penal brasileiro*, 2nd ed. (São Paulo: Revista do Tribunais, 2005), 139.

59. Camargo, *Direito penal brasileiro*.

60. Camargo, *Direito penal brasileiro*, 243.

61. Camargo, *Direito penal brasileiro*, 299.

62. See Salgado Martins, *Sistema de direito penal brasileiro: Introducao e parte geral* (Rio de Janeiro: Editora Jose Kofino, 1957).

63. For a comprehensive analysis of the origins and evolution of Brazilian rape law in the twentieth century as it relates to women, see Sueann Caulfield's *In Defense of Honor: Sexual Morality, Modernity, and Nation in Early-Twentieth-Century Brazil* (Durham, NC: Duke University Press, 2000).

64. See Francis Wharton, *A Treatise on Criminal Law* (Philadelphia: Kay and Brother, 1880).

65. Lorenne Clarke and Debra Lewis, "Women, Property, and Rape," in *The Sociology of Crime and Deviance: Selected Issues*, ed. Susan Caffrey and Gary Mundy (Dartford, UK: Greenwich University Press, 1995), 152.

66. Male rape survivor and activist Michael Scarce has rightfully shown that today most US states categorize vaginal and anal rape differently. The term *sexual intercourse* refers only to penetration of the vagina by the penis. Scarce asserts, "A reluctance to define anal rape of men as a 'sex' crime may be related, in part, to societal homophobia. If one recognizes the forced penetration of a man's anus as sexual assault, one is also forced to consider its opposite, that is, anal rape as defined by a lack of consent and therefore distinguished from consensual anal sex." Michael Scarce, *Male on Male Rape: The Hidden Toll of Stigma and Shame* (New York: Insight Books, 1997), 207.

67. Saint Thomas Aquinas, *Summa Theologica*, transl. by Fathers of the English Dominican Province, vol. 4, part 3, sect. 1 (1911; New York: Cosimo Classics, 2007), 1820.

68. Winthrop Jordan, *White over Black: American Attitudes toward the Negro, 1550–1812* (Chapel Hill: University of North Carolina Press, 1968), 141.

69. Gilberto Freyre, *The Masters and the Slaves: A Study in the Development of Brazilian Civilization*, trans. Samuel Putnam (Berkeley: University of California Press, 1986), 75.

70. Henry Koster, *Travels in Brazil* (London: Longman, Hurst, Rees, Orme, and Brown, 1816), 388–89.

71. José Veríssimo, *A educação nacional* (Rio de Janeiro: Livraria F. Alves, 1906), 34.

72. Arquivo Nacional da Torre do Tombo, Lisbon, Processo 14326, Arquivo Nacional da Torre do Tombo.

73. Richard C. Trexler, "Gender Subordination and Political Hierarchy in Pre-Hispanic America," in *Infamous Desire: Male Homosexuality in Colonial Latin America*, ed. Pete Sigal (Chicago: University of Chicago Press, 2003), 70.

74. Freyre's description of the sexual initiations of the young white master ties in with what Saidiya Hartman has termed the "doctrine of perfect submission," which "reconciled violence and the claims of mutual benevolence between master and slave" and "enchanted the brutal and direct violence of master-slave relations." Hartman, *Scenes of Subjection*, 88.

75. Jeffrey D. Needell, "Identity, Race, Gender, and Modernity in the Origins of Gilberto Frey's Oeuvre," *American Historical Review* 100, no. 1 (February 1995): 70.

76. Cited in Mott, "Pagode Português," 125.

77. Pete Sigal, "Introduction: (Homo)Sexual Desire and Masculine Power in Colonial Latin America: Notes toward an Integrated Analysis," in Sigal, *Infamous Desire*, 6.

78. Trexler, "Gender Subordination," in Sigal, *Infamous Desire*, 70–102; and Serge Gruzinski, "The Ashes of Desire: Homosexuality in Mid-Seventeenth-Century New Spain," trans. Ignacio López-Calvo, in Sigal, ed., *Infamous Desire*, 197–211.

79. See, for example, Luiz Mott, *Escravidão, homossexualidade, e demonologia* (São Paulo: Editora Ícone, 1988); Mott, *O sexo proibido*; Mott, "Crypto-Sodomites in Colonial Brazil," in Sigal, ed., *Infamous Desire*, 168–96; João Silvério Trevisan, *Devassos no paraíso: A homossexualidade no Brasil, da colônia à atualidade* (Rio de Janeiro: Editora Record, 2007); and Amílcar Torrão Filho, *Tribades galantes, fanchonos militantes: Homossexuais que fizeram história* (São Paulo: Edições GLS, 2000).

80. Scarce, *Male on Male Rape*, 85.

81. Elizabeth Jane Ward, *Not Gay: Sex between Straight White Men* (New York: New York University Press, 2015), 5–6.

82. Richard G. Parker, *Beneath the Equator: Cultures of Desire, Male Homosexuality, and Emerging Gay Communities in Brazil* (New York: Routledge, 1999), 30–31.

83. Parker, *Beneath the Equator*, 30.

84. Don Kulick, *Travesti: Sex, Gender, and Culture among Brazilian Transgendered Prostitutes* (Chicago: University of Chicago Press, 1998), 126.

85. Florence Rush, "The Many Faces of the Backlash," in *The Sexual Liberals and the*

Attack on Feminism, ed. Dorchen Leidholdt and Janice G. Raymond (Oxford: Pergamon Press, 1990), 169–70.

86. Sociologist Michael Kaufman also shows that rape is a crime that articulates physical power in the language of male-female relations. Michael Kaufman, "The Construction of Masculinity and the Triad of Men's Violence," in *Gender Violence: Interdisciplinary Perspectives*, ed. Laura O'Toole, Jessica R. Schiffman, and Margie L. Kiter Edwards (New York: New York University Press, 1997), 30. Rush's and Kaufman's observations reveal that male rape is an act of gendering, and therefore the language that we use to speak of sexual domination is gendered as well. It is possible to speak of male domination only in reference to the female body. Thus rape—even the rape of males—is correlated with womanhood for both the rapist and the victim.

87. See Scarce, *Male on Male Rape*; Claire Cohen, *Male Rape Is a Feminist Issue: Feminism, Governmentality, and Male Rape* (New York: Palgrave Macmillan, 2014); John M. Preble and A. Nicholas Groth, *Male Victims of Same-Sex Abuse: Addressing Their Sexual Response* (New York: Sidran Press, 2002); A. Nicholas Groth, *Men Who Rape: The Psychology of the Offender* (New York: Plenum Press, 1979); and Mic Hunter, *Abused Boys: The Neglected Victims of Sexual Abuse* (New York: Ballantine Books, 1991).

88. See Cohen, *Male Rape*; Sue Lees, *Ruling Passions: Sexual Violence, Reputation, and the Law* (Buckingham, UK: Open University Press, 1997); and Richie J. McMullen, *Male Rape: Breaking the Silence of the Last Taboo* (London: Heretic Books, 1990).

89. C. I. Ford Hickson, et al., "Gay Men as Victims of Nonconsensual Sex," *Archives of Sexual Behavior* 23, no. 3 (1994): 281–94.

90. Groth, *Men Who Rape*, 26.

91. A. Nicholas Groth and Ann Burgess, "Male Rape: Offenders and Victims," *American Journal of Psychiatry* 137, no. 7 (July 1980): 809.

92. Groth and Burgess, "Male Rape," 809.

93. Groth and Burgess, "Male Rape," 809.

94. Stephen Donaldson, "Sex Among Male Prisoners and Its Implications for Concepts of Sexual Orientation: A Million Jockers, Punks and Queens," lecture delivered at Columbia University, February 4, 1993; cited in Scarce, *Male on Male Rape*, 39.

95. Scarce, *Male on Male Rape*, 36.

96. Denise Donnelly and Stacy Kenyon, "'Honey, We Don't Do Men': Gender Stereotypes and the Provision of Services to Sexually Assaulted Males," *Journal of Interpersonal Violence* 11, no. 3: 441–48.

97. Male rape inside and outside of prisons is equally as shameful and violent today as it was for the enslaved men and boys presented in this chapter. Because of the degree of shame, scorn, and often disbelief that male rape survivors in contexts such as prisons experience, many live with their trauma and do not report it to officials. Scarce shows that most prison-rape survivors will not report their assault to correctional facilities because officers frequently respond, "You must have wanted it because you allowed it to happen." Once officials redefine prisoners' rape experiences as homosexuality, rape survivors are punished for confessing to a violation of rules. Decriminalization of consensual behavior would also symbolically diminish a great deal of the disgrace associated with all sexual activity, including sexual violence. This present-day attitude is identical to the

stance that inquisitors took with enslaved male rape victims. Scarce, *Male on Male Rape*, 41.

98. Similarly, Hortense J. Spillers asks regarding the man-woman reproductive model and slavery, "How does this model, or does this model, suffice for occupied or captive persons and communities in which the rites and rights of gender-function have been exploded historically into sexual neutralities?" Spillers, "The Permanent Obliquity of an In[pha]llibly Straight: In the Time of the Daughters and the Fathers," in *Daughters and Fathers*, ed. Lynda E. Boose and Betty S. Flowers (Baltimore: Johns Hopkins University Press, 1989), 158–59.

99. Fanon, *Black Skin, White Masks*, 159.

100. Groth and Burgess, "Male Rape," 806–10; Gillian Mezey and Michael B. King, "The Effects of Sexual Assault on Men: A Survey of 22 Men," *Psychological Medicine* 19, no. 1 (February 1989): 205–9; A. Nicholas Groth, *Male Victims of Sexual Assault* (Oxford: Oxford University Press, 1993).

101. P. L. Huckle, "Male Rape Victims Referred to a Forensic Psychiatric Service," *Medicine, Science, and the Law* 35, no. 3 (July 1995): 197–92.

102. Shoshana Felman and Dori Laub, *Testimony: Crises in Witnessing in Literature, Psychoanalysis, and History* (New York: Routledge, 1992), xiv.

103. The project of memorializing black male sexual passivity and plantation culture characters during Brazilian slavery would continue in the early twentieth century. This phenomenon is depicted in several novels, histories, and films, most notably in José Lins do Rego's novel *O Moleque Ricardo* (1935) and in the work of Gilberto Freyre.

THREE. The White Mistress and the Slave Woman

1. This chapter is not making the claim that *all* white women or white mistresses engaged in sexual activity with enslaved women, nor does it assert that all white mistresses tortured their slave women and forced them into prostitution. This chapter focuses on the documentation of these three realities as found in several period sources. As with the rape of the enslaved men, we are unable to know for certain how frequently these acts occurred.

2. See, for example, Sonia Maria Giacomini, *Mulher e escrava* (Petropolis, Brazil: Vozes, 1988); Nell Irvin Painter, *Southern History across the Color Line* (Chapel Hill: University of North Carolina Press, 2002); Deborah Gray White, *Ar'n't I a Woman?: Female Slaves in the Plantation South* (New York: Norton, 1999); Elizabeth Fox-Genovese, *Within the Plantation Household: Black and White Women of the Old South* (Chapel Hill: University of North Carolina Press, 1988).

3. Sueann Caulfield, *In Defense of Honor: Sexual Morality, Modernity, and Nation in Early-Twentieth-Century Brazil* (Durham, NC: Duke University Press, 2000), 24.

4. Caulfield, *In Defense of Honor*, 27.

5. See Jonathan Katz's *Miss Marianne Woods and Miss Jane Pirie against Dame Helen Cumming Gordon* (New York: Arno Press, 1975).

6. *Records of the Colony of New Plymouth*, vol. 1 (Boston: William White, 1855), 137, 163.

7. *Records and Files of the Quarterly Courts of Essex County*, vol. 1 (Salem, MA: Essex Institute, 1911), 44.

8. Ligia Bellini, *A coisa obscura: Mulher, sodomia e Inquisição* (São Paulo: Editora Brasilense, 1989), 67.

9. Bellini, *A coisa obscura*, 67.

10. Dom Sebastião Monteiro da Vide, *Constituições primeiras do arcebispdo da Bahia, 1707* (São Paulo: Typographia 2 de Dezembro, 1853), 332–34.

11. Monteiro da Vide, *Constituições primeiras*, 332–34.

12. Ludovico Maria Sinistrari, *De sodomia tractatus, in quo exponitur doctrina nova de sodomia foeminarum a tribadismo distincta* (Paris: Bibilothèque des Curieux, 1921).

13. Sinistrari, *De sodomia tractatus*, 39–41.

14. Sinistrari, *De sodomia tractatus*, 101.

15. Bernadette J. Brooten, *Love between Women: Early Christian Responses to Female Homoeroticism* (Chicago: University of Chicago Press, 1996), 7.

16. Sinistrari, *De sodomia tractatus*, 35–36.

17. Sinistrari, *De sodomia tractatus*, 49.

18. These views continued well into the nineteenth century. In 1877 German author Hugo Hildebrandt, referring to women in general, argued that the overdevelopment of the clitoris led to "excesses" that "are called lesbian love." Hugo Hildebrandt, *Die Krankheiten der äusseren weiblichen Genitalien*, in *Handbuch der Frauenkrankheiten III*, ed. Theodor Billroth (Stuttgart: Enke, 1877), 11–12.

19. Sander L. Gilman, *Difference and Pathology: Stereotypes of Sexuality, Race, and Madness* (Ithaca, NY: Cornell University Press, 1985), 89. This pathology around black women's bodies would continue well into the nineteenth century, most notably with the Venus Hottentot, a Khosian woman who was displayed throughout Europe. Upon her death, her genitals and buttocks were dissected by French scientist Georges Cuvier. For more information, see Tracy Denean Sharpley-Whiting's *Black Venus: Sexualized Savages, Primal Fears, and Primitive Narratives in French* (Durham, NC: Duke University Press, 1999).

20. Nell Irvin Painter, *Sojourner Truth: A Life, A Symbol* (New York: Norton, 1997).

21. Gilbert Vale, *Fanaticism: Its Source and Influence*, part 2 (New York: G. Vale, 1835), 90–91.

22. Sojourner Truth, *Narrative of Sojourner Truth: A Bondswoman of Olden Time, with a History of Her Labors and Correspondence Drawn from Her Book of Life* (New York: Penguin Books, 1998), 55–56.

23. Linda Brent [Harriet Ann Jacobs], *Incidents in the Life of a Slave Girl* (Boston: 1861).

24. Ronaldo Vainfas, "Homoerotismo feminino e o Santo Oficio," in *História das mulheres no Brasil* (São Paulo: Editora Contexto: Editora Unesp Fundação, 1997), 120.

25. Sinistrari strongly disagreed and argued, "Let not the authors of this sin deceive themselves by thinking that in the innominate act the passive does not sin as gravely as the active." Sinistrari, *De sodomia tractatus*, 101.

26. Once an inquisitor read the list of possible heresies after Mass, the faithful were given a period of grace of about one month during which they could confess their sins and avoid severe punishment.

27. *Processos da Inquisição, Inquisição de Lisboa,* processo 11061, Arquivo Nacional da Torre do Tombo, Lisbon. Hereafter Inquisition court records will be abbreviated as "*Processos da Inquisição,*" followed by the trial number.

28. *Processos da Inquisição,* 1289.

29. *Primeira visitação do Santo Ofício às partes do Brasil: Denunciações e confissões de Pernambuco, 1593–1595* (Recife, Brazil: Secretaria de Turismo, Cultura e Esportes/Fundarpe, 1984), 52–53.

30. *Santo Ofício da Inquisição de Lisboa: Confissões da Bahia* (São Paulo: Companhia das Letras, 1997), 259.

31. *Primeira visitação do Santo Ofício as partes do Brasil: Denunciações de Pernambuco,* 1618, 328–29.

32. *Primeira visitação do Santo Ofício,* 1618, 47–50.

33. Nicole von Germeten, *Violent Delights, Violent Ends: Sex, Race, and Honor in Colonial Cartagena de Indias* (Albquerque: University of New Mexico Press, 2013), 145.

34. *Denunciações de Pernambuco,* 37–38.

35. *Santo Ofício da Inquisição de Lisboa: Confissões da Bahia,* 198–99.

36. *Processos da Inquisição,* 1267; Bellini, *A coisa obscura,* 25.

37. *Santo Ofício da Inquisição de Lisboa,* 104–8.

38. *Processos da Inquisição,* 1267.

39. *Processos da Inquisição,* 1267.

40. *Processos da Inquisição,* 1267. Also see Bellini, *A coisa obscura,* 25.

41. *Processos da Inquisição,* 13787. Also see Bellini, *A coisa obscura,* 25.

42. *Processos da Inquisição,* 13787.

43. Bellini, *A coisa obscura,* 34.

44. António Vieira, *Sermões pregados no Brasil,* vol. 2, *A vida social e moral na colônia* (Lisbon: Agência Geral das Coloniais, 1940), 266–267.

45. Emanuel Araújo, "A arte da sedução: Sexualidade feminina na colônia," in *História das mulheres no Brasil,* ed. Mary Del Priore and Carla Beozzo Bassanezi (São Paulo: Editora Contexto: Editora Unesp Fundação, 1997), 52.

46. Araújo, "A arte da sedução: Sexualidade feminina na colônia."

47. Araújo, "A arte da sedução: Sexualidade feminina na colônia," 45.

48. Caulfield, *In Defense of Honor,* 4.

49. Ronaldo Vainfas, *Trópico dos pecados: Moral, sexualidade, e Inquisição no Brasil* (Rio de Janeiro: Editora Nova Fronteira, 1997), 139.

50. Sander L. Gilman, *Difference and Pathology,* 211.

51. José Bonifácio de Andrada e Silva, "A escravatura," in *A abolição no parlamento: 65 anos de luta, 1823–1888,* vol. 1, 2nd ed. (Brasília: Senado Federal, 2012), 34. This speech was never presented, as Bonifácio was imprisoned and deported along with other deputies by Dom Pedro I for his involvement in the Brazilian movement to separate from Portugal. The speech was subsequently published in Paris in 1845, and excerpts were published in Brazilian newspapers, mostly notably *O americano.*

52. Joaquim Manuel de Macedo, *As vítimas algozes: Quadros da escravidão* (São Paulo, Brazil: Editora Scipione, 1991), 164–65. All translations from this book are mine.

53. Macedo, *As vítimas algozes,* xiv–xv.

54. David T. Haberly, "Abolitionism in Brazil: Anti-Slavery and Anti-Slave," *Luso-Brazilian Review* 9, no. 2 (1972): 31.

55. Macedo, *As vítimas algozes*, 165.

56. Caulfield, *In Defense of Honor*, 3.

57. Macedo, *As vítimas algozes*, 177.

58. Frantz Fanon, *Black Skin, White Masks*, trans. Charles Lam Markmann (New York: Grove Press, 1967), 151.

59. Francisco Pacifico de Amaral, *Escavações: Factos da história de Pernambuco* (Recife, Brazil: Typographia do Jornal do Recife, 1884), 65. French traveler Adèle Toussaint-Samson also concurred with these racist views of black women and reported, "The negresses, with their African ardors, demoralize the young people of Rio de Janeiro and her provinces. There is in their blood a bitter principle which kills the white man." Adèle Toussaint-Samson, *A Parisian in Brazil: The Travel Account of a French Woman in Nineteenth-Century Rio de Janeiro*, trans. Emma Toussaint (Wilmington, DE: Scholarly Resources, 2001), 46.

60. Macedo, *As vítimas algozes*, 165.

61. André João Antonil, *Cultura e opulência do Brasil pelas minas do ouro* (São Paulo: Obelisco, 1964), 92–93.

62. Gilberto Freyre, *Casa-grande e senzala: Formação da família brasileira sob o regime da economia patriarcal* (Rio de Janeiro: Editora Record, 1998), 354.

63. Macedo, *As vítimas algozes*, 164.

64. Macedo, *As vítimas algozes*, 229.

65. Roger Bastide, *Sociologia do foclore brasileiro* (São Paulo: Editora Anhambi, 1959), 320.

66. Thomas Lindley, *Narrative of a Voyage to Brasil . . .* (London: J. Johnson, 1805), 34–35.

67. Charles Expilly, *Les femmes et les moeurs du Brésil* (Paris: Charlieu et Huillery, 1863), 340.

68. Lindley, *Narrative*, 34.

69. Expilly, *Les femmes et les moeurs*, 340.

70. Gilberto Freyre, *Sobrados e mocambos: Decadência do patriarcado rural e desenvolvimento urbano* (Rio de Janeiro: Editora Record, 1996), 469.

71. Bastide, *Sociologia*, 318.

72. Bastide, *Sociologia*, 320.

73. Freyre, *Casa-grande e senzala*, 455.

74. Brent, *Incidents*, 48.

75. Brent, *Incidents*, 49.

76. José Ricardo Pires de Almeida, *Homosexualismo: A libertinagem no Rio de Janeiro: Estudos sobre as perversões do instinto genital* (Rio de Janeiro: Laemmert, 1906), 232–33.

77. Pires de Almeida, *Homosexualismo*), 220.

78. Pires de Almeida, *Homosexualismo*), 198–99.

79. Francisco José Viveiros de Castro, *Atentados ao pudor: Estudos sobre as aberrações do instinto sexual* (Rio de Janeiro: Livraria Editora Freitas Bastos, 1932), 199.

80. Viveiros de Castro, *Atentados ao pudor*, 205.

81. Almeida, *Homosexualismo*, 257–58.

82. The Christian rhetoric of separatism is exemplified in the following passage: "Wherefore come out from among them, and be ye separate, saith the Lord, and touch not the unclean thing; and I will receive you" (2 Corinthians 6:17). This passage points to the importance for Christians to separate themselves from sin and sinners in order to be in God's favor. Engagement in sin and contact with sinners imperiled the soul and could ultimately lead to eternal damnation. This same logic around sexual deviance became packaged scientifically and depicted in medical studies and literature that depicted the fatal consequences of contact with "contaminative persons."

83. Aluísio Azevedo, *O cortiço* (São Paulo Editora Martin Claret, 2012), 128–29.

84. Mary Karasch, *Slave Life in Rio de Janeiro, 1808–1850* (Princeton, NJ: Princeton University Press, 1987), 295.

85. Charles R. Boxer, *Women in Iberian Expansion Overseas, 1415–1815: Some Facts, Fancies, and Personalities* (New York: Oxford University Press, 1975), 59.

86. *Código de posturas da illustrissima câmara municipal do Rio de Janeiro* (Rio de Janeiro: Typographia Dous de Dezembro, 1854), 49.

87. Charles Expilly, *Le Brésil tel qu'il est* (Paris: Arnauld de Vresse, Libraire Éditeur, 1862), 290.

88. Expilly, *Le Brésil tel qu'il est*, 291.

89. *A abolição no parlamento: 65 anos de luta, 1823–1888*, 2nd ed. (Brasília: Senado Federal, Secretaria Especial de Editoração e Publicações, 2012), 687.

90. Herculano Augusto Lassance Cunha, "Dissertação sobre a prostituição, em particular na cidade do Rio de Janeiro" (Rio de Janeiro: Typographia Imparcial de Paula Brito, 1845), 23–24.

91. João Álvares de Macedo Junior, *Da prostiuição no Rio de Janeiro e da sua influência sobre a saúde pública* (Rio de Janeiro: Typographia Americana, 1869), 12–13.

92. According to Caulfield, "By the late nineteenth century, the vast majority of Brazil's public health physicians opposed both criminalization and state regulation of prostitution, a position that coincided with progressive European health professionals. Legislators of the First Republic thus followed their imperial predecessors: they neither criminalized nor regulated prostitution, but left the messy work of prostitution control to the Federal District chief of police, who worked under (or around) a series of nebulous municipal ordinances." Caulfield, *In Defense of Honor*, 39.

93. "Relatório do chefe de policia da corte," legal case presented to the General Assembly by attorney Francisco de Paula de Negreiros Sayão Lobato, in *Relatório da repartição dos negocios da justiça apresentado a assemblea geral legislativa, annexos* (Rio de Janeiro, 1871), 21.

94. "Relatório do chefe de policia," 22.

95. Sidney Chaloub, *Visões da liberdade: Uma história das últimas décadas da escravidão na corte* (São Paulo: Companhia da Letras, 1990), 152–55.

96. "Habeas Corpus," 1879 Arquivo Nacional do Rio de Janeiro, RJ, vol. 1, 720, no. 2.468 (Gallery A). A house of corrections was a prison where slaves were sent to be punished and tortured.

97. Joaquim Nabuco, *O abolicionismo* (Petrópolis, Brazil: Editora Vozes, 1977), 131–32.

98. Hazel V. Carby, *Reconstructing Womanhood: The Emergence of the Afro-American Woman Novelist* (New York: Oxford University Press, 1987), 55.

99. Jacobs, *Incidents*, 140.

100. Fox-Genovese, *Within the Plantation Household*, 29–30, 43–45, 313–15. Also see Painter, *Southern History*; and White, *Ar'n't I a Woman?*

101. Gilberto Freyre, *The Masters and the Slaves: A Study in the Development of Brazilian Civilization*, trans. Samuel Putnam (Berkeley: University of California Press, 1986), 352.

102. Freyre, *Masters and Slaves*, 351.

103. Henry Koster, *Travels in Brazil* (London: Longman, Hurst, Rees, Orme, and Brown, 1816), 388.

104. Thaviola Glymph, *Out of the House of Bondage: The Transformation of the Plantation Household* (New York: Cambridge University Press, 2008), 35.

105. Frederick Douglass, *Narrative of the Life of Frederick Douglass, an American Slave, Written by Himself*, ed. David W. Blight (New York: Bedford/St. Martin's Press, 1993), 41.

106. Douglass, *Narrative*, 53.

107. Expilly, *Le Brésil tel qu'il est*, 149–51.

108. Joseph F. Friedrich von Weech, *Reise über England und Portugal nach Brasilien und den Vereinigten Staaten des La-Plata-Stromes während den Jahren 1823 bis 1827*, vol. 2 (Munich: Auer, 1831), 13–14.

109. Adèle Toussaint-Samson, *Une Parisienne au Brésil* (Paris: Paul Ollendorff, 1883), 68–69.

110. Toussaint-Samson, *Une Parisienne au Brésil*.

111. Machado de Assis, *Machado de Assis afro-descendente: Escritos de caramujo*, ed. Eduardo de Assis Duarte (Rio de Janeiro: Pallas, 2007), 136.

112. See Freyre, *Masters and Slaves*; Karasch, *Slave Life*; Giacomini, *Mulher e escrava*; White, *Ar'n't I a Woman?*; Fox-Genovese, *Within the Plantation Household*; Glymph, *Out of the House of Bondage*; Victoria E. Bynum, *Unruly Women: The Politics of Social and Sexual Control in the Old South* (Chapel Hill: University of North Carolina Press, 1992); and Catherine Clinton, *The Plantation Mistress: Woman's World in the Old South* (New York: Pantheon Books, 1984).

113. Lassance Cunha, "Dissertação sobre a prostituição," 24.

114. Expilly, *Les femmes et les moeurs*, 122.

115. Toussaint-Samson, *Une Parisienne au Brésil*, 147–48.

116. Painter, *Southern History*, 108.

117. Painter, *Southern History*, 122–23.

118. Freyre, *Masters and Slaves*, 351. Frederico Leopoldo Cezar Burlamaqui further observes, "Among us, the most common phrases, when a woman is suspicious of her husband or her lover, are 'I'll have her fried, I'll roast her alive, I'll burn her, or I'll cut out such and such part,' etc. And how many times are these threats even put into execution, and all because of mere suspicion?" Frederico Leopoldo Cezar Burlamaqui, in *Memória analytica acerca do commércio d'escravos e acerca da escravidão doméstica* [Analytical Memoir of Slave Trafficking and Domestic Slavery] (Rio de Janeiro, Brazil: Typographia Commercial Fluminense, 1837), 32.

119. Japi Freire, *Que sabe você sôbre o Brasil?* (Rio de Janeiro: Conquista, 1966), 41.

120. Johann Baptist Emanuel Pohl, *Viagem no interior do Brasil*, vol. 1 (Rio de Janeiro, Brazil: Ministério da Educação e Saúde, 1951), 302.

121. Aluísio Azevedo, *O mulato*, trans. Murray Graeme MacNicoll (Austin: University of Texas Press, 1993), 62.

122. Azevedo, *O mulato*, 62–63.

FOUR. Social Whiteness

1. Dauril Alden, "The Population of Brazil in the Eighteenth Century: A Preliminary Study," *Hispanic American Historical Review* 43 (May 1963): 173–205; E. Bradford Burns, *Latin America: A Concise Interpretive History* (Englewood Cliffs, NJ: Prentice Hall, 1970), 103; Maria Luisa Marcílio, "The Population of Colonial Brazil," in *Colonial Latin America*, vol. 2 of *The Cambridge History of Latin America*, ed. Leslie Bethell (New York: Cambridge University Press, 1984).

2. Francisco Vidal Luna and Herbert S. Klein, *Slavery and the Economy of São Paulo, 1750–1850* (Stanford, CA: Stanford University Press, 2003), 227–80, 230; G. Reginald Daniel, *Race and Multiraciality in Brazil and the United States: Converging Paths?* (University Park: Pennsylvania University Press, 2006), 30–31.

3. Luna and Klein, *Slavery*, 170.

4. John Burdick, "The Myth of Racial Democracy," *North American Congress on Latin America Report on the Americas* 25, no. 4 (February 1992): 40–42; David W. Cohen and Jack P. Greene, introduction to *Neither Slave nor Free: The Freemen of African Descent in the Slave Societies of the New World*, ed. David W. Cohen and Jack P. Greene (Baltimore: Johns Hopkins University Press, 1972), 1–23; Herbert S. Klein, "Nineteenth-Century Brazil," in Cohen and Greene, *Neither Slave nor Free*, 309–34; A. J. R. Russell-Wood, "Colonial Brazil," in Cohen and Greene, *Neither Slave nor Free*, 84–133; Herbert S. Klein, *African Slavery in Latin America and the Caribbean* (New York: Oxford University Press, 1986), 227–28, 230, 309–34.

5. Melissa Nobles, *Shades of Citizenship: Race and the Census in Modern Politics* (Stanford, CA: Stanford University Press, 2000), 89; Edith Piza and Fúlvia Rosemberg, "Color in the Brazilian Census," in *Race in Contemporary Brazil: From Indifference to Equality*, ed. Rebecca Reichmann (University Park: Pennsylvania State University Press, 1999), 40–41.

6. It is difficult to determine accurate demographics for this period due to Brazil's great racial diversity and the complexity of how individuals classified themselves racially, regardless of their skin color.

7. Daniel, *Race and Multiraciality*, 30–31; Hartimus Hoetink, *Slavery and Race Relations in the Americas: Comparative Notes on Their Nature and Nexus* (New York: Harper and Row, 1973), 23.

8. Directoria Geral da Estatística, *Relatório e trabalhos estatísticos* (Rio de Janeiro, 1875), 46–62; *Relatório do Ministério da Agricultura*, May 10, 1883, 10.

9. Luna and Klein, *Slavery*, 158.

10. Luna and Klein, *Slavery*, 159, 178.

11. Historian Ann Twinam has studied at length the existence of social whitening in Spanish America through a system known as *gracias al sacar* (thanks for the exclusion) in which mixed-race individuals could purchase a royal exemption that provided them with white status. See Ann Twinam, *Purchasing Whiteness: Pardos, Mulattos, and the Quest for Social Mobility in the Spanish Indies* (Stanford, CA: Stanford University Press, 2014); and *Public Lives, Private Secrets: Gender, Honor, Sexuality, and Illegitimacy in Colonial Spanish America* (Stanford, CA: Stanford University Press, 1999).

12. Carl N. Degler, *Neither Black nor White: Slavery and Race Relations in Brazil and the United States* (New York: Macmillan, 1971).

13. Johann Moritz Rugendas arrived in Brazil in 1821 at the age of eighteen, contracted as an artist for a scientific expedition by Georg Heinrich von Langsdorff, the Baron of Langsdorff. The expedition went to Minas Gerais, São Paulo, the central west, and the Amazon. Johann Moritz Rugendas, *Viagem pitoresca através do Brasil* (Belo Horizonte, Brazil: Itatiaia, 1979), 193.

14. Hoetink, *Slavery and Race Relations*, 8–37; Katia M. de Queirós Mattoso, *To Be a Slave in Brazil, 1550–1888* (New Brunswick, NJ: Rutgers University Press, 1986), 182, 191–92.

15. Donald Pierson, *Negroes in Brazil: Study of Race Contact at Bahia* (Carbondale: Southern Illinois University Press, 1967), 139; Kim D. Butler, *Freedoms Given, Freedoms Won: Afro-Brazilians in Post-Abolition São Paulo and Salvador* (New Brunswick, NJ: Rutgers University Press, 1998), 53–54; Degler, *Neither Black nor White*, 103, 140, 196–99; Mattoso, *To Be a Slave in Brazil*, 191; Daniel, *Race and Multiraciality*, 42–43; Mieko Nishida, "From Ethnicity to Race and Gender: Transformation of Black Lay Sodalities in Salvador, Brazil," *Journal of Social History* 32, no. 2 (winter 1998): 329–48.

16. George Reid Andrews, *Blacks and Whites in São Paulo* (Madison: University of Wisconsin Press, 1991), 247; Petrônio Domingues, *Uma história não contada: Negro, racismo e branqueamento em São Paulo na pós-abolição* (São Paulo: Senac, 2004), 188; Daniel, *Race and Multiraciality*, 44–47.

17. Emília Viotti da Costa, *The Brazilian Slave Empire: Myths and Histories* (Chapel Hill: University of North Carolina Press, 2000), 241–42.

18. João Costa Vargas and Jaime Ampara Alves, "Geographies of Death: Intersectional Analysis of Police Lethality and the Racialized Regimes of Citizenship in São Paulo," *Ethnic and Racial Studies* 33, no. 4 (April 2010): 613.

19. Viotti da Costa, *Brazilian Slave Empire*, 240.

20. Quoted in Jean-Michel Massa, *La jeunesse de Machado de Assis, 1839–1870: Essai de biograpahie intéllectuelle*, vol. 1 (Université de Poitiers: Rennes, 1969), 47.

21. Viotti da Costa, *Brazilian Slave Empire*, 241–42.

22. Lamonte Aidoo and Daniel F. Silva, eds., *Emerging Dialogues on Machado de Assis* (New York: Palgrave Macmillan, 2016).

23. João Costa Vargas, "Hyperconsciousness of Race and Its Negation: The Dialectic of White Supremacy in Brazil," *Identities: Global Studies in Culture and Power* 11 (2004): 449.

24. Daniel, *Race and Multiraciality*, 39.

25. Homi K. Bhabha, *The Location of Culture* (New York: Routledge, 1994), 86.

26. Bhabha, *Location of Culture*, 88.

27. Sharon Patricia Holland, *The Erotic Life of Racism* (Durham, NC: Duke University Press, 2012), 3.

28. G. Reginald Daniel, *Machado de Assis: Multiracial Identity and the Brazilian Novelist* (University Park: Pennsylvania University Press, 2012), 21.

29. Daniel, *Machado de Assis*, 18.

30. Degler, *Neither Black nor White*, 84.

31. Reverend Robert Walsh, *Notices of Brazil in 1828–1829*, vol. 2 (London: F. Westley and A. H. Davis, 1830), 465.

32. Maria Dundas Graham, *Journal of a Voyage to Brazil, and Residence There during Part of the Years 1821, 1822, 1823* (London: Longman, Hurst, Rees, Orme, Brown, and Green, 1824), 125. While in Pernambuco Graham also noted, "By the last census, the population of Pernambuco, including Olinda, was seventy thousand, of which not above one third are white: the rest are mulatto or negro" (125).

33. Graham, *Journal*, 126.

34. Adèle Toussaint-Samson, *A Parisian in Brazil: The Travel Account of a French Woman in Nineteenth-Century Rio de Janeiro*, trans. Emma Toussaint (Wilmington, DE: Scholarly Resources, 2001), 47. In Recife in 1824, a military faction of mulattos lodged a revolt along with a group of insurgent slaves. The leader of the revolt, illustrating the impact of the Haitian revolution, issued a manifesto that read:

As I imitate Christopher
That immortal Haitian
Hey! Imitate his people
O my sovereign people!

Clóvis Moura, *O negro-de bom escravo a mau cidadão* (Rio de Janeiro: Editora Conquista, 1977), 116.

35. Walsh, *Notices of Brazil*, 329.

36. Jorge Andrade, "Quatro Tiradentes Baianos," *Realidade* (São Paulo, November 1971): 34–53; Kenneth R. Maxwell, *Conflicts and Conspiracies: Brazil and Portugal, 1750–1808* (Cambridge: Cambridge University Press, 1974); Donald Ramos, "Social Revolution Frustrated: The Conspiracy of the Tailors in Bahia, 1798," *Luso-Brazilian Review* 13, no. 1 (summer 1976): 74–90; Stuart B. Schwartz, *Sugar Plantations in the Formation of Brazilian Society: Bahia, 1550–1835* (Cambridge, UK: Cambridge University Press, 1985).

37. Moura, *O negro-de bom escravo*, 139.

38. Luiz Luna, *O negro na luta contra abolição* (Rio de Janeiro: Leitura 1976), 213; Michael R. Trochim, "The Black Guard: Racial Conflict in Post-Abolition Brazil," *Americas* 44, no. 3 (January 1988): 287–88; Butler, *Freedoms Given*, 53, 147–50.

39. Charles Expilly, *Les femmes et les moeurs du Brésil* (Paris: Charlieu et Huillery Libraires Editeurs, 1863), 256.

40. Daniel, *Machado de Assis*, 35.

41. Expilly, *Les femmes et les moeurs*, 264.

42. Renting slaves was a common practice in Brazil, especially in large cities such as

Rio de Janeiro. To earn extra money, masters would often rent out some of their slaves for day work or for short periods of time. They would place ads in local newspapers advertising the slave and the services that they offered, such as cleaning, cooking, manual labor, and caring for children. Europeans like Expilly who were staying in Brazil temporarily often rented slaves to work in their houses. These slaves were called *escravos de ganho* (slaves for gain or profit), as they would give all the proceeds from their work to their masters. Many of the slave women, in addition to performing domestic duties, were also prostituted by their masters. Newspaper advertisements included physical references alluding to prostitution, such as these from 1860: "A beautiful little black girl is for sale, with basic sewing skills; her skills will certainly not displease the buyer"; and "On Ouvidor Street a beautiful little black girl is for sale to give as a gift, who knows how to sew well and care for children, and who is very affectionate." *Indústria, escravidão, sociedade: Uma pesquisa historiográfica do Rio de Janeiro no século XIX* (Rio de Janeiro: Editora Civilização Brasileira, 1976), 99. See also Delso Renault, *Rio de Janeiro: A vida da cidade refletida nos jornais, 1850–1870* (Rio de Janeiro: Editora Civilização Brasileira, 1978).

43. Charles Expilly, *Le Brésil tel qu'il est* (Paris: Arnauld de Vresse, Libraire Éditeur, 1862), 198–200.

44. Expilly, *Les femmes et les moeurs*, 264.

45. Burdick, "Myth of Racial Democracy," 40–42; Daniel, *Race and Multiraciality*, 32–33; Viotti da Costa, *Brazilian Slave Empire*, 239–43; Luna and Klein, *Slavery*, 169–72.

46. Daniel, *Race and Multiraciality*, 33.

47. Luiz Anselmo da Fonseca, *A escravidão, o clero e o abolicionismo* (Bahia, Brazil: Imprensa Econômica, 1887), 150.

48. See Expilly, *Les femmes et les moeurs*, 222. Several slave revolts and uprisings occurred throughout the eighteenth century in Minas Gerais. Records indicate that revolts occurred almost yearly. A similar version of the capitão do mato, known as *ranchadores*, who caught fugitive slaves, emerged in Cuba a century earlier. See Fernando Ortiz, *Hampa afro cubana: Los negros esclavos: Estudio sociológico y de derecho público* (Havana: Revista Bimestre Cubana, 1916), 397; and D. José Antonio Saco, *História de la esclavitud de la raza africana en el nuevo mundo* (Barcelona: Jaime Jepús, 1879), 221–22.

49. The military equivalent of the capitão do mato.

50. Henry Koster, *Travels in Brazil* (London: Longman, Hurst, Rees, Orme, and Brown, 1816), 391.

51. Expilly, *Les femmes et les moeurs*, 261–67.

52. Koster, *Travels in Brazil*, 431.

53. Expilly, *Le Brésil tel qu'il est*, 187.

54. David Roediger, *Towards the Abolition of Whiteness: Essays on Race, Politics, and Working Class History* (New York: Verso, 1994), 13.

55. Viotti da Costa, *Brazilian Slave Empire*, 240.

56. Luna and Klein, *Slavery*, 177.

57. Luna and Klein, *Slavery*.

58. Daniel, *Race and Multiraciality*, 40–41.

59. João José Reis, *O rol dos culpados: Notas sobre um documento da rebelião de 1835*, Anais do Arquivo Público do estado da Bahia, vol. 48, 1996, 301–4.

60. Luiz Gonzaga Pinto da Gama, "Sortimento de gorras para a gente do grande tom," in *Trovas burlescas e escritos em prosa*, ed. Fernando Góes (São Paulo: Editora Cultura, 1944), 24–26. For more information on the life of Luiz Gama see Nelson Camara Azevedo, *O advogado dos escravos — Luiz Gama* (São Paulo: Editora Lettera, 2010); Elciene Azevedo, *Orfeu da Carapinha: A trajetória de Luiz Gama na imperial cidade de São Paulo* (São Paulo: Editora Unicamp, 1999); Sud Mennuci, *O precursor do abolicionismo no Brasil: Luiz Gama* (São Paulo: Companhia Editora Nacional, 1938).

61. Elizabeth Abbott, *Haiti: The Duvaliers and Their Legacy* (New York: McGraw-Hill, 1988); C. L. R. James, *The Black Jacobins: Toussaint L'Ouverture and the San Domingo Revolution* (New York: Vintage: 1989); Laurent Dubois, *Avengers of the New World: The Story of Haitian Revolution* (Boston: Belknap Press, 2005).

62. Wilhelm Ludwig von Eschwege, *Pluto brasiliensis* (São Paulo, Brazil: Companhia Editora Nacional, 1944), 447.

63. Graham, *Journal*, 127.

64. Graham, *Journal*, 165.

65. Joaquim Nabuco, *O abolicionismo* (1883; repr., Brasília: Fundação Universidade de Brasília Editora, 2003), 196.

66. Nabuco, *O abolicionismo*, 196.

67. Mahommah Gardo Baquaqua, *The Biography of Mahommah Gardo Baquaqua: His Passage from Slavery to Freedom in Africa and America*, ed. Robin Law and Paul E. Lovejoy (Princeton, NJ: Markus Wiener, 2007), 162.

68. Koster, *Travels in Brazil*, 427.

69. John Hope Franklin, *The Free Negro in North Carolina, 1790–1860*, 2nd ed. (Chapel Hill: University of North Carolina Press, 1995), 159.

70. Franklin, *Free Negro*, 159.

71. Franklin, *Free Negro*, 161. Author Edward P. Jones offers a very interesting depiction of African American slaveholders in the antebellum South in his novel *The Known World* (New York: HarperCollins, 2009).

72. Koster, *Travels in Brazil*, 431.

73. Expilly, *Les femmes et les moeurs*, 424.

74. Koster, *Travels in Brazil*, 424.

75. See, for example, Saidiya V. Hartman, *Scenes of Subjection: Slavery, Terror, and Self-Making in Nineteenth-Century America* (New York: Oxford University Press, 1996); Saidiya V. Hartman, *Lose Your Mother: A Journey along the Atlantic Slave Route* (New York: Farrar, Straus and Giroux, 2008); Aliyyah Abdur-Rahman, *Against the Closet: Black Political Longing and the Erotics of Race* (Durham, NC: Duke University Press, 2012); Christina Sharpe, *Monstrous Intimacies: Making Post-Slavery Subjects* (Durham, NC: Duke University Press, 2010); Vincent Woodard, *The Delectable Negro: Human Consumption and Homoeroticism within US Slave Culture* (New York: NYU Press, 2014); David Sartorious, *Ever Faithful: Race, Loyalty, and the Ends of Empire in Spanish Cuba* (Durham, NC: Duke University Press, 2014); Camilia Cowling, *Conceiving Freedom: Women of Color, Gender, and the Abolition of Slavery in Havana and Rio de Janeiro* (Chapel Hill: University of North Carolina Press, 2013).

76. Júnia Ferreira Furtado, *Chica da Silva: A Brazilian Slave of the Eighteenth Century* (New York: Cambridge University Press, 2009), 146.

77. Furtado, *Chica da Silva*, 147.

78. Machado de Assis, *Memórias póstumas de Brás Cubas* (São Paulo: Ateliê Editorial, 1998), 169–70.

79. José Antônio Gonsalves de Mello, *Henrique Dias: Governador dos crioulos, negros, e mulatos do Brasil* (Rio de Janeiro: Editora Fundação Joaquim Nabuco, 1988); Hebe Mattos, "'Pretos' and 'Pardos' between the Cross and the Sword: Racial Categories in Seventeenth-Century Brazil," *European Review of Latin American and Caribbean Studies/Revista Europea de Estudios Latinoamericanos y del Caribe* 80 (April 2006): 43–55.

80. Fonseca, *A escravidão*, 143, 154.

81. Fonseca, *A escravidão*, 152.

82. Fonseca, *A escravidão*, 154.

83. Fonseca, *A escravidão*, 148.

84. Audre Lorde, "The Transformation into Language and Action," in *Sister Outsider: Essays and Speeches* (Berkeley, CA: Crossing Press, 2007), 40–44.

85. Daniel, *Race and Multiraciality*, 33.

86. Joaquim Nabuco, *Campanha abolicionista no recife, eleições de 1884* (Brasília: Senado Federal, 2005), 27–28.

87. Antônio Bento, "Negros e mulatos," *Correio Paulistano*, October 13, 1883.

88. Though passing became woven into the Brazilian social structure, neither this structure nor its consequences are (see: http://grammarguide.copydesk.org/2012/01/10/a-tricky-agreement-problem-neither-nor/) entirely unique to Brazil. Mulatto privilege and its resultant intraracial division can be found in slave societies throughout the Americas, although not on a systemic level. In the Caribbean and the United States, for example, division between blacks as a result of mulatto privilege has historically been the source of great conflict and presented significant challenges to unified conceptions of black identity and community formation. In 1918 Edward Reuter reported in a study that out of 4,267 US blacks who had had any notable success in life, 3,820 were mulattos. Edward Byron Reuter, *The Mulatto in the United States, Including a Study of the Role of Mixed-Blood Races around the World* (Boston: Gorham Press, 1918), 312. Additionally, as philosopher Naomi Zack has shown, what W. E. B. Du Bois called the "talented tenth" was predominately composed of a mulatto elite. Naomi Zack, *Race and Mixed Race* (Philadelphia: Temple University Press, 1993), 96. This early twentieth-century American mulatto elite was excluded from white society and was both revered and resented by less economically and culturally advantaged blacks. It was tradition, as in Brazil, that many of the US mulatto elite would maintain a distance from the black masses. As many descended from prominent white ancestors and had long histories of freedom that predated the Civil War, they sought to sustain their privilege and social standing, often refusing to marry partners of darker complexion or of a lower socioeconomic background.

89. Randall Kennedy, *Sellout: The Politics of Racial Betrayal* (New York: Pantheon Books, 2008). Randall Kennedy uncovered a number of documented instances of blacks aiding whites to suppress slave uprisings. Kennedy, *Sellout*, 32–42. In 1739 in South

Carolina, in the Stono Rebellion, referred to as the "most serious slave uprising in colonial America," approximately thirty slaves, including one named July, fought against the rebelling slaves to save whites and were rewarded for their loyalty. July was emancipated and given a suit and other clothes. Darold D. Wax, "'The Great Risque We Run': The Aftermath of the Slave Rebellion at Stono, South Carolina, 1739–1745," *Journal of Negro History* 67 (summer 1982): 136–47. In 1800 in Richmond, Virginia, what was reputed to have been one of the largest slave revolts in the United States, lead by Gabriel Prosser, was quelled by several slaves who told their masters of Prosser's plans. Prosser tried to escape with the help of a former overseer but was seen by a slave who turned him in. The slave was awarded fifty dollars. Douglas R. Egerton, *Gabriel's Rebellion: The Virginia Slave Conspiracies of 1800 and 1802* (Chapel Hill: University of North Caroline Press, 1993), 105–7.

90. Amy Jacques Garvey, *Philosophy and Opinions of Marcus Garvey*, ed. and with an introduction by Robert A. Hill, vol. 1 (1923; repr., New York: Atheneum, 1992), 29.

91. David Walker, *Walker's Appeal, in Four Articles: Together with a Preamble, to the Coloured Citizens of the World, but in Particular, and Very Expressly, to Those of the United States of America, Written in Boston, State of Massachusetts, September 28, 1829* (Boston: David Walker, 1830; electronic edition, Chapel Hill: University of North Carolina Library, 2011), 26.

92. Walker, *Walker's Appeal*, 25.

93. Vargas and Alves, "Geographies of Death," 613.

94. Vargas and Alves, "Geographies of Death," 614.

95. Sérgio Corrêa Da Costa, *Brasil, segredo de estado*, Rio de Janeiro: Record, 2001; Maria Helena Farelli, *Malês: Os negros Bruxos* (São Paulo: Madras, 2002); João José Reis, *Rebelião escrava no Brasil: A história do levante dos malês em 1835* (São Paulo: Companhia das Letras, 2003).

96. Zita Nunes, *Cannibal Democracy: Race and Representation in the Literature of the Americas* (Minneapolis: University of Minnesota Press, 2008), 73.

97. Martha Elizabeth Hodes, *White Women, Black Men: Illicit Sex in the Nineteenth-Century South* (New Haven, CT: Yale University Press, 1997), 117, 207.

98. W. C. Benet, "Is the Negro a Failure? A Review of the Question," *Augusta* (Georgia) *Chronicle*, April 1886, 6.

99. Ariel [Buckner H. Payne], *The Negro: What Is His Ethnological Status?* (Cincinnati: Author, 1867), 23.

100. Graham, *Journal*, 126.

101. Expilly, *Les femmes et les moeurs*, 254–55.

102. Expilly, *Les femmes et les moeurs*, 254–55.

103. Thales de Azevedo, *Social Change in Brazil* (Gainesville: University of Florida Press, 1963), 32.

104. Catherine Clinton and Michelle Gillespie, eds., *The Devil's Lane: Sex and Race in the Early South* (New York: Oxford University Press, 1997); David H. Fowler, *Northern Attitudes toward Interracial Marriage: Legislation and Public Opinion in the Middle States of the Old Northwest, 1780–1930* (New York: Garland, 1987); Calvin C. Hernton, *Sex and Racism in America* (New York: Double Day, 1965, 1981); Martha Hodes, ed. *Sex, Love,*

Race: Crossing Boundaries in North American History (New York: NYU Press, 1999); Randall Kennedy, *Interracial Intimacies: Sex, Marriage, Identity, and Adoption* (New York: Pantheon Books, 2003); James Kinney, *Amalgamation!: Race, Sex, and Rhetoric in the Nineteenth-Century American Novel* (Westport, CT: Greenwood Press, 1985); Scott L. Malcomson, *One Drop of Blood: The American Misadventure of Race* (New York: Farrar, Straus and Giroux, 2000); Rachel F. Moran, *Interracial Intimacy: The Regulation of Race and Romance* (Chicago: University of Chicago Press, 2001); Nell Irvin Painter, *Southern History across the Color Line* (Chapel Hill: University of North Caroline Press, 2002); Renée C. Romano, *Erosion of a Taboo: Black-White Marriage in the United States from World War II to the Present* (Cambridge, MA: Harvard University Press, 2003); Maria P. P. Root, *Love's Revolution: Interracial Marriage* (Philadelphia: Temple University Press, 2001); Joshua D. Rothman, *Notorious in the Neighborhood: Sex and Families across the Color Line in Virginia, 1787–1861* (Chapel Hill: University of North Carolina Press, 2003); Werner Sollers, ed., *Interracialism: Black-White Intermarriage in American History, Literature, and Law* (New York: Oxford University Press, 1997).

105. Robyn Wiegman, *American Anatomies: Theorizing Race and Gender* (Durham, NC: Duke University Press, 1995), 90.

106. Graça Aranha, *O meu próprio romance* (Rio de Janeiro, Brazil: Companhia Editora Nacional, 1931), 110–11.

107. Expilly, *Les femmes et les moeurs*, 254. Peter Wade has argued, "The articulation of race and sex shows a dynamic process of mutual constitution: sexual virtue (sex) was important to status; blood connections and purity of blood (race) also defined status; what connected sex and race was the process of regulating sexual exchanges through marriage (while sexual exchanges outside marriage enacted the dominant position of white men)." Peter Wade, *Race and Sex in Latin America* (New York: Pluto Press, 2009), 92.

108. Furtado, *Chica da Silva*, 261.

109. Furtado, *Chica da Silva*, 263.

110. Furtado, *Chica da Silva*.

111. Ralph Beals, "Social Stratification in Latin America," *American Journal of Sociology* 58 (1953): 334.

112. Thales de Azevedo, *Les élites de couleur dans une ville brésilienne* (Paris: UNESCO, 1953), 45.

113. Josué Montello, *Aluísio Azevedo e a polêmica d'O Mulato* (Rio de Janeiro: J. Olympio; Brasília, DF), 1975; José Verissimo, *História da literatura brasileira: De Bento Teixeira (1601) a Machado de Assis (1908)* (Rio de Janeiro: Francisco Alves, 1916); Jean-Yves Mérian, *Aluísio Azevedo, vida, e obra, 1857–1913: O verdadeiro Brasil do século XIX* (Rio de Janeiro: Editora Espaço e Tempo, 1988); Alfredo Bosi, *História concisa da literatura brasileira* (São Paulo: Editora Cultrix), 188–92.

114. Aluísio Azevedo, *O mulato*, trans. Murray Graeme MacNicoll (Austin: University of Texas Press, 1993), 203–4.

115. Azevedo, *O mulato*, 226–27.

116. Azevedo, *O mulato*, 275–76.

FIVE. *O Diabo Preto* (The Negro Devil)

1. Miguel Pereira, *Á margem da medicina* (Rio de Janeiro: Castro, Mendonça, 1922), 124.

2. Sander L. Gilman, *Difference and Pathology: Stereotypes of Sexuality, Race, and Madness* (Ithaca, NY: Cornell University Press, 1985), 24.

3. Gilberto Freyre, *The Masters and the Slaves: A Study in the Development of Brazilian Civilization*, trans. Samuel Putnam (Berkeley: University of California Press, 1986), 71.

4. Herculano Augusto Lassance Cunha, "Dissertação sobre a prostituição em particular na cidade do Rio de Janeiro" (PhD diss., University of Rio de Janeiro, 1845).

5. Émile Béringer, *Recherches sur le climat et la mortalité de la ville du Recife ou Pernambuco (Brésil)* (Versailles: E. Aubert, 1878), 45.

6. Johann Baptist von Spix and Carl Friedrich Philipp von Martius, *Travels in Brazil in the years 1817–1820: Undertaken by Command of His Majesty King of Bavaria*, vol. 2 (London: Longman, Hurst, Rees, Orme, Brown, and Green, 1824), 126–27.

7. Spix and Martius, *Travels in Brazil*, 2:127.

8. Spix and Martius, *Travels in Brazil*, 2:127.

9. Spix and Martius, *Travels in Brazil*, 2:70. Also see Spix and Martius, *Travels in Brazil*, vols. 1 and 2; Oscar Clark, "Sífilis no Brasil e suas manifestações viscerais," in *2° Boletim do VIII Congresso brasileiro de Medicina, 1° Congresso Sul-Americano de Dermatologia de Siflografia etc.* (Rio de Janeiro: Imprensa Nacional, 1928); Oscar da Silva Araújo, *Alguns comentários sobre a syphilis no Rio de Janeiro* (Rio de Janeiro: Empreza Gráphica Editora Paulo Pongetti, 1928); Oscar da Silva Araújo, "A prophylaxia da lepra e das doenças venéreas no Brasil e a actuação do Departamento Nacional de Saúde Pública," *Archivos de hygiene* (Rio de Janeiro) 1, no. 2 (1927): 195–293; Sérgio Carrara, *Tributo a Vênus: A luta contra sífilis no Brasil, da passagem do século aos anos 40* (Rio de Janeiro: Editora Fiocruz, 1996).

10. Freyre, *The Masters and the Slaves*, 324, Spix and Martius, *Travels in Brazil*, 2:70.

11. João Álvares de Macedo Junior, *Da prostiuição no Rio de Janeiro e da sua influência sobre a saúde pública* (Rio de Janeiro: Typographia Americana, 1869), 12–13.

12. Robert J. C. Young, *Colonial Desire: Hybridity in Theory, Culture, and Race* (London: Routledge, 1995), 181.

13. José Ricardo Pires de Almeida, *Homosexualismo: A libertinagem no Rio de Janeiro: Estudos sobre as perversões do instinto genital* (Rio de Janeiro: Laemmert, 1906), 32–34.

14. Joaquim Nabuco, *O abolicionismo* (1883; repr., Brasília: Fundação Universidade de Brasília, 2003), 172.

15. Nabuco, *O abolicionismo*, 170.

16. Carrara, *Tributo a Vênus*, 26.

17. See pertinent discussions of the conflation of the Brazilian citizen and the white man in Richard Miskolci, *O desejo da nação: Masculinidade e branquitude no Brasil de fins do XIX* (São Paulo: Annablume, 2012); Sueann Caulfield, *In Defense of Honor: Sexual Morality, Modernity, and Nation in Early-Twentieth-Century Brazil* (Durham, NC: Duke University Press, 2000); Jerry Dávila, *Diploma of Whiteness: Race and Social Policy in Brazil, 1917–1945* (Durham, NC: Duke University Press, 2003).

18. Sérgio Buarque de Hollanda, *Raízes do Brasil* (São Paulo: Companhia das Letras, 1996).

19. For a nuanced discussion of the evolution of the Brazilian citizen and notions of

citizenship in Brazil, see José Murilo Carvalho, *Cidadania no Brasil: O longo caminho* (Rio de Janeiro: Civilização Brasileira, 2001); Andrei Koerner, *Judiciário e cidadania na constituição da república brasileira, 1841–1920* (Curitiba, Brazil: Editora Jurua, 2010); André Botelho and Lília Mortiz Schwarcz, *Cidadania, um projeto em construção: Minorias, justiça, e direitos* (São Paulo: Editora Claro Enigma, 2012).

20. Miskolci, *O desejo da nação*, 42.

21. Macedo Júnior, *Da prostiuição no Rio de Janeiro, 13.*

22. Antônio da Fonseca Viana, "Considerações higiênicas e médico-legais sobre o casamento relativamente à mulher." Medical Thesis, Faculdade de Medicina do Rio de Janeiro, 1872: Typographia Americana, 1842, 18.

23. Freyre, *Masters and Slaves*, 395.

24. Freyre, *Masters and Slaves.*

25. Freyre, *Masters and Slaves*, 155.

26. Freyre, *Masters and Slaves*, 395.

27. Freyre, *Masters and Slaves*, 155.

28. Jeffrey D. Needell, "Identity, Race, Gender, and Modernity in the Origins of Gilberto Freyre's Oeuvre," *American Historical Review* 100, no. 1 (February 1995): 70.

29. Almeida, *Homosexualismo*, 32–34.

30. Viriato Fernando Nunes, "As perversões sexuais em medicina legal" (PhD diss., University of São Paulo, 1928), 37.

31. Michel Foucault, *The History of Sexuality*, trans. Robert Hurley, vol. 1, *An Introduction* (New York: Vintage Books, 1990), 43.

32. Leonídio Ribeiro, *Homossexualismo e Endocrinologia* (Rio de Janeiro: Livraria Francisco Alves, 1938), 168.

33. Francisco Ferraz de Macedo, "Da prostituição em geral e em particular em relação ao Rio de Janeiro," thesis, Faculdade de Medicine do Rio de Janeiro, 1872.

34. James N. Green, *Beyond Carnival: Male Homosexuality in Twentieth-Century Brazil* (Chicago: University of Chicago Press, 1999), 34.

35. Macedo, "Da prostituição em geral," 40.

36. Pires de Almeida, *Homosexualismo*, 49–50.

37. Pires de Almeida, *Homosexualismo*, 73.

38. Pires de Almeida, *Homosexualismo*, 50–57.

39. Macedo, "Da prostituição em geral," 44.

40. Talisman Ford, "Passion in the Eye of the Beholder: Sexuality as Seen by Sexologists, 1900–1940" (PhD diss., Vanderbilt University, 1995), 162–70, 183–84.

41. Green, *Beyond Carnival*, 144.

42. Francisco José Viveiros de Castro, *Atentados ao pudor: Estudos sobre as aberrações do instinto sexual* (Rio de Janeiro: Livraria Editora Freitas Bastos, 1932), 228–29.

43. Castro, *Atentados ao pudor.*

44. Ribeiro, "Homossexualismo e endicronologia," 123.

45. Pires de Almeida, *Homosexualismo*, 168.

46. Pires de Almeida, *Homosexualismo*, 81.

47. Siobhan B. Somerville, *Queering the Color Line: Race and the Invention of Homosexuality in American Culture* (Durham, NC: Duke University Press, 2000), 17.

48. Somerville, *Queering the Color Line*, 3.

49. Nabuco, *O abolicionismo*, 194.

50. Green, *Beyond Carnival*, 122.

51. Leonídio Ribeiro, *Homossexualismo e Endocrinologia*, 163.

52. José Henrique Pierangelli, *Códigos penais do Brasil: Evolução histórica* (São Paulo: Editora Javoli, 1980), 168.

53. Afonso Henrique de Lima Barreto, *Diário do hospício: O cemitério dos vivos* (Rio de Janeiro: Secretaria Municipal de Cultura, Departamento Geral de Documentação e Informação Cultural, Divisão de Editoração, 1993).

54. Sérgio Adorno, *Os aprendizes do poder: O bacharelismo liberal na política brasileira* (Rio de Janeiro: Paz e Terra, 1988); André Paulo Castnaha, *Pedagogia da moralidade: O estado e a organização da instrução pública na província do Mato Grosso, 1834–1873* (master's thesis, Universidade Federal de Mato Grosso, 1999); Viveiros de Castro, *Os delictos contra a honra da mulher* (Rio de Janeiro: João Lopes da Cunha Editora, 1897); Boris Fausto, *Crime e cotidiano: A criminalidade em São Paulo, 1880–1924*, 2nd edition (São Paulo: Editora da Universidade de São Paulo, 2001).

55. Green, *Beyond Carnival*, 22.

56. Michel Foucault, *Abnormal: Lectures at the Collège de France, 1974–1975* (New York: Picador, 2003), 316–17.

57. Aldo Sinisgalli, "Considerações gerais sobre o homossexualismo," in *Arquivos de polícia e identificação* (São Paulo), vol. 3 (1938–40), 292.

58. Sinisgalli, "Considerações," 292.

59. Gilman, *Difference and Pathology*, 112.

60. Zita Nunes, *Cannibal Democracy: Race and Representation in the Literature of the Americas* (Minneapolis: University of Minnesota Press, 2008), 72.

61. Idelber Avelar, "Cenas dizíveis e indizíveis: Raça e sexualidade em Gilberto Freyre," *Luso-Brazilian Review* 49, no. 1 (November 2012): 176.

62. Needell, "Identity, Race, Gender," 51.

63. Ricardo Noblat, "Playboy entrevista Gilberto Freyre," *Playboy*, March 1980, 29–30.

64. Freyre, *Masters and Slaves*, 323.

65. Freyre, *Masters and Slaves*, 97.

66. Gilberto Freyre, *Sobrados e mocambos: Decadência do patriarcado rural e desenvolvimento urbano* (Rio de Janeiro: Editora Record 1996), 289.

67. Freyre, *Sobrados e mocambos*, 96.

68. Freyre, *Masters and Slaves*, 119.

69. Freyre, *Masters and Slaves*.

70. Freyre, *Masters and Slaves*, 323.

71. Freyre, *Masters and Slaves*, 329.

72. Freyre, *Masters and Slaves*, 98.

73. Freyre, *Masters and Slaves*, 428.

74. Freyre, *Masters and Slaves*, 429.

75. Freyre, *Masters and Slaves*.

76. Freyre, *Masters and Slaves*.

77. Freyre, *Masters and Slaves*.

78. Freyre, *Masters and Slaves*, 97.

79. Freyre, *Masters and Slaves*, 98.

80. Freyre, *Masters and Slaves*, 647.

81. Nunes, *Cannibal Democracy*, 73.

82. Freyre, *Masters and Slaves*, 124.

83. *Primeira visitação do Santo Oficio ás partes do Brasil pelo licenciado Heitor Furtado de Mendonça denunciações de Pernambuco, 1593–1595* (São Paulo: P. Prado, 1929), 399.

84. Luiz Mott, "Relações raciais entre homossexuais no Brasil Colônia," *Revista Brasileira de História* (São Paulo) 5, no. 10 (March/August 1985): 99–122.

85. E. L. McCallum, *Object Lessons: How to Do Things with Fetishism* (Albany: SUNY Press, 1999).

86. Sigmund Freud, *New Introductory Lectures on Psycho-analysis* (New York: W. W. Norton, 1990; 1933), 158–63.

87. Frantz Fanon, *Black Skin, White Masks*, trans. Charles Lam Markmann (New York: Grove Press, 1967), 156, 110.

88. Fanon, *Black Skin, White Masks*, 159.

89. Nunes, *Cannibal Democracy*, 73.

90. Sônia Breyner, *A metáfora do corpo no romance naturalista* (Rio de Janeiro: Livraria São José, 1973), 20.

91. Carlos Figari, *@s "@utros" cariocas: interpelaçes, experiências, e identidades homoeróticas no Rio de Janeiro: Séculos XVII ao XX* (Belo Horizonte, Brazil: Editora UFMG, 2007), 40.

92. Miskolci, *O desejo da nação*, 38.

93. Alessandra El Far, "Crítica social e ideias médicas nos excessos do desejo: Uma ánalise dos 'romances para homens' de finais d século XX e ínicio do XX," *Núcleo de Estudos de Gênero Pagu-Unicamp* 28 (2007): 285–312; Alessandra El Far, *Páginas de sensasão: Literatura popular e pornografia no Rio de Janeiro, 1870–1924* (São Paulo: Companhia das Letras, 2004).

94. Miskolci, *O desejo da nação*, 54.

95. Valentim Magalhães, "Semana literária," *A notícia* (Rio de Janeiro), November 20–21, 1895, 1.

96. The article was originally unsigned but was attributed to José Veríssimo. *Jornal do comércio* (Rio de Janeiro), November 27, 1895, 2. Also see Sânzio de Azevedo's *Adolfo Caminha: Vida e obra* (Fortaleza, Brazil: UFC Edições, 1999), 123.

97. Adolfo Caminha, "Um livro condenado," *A nova revista* (Rio de Janeiro) 1, no. 2 (February 1896): 40–42.

98. Caminha, "Um livro condenado," 41.

99. Adolfo Caminha, *The Black Man and the Cabin Boy*, trans. E. A. Lacey (San Francisco: Gay Sunshine Press, 1982). All quotations in this chapter are from this edition of the novel. Further page numbers are cited in the text.

100. Castro, *Atentados ao pudor*, 227.

101. Kim D. Butler, *Freedoms Given, Freedoms Won: Afro-Brazilians in Post-Abolition São Paulo and Salvador* (New Brunswick, NJ: Rutgers University Press, 1998); George Reid Andrews, *Blacks and Whites in São Paulo* (Madison: University of Wisconsin Press,

1997); Florestan Fernandes, *A integração do negro na sociedade de classes* (São Paulo, Do-
minus Editôra, 1965).

102. *Código Penal da República dos Estados Unidos do Brasil* (Rio de Janeiro: Editora
H. Garnier, 1904), 587.

103. Antônio Carlos Pacheco e Silva, *Psiquiatria clínica e forense* (São Paulo: Companhia Editora Nacional, 1940), 23.

104. Processo-crime #1670–1927, "Dr. Coriolano Nogueira Cobra," Museu do Crime
da Academia de Polícia de São Paulo.

105. Paulo Fernando de Souza Campos, "Os crimes de Preto Amaral: Representações
da degenerescência em São Paulo 1920" (PhD diss., Universidade Estadual Paulista,
2003).

106. Winthrop Jordan, *White over Black: American Attitudes toward the Negro,
1550–1812* (Chapel Hill: University of North Carolina Press, 1968), 151–52.

107. Ellen Barret Ligon, "The White Woman and the Negro," *Good Housekeeping*, November 1903, 135–39.

108. Laura Moutinho, *Razão, "cor" e desejo* (São Paulo: Editora Unesp, 2004),
200–205.

109. Twelve years before Amaral's case, highly influential Paulista author Monteiro
Lobato, who made no qualms about his hatred of blacks, wrote a story titled "Boca torta"
(Crooked Mouth), about a repulsive exslave who was found engaging in necrophilia on
the corpse of a white woman that he dug up. Lobato wrote, "Hideousness was personified
in him. . . . This twisted mouth set obliquely in his face smiled diabolically, illustrating
how the ugly may be made up of the horrifying. So ugly a monster. . . . Everyone says that
he has done horrible things—that he eats children, he's a witch, and that he has a pact
with the devil. All of the misfortunes that have occurred in the village are because of
him." Monteiro Lobato, *Urupês* (São Paulo: Editora Brasilense, 1966), 224.

AFTERWORD

1. Joaquim Felício dos Santos, *Memórias do Distrito Diamantino* (Rio de Janeiro: Typ.
Americana, 1868).

2. André João Antonil, *Cultura e opulência do Brasil pelas minas do ouro* (São Paulo,
Brazil: Obelisco, 1964), 92–93.

3. Júnia Ferreira Furtado, *Chica da Silva: A Brazilian Slave of the Eighteenth Century*
(New York: Cambridge University Press, 2009).

4. Furtado, *Chica da Silva*, 46.

5. Elisa Lucinda, *O semelhante* (Rio de Janeiro: Record, 2002), 20.

Bibliography

ARCHIVAL COLLECTIONS

Arquivo Nacional da Torre do Tombo, Lisbon, Portugal
Arquivo Nacional do Rio de Janeiro
Fundação Casa Rui Barbosa, Rio de Janeiro
Museu do Crime, São Paulo
Museu Paulista São Paulo

PORTUGUESE ARCHIVAL SOURCES

The verbatim transcripts of cases from the Portuguese Inquisition (1536–1821) are extracted from the Arquivo Nacional Torre do Tombo in Lisbon, Portugal.

Livro das confissões e reconciliações que se fizeram na visitação do Santo Ofício na cidade do Salvador da Baía de Todos os Santos, do estado do Brasil, 1618–1620.
Livro das denunciações feitas numa visitação em Lisboa, 1583–1588.
Livro da visitação do Santo Ofício da Inquisição ao estado do Grão-Pará, 1763–1769.
Livro 2 de denúncias dos casados duas vezes, dos do pecado nefando, e de demonstrações de crimes contra a fé, nos Açores e Continente, 1575–1580.
Livro 3 de confissões da primeira visitação ao Brasil, Heitor Furtado de Mendonça, 1594–1595.
Primeira visitação do Santo Ofício às partes do Brasil: Denunciações de Pernambuco, 1618.
Primeira visitação do Santo Ofício às partes do Brasil: Denunciações e confissões de Pernambuco, 1593–1595. Edited by Mello, José Antônio Gonçalves. Recife, Brazil: Secretaria de Turismo, Cultura e Esportes/Fundarpe, 1984.
Primeira visitação do Santo Ofício às partes do Brasil pelo licenciado Heitor Furtado de Mendonça denunciações de Pernambuco, 1593–1595.
Primeira visitação do Santo Ofício às partes do Brasil pelo licenciado Heitor Furtado de Mendonça denunciações de Pernambuco, 1593–1595. Edited by João Capistrano de Abreu. São Paulo: Paulo Prado, 1929.
Quarto livro das denunciações da primeira visitação do Santo Ofício da Inquisição do Brasil,

*a qual fez o licenciado Heitor Furtado de Mendonça, por especial comissão de sua alteza,
1593–1595.*

Santo Ofício da Inquisição de Lisboa: Confissões da Bahia. Edited by Ronaldo Vainfas. São
Paulo: Companhia das Letras, 1997.

*Segunda visitação do Santo Ofício as partes do Brasil pelo inquisidor e visitador o licenciado
Marcos Teixeira: Livro das confissões e ratificações da Bahia, 1618–1620.*

BRAZILIAN ARCHIVAL SOURCES

"Habeas Corpus." 1879. Arquivo Nacional do Rio de Janeiro, vol. 1, 720, no. 2.468
(Gallery A).

*Polícia: Ofícios e ordens: Registro dos ofícios e ordens expedidos aos juizes do crime dos
bairros, 1811–1812.* Arquivo Nacional do Rio de Janeiro, Códice 329, vol. 1.

PORTUGUESE NEWSPAPERS

Correio Paulistano
Gazeta da Tarde
Jornal do Commercio
O Cruzeiro
O Paiz
Rio News

PRIMARY SOURCES

A abolição no parlamento: 65 anos de luta, 1823–1888. 2nd ed. Brasília: Senado Federal,
Secretaria Especial de Editoração e Publicações, 2012. Parliamentary proceedings.

Agassiz, Louis J. R., and Elizabeth Cary Agassiz. *A Journey in Brazil.* Boston: Ticknor
and Fields, 1868.

Alencar, José Martiniano de. *Cartas à favor da escravidão.* São Paulo: Hedra, 2008.

Almeida, José Ricardo Pires de. *Homosexualismo: A libertinagem no Rio de Janeiro:
Estudos sobre as perversões do instinto genital.* Rio de Janeiro: Laemmert, 1906.

Alves, Castro. *Obras completas de Castro Alves.* Vol. 2. São Paulo: Companhia Editora
Nacional, 1942.

Amaral, Francisco Pacifico de. *Escavações: Factos da história de Pernambuco.* Recife,
Brazil: Typographia do Jornal do Recife, 1884.

Annães da Assemblea Legislativa Provincial de São Paulo, March 27, 1878, 90.

Annaes da Câmara e Senado. 1871. Vols. 3 and 4. Rio de Janeiro: Typographia do Diário
do Rio de Janeiro, 1871.

———. 1875. Vol. 4. Rio de Janeiro: Typographia do Diário do Rio de Janeiro, 1875.

Antonil, André João. *Cultura e opulência do Brasil pelas minas do ouro.* São Paulo:
Obelisco, 1964.

Aranha, Graça. *O meu próprio romance.* Rio de Janeiro: Companhia Editora Nacional,
1931.

Araújo, José Thomaz Nabuco de, and José Antônio Pimento Bueno. *Trabalho sôbre a extinccão da escravatura no Brasil*. Rio de Janeiro: TYP Nacional, 1868.

Araújo, Oscar da Silva. *Alguns comentários sobre a syphilis no Rio de Janeiro*. Rio de Janeiro: Paulo Pongetti, 1928.

———. "A prophylaxia da Lepra e das doenças venéreas no Brasil e a actuação do Departamento Nacional de Saúde Pública." *Archivos de hygiene* (Rio de Janeiro) 1, no. 2 (1927): 195–293.

Assis, Machado de. *Machado de Assis afro-descendente escritos de caramujo*. Edited by Eduardo de Assis Duarte. Rio de Janiero: Pallas, 2007.

———. *Memórias póstumas de Brás Cubas*. São Paulo, Brazil: Ateliê Editorial, 1998.

Azevedo, Aluísio. *O cortiço*. São Paulo: Editora Martin Claret, 2012.

———. *O mulato*. Translated by Murray Graeme MacNicoll. Austin: University of Texas Press, 1993.

Azevedo, Artur de, and Urbano Duarte. *O escravocrata*. Rio de Janeiro: A. Guimarães, 1884.

Baquaqua, Mahommah Gardo. *The Biography of Mahommah Gardo Baquaqua: His Passage from Slavery to Freedom in Africa and America*. Edited by Robin Law and Paul E. Lovejoy. Princeton, NJ: Markus Wiener, 2007.

Benci, Jorge. *Economia cristã dos senhores no governo dos escravos: Livro brasileiro de 1700*. São Paulo: Editora Grijalbo, 1977.

Bento, Antônio. "Negros e mulatos." *Correio Paulistano*, October 13, 1883.

Béringer, Émile. *Recherches sur le climat et la mortalité de la ville du Recife ou Pernambuco (Brésil)*. Versailles: E. Aubert, 1878.

Brandão, Francisco Antônio Jr. *A escravatura no Brasil*. Brussels: Thiry-Van Buggenhoudt, 1865.

Brito, Félix Peixoto de. *Considerações geraes sobre a empanicação dos escravos no império do Brasil*. Lisbon: Typographia Portugueza, 1870.

Burlamaqui, Frederico Leopoldo Cezar. *Mémória analytica acerca do commércio d'escravos e acerca da escravidão doméstica*. Rio de Janeiro: Typographia Commercial Fluminense, 1837.

Caminha, Adolfo. *Bom-Crioulo: The Black Man and the Cabin Boy*. Translated by E. A. Lacey. San Francisco: Gay Sunshine Press, 1982.

———. "Um livro condenado." *A nova revista* (Rio de Janeiro) 1, no. 2 (February 1896): 40–42.

Carneiro, João Fernando. "Interpretação da política imigratória brasileira." *Digesto Econômico* 4, no. 46 (1948): 110–25.

Carrara, Sérgio. *Tributo a Vênus: A luta contra sífilis no Brasil, da passagem do século aos anos 40*. Rio de Janeiro: Editora Fiocruz, 1996.

Carvalho, Augusto de. *O Brasil: Colonização e emigração*. Porto, Portugal: B. H. de Morães, 1876.

Castro, Francisco José Viveiros de. *Atentados ao pudor: Estudos sobre as aberrações do instinto sexual*. Rio de Janeiro: Livraria Editora Freitas Bastos, 1932.

Clark, Oscar. "Sífilis no Brasil e suas manifestações viscerais." In *2° Boletim do VIII Congresso Brasileiro de Medicina, 1° Congresso Sul-Americano de Dermatologia de Siflografia etc*. Rio de Janeiro: Imprensa Nacional, 1928.

Código de posturas da illustrissima câmara municipal do Rio de Janeiro. Rio de Janeiro: Typographia Dous de Dezembro, 1854.

Código Penal da República dos Estados Unidos do Brasil. Rio de Janeiro: Editora H. Garnier, 1904.

Congresso Agrícola, Rio de Janeiro. 1878. *Anais.* Rio de Janeiro: Fundação Casa Rui Barbosa, 1988.

Cooper, Clayton Sedgwick. *The Brazilians and Their Country.* New York: Frederick A. Stokes, 1917.

Cunha, Herculano Augusto Lassance. "Dissertação sobre a prostituição em particular na cidade do Rio de Janeiro." PhD diss., University of Rio de Janeiro. Rio de Janeiro: Typographia Imparcial de Paula Brito, 1845.

Diretoria Geral da Estatística. *Relatório e trabalhos estatísticos.* In *Relatórios do Ministério da Agricultura*, May 10, 1883. Rio de Janeiro: N. p., 1875.

Douglass, Frederick. *My Bondage and My Freedom.* New York: Dover, 1969.

———. *Narrative of the Life of Frederick Douglass, an American Slave, Written by Himself.* Edited by David W. Blight. New York: Bedford/St. Martin's Press, 1993.

Du Bois, W. E. B. *The Negro.* 1915. Millwood, NY: Kraus-Thomson, 1974.

———, ed. *The Negro American Family.* New York: Negro University Press, 1969. First published 1908 by Atlanta University Press.

———. *The Souls of Black Folk.* New York: Modern Library, 2003.

Eschwege, Wilhelm Ludwig von. *Pluto Brasiliensis.* São Paulo: Companhia Editora Nacional, 1944.

Expilly, Charles. *Le Brésil tel qu'il est.* Paris: Arnauld de Vresse, Libraire Éditeur, 1862.

———. *Les femmes et les moeurs du Brésil.* Paris: Charlieu et Huillery, 1863.

———. *Mulheres e costumes do Brasil.* São Paulo: Editora Nacional, 1935.

Fernandes, João Ribeiro de Andrade. *História do Brasil: Curso médio.* 17th edition. Rio de Janeiro: Livraria Francisco Alves, 1935.

Fletcher, Rev. James C., and Rev. D. P. Kidder. *Brazil and the Brazilians Portrayed in Historical and Descriptive Sketches.* Boston: Little, Brown, 1868.

Fonseca, Luiz Anselmo da. *A escravidão, o clero e o abolicionismo.* Bahia, Brazil: Imprensa Economica, 1887.

Freyre, Gilberto. *Casa-grande e senzala: Formação da família brasileira sob o regime da economia patriarcal.* Edited by Guillermo Giucci et al. Madrid: Archivos/UNESCO, 2002.

———. *The Masters and the Slaves: A Study in the Development of Brazilian Civilization.* Translated by Samuel Putnam. Berkeley: University of California Press, 1986.

———. *Sobrados e mocambos: Decadência do patriarcado rural e desenvolvimento urbano.* Rio de Janeiro: Editora Record, 1996.

Gama, Luiz Gonzaga Pinto. "Sortimento de gorras para a gente do grande tom." In *Trovas burlescas e escritos em prosa*, edited by Fernando Góes, 24–26. São Paulo, Brazil: Editora Cultura, 1944.

Graham, Maria Dundas. *Journal of a Voyage to Brazil, and Residence There during Part of the Years 1821, 1822, 1823.* London: Longman, Hurst, Rees, Orme, Brown, and Green, 1824.

Guimarães, Francisco Pinheiro. *História de uma moça rica: Drama en quatro actos*. Rio de Janeiro: Typographia do Diário do Rio de Janeiro, 1861.

Hildebrandt, Hugo. *Die Krankheiten der äusseren weiblichen Genitalien*. In *Handbuch der Frauenkrankheiten III*, edited by Theodor Billroth, 11–12. Stuttgart: Enke, 1877.

Koster, Henry. *Travels in Brazil*. London: Longman, Hurst, Rees, Orme, and Brown, 1816.

Lacerda, João Batista de. "Sur les métis au Brésil." *Premier Congrès Universel des Races*. Paris: Imprimerie Devouge, 1911.

Lapa, José Roberto do Amaral, ed. *Livro da visitação do Santo Ofício da Inquisição ao estado do Grão-Pará, 1763–1769*. Petrópolis, Brazil: Vozes, 1978.

Lemos, Francisco de. "Relatório do chefe de policia da corte." In Francisco de Paula de Negreiros Sayão Lobato, *Relatório da repartição dos negocios da justiça apresentado a assemblea geral legislativa, annexos*. Rio de Janeiro, Typographia Nacional, 1871.

Lima, Alexandre Jose Barbosa. "Mensagem do governador de Pernambuco." March 6, 1893, 28–29. In Robert Brent Toplin, *The Abolition of Slavery in Brazil*. New York: Atheneum, 1972.

Lima, Manoel de Oliveira. *Nos Estados Unidos: Impressões políticas e sociais*. Leipzig: Brockhaus, 1899.

Lindley, Thomas. *Narrative of a Voyage to Brasil . . .* London: J. Johnson, 1805.

Lobato, Monteiro. *Urupês*. São Paulo: Editora Brasilense, 1966.

Lobo, Bruno. *Japonezes no Japão, no Brasil*. Rio de Janeiro: Imprensa Nacional, 1926.

Macedo, Francisco Ferraz de. "Da Prostituição em geral e em particular em relação ao Rio de Janeiro." Thesis, Faculdade de Medicina do Rio de Janeiro, 1872.

Macedo, Joaquim Manuel de. *As vítimas algozes: Quadros da escravidão*. São Paulo, Brazil: Editora Scipione, 1991.

Macedo Junior, João Álvares de. *Da prostiuição no Rio de Janeiro e da sua influência sobre a saúde pública*. Rio de Janeiro: Typographia Americana, 1869.

Magalhães, Valentim. "Semana literária." *A Notícia* (Rio de Janeiro), November 20–21, 1895.

Mello, Jose Antonio Gonsalves. *Confissões de Pernambuco, 1594–1595: Primeira visitação do santo oficio às Partes do Brasil*. Recife, Brazil: Editora Universidade Federal de Pernambuco, 1970.

Menezes, Caio de. *A raça Allemã*. Porto Alegre, Brazil: Verband Deutscher Vereine, 1914.

Nabuco, Joaquim. *Campanha abolicionista no recife, eleições de 1884*. Brasília: Senado Federal, 2005.

———. *Discursos Parlamentares, 1879–1889*. Brasília: Câmara dos Deputados, 1983.

———. 1883. *O abolicionismo*. Brasília: Fundação Universidade de Brasília, 2003.

———. *O Brasil e as colônias portuguesas*. 2nd ed. Lisbon: Parceria A. M. Pereira, 1881.

Nascimento, Abdias do. *Brazil, Mixture or Massacre? Essays in the Genocide of a Black People*. 2nd ed. Dover, MA: Majority Press, 1989.

———. *O negro revoltado*. Rio de Janeiro: Editora GRD, 1968.

———. *Racial Democracy in Brazil, Myth or Reality? A Dossier of Brazilian Racism*. Ibadan, Nigeria: Sketch, 1977.

Nelson, Thomas. *Remarks on the Slavery and Slave Trade of the Brazils*. London: J. Halchard and Son, 1846.

Neto, Coelho. *Rei negro: Romance barbaro*. Porto, Portugal: Livraria Lello & Irmão, 1912.

Nunes, Viriato Fernandes. "As perversões sexuais em medicina legal." PhD diss., University of São Paulo, Brazil, 1928.

Ortiz, Fernando. *Hampa afro cubana: Los negros esclavos: Estudio sociológico y de derecho público*. Havana: Revista Bimestre Cubana, 1916.

Patrocínio, José do. "A imigração Europeia." *Gazeta da Tarde*, April 30, 1884.

Peixoto, Afrânio. *Novos rumos da medicina legal: Parentesco e exame pre-nupcial. Casamento e contracepção. Investigação da paternidade. Missexualismo. Endocrinologia e psicánalise. Psicologia do testemunho. Medicina legal e leis sociaes*. 2nd ed. Rio de Janeiro: Editora Guanabara, 1933.

Peixoto, Manuel Rodrigues. *A crise do açúcar e a transformação do trabalho*. Rio de Janeiro: Typographia de G. Leuzinger & Filhos, 1885.

Pereira, Miguel. *Á margem da medicina*. Rio de Janeiro: Castro, Mendonça, 1922.

Pessoa, Fernando. "Ulysses." In *Mensagem*. Lisbon: Edições Ática, 1967.

Pohl, Johann Emanuel Baptist. *Viagem no interior do Brasil*. Vol. 1. Rio de Janeiro: Ministério da Educação e Saúde, 1951.

Rebouças, André. *A agricultura nacional*. Rio de Janeiro: A. J. Lamoureux, 1883.

Records and Files of the Quarterly Courts of Essex County. Vol. 1. Salem, MA: Essex Institute, 1911.

Records of the Colony of New Plymouth. Vol. 1. Boston: William White, 1855.

Relatório do Ministério da Agricultura. May 10, 1883. Rio de Janeiro: Typografia Nacional, 1883.

Report from the Select Committee of the House of Lords, Appointed to Consider the Best Means Which Great Britain Can Adopt for the Final Extinction of the African Slave Trade, Session 1849. London: House of Commons, 1849.

Ribeiro, Leonídio. *Homossexualismo e Endocrinologia*. Rio de Janeiro: Livraria Francisco Alves, 1938.

Rodrigues, Antônio Coelho. *Manual de um subdito fiel ou cartas de um lavrador a sua magestade o imperador sôbre a questão do elemento servil*. Rio de Janeiro: Lith. De Moreira, Maximo, 1884.

Romero, Sílvio. *História da literatura brasileira*. Rio de Janeiro: H. Garnier, 1883.

Rugendas, Johann Moritz. *Viagem pitoresca através do Brasil*. Belo Horizonte, Brazil: Itatiaia, 1979.

Saco, D. José Antonio. *História de la esclavitud de la raza africana en el nuevo mundo*. Barcelona: Jaime Jepús, 1879.

Schlichthorst, Carl. *O Rio de Janeiro como é, 1824–1826*. Rio de Janeiro: Senado Federal, 2000.

Silva, Antônio Carlos Pacheco e. *Psiquiatria clínica e forense*. São Paulo: Companhia Editora Nacional, 1940.

Silva Araújo, Oscar da. *Alguns comentários sobre a syphilis no Rio de Janeiro*. Rio de Janeiro: Empreza Gráphica Editora Paulo Pongetti, 1928.

———. "A prophylaxia da lepra e das doenças venéreas no Brasil e a actuação do Departamento Nacional de Saúde Pública." *Archivos de hygiene* (Rio de Janeiro) 1, no. 2 (1927): 195–293.

Silva, José Bonifácio de Andrada e. "A escravatura." In *A abolição no parlamento: 65 anos de luta, 1823–1888*. Vol. 1. 2nd ed. Brasília: Senado Federal, 2102.

Sinistrari, Ludovico Maria. *De sodomia tractatus, in quo exponitur doctrina nova de sodomia foeminarum a tribadismo distincta*. Paris: Bibliothèque des Curieux, 1921.

Souza, João Menezes de. *Theses sobre colonização do Brazil: Projecto de solução as questões sociaes, que se predendem a este difícil problema—Relatório apresentado ao ministério da agricultura, commércio e obras públicas em 1873*. Rio de Janeiro: Typographia Nacional, 1875.

Spix, Johann Baptist Ritter von, and Carl Friedrich Philipp von Martius. *Travels in Brazil in the Years 1817–1820: Undertaken by Command of His Majesty King of Bavaria*. Vols. 1 and 2. London: Longman, Hurst, Rees, Orme, Brown, and Green, 1824.

Toussaint-Samson, Adèle. *A Parisian in Brazil: The Travel Account of a French Woman in Nineteenth-Century Rio de Janeiro*. Translated by Emma Toussaint. Wilmington, DE: Scholarly Resources, 2001.

———. *Une Parisienne au Brésil*. Paris: Paul Ollendorff, 1883.

Truth, Sojourner. *Narrative of Sojourner Truth: A Bondswoman of Olden Time, with a History of Her Labors and Correspondence Drawn from Her Book of Life*. New York: Penguin Books, 1998.

Vale, Gilbert. *Fanaticism: Its Source and Influence*. Part 2. New York: G. Vale, 1835.

Veríssimo, José. *A educação nacional*. Rio de Janeiro: Livraria F. Alves, 1906.

Viana, Antônio da Fonseca, "Considerações higiênicas e médico-legais sobre o casamento relativamente à mulher." Medical Thesis, Faculdade de Medicina do Rio de Janeiro, 1872: Typographia Americana, 1842.

Vide, Dom Sebastião Monteiro da. *Constituições primeiras do arcebispdo da Bahia, 1707*. São Paulo: Typographia 2 de Dezembro, 1853.

Walker, David. *Walker's Appeal, in Four Articles: Together with a Preamble, to the Coloured Citizens of the World, but in Particular, and Very Expressly, to Those of the United States of America, Written in Boston, State of Massachusetts, September 28, 1829*. Boston: David Walker, 1830; electronic edition, Chapel Hill: University of North Carolina Library, 2011.

Walsh, Reverend Robert. *Notices of Brazil in 1828–1829*. Vol. 2. London: F. Westley and A. H. Davis, 1830.

Weech, F. Friedrich von. *Reise über England und Portugal nach Brasilien und den Vereinigten Staaten des La-Plata-Stromes während den Jahren 1823 bis 1827*. Vol. 2. Munich: Auer, 1831.

Werneck, Luiz Peixoto de Lacerda. *Ideas sobre colonizacação precididas de uma succinta exposição dos princípios geraes que regem a população*. Rio de Janeiro: Typographia Universal de Laemert, 1855.

Wharton, Francis. *A Treatise on Criminal Law*. Philadelphia: Kay and Brother, 1880.

SECONDARY SOURCES

Abdur-Rahman, Aliyyah. *Against the Closet: Black Political Longing and the Erotics of Race*. Durham, NC: Duke University Press, 2012.

Alberto, Paulina. *Terms of Inclusion: Black Intellectuals in Twentieth-Century Brazil*. Chapel Hill: University of North Carolina Press, 2011.

Albuquerque, Wlamyra R. de. *O jogo da dissimulação: Abolição e cidadania negra no Brasil*. São Paulo, Brazil: Companhia das Letras, 2009.

Alden, Dauril. "The Population of Brazil in the Eighteenth Century: A Preliminary Study." *Hispanic American Historical Review* 43 (May 1963): 173–205.

Almeida, Miguel Vale de. *An Earth-Colored Sea: "Race," Culture, and the Politics of Identity in the Postcolonial Portuguese-Speaking World*. New York: Berghahn Books, 2003.

———. "Not Quite White: Portuguese People in the Margins of Lusotropicalism, the Luso-Afro-Brazilian Space, and Lusophony." Unpublished paper presented at "António Vieira and the Futures of Luso-Afro-Brazilian Studies," Center for Portuguese Studies and Culture, University of Massachusetts-Dartmouth, May 2, 2008.

Aminoff, Michael J. *Brown-Séquard: An Improbable Genius that Transformed Medicine*. New York: Oxford University Press, 2010.

Andrews, George Reid. *Blacks and Whites in São Paulo*. Madison: University of Wisconsin Press, 1991.

Aquinas, Saint Thomas. *Summa Theologica*. Translated by Fathers of the English Dominican Province. Vol. 4, part 3, sect. 1. 1911; New York: Cosimo Classics, 2007.

Araújo, Emanuel. "A arte da sedução: Sexualidade feminina na colônia." In *História das mulheres no Brasil*, edited by Mary Del Priore and Carla Beozzo Bassanezi, 45–77. (São Paulo: Editora Contexto/Editora Unesp Fundação, 1997.

Araújo, Ricardo Benzaquen de. *Guerra e Paz: Casa grande e senzala e a obra de Gilberto Freyre nos anos 30*. Rio de Janeiro: Editora 34, 1994.

Arnold, John. "The Historian as Inquisitor: The Ethics of Interrogating Subaltern Voices." *Rethinking History* 2 (1998): 379–86.

Avelar, Idelber. "Cenas dizíveis e indizíveis: Raça e sexualidade em Gilberto Freyre." *Luso-Brazilian Review* 49, no. 1 (November 2012): 168–86.

Azevedo, Elciene. *Orfeu da carapinha: A trajetória de Luiz Gama na imperial cidade de São Paulo*. São Paulo, Brazil: Editora Unicamp, 1999.

Azevedo, João Lúcio de. *História de Antônio Vieira*. São Paulo: Alameda, 2008.

Azevedo, Nelson Camara. *O advogado dos escravos: Luiz Gama*. São Paulo, Brazil: Editora Lettera, 2010.

Azevedo, Sânzio de. *Adolfo Caminha: Vida e obra*. Fortaleza, Brazil: UFC Edições, 1999.

Azevedo, Thales de. *Les élites de couleur dans une ville brésilienne*. Paris: UNESCO, 1953.

———. "Os grupos negro-africanos." In *História da cultura brasileira,* 80–93. Rio de Janeiro: Ministério da Educação e Cultura, 1975.

———. *Social Change in Brazil*. Gainesville: University of Florida Press, 1963.

Balán, Jorge, ed. *Centro e periferia no desenvolvimento brasileiro*. São Paulo: DIFEL, 1974.

Barbosa, Rui. *Obras completas de Rui Barbosa*. Vol. 17. Rio de Janeiro: Ministério de Educação e Saúde, 1942.

Barreto, Afonso Henrique de Lima. *Diário do hospício: O cemitério dos vivos*. Rio de Janeiro: Secretaria Municipal de Cultura, Departamento Geral de Documentação e Informação Cultural, Divisão de Editoração, 1993.

Bastide, Roger. *Sociologia do foclore brasileiro*. São Paulo: Editora Anhambi, 1959.

Bataille, Georges. *Eroticism: Death and Sensuality*. San Francisco, CA: City Light Books, 1986.

Beals, Ralph. "Social Stratification in Latin America." *American Journal of Sociology* 58 (1953): 327–39.

Beattie, Peter M. *The Human Tradition in Modern Brazil*. Wilmington, DE: SR Books, 2004.

———. *The Tribute of Blood: Army, Honor, Race, and Nation in Brazil, 1864–1945*. Durham, NC: Duke University Press, 2001.

Bellini, Ligia. *A coisa obscura: Mulher, sodomia, e Inquisição*. São Paulo: Editora Brasilense, 1989.

Bender, Gerald J. *Angola under the Portuguese: The Myth and the Reality*. Berkeley: University of California Press, 1978.

Bethell, Leslie. *The Abolition of the Brazilian Slave Trade: Britain, Brazil, and the Slave*. New York: Cambridge University Press, 1970.

Bhabha, Homi K. *The Location of Culture*. New York: Routledge, 1994.

Bodian, Miriam. *Dying in the Law of Moses: Crypto-Jewish Martyrdom in the Iberian World*. Bloomington: University of Indiana Press, 2007.

Bonnycastle, Kevin Denys. *Stranger Rape: Rapists, Masculinity, and Penal Governance*. Toronto: University of Toronto Press, 2012.

Borges, Dain E. *The Family in Bahia, 1870–1945*. Stanford, CA: Stanford University Press, 1992.

Bosi, Alfredo. *Dialética da colonização*. São Paulo, Brazil: Companhia das Letras, 1992.

———. *História concisa da literatura brasileira*. São Paulo: Editora Cultrix, 1976.

Boxer, Charles R. *Women in Iberian Expansion Overseas, 1415–1815: Some Facts, Fancies, and Personalities*. New York: Oxford University Press, 1975.

Brent, Linda [Harriet Ann Jacobs]. *Incidents in the Life of a Slave Girl*. Boston: 1861.

Breyner, Sônia. *A metáfora do corpo no romance naturalista*. Rio de Janeiro: Livraria São José, 1973.

Brookshaw, David. *Race and Color in Brazilian Literature*. Metuchen, NJ: Scarecrow Press, 1986.

Brooten, Bernadette J. *Love between Women: Early Christian Responses to Female Homoeroticism*. Chicago: University of Chicago Press, 1996.

Brown, Judith. *Immodest Acts: The Life of a Lesbian Nun in Renaissance Italy*. New York: Oxford University Press, 1986.

Bruner, Jerome S. *Acts of Meaning*. Cambridge, MA: Harvard University Press, 1990.

Burdick, John, "The Myth of Racial Democracy." *North American Congress on Latina America Report on the Americas* 25, no. 4 (February 1992): 40–42.

Burns, E. Bradford, ed. *A Documentary History of Brazil*. New York: Alfred A. Knopf, 1966.

———. *Latin America: A Concise Interpretive History*. Englewood Cliffs, NJ: Prentice Hall, 1970.

Burton, Antoinette. *Archive Stories: Facts, Fictions, and the Writing of History*. Durham, NC: Duke University Press: 2006.

———. *Dwelling in the Archive: Women Writing House, Home, and History in Late Colonial India*. New York: Oxford University Press, 2006.

Butler, Judith. *Bodies that Matter: On the Discursive Limits of "Sex."* New York: Routledge, 1993.

———. *Gender Trouble: Feminism and the Subversion of Identity*. New York: Routledge, 1990.

Butler, Kim D. *Freedoms Given, Freedoms Won: Afro-Brazilians in Post-Abolition São Paulo and Salvador*. New Brunswick, NJ: Rutgers University Press, 1998.

Bynum, Victoria E. *Unruly Women: The Politics of Social and Sexual Control in the Old South*. Chapel Hill: University of North Carolina Press, 1992.

Caldwell, Kia Lilly. *Negras in Brazil: Re-Envisioning Black Women, Citizenship, and the Politics of Identity*. New Brunswick, NJ: Rutgers University Press, 2007.

Calógeras, João Pandiá. *A History of Brazil*. São Paulo, Brazil: Companhia Editora Nacional, 1938; New York: Russell & Russell, 1963, trans. Percy Alvin Martin.

Camargo, Joaquim Augusto de. *Direito penal brasileiro*. 2nd ed. São Paulo: Revista do Tribunais, 2005.

Carby, Hazel V. *Reconstructing Womanhood: The Emergence of the Afro-American Woman Novelist*. New York: Oxford University Press, 1987.

Carlson, Cindy L., Robert L. Mazzola, and Susan M. Bernardo. *Gender Reconstructions: Pornography and Perversions in Literature and Culture*. Burlington, VT: Ashgate, 2002.

Carrara, Sérgio. *Tributo a Vênus: A luta contra sífilis no Brasil, da passagem do século aos anos 40*. Rio de Janeiro: Editora Fiocruz, 1996.

Carrasco, Rafael. *Inquisición y represión sexual en Valencia: Historia de los sodomitas, 1565–1785*. Barcelona: Laertes, 1985.

Caruth, Cathy. *Trauma: Explorations in Memory*. Baltimore: Johns Hopkins University Press, 1995.

Carvalho, Gilberto de Abreu Sodré. *A Inquisição no Rio de Janeiro no começo do século XVII*. Rio de Janeiro: Imago, 2008.

Caulfield, Sueann. *In Defense of Honor: Sexual Morality, Modernity, and Nation in Early-Twentieth-Century Brazil*. Durham, NC: Duke University Press, 2000.

Celestin, Louis-Cyril. *Charles Édouard Brown-Séquard: The Biography of a Tormented Genius*. New York: Springer, 2014.

Chaloub, Sidney. *Machado de Assis Historiador*. São Paulo: Companhia das Letras, 2003.

———. *Visões da liberadade: Uma história das últimas décadas da escravidão na corte*. São Paulo: Companhia das Letras, 1990.

Clarke, Lorenne, and Debra Lewis. "Women, Property, and Rape." In *The Sociology of Crime and Deviance: Selected Issues*, edited by Susan Caffrey and Gary Mundy, 151–61. Dartford, UK: Greenwich University Press, 1995.

Clinton, Catherine. *The Plantation Mistress: Woman's World in the Old South*. New York: Pantheon Books, 1984.

Cohen, Claire. *Male Rape Is a Feminist Issue: Feminism, Governmentality, and Male Rape*. New York: Palgrave Macmillan, 2014.

Cohen, David W., and Jack P. Greene. Introduction to *Neither Slave nor Free: The Freemen of African Descent in the Slave Societies of the New World*, edited by David W. Cohen and Jack P. Greene, 1–23. Baltimore: Johns Hopkins University Press, 1972.

Conrad, Robert. *The Destruction of Brazilian Slavery, 1850–1888*. Berkeley: University of California Press, 1972.

Costa, Emília Viotti da. *The Brazilian Slave Empire: Myths and Histories*. Chapel Hill: University of North Carolina Press, 2000.

Costa, Haroldo. *Fala, Crioulo*. Rio de Janeiro: Editora Record, 1982.

Costa, Jurandir Freire. *Ordem médica e norma familiar*. Rio de Janeiro: Graal, 1983.

Cowling, Camilia. *Conceiving Freedom: Women of Color, Gender, and the Abolition of Slavery in Havana and Rio de Janeiro*. Chapel Hill: University of North Carolina Press, 2013.

Crawford, Katherine. *The Sexual Culture of the French Renaissance*. New York: Cambridge University Press, 2010.

Crawford, Margo Natalie. *Dilution Anxiety and the Black Phallus*. Columbus: Ohio State University Press, 2008.

Daniel, G. Reginald. *Machado de Assis: Multiracial Identity and the Brazilian Novelist*. University Park: Pennsylvania University Press, 2012.

———. *More Than Black: Multiracial Identity and New Racial Order*. Philadelphia: Temple University Press, 2001.

———. *Race and Multiraciality in Brazil and the United States: Converging Paths?* University Park: Pennsylvania University Press, 2006.

Dávila, Jerry. *Diploma of Whiteness: Race and Social Policy in Brazil, 1917–1945*. Durham, NC: Duke University Press, 2003.

———. *Hotel Trópico: Brazil and the Challenge of African Decolonization*. Durham, NC: Duke University Press, 2010.

Debord, Guy. *The Society of the Spectacle*. New York: Zone Books, 1994.

Degler, Carl N. *Neither Black nor White: Slavery and Race Relations in Brazil and the United States*. New York: Macmillan, 1971.

D'Emilio, John, and Estelle Freedman. *Intimate Matters: A History of Sexuality in America*. 2nd ed. Chicago: University of Chicago Press, 1997.

Domingues, Petrônio. *Uma história não contada: Negro, racismo e branqueamento em São Paulo na pós-abolição*. São Paulo: Editora Senac, 2004.

Donnelly, Denise, and Stacy Kenyon. "'Honey, We Don't Do Men': Gender Stereotypes and the Provision of Services to Sexually Assaulted Males." *Journal of Interpersonal Violence* 11, no. 3 (September 1996): 441–48.

Drescher, Seymour. "The Atlantic Slave Trade and the Holocaust: A Comparative Analysis." In *Is the Holocaust Unique? Perspectives on Comparative Genocide*, edited by Alan S. Rosenbaum, 98–99. 2nd ed. Boulder, CO: Westview Press, 2001.

Dunn, Christopher. "A retomada freyreana." In *Gilberto Freyre e os estudos latino-americanos*, edited by Joshua Lund and Malcolm McNee, 35–51. Pittsburgh: Instituto Internacional de Literatura Iberoamericana, 2006.

Dunning, Stefanie K. *Queer in Black and White: Interraciality, Same Sex Desire, and Contemporary African American Culture*. Bloomington: Indiana University Press, 2009.

Egerton, Douglas R. *Gabriel's Rebellion: The Virginia Slave Conspiracies of 1800 and 1802.* Chapel Hill: University of North Caroline Press, 1993.

El Far, Alessandra. "Crítica social e ideias médicas nos excessos do desejo: Uma ánalise dos 'romances para homens' de finais d século XX e ínicio do XX." *Núcleo de Estudos de Gênero Pagu-Unicamp* 28 (2007): 285–312.

———. *Páginas de sensasão: Literatura popular e pornografia no Rio de Janeiro, 1870–1924.* São Paulo: Companhia das Letras, 2004.

Eneida, Maria Mercadante Sela. *Modos de ser, modos de ver: Viajantes europeus e escravos africanos no Rio de Janeiro, 1808–1850.* Campinas, Brazil: UNICAMP, 2008.

Falcão, Joaquim, and Rosa Maria Barboza de Araújo, eds., *O imperador das idéias: Gilberto Freyre em questão.* Rio de Janeiro: Fundação Roberto Marinho: Topbooks, 2001.

Fanon, Frantz. *Black Skin, White Masks.* Translated by Charles Lam Markmann. New York: Grove Press, 1967.

Fausto, Boris. *A Concise History of Brazil*, 2nd ed. New York: Cambridge University Press, 1999.

Felman, Shoshana, and Dori Laub. *Testimony: Crises in Witnessing in Literature, Psychoanalysis, and History.* New York: Routledge, 1992.

Fernandes, Florestan. *The Negro in Brazilian Society.* New York: Columbia University Press, 1969.

Fernandez, Nadine T. *Revolutionizing Romance: Interracial Couples in Contemporary Cuba.* New Brunswick, NJ: Rutgers University Press, 2010.

Figari, Carlos. *@s "@utros" cariocas: Interpelações, experiências, e identidades homoeróticas no Rio de Janeiro: Séculos XVII ao XX.* Belo Horizonte, Brazil: Editora UFMG, 2007.

Fischer, Brodwyn M. *A Poverty of Rights: Citizenship and Inequality in Twentieth-Century Rio de Janeiro.* Stanford, CA: Stanford University Press, 2008.

Ford, Talisman. "Passion in the Eye of the Beholder: Sexuality as Seen by Sexologists, 1900–1940." PhD diss., Vanderbilt University, 1995.

Foster, William Henry. *Gender, Mastery, and Slavery: From European to Atlantic World Frontiers.* New York: Palgrave Macmillan, 2010.

Foucault, Michel. *Abnormal: Lectures at the Collège de France, 1974–1975.* New York: Picador, 2003.

———. *The History of Sexuality.* Translated by Robert Hurley. Vol. 1, An Introduction. New York: Vintage Books, 1990.

Fox-Genovese, Elizabeth. *Within the Plantation Household: Black and White Women of the Old South.* Chapel Hill: University of North Carolina Press, 1988.

Franklin, John Hope. *The Free Negro in North Carolina, 1790–1860.* 2nd ed. Chapel Hill: University of North Carolina Press, 1995.

Freedman, Estelle B. *Redefining Rape: Sexual Violence in the Era of Suffrage and Segregation.* Cambridge, MA: Harvard University Press, 2013.

Freire, Japi. *Que sabe você sôbre o Brasil?* Rio de Janeiro: Conquista, 1966.

French, Jan Hoffman. *Legalizing Identities: Becoming Black or Indian in Brazil's Northeast.* Chapel Hill: University of North Carolina Press, 2009.

Freud, Sigmund. *Sigmund Freud: Collected Papers.* Vol. 4, *Contributions to the Psychology of Love: A Neurosis of Demoniacal Possession in the 17th Century.* Translated by Joan Riviere. New York: International Psycho-Analytical Press, 1959.

Fry, Peter. "Estética e política: Relações entre 'raça,' publicidade e produção da beleza no Brasil." In *Nu e vestido: Dez antropólogos revelam a cultura do corpo carioca,* edited by Mirian Goldenberg, 303–26. Rio de Janeiro: Editora Record, 2002.

Furtado, Júnia Ferreira. *Chica da Silva: A Brazilian Slave of the Eighteenth Century.* New York: Cambridge University Press, 2009.

Garvey, Amy Jacques. *Philosophy and Opinions of Marcus Garvey.* Edited and with an introduction by Robert A. Hill. Vol. 1. 1923; repr., New York: Antheneum, 1992.

Gaulmier, Jean. "Au Brésil, il y a un siècle . . . Quelques images d'Arthur Gobineau." *Bulletin de la Faculté des Lettres de Strasbourg* 2 (May–June 1964): 483–98.

Gentilcore, David. "From Bishop to Witch: The System of the Sacred in Early Modern Terra d'Otranto." New York: Manchester University Press, 1992.

Germeten, Nicole von. *Violent Delights, Violent Ends: Sex, Race, and Honor in Colonial Cartagena de Indias.* Albuquerque: University of New Mexico Press, 2013.

Giacomini, Sonia Maria. *Mulher e escrava: Uma introdução histórica ao estudo da mulher negra no Brasil.* Petrópolis, Brazil: Vozes, 1988.

Gilliam, Angela. "Women's Equality and National Liberation." In *Third World Women and the Politics of Feminism,* edited by Chandra Talpade Mohanty, Ann Russo, and Lourdes Torres, 215–37. Bloomington: Indiana University Press, 1991.

Gilman, Sander L. *Difference and Pathology: Stereotypes of Sexuality, Race, and Madness.* Ithaca, NY: Cornell University Press, 1985.

———. *Sexuality.* New York: 1989.

Ginzburg, Carlo. *The Cheese and The Worms: The Cosmos of a Sixteenth-Century Miller.* Baltimore: Johns Hopkins University Press, 1997.

———. "The Inquisitor as Anthropologist." In *Clues, Myths, and the Historical Method,* translated by John Tedeschi and Anne C. Tedeschi, 156–64. Baltimore: Johns Hopkins University Press, 1980.

Glymph, Thaviola. *Out of the House of Bondage: The Transformation of the Plantation Household.* New York: Cambridge University Press, 2008.

Goffman, Erving. *Stigma: Notes on the Management of Spoiled Identity.* Englewood Cliffs, NJ: Prentice-Hall, 1963.

Goldenberg, David M. *The Curse of Ham: Race and Slavery in Early Judaism.* Princeton, NJ: Princeton University Press, 2003.

Goldstein, Donna M. *Laughter Out of Place: Race, Class, Violence, and Sexuality in a Rio Shantytown.* Berkeley: University of California Press, 2003.

Gomes, Albert. *Through a Maze of Colour.* Port of Spain, Trinidad: Key Caribbean Publications, 1974.

Gomes, Heloisa Toller. *O negro e o romantismo brasileiro.* São Paulo: Atual Editora, 1988.

Gomes, Odival Cassiano. *Manoel Vitorino Perreira: Médico e cirugião.* Rio de Janeiro: Agir, 1953.

Gorenstein, Lina. *A Inquisição contra as mulheres: Rio de Janeiro, século XVII e XVIII.* São Paulo: Associação Humanitas, 2005.

Green, James N. *Beyond Carnival: Male Homosexuality in Twentieth-Century Brazil.* Chicago: University of Chicago Press, 1999.

Groth, A. Nicholas. *Male Victims of Sexual Assault.* Oxford: Oxford University Press, 1993.

———. *Men Who Rape: The Psychology of the Offender.* New York: Plenum Press, 1979.

Groth, A. Nicholas, and Ann Burgess. "Male Rape: Offenders and Victims." *American Journal of Psychiatry* 137, no. 7 (July 1980): 806–10.

Gruzinski, Serge. "The Ashes of Desire: Homosexuality in Mid-Seventeenth-Century New Spain." Translated by Ignacio López-Calvo. In *Infamous Desire: Male Homosexuality in Colonial Latin America*, edited by Pete Sigal, 197–211. Chicago: University of Chicago Press, 2003.

Guimarães, Antônio Sérgio Alfredo. *Classes, raças, e democracia.* São Paulo: Editora 34, 2002.

Haberly, David T. "Abolitionism in Brazil: Anti-Slavery and Anti-Slave." *Luso-Brazilian Review* 9, no. 2 (1972): 31.

———. *Three Sad Races: Racial Identity and National Consciousness in Brazilian Literature.* New York: Cambridge University Press, 1983.

Halperin, David. *One Hundred Years of Homosexuality, and Other Essays on Greek Love.* New York: Routledge, 1990.

Hanchard, Michael. *Orpheus and Power: The Movimento Negro of Rio de Janeiro and São Paulo, Brazil, 1945–1988.* Princeton, NJ: Princeton University Press, 1994.

Hartman, Saidiya V. *Lose Your Mother: A Journey along the Atlantic Slave Route.* New York: Farrar, Straus and Giroux, 2008.

———. *Scenes of Subjection: Slavery, Terror, and Self-Making in Nineteenth-Century America.* New York: Oxford University Press, 1996.

Hickson, Ford C. I., Peter M. Davies, Andrew J. Hunt, Peter Weatherburn, Thomas J. McManus, and Anthony P. M. Coxon. "Gay Men as Victims of Nonconsensual Sex." *Archives of Sexual Behavior* 23, no. 3 (1994): 281–94.

Higgins, Kathleen J. *"Licentious Liberty" in a Brazilian Gold-Mining Region: Slavery, Gender, and Social Control in Eighteenth-Century Society, Minas Gerais.* University Park: Pennsylvania State University Press, 1999.

Higgs, David. "Tales of Two Carmelites: Inquisition Narratives from Portugal and Brazil." In *Infamous Desire: Male Homosexuality in Colonial Latin America*, edited by Peter Herman Sigal, 152–67. Chicago: University of Chicago Press, 2003.

Hodes, Martha Elizabeth. *White Women, Black Men: Illicit Sex in the Nineteenth-Century South.* New Haven, CT: Yale University Press, 1997.

Hoetink, Hartimus. *Slavery and Race Relations in the Americas: Comparative Notes on Their Nature and Nexus.* New York: Harper and Row, 1973.

Holanda, Sérgio Buarque de. *Roots of Brazil.* Translated by G. Harvey Summ. Notre Dame, IN: University of Notre Dame Press, 2012.

Holland, Sharon Patricia. *The Erotic Life of Racism.* Durham, NC: Duke University Press, 2012.

Holloway, Karla F. C. *Legal Fictions: Constituting Race, Composing Literature.* Durham, NC: Duke University Press, 2014.

Huckle, P. L. "Male Rape Victims Referred to a Forensic Psychiatric Service." *Medicine, Science, and the Law* 35, no. 3 (July 1995): 187–92.

Isfahani-Hammond, Alexandra. *White Negritude: Race, Writing, and Brazilian Cultural Identity*. New York: Palgrave Macmillan, 2005.

Jordan, Mark D. *The Invention of Sodomy in Christian Theology*. Chicago: University of Chicago Press, 1997.

———. *The Silence of Sodom: Homosexuality in Modern Catholicism*. Chicago: University of Chicago Press, 2000.

Jordan, Winthrop. *White over Black: American Attitudes toward the Negro, 1550–1812*. Chapel Hill: University of North Carolina Press, 1968.

Kagan, Richard. *Lucrecia's Dreams: Politics and Prophecy in Sixteenth-Century Spain*. Berkeley: University of California Press, 1990.

Karasch, Mary. *Slave Life in Rio de Janeiro, 1808–1850*. Princeton, NJ: Princeton University Press, 1987.

Katz, Jonathan. *Miss Marianne Woods and Miss Jane Pirie against Dame Helen Cumming Gordon*. New York: Arno Press, 1975.

Kaufman, Michael. "The Construction of Masculinity and the Triad of Men's Violence." In *Gender Violence: Interdisciplinary Perspectives*, edited by Laura O'Toole, Jessica R. Schiffman, and Margie L. Kiter Edwards, 30–52. New York: New York University Press, 1997.

Kennedy, Helena. *Eve Was Framed: Women and British Justice*. London: Chatto and Windus, 1992.

Kennedy, Randall. *Sellout: The Politics of Racial Betrayal*. New York: Pantheon Books, 2008.

Kimmel, Michael S. "Masculinity as Homophobia." In *Theorising Masculinities*, edited by Harry Brod and Michael Kaufman. London: Sage, 1994.

Klein, Herbert S. *African Slavery in Latin America and the Caribbean*. New York: Oxford University Press, 1986.

———. "Nineteenth-Century Brazil." In Cohen and Greene, *Neither Slave nor Free*, 309–34.

Klein, Herbert S., and Francisco Vidal Luna. *Slavery in Brazil*. New York: Cambridge University Press, 2010.

Kosofsky Sedgwick, Eve. *Between Men: English Literature and Male Homosocial Desire*. New York: Columbia University Press, 1985.

———. *Epistemology of the Closet*. Berkeley: University of California Press, 1990.

Kulick, Don. *Travesti: Sex, Gender, and Culture among Brazilian Transgendered Prostitutes*. Chicago: University of Chicago Press, 1998.

Ladurie, Emmanuel Le Roy. *Montaillou: Village Occitan de 1294 à 1324*. Paris: Gallimard, 1975.

Lauderdale Graham, Sandra. *Caetana Says No: Women's Stories from a Brazilian Slave Society*. New York: Cambridge University Press, 2002.

Lees, Sue. *Ruling Passions: Sexual Violence, Reputation, and the Law*. Buckingham, UK: Open University Press, 1997.

Lesser, Jeff. *Immigration, Ethnicity, National Identity in Brazil, 1808 to the Present*. New York: Cambridge University Press, 2002.

———. *Negotiating National Identity: Immigrants, Minorities, and the Struggle for Ethnicity in Brazil*. Durham, NC: Duke University Press, 1999.

Lipsitz, George. *The Possessive Investment in Whiteness: How White People Profit from Identity Politics*. Philadelphia: Temple University Press, 2006.

Lockwood, Daniel. *Prison Sexual Violence*. New York: Elsevier Science, 1980.

López, Alfred J. *Postcolonial Whiteness: A Critical Reader on Race and Empire*. Albany: State University of New York Press, 2005.

Lorde, Audre. *Sister Outsider: Essays and Speeches*. Berkeley, CA: Crossing Press, 2007.

Lucinda, Elisa. *O semelhante*. Rio de Janeiro: Record, 2002.

Luna, Francisco Vidal, and Herbert S. Klein. *Slavery and the Economy of São Paulo, 1750–1850*. Stanford, CA: Stanford University Press, 2003.

Luna, Luiz. *O negro na luta contra abolição*. Rio de Janeiro: Editora Leitura, 1976.

Lund, Joshua, and Malcolm McNee, eds. *Gilberto Freyre e os estudos latino-americanos*. Pittsburgh: Instituto Internacional de Literatura Iberoamericana, 2006.

Mara Loveman, Jeronimo O. Muniz, and Stanley R. Bailey. "Brazil in Black and White? Race Categories, the Census, and the Study of Inequality." *Ethnic and Racial Studies* (September 23, 2011): 1466–83. DOI:10.1080/01419870.2011.607503.

Marcílio, Maria Luisa. "The Population of Colonial Brazil." In *Colonial Latin America*, vol. 2 of *The Cambridge History of Latin America*, edited by Leslie Bethell. New York: Cambridge University Press, 1984.

Martins, José Salgado. *Sistema de direito penal brasileiro: Introdução e parte geral*. Rio de Janeiro: Editora José Konfino, 1957.

Massa, Jean-Michel. *La jeunesse de Machado de Assis, 1839–1870: Essai de biographie intéllectuelle*. Vol. 1. PhD diss., Université de Poitiers, 1969.

Mattoso, Kátia M. de Queirós. *To Be a Slave in Brazil, 1550–1888*. New Brunswick, NJ: Rutgers University Press, 1986.

McMullen, Richie J. *Male Rape: Breaking the Silence of the Last Taboo*. London: Heretic Books, 1990.

Mello, José Antônio Gonsalves de. *Henrique Dias: Governador dos crioulos, negros, e mulatos do Brasil*. Rio de Janeiro: Editora Fundação Joaquim Nabuco, 1988.

Mennuci, Sud. *O precursor do abolicionismo no Brasil: Luiz Gama*. São Paulo: Companhia Editora Nacional, 1938.

Mezey, Gillian, and Michael B. King. "The Effects of Sexual Assault on Men: A Survey of 22 Men." *Psychological Medicine* 19, no. 1 (February 1989): 205–9.

Miskolci, Richard. *O desejo da nação: Masculinidade e branquitude no Brasil de fins do XIX*. São Paulo: Annablume, 2012.

Moraes, Evaristo de. *A campanha aboliscionista, 1879–1888*. Brasília: Editora Universidade de Brasília, 1986.

Mott, Luiz. "Alternativas eroticas dos africanos e seus descendentes no Brasil escravista." In *O sexo proibido: Virgens, gays, e escravos nas garras, Inquisição*. Campinas, Brazil: Papirus, 1980.

———. "Crypto-Sodomites in Colonial Brazil." In *Infamous Desire: Male Homosexuality in Colonial Latin America*, edied by Pete Sigal, 168–96. Chicago: University of Chicago Press, 2003.

——. *Escravidão, homossexualidade, e demonologia*. São Paulo: Editora Ícone, 1988.

——. "The Misadventures of a Portuguese Man in Seventeenth-Century Brazil." In *Pelo Vaso Traseiro: Sodomy and Sodomites in Luso-Brazilian History*, edited by Harold Johnson and Francis A. Dutra, 293–336. Tucson, AZ: Fenestra Books, 2007.

——. *O sexo proibido: Virgins, gays, e escravos nas garras da Inquisição*. Campinas: Pairus, 1988.

——. "Pagode Português: A subcultura gay em Portugal nos tempos da Inquisição." *Ciência e Cultura* 40 (February 1980): 120–39.

Moura, Clóvis. *O negro-de bom escravo a mau cidadão*. Rio de Janeiro: Editora Conquista, 1977.

Moutinho, Laura. *Razão, "cor" e desejoi*. São Paulo: Editora Unesp, 2004.

Muir, Edward. Review of *From Bishop to Witch: The System of the Sacred in Early Modern Terra d'Otranto*, by David Gentilcore. *Journal of Modern History* 67, no. 1 (March 1995): 182–85.

——. Review of *Trent 1475: Stories of Ritual Murder Trial*, by R. Po-Chia Hisia. *Journal of Modern History* 67, no. 1 (March 1995): 182–85.

Muraro, Rose Marie. *Sexualidade da mulher brasileira: Corpo e classe social no Brazil*. 4th ed. Petrópolis, Brazil: Vozes, 1983.

Nabuco, Joaquim. *O abolicionismo*. Petrópolis, Brazil: Editora Vozes, 1977.

Nascimento, Elisa Larkin. *The Sorcery of Color: Identity, Race, and Gender in Brazil*. Philadelphia: Temple University Press, 2003.

Needell, Jeffrey D. "Identity, Race, Gender, and Modernity in the Origins of Gilberto Freye's Oeuvre." *American Historical Review* 100, no. 1 (February 1995): 51–77.

——. *The Party of Order: The Conservatives, the State, and Slavery in the Brazilian Monarchy, 1831–1871*. Stanford, CA: Stanford University Press, 2006.

——. *A Tropical Belle Epoque: Elite Culture and Society in Turn-of-the-Century Rio de Janeiro*. New York: Cambridge University Press, 1987.

Nobles, Melissa. *Shades of Citizenship: Race and the Census in Modern Politics*. Stanford, CA: Stanford University Press, 2000.

Novinsky, Anita Waingort. *A Inquisição*. São Paulo: Brasilense, 1982.

Nunes, Zita. *Cannibal Democracy: Race and Representation in the Literature of the Americas*. Minneapolis: University of Minnesota Press, 2008.

Oliveira, Emanuelle. *Writing Identity: The Politics of Afro-Brazilian Literature*. West Lafayette, IN: Purdue University Press, 2007.

Painter, Nell Irvin. *The History of White People*. 1st ed. New York: W. W. Norton, 2010.

——. *Sojourner Truth: A Life, A Symbol*. New York: W. W. Norton, 1997.

——. *Soul Murder and Slavery: Toward a Fully Loaded Cost Accounting*. Waco, TX: Markham Press Fund, 1995.

——. *Southern History across the Color Line*. Chapel Hill: University of North Carolina Press, 2002.

Parker, Richard G. *Beneath the Equator: Cultures of Desire, Male Homosexuality, and Emerging Gay Communities in Brazil*. New York: Routledge, 1999.

Pecora, Alcir. *Teatro do sacramento*. 2nd ed. São Paulo: Editora da Universidade de São Paulo, 2008.

Peggs, Martin G. "Historians and Inquisitors: Testimonies from the Early Inquisition into Heretical Depravity." In *Understanding Medieval Primary Sources: Using Sources to Discover Medieval Europe*, edited by Joel T. Rosenthal, 98–116. New York: Routledge, 2014.

Pierangelli, José Henrique. *Códigos penais do Brasil: Evolução histórica*. São Paulo: Editora Javoli, 1980.

Pierson, Donald. *Negroes in Brazil: Study of Race Contact at Bahia*. Carbondale: Southern Illinois University Press, 1967.

Piza, Edith, and Fúlvia Rosemberg. "Color in the Brazilian Census." In *Race in Contemporary Brazil: From Indifference to Equality*, edited by Rebecca Reichmann, 27–52. University Park: Pennsylvania State University Press, 1999.

Poliakov, León. *O mito ariano*. São Paulo: Editora da Universidade de São Paulo, 1974.

Prado, Paulo. *Retrato triste do Brasil*. Rio de Janeiro: José Olympio, 1972.

Quinlan, Susan Canty, and Fernando Arenas, eds. *Lusosex: Gender and Sexuality in the Portuguese-Speaking World*. Minneapolis: University of Minnesota Press, 2002.

Rabassa, Gregory. *O negro na ficção brasileira*. 4 vols. Rio de Janeiro: Editora Tempo Brasileiro, 1965.

Raeders, Georges. *O inimigo cordial do Brasil: O conde de Gobineau no Brasil*. Rio de Janeiro: Paz e Terra, 1988.

Rago, Margareth. *Os prazeres da noite: Prostituição e códigos da sexualidade feminina em São Paulo, 1890–1930*. Rio de Janeiro: Paz e Terra, 1991.

Reis, João José. *O rol dos culpados: Notas sobre um documento da rebelião de 1835*. Anais do Arquivo Público do estado da Bahia. Vol. 48. 1996.

Reis, João José, Flávio dos Santos Gomes, Marcus Joaquim de Carvalho. *O Alufá Rufino: Tráfico, escravidão, e liberdade no atlântico negro, 1822–1853*. São Paulo: Companhia das Letras, 2010.

———. *Slave Rebellion in Brazil: The Muslim Uprising of 1835 in Bahia*. Baltimore, MD: Johns Hopkins University Press, 1993.

Renault, Delso. *Indústria, escravidão, sociedade: Uma pesquisa historiográfica do Rio de Janeiro no século XIX*. Rio de Janeiro: Editora Civilização Brasileira, 1976.

———. *Rio de Janeiro: A vida da cidade refletida nos jornais, 1850–1870*. Rio de Janeiro: Editora Civilização Brasileira, 1978.

Reuter, Edward Byron. *The Mulatto in the United States, Including a Study of the Role of Mixed-Blood Races around the World*. Boston: Gorham Press, 1918.

Rideau, Wilbert, and Billy Sinclair. "Prison: The Sexual Jungle." In *Male Rape: A Casebook of Sexual Aggression*, edited by Antony M. Sacco, Jr., 3–30. New York: AMS Press, 1982.

Roberts, Dorothy E. *Killing the Black Body: Race, Reproduction, and the Meaning of Liberty*. New York: Pantheon Books, 1997.

Roediger, David. *Towards the Abolition of Whiteness: Essays on Race, Politics, and Working Class History*. New York: Verso, 1994.

Rosaldo, Renato. "From the Door of His Tent: The Fieldworker and the Inquisitor." In *Writing Culture: The Poetics and Politics of Ethnography*, edited by James Clifford and G. E. Marcus, 77–97. Berkeley: University of California Press, 1986.

Rush, Florence. "The Many Faces of the Backlash." In *The Sexual Liberals and the Attack on Feminism*, edited by Dorchen Leidholdt and Janice G. Raymond, 165–74. Oxford: Pergamon Press, 1990.

Russell-Wood, A. J. R. "Colonial Brazil." In *Neither Slave nor Free: The Freemen of African Descent in the Slave Societies of the New World*, edited by David W. Cohen and Jack P. Greene, 84–133. Baltimore: Johns Hopkins University Press, 1972.

Sagarin, Edward. "Prison Homosexuality and Its Effect on Post-Prison Sexual Behavior." *Psychiatry* 39, 1976: 245–57.

Sánchez-Eppler, Karen. *Touching Liberty: Abolition, Feminism, and the Politics of the Body*. Berkeley: University of California Press, 1993.

Santos, Boaventura de Sousa. "Entre Próspero e Caliban: Colonialismo, pós-colonialismo e inter-identidade." In *Entre ser e estar: Raízes, percursos, e discursos da identidade*, edited by Maria Irene Ramalho and António Sousa Ribeiro, 23–85. Porto, Portugal: Edições Afrontamento, 2001.

Santos, Wanderley Guilherme dos. "A imaginação politico-social brasileira." *Revista Dados* 2/3 (1967): 182–93.

Sartorius, David. *Ever Faithful: Race, Loyalty, and the Ends of Empire in Spanish Cuba*. Durham, NC: Duke University Press, 2014.

Sartwell, Crispin. *Act Like You Know: African-American Autobiography and White Identity*. Chicago: University of Chicago Press, 1998.

Scarce, Michael. *Male on Male Rape: The Hidden Toll of Stigma and Shame*. New York: Insight Books, 1997.

Schepper-Hughes, Nancy. *Death without Weeping: The Violence of Everyday Life in Brazil*. Berkeley: University of California Press, 1993.

Schwarcz, Lilia K. Moritz. *As barbas do imperado: D. Pedro II, um monarca nos trópicos*. São Paulo: Companhia das Letras, 1998.

———. *Nicolas-Antoine Taunay no Brasil: Uma leitura dos trópicos*. Rio de Janeiro: Sextante, 2008.

———. *O espetáculo das raças: Cientistas, instituições, e questão racial no Brasil, 1870–1930*. São Paulo: Companhia das Letras, 1993.

———. *Os guardiões da nossa história oficia: Os institutos histíricos e geográficos brasileiros*. São Paulo: Instituto de Estudos Econômicos, Sociais e Políticos de São Paulo, 1989.

———. *Racismo no Brasil*. São Paulo: Publifolha, 2001.

———. *Retrato em branco e negro: Jornais, escravos, e cidadãos em São Paulo no final do século XIX*. São Paulo: Companhia das Letras, 1987.

Schwartz, Stuart B. *Slaves, Peasants, and Rebels: Reconsidering Brazilian Slavery*. Urbana: University of Illinois Press, 1995.

Schwarz, Roberto, and John Gledson. *Misplaced Ideas: Essays on Brazilian Culture*. London: Verso, 1992.

Scott, Rebecca J. *Abolition of Slavery and the Aftermath of Emancipation in Brazil*. Durham, NC: Duke University Press, 1988.

———. *Slave Emancipation in Cuba: The Transition to Free Labor, 1860–1899*. Pittsburgh: University of Pittsburgh Press, 2000.

Searles, Patricia, and Ronald J. Berger. *Rape and Society: Readings on the Problem of Sexual Assault*. Boulder, CO: Westview Press, 1995.

Seigel, Micol. *Uneven Encounters: Making Race and Nation in Brazil and the United States*. Durham, NC: Duke University Press, 2009.

Sharpe, Christina. *Monstrous Intimacies: Making Post-Slavery Subjects*. Durham, NC: Duke University Press, 2010.

Sigal, Peter Herman. *Infamous Desire: Male Homosexuality in Colonial Latin America*. Chicago: University of Chicago Press, 2003.

Simonsen, Roberto Cochrane. "As econômicas consequências da abolição." *Revista do Arquivo Municipal de São Paulo* (May 1938): 257–68.

Siqueira, Sonia A. *A Inquisição portuguesa e a sociedade colonial*. São Paulo: Editora Ática, 1978.

Skidmore, Thomas E. *Brazil, Black into White: Race and Nationality in Brazilian Thought*. Durham, NC: Duke University Press, 2003.

———. "The Death of Brazilian Slavery, 1866–68." In *Latin American History: Select Problems, Identity, Integration, and Nationhood*, edited by Frederick Pike, 134–71. New York: Harcourt, Brace & World, 1968.

Sollors, Werner. *Interracialism: Black-White Intermarriage in American History, Literature, and Law*. New York: Oxford University Press, 2000.

———. *Neither Black nor White Yet Both: Thematic Explorations of Interracial Literature*. New York: Oxford University Press, 1997.

Somerville, Siobhan B. *Queering the Color Line: Race and the Invention of Homosexuality in American Culture*. Durham, NC: Duke University Press, 2000.

Sontag, Susan. *Regarding the Pain of Others*. New York: Farrar, Straus and Giroux, 2003.

Souza, Laura de Mello e. *The Devil and the Land of the Holy Cross: Witchcraft, Slavery, and Popular Religion in Colonial Brazil*. Austin: University of Texas Press, 2004.

Souza, Neusa Santos. *Tornar-se negro: As vicissitudes da identidade do negro brasileiro em acensão social*. Rio de Janeiro: Graal, 1983.

Soyer, François. *Ambiguous Gender in Early Modern Spain and Portugal: Inquisitors, Doctors, and the Transgression of Gender Norms*. Leiden: Brill Press, 2012.

Spillers, Hortense J. "The Permanent Obliquity of an In[pha]llibly Straight: In the Time of the Daughters and the Fathers." In *Daughters and Fathers*, edited by Lynda E. Boose and Betty S. Flowers, 157–80. Baltimore: Johns Hopkins University Press, 1989.

Stepan, Nancy Leys. *The Hour of Eugenics: Race, Gender, and Nation in Latin America*. Ithaca, NY: Cornell University Press, 1991.

Stockton, Kathryn Bond. *Beautiful Bottom, Beautiful Shame: Where "Black" Meets "Queer."* Durham, NC: Duke University Press, 2006.

Stoler, Ann Laura. *Race and the Education of Desire: Foucault's "History of Sexuality" and the Colonial Order of Things*. Durham, NC: Duke University Press, 1995.

Sweet, James H., *Domingos Álvares, African Healing, and the Intellectual History of the Atlantic World*. Chapel Hill: University of North Carolina Press, 2011.

———. *Recreating Africa: Culture, Kinship, and Religion in the African-Portuguese World, 1441–1770*. Chapel Hill: University of North Carolina Press, 2003.

Tannenbaum, Frank. *Slave and Citizen: The Classic Comparative Study of Race Relations in the Americas*. Boston: Beacon Press, 1992. First published 1946 by Alfred A. Knopf.

Tate, Claudia. *Domestic Allegories of Political Desire*. New York: Oxford University Press, 1998.

———. *Psychoanalysis and Black Novels: Desire and the Protocols of Race*. New York: Oxford University Press, 1998.

Tillet, Salamishah. *Sites of Slavery: Citizenship and Racial Democracy in the Post-Civil Rights Imagination*. Durham, NC: Duke University Press, 2013.

Toplin, Robert Brent. *The Abolition of Slavery in Brazil*. New York: Atheneum, 1972.

Torrão Filho, Amílcar. *Tríbades galantes, fanchonos militantes: Homossexuais que fizeram história*. São Paulo: Edições GLS, 2000.

Trevisan, João Silvério. *Devassos no paraíso: A homossexualidade no Brasil, da colônia à atualidade*. 7th edition. Rio de Janeiro: Editora Record, 2007.

Trexler, Richard C. "Gender Subordination and Political Hierarchy in Pre-Hispanic America." In *Infamous Desire: Male Homosexuality in Colonial Latin America*. Edited by Peter Herman Sigal. Chicago: University of Chicago Press, 2003.

Trochim, Michael R. "The Black Guard: Racial Conflict in Post-Abolition Brazil." *Americas* 44, no. 3 (January 1988): 287–88.

Trouillot, Michel-Rolph. *Silencing the Past: Power and the Production of History*. Boston: Beacon Press, 1995.

Twinam, Ann. *Public Lives, Private Secrets: Gender, Honor, Sexuality, and Illegitimacy in Colonial Spanish America*. Stanford, CA: Stanford University Press, 1999.

———. *Purchasing Whiteness: Pardos, Mulattos, and the Quest for Social Mobility in the Spanish Indies*. Stanford, CA: Stanford University Press, 2014.

Twine, France Widdance. *Racism in a Racial Democracy: The Maintenance of White Supremacy in Brazil*. New Brunswick, NJ: Rutgers University Press, 1998.

Vainfas, Ronaldo. "Homoerotismo feminino e o Santo Ofício." In *História das mulheres no Brasil*. São Paulo: Editora Contexto: Editora Unesp Fundação, 1997.

———. "Inquisição como fábrica de hereges: Os sodomitas foram exceção?" In *A Inquisição em xeque: Temas, controvérsias, estudos de caso*, edited by Ronaldo Vainfas, Bruno Feitler, and Lana Lage da Gama Lima, 267–80. Rio de Janeiro: Editora UERJ, 2006.

———. "The Nefarious and the Colony." In *Pelo Vaso Traseiro: Sodomy and Sodomites in Luso-Brazilian History*, edited by Harold Johnson and Francisco A. Dutro, 337–69. Tucson, AZ: Fenestra Books, 2006.

———. "Sodomy, Love, and Slavery in Colonial Brazil: A Case Study of Minas Gerais during the Eighteenth Century." In *Sex, Power, and Slavery*, edited by Gwyn Campbell and Elizabeth Elbourne, 526–40. Athens: Ohio University Press, 2015.

———. *Trópico dos pecados: Moral, sexualidade, e Inquisição no Brasil*. Rio de Janeiro, Brazil: Editora Nova Fronteira, 1997.

Vainfas, Ronaldo, Bruno Feitler, and Lana Lage da Gama Lima, eds. *A Inquisição em xeque: Temas, controvérsias, estudos de caso*. Rio de Janeiro: Editora UERJ, 2006.

Vargas, João Costa. "Hyperconsciousness of Race and Its Negation: The Dialectic of White Supremacy in Brazil." *Identities: Global Studies in Culture and Power* 11 (2004): 443–70.

Vargas, João Costa, and Jaime Ampara Alves. "Geographies of Death: Intersectional Analysis of Police Lethality and the Racialized Regimes of Citizenship in São Paulo." *Ethnic and Racial Studies* 33, no. 4 (April 2010): 613.

Vianna, Hermano. "A meta mitológica da democracia racial." In *O imperador das idéias: Gilberto Freyre em questão*, edited by Joaquim Falcão and Rosa Maria Barboza de Araújo, 215–21. Rio de Janeiro: Fundação Roberto Marinho/Topbooks, 2001.

Vieira, António. *Sermões pregados no Brasil*. Vol. 2, *A vida social e moral na colônia*. Lisbon: Agência Geral das Colônias, 1940.

Vieira, Nelson H. *Brasil e Portugal, a imagem recíproca: O mito e a realidade na espressão literária*. Lisbon: Ministério da Educação, Instituto de Cultura e Língua Portuguesa, 1991.

Wade, Peter. *Race and Ethnicity in Latin America*. London: Pluto Press, 2010.

———. *Mestizo Genomics: Race Mixture, Nation, and Science in Latin America*. Durham, NC: Duke University Press, 2014.

———. *Race and Sex in Latin America*. London: Pluto Press, 2009.

Ward, Elizabeth Jane. *Not Gay: Sex between Straight White Men*. New York: New York University Press, 2015.

Weinstein, Barbara. *The Color of Modernity: São Paulo and the Making of Race and Nation in Brazil*. Durham, NC: Duke University Press, 2015.

West, Cornel. *Race Matters*. Boston: Beacon Press, 2001.

White, Deborah Gray. *Ar'n't I a Woman? Female Slaves in the Plantation South*. New York: Norton, 1999.

Wiegman, Robyn. *American Anatomies: Theorizing Race and Gender*. Durham, NC: Duke University Press, 1995.

Williams, Erica Lorraine. *Sexual Tourism in Bahia: Ambiguous Entanglements*. Urbana: University of Illinois Press, 2013.

Wood, Marcus. *Slavery, Empathy, and Pornography*. New York: Oxford University Press, 2002.

Woodard, Vincent. *The Delectable Negro: Human Consumption and Homoeroticism within US Slave Culture*. New York: NYU Press, 2014.

Yancy, George. *Black Bodies, White Gazes: The Continuing Significance of Race*. Lanham, MD: Rowman & Littlefield, 2008.

Young, Robert J. C. *Colonial Desire: Hybridity in Theory, Culture, and Race*. London: Routledge, 1995.

Zack, Naomi. *Race and Mixed Race*. Philadelphia: Temple University Press, 1993.

O abolicionismo (*Abolitionism*) (Nabuco, J.),
24, 161
abolitionism, 2, 14–17, 24, 87–89, 112, 136–41
Abolitionism (*O abolicionismo*) (Nabuco, J.),
24, 161
Abramo, Livio, 93
affection, between women, 73–74. *See also*
lesbianism
Alberto, Paulina, 27
Alencar, José Martiniano de, 14, 16, 18, 47, 180,
199n11
Alfaiates revolt (Revolt of the Tailors), 121
Alfonso V (King), 42
Almeida, José Ricardo Pires de, 97, 152–53,
157–60
Almeida, Vale de, 26
Amaral, Francisco Pacífico de, 89–90
Amaral, José Augusto do (Preto), 163, 180–83,
226n109
amizade de pouco saber (friendship of little
knowledge), 68
amizade deshonesta (dishonest friendship), 68,
90–96
amizade nefanda (nefarious friendship), 68
amizade tola (foolish friendship), 68
Ampara Alves, Jaime, 115, 139
Andrews, George Reid, 181
antiracism, 27–28, 195
Antônia, Isabel (the Velvet One), 82–83
Antonil, André João, 90, 188
Antonio, Joaquim, 29, 35–38
Antunes, Paula, 80
*Appeal to the Colored Citizens of the World but
in Particular, and Very Expressly, to Those of
the United States of America* (Walker), 138
Aquinas, Thomas (Saint), 53
Aragão, Garcia Dávila Perreira, 40–41
Aranha, Graça, 144–45
Araújo, Emanuel, 85
Araújo, Taís, 192
Arnold, John, 7–8
Assaults on Modesty: Studies on Sexual Aber-
rations (*Atentados ao pudor: Estudos sobre
as aberrações do instinto sexual*) (Viveiros de
Castro), 97
Assis, Machado de, 116–17, 124–25, 129–30,
134–35, 140–41
"Assortment of Hats for People of High Style"
(Sortimento de gorras para a gente do
grande tom), 130–31
asylums, for homosexuals, 162
*Atentados ao pudor: Estudos sobre as aberrações
do instinto sexual* (Assaults on Modesty:
Studies on Sexual Aberrations) (Viveiros de
Castro), 97
Avancini, Walter, 192
Avelar, Idelber, 21, 164
Azevedo, Aluísio, 98–99, 108, 129–30,
147–48
Azevedo, Amélia Francelina Cabral de, 102–3

Balaio, Manuel, 121
baptism, 44, 78
Baquaqua, Mahommah Gardo, 19, 132
Barbosa, Iria, 76

Barbosa, Rui, 11
Baroa, Catarina, 75
Barreto, Estevão Velho, 55
Bastide, Roger, 21, 94
Bellini, Ligia, 84
Bem-te-vis, 121
Benci, Jorge, 19, 44
Bender, Gerald, 25
Bento, Antônio, 137
Béringer, Émile, 151
bestiality, 53
black freedom, 21, 42, 113–17, 148, 175
The Black Man and the Cabin Boy (Bom-
    Crioulo) (Caminha), 173–80
blacks: as diseased, 180; as eliminated from re-
    production, 183–85; mulattos distinguished
    from, 167–68; population diversity and
    growth of, 13, 111–12, 140; preponderance
    of, 120; scientific studies on, 161–62; sexual
    inferiority of, 165–72, 177; sexuality of, as
    impure, 51; sin associated with, 48; white
    sexuality compared to sexuality of, 88,
    166–67. See also free blacks
black slaveholders, slaves treatment by, 131–36
black women: lack of honor of, 77; penetra-
    bility capacity of, 70–71; white women
    corrupted by, 75, 86, 89–90; white women
    relationship elements with, 75–83, 86–91
Boas, Franz, 21–22
Bom-Crioulo (The Black Man and the Cabin
    Boy) (Caminha), 173–80
Boxer, Charles R., 99
Brazilian Imperial Criminal Code (1830),
    50–51
Brent, Linda, 78
Breyner, Sônia, 172
Brito, Félix Peixoto de, 14
Brooten, Bernadette J., 71
Burgess, Ann, 62, 64
Burlamaqui, Frederico Leopoldo Cezar,
    213n118
Burton, Antoinette, 7
Butler, Kim, 181

Cabral, Manoel Alves, 34–35
Cabral, Manuel Álvares, 39
cafuné (caress), 92–93
Caminha, Adolfo, 173–80

Campos, Jacinto Ferreira dos, 59
Campos, Martinho, 20
Campos, Paulo Fernando de Souza, 182
capitão do mato (slave catcher), 124–26
caress (cafuné), 92, 93
carnal women (mundanas), 97
A carne (The Flesh) (Ribeiro, J.), 173
Carrara, Sérgio, 153
Carrasco, Walcyr, 192
Carvalho, Manuel Alves, 39
Casa-Grande e Senzala (The Masters and the
    Slaves) (Freyre), 21–22, 54–55, 163–65
The Case of the Whip ("O caso da vara"), 106
Castro, Álvaro Soares de, 70
Castro, Francisco Serrão de, 29, 35–37
Catholic Church, 13; abuses denounced to,
    121; distrust and espionage incited by,
    32–33; rape tolerated by, 50; reach of influ-
    ence of, 109; sexual activity prohibited by,
    26, 31; sin as main concern of, 83; slavery
    relationship with, 36, 40–43; supreme
    reign of, 59
Caulfield, Sueann, 69, 212n92
Cemetério dos Negros Novos (New Negro
    Cemetery), 18
Chaloub, Sidney, 102
Chevalier, Julien, Dr., 156
Chica da Silva (Oliveira, Francisca da Silva
    de), 134, 145–46
children: legal status inherited by, 67, 142–44;
    masters legal obligation to, 20–21; slaves
    given as plaything to, 55; white mistresses
    murdering, 108
citizenship, 12, 15
City of God (Augustine), 41
Clarke, Lorenne, 51
clitoris, 70–71, 74, 209n18
clitorismo, 97
Coelho Rodrigues, Antônio, 20
colonialism, 3, 22–23, 26, 153
Confederate Abolitionist Manifesto of Rio de
    Janeiro, 100
Conrad, Robert, 19
consent, 95; desire and, 53; fear provoking,
    49–50; in interracial, same-sex relations,
    82; racial passing as function of white, 119;
    of sex between masters and slaves, 194; of
    sex between women, 77

Cordial Man, theory of, 26
corretor de escravos (slave punisher), 124,
    126–28
O cortiço (The Slum) (Azevedo), 98–99, 129
Cosme, Preto, 121
Costa, João Nunes da, 102
Costa, Luiz da, 34–35
Costa, Viotti da, 116
criminality, 8, 183
crioulos (native-born Afro-Brazilians), 13, 41
culpability, 49–50, 54, 67, 80
Cunha, Herculano Augusto Lassance, 100,
    106, 151
curumins (indigenous slave boys), 55

Daniel, G. Reginald, 117, 129, 137
Dantas, Lucas, 121
Darwin, Charles, evolution theory of, 172
Dávila, Jerry, 21
Décianus, Tibérius, 71
Degler, Carl, 114
deheterosexualization, 163–69, 184
Delgado, Luiz, 39
desire, 26–28; consent and, 53; as individual,
    140–41; male rape connected to, 48–49;
    regulation of, 91; as shameful, 85; slavery as
    institution of, 95; sodomy as, 156. *See also*
    same-sex desire
Dias, Felipe, 76
Dias, Henrique, 136
Dias, José Ribeiro, 40
Diegues, Carlos, 189, 192
dildos, 71, 74, 82, 86
dishonest friendship (*amizade deshonesta*), 68,
    74, 90–96
displacement, of white men, 68, 83, 86–87
"doctrine of perfect submission," 206n74
dominance, 26, 38, 54–56, 94, 104, 109, 183
Dom Pedro II, 15, 126
Donaldson, Stephen, 62
Douglass, Frederick, 105, 130
Du Bois, W. E. B., 219n88
Dum Diversas, 42
Dumont, Sally, 72

effeminacy, 159, 167–72
El Far, Alessandra, 174

equality, 2–3, 6, 26–27, 122, 132, 144
Eschwege, Wilhelm von, 132
escravos de ganho (slaves for profit), 216n42
Estaço, João, 70
Ethiopia, standing for Africa, 204n50
exceptionalism, of slavery, 17–23, 163, 187, 191
Expilly, Charles, 8, 92, 99–100, 105, 121–26,
    143–45
"Exportation Mulatta" (Mulata exportação),
    195

Fanon, Frantz, 28, 48, 89, 171
"Father Versus Mother" (Pai contra mãe),
    129–30
Felman, Shoshana, 64
Fernandes, Ana, 76
Fernandes, Clara, 76, 78
Fernandes, Florestan, 181
Fernandes, Manoel, 75
Figari, Carlos, 173
Filho, Amílcar Torrão, 58
Filipine Code of Portuguese criminal law
    (1603), 32, 50
film, 187, 189–91
The Flesh (*A carne*) (Ribeiro, J.), 173
Folger, Ann, 72
Fonseca, Luiz Anselmo da, 124, 136
foolish friendship (*amizade tola*), 68
Ford, Talisman, 158
Foucault, Michel, 31, 163
Franklin, John Hope, 133
free blacks, 111–14, 118–21, 124–30, 137–38,
    192
freedom, 43, 90, 126, 140, 188; transition to,
    52
Freitas de Azevedo, Matheus de, 78
French Emancipation Committee, 15
Freud, Sigmund, 169–72
Freyre, Gilberto de Mello, 90–91, 94, 104,
    151–55, 206n74; *The Masters and the Slaves*
    by, 21–22, 54–56, 163–65; penis envy of,
    169–72
friendship: as dishonest (*amizade deshonesta*),
    68, 90–96; as foolish (*amizade tola*), 68; of
    little knowledge (*amizade de pouco saber*),
    68; as nefarious (*amizade nefanda*), 68
friendship of little knowledge (*amizade de
    pouco saber*), 68

Fruchot, Justino, 125
Fry, Peter, 197n1
fugitive slave communities (*quilombos*),
120–21, 124
Furtado, Júnia Ferreira, 134, 145, 189
<#>
Gama, Luiz Gonzaga Pinto da, 130–31
Garcia, Pero, 38–39
gender, 8, 52–54, 56–61, 68, 74, 83–87, 96–98
genital mutilation, 70–71
Geraldes, Inácio, 39–40
Germeten, Nicole von, 77
Gilliam, Angela, 27
Gilman, Sander, 48, 71, 88, 150, 163
Goldstein, Donna, 27–28
Gomes, Albert, 26
Gonzaga da Virgens, Luis, 121
Grace Period (Tempo de Graça), 32, 209n26
Graham, Maria Dundas, 8, 120, 132, 143,
200n32, 216n32
Green, James, 157, 161–63
Gregory XVI (Pope), 42
Groth, A. Nicholas, 62, 64
Gruzinski, Serge, 58
Guimarães, Antônio Sérgio, 21
Guimarães, Manuel Pereira, 41

Haitian revolution, 112, 120, 216n34
Hammon, Mary, 69
Hartman, Saidiya, 41, 49, 206n74
Hesedo, Maria de, 76–79
heteronormativity, 83, 86, 163, 172, 193; miscegenation, reproduction and, 9; sexual
coercion framed within classed, 54; sexual
violence as beyond domain of, 6; violence
within framework of, 64
heterosexuality, 6, 22; bending barriers of, 84;
outlets for, 157; preoccupation with white
male, 176; as presumed, 84; rape legislation
focused on, 52; supremacy of, 161; undermining of, 83; white male supremacy connected to, 90
Higgs, David, 198n4
Hildebrandt, Hugo, 209n18
Holanda, Sérgio Buarque de, 26, 153
*Homosexualismo: A libertinagem no Rio de Ja-
neiro: Estudos sobre as perversões do instinto
genital* (Homosexuality: Libertinage in Rio

de Janeiro: A Study of the Perversions of
Genital Instincts) (Almeida, J.), 159–60
homosexuality, 2, 22, 150; constructions of and
predisposition to black, 57–58, 160–69;
creation of, 79; curing of, 162–63; depicted
in literature, 173–80; effeminacy and,
168–72; fear of, 184; of females, 75, 95–96;
historicization of race and, 169–71; of indigenous men, 166–69; male rape as manifestation of, 53–54, 58; masculinity and, 60,
158; medical studies on, 156–60; as mental
illness, 159–61; mulattos and, 164–68; naturalism and, 172–73; negative embodiment
of, 183; passivity and, 166–67; physical
symptoms of, 97; poverty related to, 98; as
racialized, 5, 6, 87–88, 160, 163–64, 169;
sex transmitting, 179–80; as sexual category, 34, 83–84, 87, 156; singular nature of,
156; sodomy distinguished from, 178
Homosexuality: Libertinage in Rio de Janeiro:
A Study of the Perversions of Genital Instincts (*Homosexualismo: A libertinagem no
Rio de Janeiro: Estudos sobre as perversões do
instinto genital*) (Almeida J.), 159–60
honest woman (*mulher honesta*), 50–51
Hottentot, Venus, 209n19
Huckle, P. L., 64
"A huma dama que macehavea outras damas"
(To a Woman Who Copulates with Other
Women), 87
humanity, of slaves, 43–48, 49
hypersexuality, 52, 64, 107, 165–66

imperfect sodomy (sodomia imperfeita),
33–36, 39
incest, 31
*Incidents in the Life of a Slave Girl, Written by
Herself* (Jacobs, Harriet), 1, 72
íncuba (incubator), 74
incubator (*íncuba*), 74
independence, of 1822, 16, 24
individuality, 139–40
In Plurimis (1888), 42
Inquisition. *See* Portuguese Inquisition
In supremo apostolatus (1839), 42
insurrection, 120–21
intendente (overseer), 124
interracial sex, 3, 27, 88, 142; equality symbol-

ized by, 26; as harmonious, 25; political and personal forms of, 28; rape overshadowed by narrative of, 191; for slave reproduction, 12; strategic uses of, 4

intimacy, 26, 91, 196; barriers to, 148; sex as act of, 3, 23, 53; sexual violence turned into, 164–65

Jacobs, Harriet A., 1, 72, 94–95, 104
João III (King), 30
Johnson, Elizabeth, 69
Jordan, Winthrop, 54, 183

Kaufman, Michael, 207n86
Kennedy, Randall, 138, 219n89
Kertbeny, Karl-Maria, Dr., 156
King, Michael B., 64
Klein, Herbert S., 112, 113, 132
Koster, Henry, 8, 55, 104, 124–26, 132–33, 135
Krafft-Ebing, Richard von, 156
Kulick, Don, 60

Lacerda, João Batista de, 22
Langsdorff, Georg Heinrich von, 215n13
Laub, Dori, 64
Law of the Free Womb (Lei do Ventre Livre), 20, 89
Leitão, Homem, 70
Lemos, Francisco de Faria, 101
Lemos, Micia de, 76
Leo XIII (Pope), 42–43
lesbianism, creation of, 96–99
Lewis, Debra, 51
Ligon, Ellen Barret, Dr., 183
Lima, Manoel de, 34
Lindley, Thomas, 92
Lira, Manuel Faustino dos Santos, 121
literature for men (*literatura para homens*), 174–75
Lobato, Monteiro, 226n109
Lomba, Balthazar da, 168–69
Lorde, Audre, 137
Lourenço, Maria, 81
Love between Women: Early Christian Response to Female Homoeroticism (Brooten), 71
Loving v. State of Virginia (1967), 142

Lucena, Maria de, 76–79
Lucinda, Elisa, 195
"Lucinda, the Slave Maid," 91–92
Luiz, Francisca, 82–83, 84
Luna, Francisco Vidal, 112–13, 132
Lusotropicalism, 21
lust (*luxuria*), 53

Macedo, Francisco Ferraz de, Dr., 157
Macedo, Joaquim Manuel de, 88, 90, 91
Macedo Junior, João Álvares de Azevedo, Dr., 100–101, 152, 154–58
Madeira, Pero, 79
Magalhães, Manoel de, 70
Magalhães, Valentim, 175
male rape, 5, 27, 60–65, 196; active/passive roles in, 57–58; case records of, 34–41; deaths from, 29–31; desire connected to, 48–49; dramatization of history of, 179; legal understanding of, 50; as manifestation of homosexuality, 52–54; modern day prison experience of, 207n97; victims of, 8
Malê revolt of 1835, 130, 140
malnutrition, 18–19, 20
The Mansions and the Shanties: The Making of Modern Brazil (Freyre), 22, 163–64, 166
Marimba, João, 38
Marques, Isabel, 75
marriage, 85, 96, 143–48, 184, 221n107
Martius, Friedrich Philipp von, 151
masculinity: enhancing of, 83; homosexuality and, 60, 158; power as proof of, 55–57; protecting of, 184; trauma, male rape and, 62, 64–65
The Masters and the Slaves (Casa-Grande e Senzala) (Freyre), 21–22, 54–55, 163–65
masturbation, 31, 34, 156, 177
Matos, Gregório de, 87
Maximilian I (King), 151
Memórias póstumas de Brás Cubas (The Posthumous Memoirs of Brás Cubas) (Assis), 134–35
Memories from the Diamond District (*Memórias do Distrito Diamantino*) (Santos, J.), 188
mestiço (mixed-race), 25–26
Mezey, Gillian, 64
mining industry, 13

Miranda, Felipe Thomaz de, 38
miscegenation, 9, 22, 24, 65, 111. *See also* reverse miscegenation
Miskolci, Richard, 153–54, 173
mixed-race (*mestiço*), 25–26
moleques (slave boys), 55
molície, 34–35, 70, 167–68
Moll, Albert, 156
morality, 37, 48, 88, 100
Mott, Luiz, 31, 58, 169
Motta, Zezé, 189, 192
Moutinho, Laura, 184
Muir, Edward, 7
"Mulata exportação" (Exportation Mulatta), 195
The Mulatto (*O mulato*) (Azevedo), 108, 129, 147–48
"mulatto escape hatch," 114–15
mulattos, 13, 26–27, 144–45; abolitionism and, 136–37; blacks distinguished from, 167–68; children as, 142–43; homosexuality and, 164–68; influence of racial passing on, 128–30; population of, 112, 120–21; privilege of, 219n88; revolt by, 216n34; scientific studies on, 161–62; slaveholders as, 131–32; social realities for, 147–48; social whiteness of, 118–26, 141, 146; white male sex with, 196
mulher honesta (honest woman), 50–51
multiracial identity politics, 117
mundanas (carnal women), 97
murder: of children by white mistresses, 108; by slaveholders, 38, 105

Nabuco, Joaquim, 16, 23–24, 103, 116–17, 137, 160; on absence of racism, 135; equality perspective of, 132; Portuguese blamed by, 152–53
Narrative of Sojourner Truth (Truth), 1
Nascimento, João de Deus, 121
native-born Afro-Brazilians (*crioulos*), 13, 41
naturalism, 172–80
natural vessel (*vaso natural*), 74
necrophilia, 181–84, 226n109
Needell, Jeffrey, 56, 155, 165
nefarious friendship (*amizade nefanda*), 68
The Negro Devil (*O Diabo Preto*). *See* Amaral, José Augusto do

negrophobia, 171
Neither Black nor White: Slavery and Race Relations in Brazil and the United States (Degler), 114
Nelson, Thomas, 19
New Testament, 204n47
Nicholas V (Pope), 42
Noblat, Ricardo, 165
Norman, Sara, 69
Not Gay: Sex between Straight White Men (Ward), 59–60
Nunes, Viriato Fernandes, Dr., 156
Nunes, Zita, 164, 171

Old Testament, 41
Oliveira, Francisca da Silva da (Chica da Silva), 134, 145–46, 187–96
Oliveira, João Fernandes de, 145–46, 188, 190
"one-drop rule," 115, 140
Order and Progress: Brazil from Monarchy to Republic (Freyre), 22
orgasms, 74, 75, 80, 81, 86, 155–56
orgies, 41
Otoni, Cristiano, 19
overseer (*intendente*), 124

Pacheco e Silva, Antônio Carlos, 181–82
paciente (passive woman), 74
"Pai contra mãe" (Father Versus Mother), 129–30
Painter, Nell Irvin, 72
palmatória, 106
Paraguayan War, 15
Parda, Catarina, 102
pardos (descended from *pretos* and *brancos*), 112
Parker, Richard G., 60
passive woman (*paciente*), 74
passivity, 60, 208n103
paternalism, 17
Patrocínio, José do, 24
Paula Barros, Isabel Jutaí de, 174
Payne, Buckner H., 143
peças (pieces), 18
penetrability, 56–61, 85, 155; slavery framing, 158, 164; women capacity for, 70–71, 76

penis: clitoris functioning as, 70–71; masters inspecting, 167; race influencing size of, 167, 181; white male supremacy influenced by, 170

penis envy, 169–72

Peralta, Maria de, 80

Pereira, Miguel, 149

perfect sodomy (*sodomia perfeita*), 33–34

Philip I (King), 50

pieces (*peças*), 18

Pimentel, Madalena, 76

Pimentel, Souza, 105

Pinheira, Guiomar, 79

Pisçarra, Guiomar, 75

plantations, conditions of, 18

pleasure: hyperestheticized genitals producing, 97; of masters command, 14; over obedience, 77; power dynamics concealed by, 93–95; from rape, 40–41; right to, 26; sex as not about, 84–85; torture as, 127; violence and sexual coercion in pursuit of, 86; women divulging reception of, 74

Pohl, Johann Baptist Emanuel, 108

Portuguese Inquisition, 4–7; female same-sex relations confessed to, 75–83; same-sex relations documented by, 68–83; same-sex sexual violence proceedings of, 29–41

The Posthumous Memoirs of Brás Cubas (*Memórias póstumas de Brás Cubas*) (Assis), 134–35

poverty, 98, 129, 181

power: abuse of, 2, 40; boundaries and, 62; denial of dynamics of, 190; fear of loss of, 15; of gender, 54; invisibility and, 10; of miscegenation, as transcendental, 24; pleasure concealing dynamics of, 93–95; as proof of masculinity, 55–57; public display of, 31; relations of, between slave women and white mistresses, 94; sexual desire as transfer point of, 26; sexual violence as about, 61, 83; of violence, 28, 104; white male supremacy relations of, 196

pretos (blacks of pure African descent), 112

Prosser, Gabriel, 219n89

prostitution, 2, 90, 179, 188–89; forced on slave women by white mistresses, 99–103, 196, 216n42; income from, 100; of males, 157–58; regulation of, 212n92

Provincial Assembly of Pernambuco (1884), 89–90

Punitions publiques sur la Place Ste. Anne, 126–27

Quaresma, Catarina, 75

Queixada, Cristovão, 76

quilombos (fugitive slave communities), 120–21, 124

race, 10, 183; active/passive binaries of, 56–57; class, sexual deviance and, 97; families as mixed, 194–95; historicization of homosexuality and, 169–71; individual transcendence of, 136–41; love between, 142; mutations of, 124–25; penis size influenced by, 167, 181; sex, national identity and, 150; sexual discourses around, 163; signs of separation of, 71

race relations: challenges to Brazilian, 139; construction of, 6; democratic view of, 12; as harmonious, 3; history of Brazilian, 21–22; racial identity and, 113–17; sexual history and, 28

racial democracy, myth of, 3, 9, 21–25, 27, 95, 187–89, 197n1

racial exceptionalism, 3, 4, 12, 28

racial passing, 121–22; as function of white consent, 119; mulattos influenced by, 128–30; in societies of Americas, 219n88; US association with, 113–17

racism: against abnormality, 163; absence of, 23–27

Ramos, Arthur, 21

Rangel, Maria, 76

rape, 2, 27, 94; application of term, 27; Brazilian law defining, 50–51; categorizations of vaginal and anal, 205n66; Catholic Church tolerance of, 50; as correlated with womanhood, 207n86; film representation of, 190; interracial sex narrative overshadowing, 191; legal, religious and social constructions of, 50–54; legislation of, focused on heterosexuality, 52; moral depravity affirmed by, 48; pleasure from, 40–41; punishment for victims of, 50; of slave boys, 55–56; slave women vulnerability to legalized, 51; white male supremacy preserved by, 61. *See also* male rape

rape laws, 50–52, 95

Reis, João, 130

reproduction: elimination of blacks from, 183–85; gender hierarchies cemented by, 86; heteronormativity, miscegenation and, 9; slavery, visible sexual violence and, 63–64; of white elites, 67, 84

reputation, concern for international, 14–16

Response of the Congregation of the Holy Office, 42

Reuter, Edward Byron, 219n88

reverse miscegenation, 141–46

Revolt of the Tailors (Alfaiates revolt), 121

Ribeiro, Júlio, 173

Ribeiro, Leonídio, 156, 159

Rodrigues, Gaspar, 38

Roediger, David, 128

Roiz, Maria, 75

Romanus Pontifex (1454), 42

Rosaldo, Renato, 7

Rugendas, Johann Moritz, 114, 125–27, 215n13

Rush, Florence, 60–61

sadism, 56

sameness, 2–3, 196

same-sex desire, 75, 79–81, 83–87, 90

same-sex gaze, 48, 205n56

same-sex relations, 6; consent for interracial, 82; of females, confessions to Portuguese Inquisition, 75–83; as against nature, 84; Portuguese Inquisition documenting, 68–83; punishments for women in, 81; as scandalous, 82; shame in, 75; slavery and, in the telenovela, 192–95; written records of, 109

Santiago, Filipe, 40

Santos, Boaventura de Sousa, 26–27

Santos, Joaquim Felício dos, 188

Saraiva, José Antônio, 11

Sardinha, Manuel Pires, 190

Scarce, Michael, 58, 62, 205n66

Seca, Quitéria, 79

segregationist system, of US, 23, 24

The Semblance (*O semelhante*) (Lucinda), 195

separatism, 212n82

sex, 2, 54, 183; as act of intimacy, 53; under colonialism, 26; consent of, between masters and slaves, 194; consent to, between women, 77; decriminalization of acts of, 162; as duty, 33; freedom obtained through, 90, 188; homosexuality transmitted through, 179–80; intimacy connected to, 3, 23; language for, between women, 69–70; masters promoting, 154; between mulatta and white male, 196; as not about pleasure, 84–85; race, national identity and, 150; slaves for sole purpose of, 39–40; social hygiene and, 152–53; as weapon, 9; white male supremacy and, 152–56; between women and female body, 68–71. *See also* interracial sex

Sexagenarian Law of 1885, 21

sexual abuse: as concealed, 189, 191; legality of, 43; slavery separation from, 33; of slave women by white women, 72; uncertainty of frequency of, 208n1; by white mistresses, 76–77

sexual coercion: within classed heteronormativity, 54; conditions of, between women, 73; sodomy not implying, 63; violence and, in pursuit of pleasure, 86

sexual deviance, 97, 152, 212n82

sexual exploitation, 2, 27, 103, 196

sexual identity, 58, 84

sexual inferiority, of blacks and indigenous peoples, 167–72, 177

sexually transmitted diseases, 87, 100, 150–52

sexual repression, 93–94

sexual revenge, 64

sexual violence: camouflaging of, 4, 64; contemporary rendering of history of, 187; documentation of, 30; as beyond domain of heteronormativity, 6; erasing of, 52; Portuguese Inquisition proceedings on, 29–41; as about power, 61, 83; as slavery norm, 103; turned into intimacy, 164–65

shame, 5, 37, 72, 75, 85, 137–38

Silva, Domingos da, 136

Silva, João da, 39

Silva, José Bonifácio de Andrada e, 88, 210n51

Sinisgalli, Aldo, 163

Sinistrari, Ludovico Maria, 70, 209n25

Siqueira, Paula de, 80–81

slave auctions, 15–16

slave boys (*moleques*), 55–56

slave catcher (*capitão do mato*), 124–26

slaveholders, 2, 38; as careless, 19; cruelty denied by, 20; identity of, 17; informants for,

124; legal property rights of, 44; as mulattos, 131–32; murder by, 38, 105; as possibility for all people, 132

slave masters: accountability of, 37; command pleasure of, 14; consent to sex between slaves and, 194; as fathers, 17–18; legal obligation of, to children, 20–21; male rape and initiation of white, 54–56; penis inspection by, 167; prosecution of, 49–50; religious responsibility of, 44; sex promoted by, 154; sodomy active role of, 59

slave population: in 1798, 19; in 1860, 14; mortality rate of, 13

slave punisher (*corretor de escravos*), 124, 126–28

Slavery. *See specific topics*

slaves: abuse of, as will of God, 45–47; black slaveholders treatment of, 133–34; Catholic Church protecting, 43; children given, as plaything, 55; consent to sex between masters and, 194; criminal liability of, 49; cruel punishments for, 40; death of, from work conditions, 13; fear of punishment of, 33, 35, 39, 73; humanity of, 43–48, 49; interracial sex for reproduction of, 12; labor and wealth represented by, 14; laws protecting, 20; as left to die when unable to work, 200n32; liberation of, 20; mortality rate of, 18–19; naming violence not allowed for, 61; negative roles of, 180; penetrability of body of, 56–61, 85; prevented from religious participation, 36, 45; as property, 25, 103; as rented, 216n42; replacing of, 19; resistance of, 77, 120–21, 130–31, 194; revolts by, 217n48; sexual vulnerability of, 35, 40; silencing of violence towards, 28; sin understood by, 78; slavery as benefit to, 140; for sole purpose of sex, 39–40; suppression of uprisings of, 219n89; trial recordings control of, 8; unconditional obedience of, 46; as unseen, 2, 4, 196; used for farming, 12–13

slave trade, 14, 19, 111

slave women: culpability ascribed to, 67; erotic practices between white mistresses and, 92; forced prostitution of, by white mistresses, 99–103, 196, 216n42; lack of bodily control of, 53; manipulation tactics of, 191; relations of power between white mistresses and, 94; sexual abuse by white women of, 72; sexual

exploitation of, by white men, 2, 27; as threat, 88; violence of white mistresses towards, 104–8; vulnerability of, to legalized rape, 51; white mistresses relationship with, 68, 91, 196; white victimhood and, 87–90; white women rivalry with, 107

The Slum (*O cortiço*) (Azevedo), 98–99, 129

Smith, Herbert H., 20

social-hygiene movement, 149–50, 172

social isolation, 104

social whiteness and whitening, 2, 86, 114–28, 141–42, 146, 215n11

sodomia imperfeita (imperfect sodomy), 33–36, 39

sodomia perfeita (perfect sodomy), 33–34

sodomy: categorization of, 31, 53; deaths from, 36; description of cases of, 34–36; as desire, 156; as expected obligation, 57; of females, 69–72, 76–83; as grave sin, 33, 39, 59; historical ambiguity surrounding, 61; homosexuality distinguished from, 178; of indigenous men, 168–69; male honor compromised by, 203n21; masters active role in, 59; sexual coercion not implied by, 63. *See also* imperfect sodomy; male rape; perfect sodomy

Somerville, Siobhan, 160

"Sortimento de gorras para a gente do grande tom" (Assortment of Hats for People of High Style), 130–31

Souza, Felipa de, 79–81, 84

Spanish Inquisition, 30

Spillers, Hortense J., 208n98

Spurling, Geoffrey, 203n21

Stoler, Ann Laura, 26

Stono Rebellion, 219n90

sugar plantations, 13

Summa Theologica (Aquinas), 53

Sweet, James, 19, 44

syphilis epidemic, 150–52, 157

Tavares, Miguel José, 101–2

Tempo de Graça (Grace Period), 32, 209n26

"To a Woman Who Copulates with Other Women" (A huma dama que macehavea outras damas), 87

torture, 9; free blacks as agents of, 128; as pleasure, 127; as public, 64

Toussaint-Samson, Adèle, 8, 15–16, 106, 120, 211n59
trauma, male rape, masculinity and, 62, 64–65
Travesti: Sex, Gender, and Culture among Brazilian Transgendered Prostitutes (Kulick), 60
Trevisan, João Silvério, 58
Trexler, Richard, 55, 58
Trouillot, Michel-Rolph, 10
Truth, Sojourner, 1, 72–73, 77–78, 196
Twinam, Ann, 215n11

unification, prevention of, 13, 121
United States (US), 10; Brazilian slavery compared to, 17–18, 24–25, 140; racial passing association with, 113–17; rape laws of, 51; segregationist system of, 23, 24; slavery context of, 72
unseen, slaves as, 2, 4, 196

Vainfas, Ronaldo, 23, 26, 33, 73, 85
Valle, Manoel do, 70
Vargas, João Costa, 115, 139
vaso natural (natural vessel), 74
The Velvet One (Antônia, Isabel), 82–83
Veríssimo, José, 55, 116, 175–76
Viana, Antônio da Fonseca, Dr., 154
Vianna, Paulo Fernandes, 18
Victim Executioners: Portraits of Slavery (*As vítimas algozes: Quadros da escravidão*) (Macedo), 89, 91
victimhood, 50, 52, 87–90, 104
Vieira, António, 45–47, 84–85
Vieira Couto, Manuel, 190
violence: as cathartic, 135; description of slave, 19–20; eroticization of, 190–92; forms of, 104–5; within heteronormative framework, 64; hypervisibility of, 135–36; intimacy coexisting with, 26; of law, 49; power of, 28, 104; public display of, 126–27; sexual coercion and, in pursuit of pleasure, 86; ties to, of slavery, 124; of white mistresses towards slave women, 104–8; whiteness asserted through, 123; from white women, 68. *See also* sexual abuse; sexual violence
As vítimas algozes: Quadros da escravidão (Victim Executioners: Portraits of Slavery) (Macedo), 89, 91

Vitorino, Manoel, 16–17
Viveiros de Castro, Francisco José, Dr., 97, 159, 163, 179
Von Spix, Johann Baptist, 151
vulnerability: of body, 52; control of, 48; slaves sexual, 35, 40; of white women, 88

Wade, Peter, 221n107
Walker, David, 138
Walsh, Robert, 8, 120
Ward, Jane, 59–60
wealth, 14, 145
Weech, Joseph F. Friedrich von, 105–6
Werneck, Luiz Peixoto de Lacerda, 14
white elites, 3; anxieties of, 111; control of, 128; entry into, 114; reproduction of, 67
white male supremacy, 2, 45–46, 67, 109, 163, 184; heterosexuality connected to, 90; inferior existence necessary for, 55; maintaining, 3, 142; national progress and, 152–56; penis size influence on, 170; power relations of, 196; promoting of, 175; rape preserving, 61; reinforcing of, 59; sex and, 152–56; slavery maintaining, 117; structures of, 3
white mistresses, 109; children murdered by, 108; erotic practices between slave women and, 92; forced prostitution of slave women by, 99–103, 196, 216n92; police resented by, 102; relations of power between slave women and, 94; sexual abuse by, 76–77; slave women relationship with, 68, 91, 196; violence of, towards slave women, 104–8
The Whitening Project, 183–85
white women: black women corrupting, 75, 86, 89–90; black women relationship elements with, 75–83, 86–91; initiatives taken by, 85; purity of, 67, 90; sexual abuse of slave women by, 72; slave women rivalry with, 107; victimhood of, 104; violence from, 68; vulnerability of, 88
Wiegman, Robyn, 144
Williams, Erica Lorraine, 26

Xica da Silva: film (1976), 189–91; telenovela (1996), 191, 192–95

Zack, Naomi, 219n88